QUALITATIVE RESEARCH IN CLINICAL HEALTH PSYCHOLOGY

Also by Antonia Lyons

Health Psychology: A Critical Introduction (with K. Chamberlain)
*Pleasure, Pain and Profit: Alcohol in New Zealand and the Contemporary
   Culture of Intoxication* (with B. McEwan, M. Campbell & D. Swain)

Also by Poul Rohleder

Critical Issues in Clinical and Health Psychology
HIV/AIDS in South Africa 25 Years On: Psychosocial Perspectives
   (with L. Swartz, S. Kalichman & L. Simbayi)

Qualitative Research in Clinical and Health Psychology

Edited by

*Poul Rohleder (DPhil) and
Antonia C. Lyons (PhD)*

First published 2015 by
PALGRAVE MACMILLAN

Palgrave Macmillan in the UK is an imprint of Macmillan Publishers Limited,
registered in England, company number 785998, of Houndmills, Basingstoke,
Hampshire RG21 6XS.

Palgrave Macmillan in the US is a division of St Martin's Press LLC,
175 Fifth Avenue, New York, NY 10010.

Palgrave Macmillan is the global academic imprint of the above companies
and has companies and representatives throughout the world.

Palgrave® and Macmillan® are registered trademarks in the United States,
the United Kingdom, Europe and other countries.

ISBN: 978–1–137–29107–3 hardback
ISBN: 978–1–137–29104–2 paperback

This book is printed on paper suitable for recycling and made from fully
managed and sustained forest sources. Logging, pulping and manufacturing
processes are expected to conform to the environmental regulations of the
country of origin.

A catalogue record for this book is available from the British Library.

A catalog record for this book is available from the Library of Congress.

Typeset by Cambrian Typesetters, Camberley, Surrey.

Printed in China.

For Mark [PR] and Esme [AL] with love

Contents

Part III: Qualitative Methods: Exploring Social Worlds

Part IV: Combining Qualitative and Quantitative Data

Acknowledgements

I would like to thank my colleagues at the Department of Psychology at Anglia Ruskin University, UK, for their support and encouragement. I am also grateful for the ongoing encouragement and guidance from valued colleagues such as Leslie Swartz, Arne Henning Eide and Nora Groce. Thanks also to the many students I have had the privilege to teach and know, and from whom I have learned so much. Thank you to Charlotte Smith and Magda Borawska-Charko for being such great PhD students. A special thank-you to Antonia for joining me in the development of this book. Finally, a lot of love and gratitude to family and friends and especially to Mark for always being by my side.

Poul Rohleder

I would like to gratefully thank the School of Psychology at Massey University, New Zealand, for their support of this work. I would also like to acknowledge and thank the great colleagues I've had the privilege to work with while at Massey University, particularly Kerry Chamberlain, Christine Stephens and John Spicer. I've also been lucky to have supervised many fantastic postgraduate students over the previous few years, from whom I've learned a lot; thanks especially to Patricia Niland, Glennis Mark, Prue Fisher, Ross Hebden, Ria Pugmire, Jessica Glen, Anna Tonks, Zoe McGavock, Jacqui Laidler and Michelle Pedersen. Lots of love and thanks to my friends and family, and especially Ian Goodwin, who has been essential in assisting me in many practical ways to bring this project to fruition. Ian has been an unwavering source of support, encouragement and childcare. Callum and Esme, you've both been totally supportive and loads of fun. Finally, a big thank-you to Poul for asking me to be involved in this project; it's been a real pleasure to work with you.

Antonia Lyons

We would both like to thank Paul Stevens and Jenny Hindley and the rest of the team at Palgrave Macmillan for their advice and support and making this such a painless journey. And finally to all the contributors – thanks for agreeing to be part of this, thanks for your excellent contributions, and thanks for your timely responses to our nagging emails. This book would not exist without this collaborative effort.

May 2014

Publisher's Acknowledgements

The publisher and authors would like to thank the organizations and people listed below for permission to reproduce material from their publications:

Box 6.1 is reprinted from *Qualitative Sociology*, 25:4, Hermanowicz, J.C., The great interview: 25 strategies for studying people in bed, 479–49, 2002, with permission from Springer Science+Business Media.

Box 7.3 is reprinted from *Sexuality Research and Social Policy*, 9:4, Terry, G., Braun, V., & Farvid, P., Structural Impediments to Sexual Health in New Zealand: Key Informant Perspectives, 317–326, 2012, with permission from Springer.

Table 7.4 is reprinted from *Qualitative Research in Psychology*, 3:2, Braun, V., & Clarke, V., Using thematic analysis in psychology, 77–101, 2006, with permission from Taylor and Francis.

Notes on Contributors

Virginia Braun is an Associate Professor in the School of Psychology at The University of Auckland, Aotearoa/New Zealand. Her research explores the intersecting areas of gender, bodies, sex/sexuality and health, and she has worked on projects on heterosex, sexual health, cervical cancer prevention policy, sexualities and higher education, women's genital meanings, female genital cosmetic surgery, body hair (removal), pornography and qualitative research methods. She is author (with Victoria Clarke) of *Successful Qualitative Research: A Practical Guide for Beginners* (Sage).

Kerry Chamberlain is Professor of Social and Health Psychology at Massey University in Auckland, New Zealand. He is a critical health psychologist with research interests in health and the everyday, with a specific focus on medications, media, materiality, mundane ailments, food and disadvantage, and in innovative qualitative research methodologies. He is co-author (with Antonia Lyons) of *Health Psychology: A Critical Introduction* (Cambridge University Press).

Victoria Clarke is an Associate Professor in Sexuality Studies in the Department of Health and Social Sciences at the University of the West of England, UK. Her research has focused on lesbian and gay parenting, same-sex and heterosexual relationships, sexual practices, sexualities and appearance, sexualities and higher education, and qualitative research methods. Her books include *Out in Psychology: Lesbian, Gay, Bisexual, Trans and Queer Perspectives* (Wiley) with Elizabeth Peel, *LGBTQ Psychology: An Introduction* (Cambridge University Press) with Sonja Ellis, Elizabeth Peel and Damien Riggs, and *Successful Qualitative Research: A Practical Guide for Beginners* (SAGE) with Virginia Braun.

Mick Finlay is a Reader in Psychology at Anglia Ruskin University, Cambridge, UK. His research interests include communication and interaction involving people with intellectual disabilities and others, and discourses of group conflict.

Juliet Foster is a Lecturer in Social Psychology in the Department of Psychology, and Senior Tutor at Murray Edwards College, University of Cambridge. She is particularly interested in common-sense understandings of health and illness, especially mental health, and in the development of qualitative analysis.

Kerry Gibson is a clinical psychologist and Senior Lecturer in the School of Psychology at the University of Auckland, New Zealand. Her research interests include clients' experiences of, and engagement with, different forms of psychological intervention. She also does research on trauma and its impact on individuals and organizations.

Michael Larkin is a Senior Lecturer in Psychology at the University of Birmingham, UK, where he works as part of the clinical psychology training team. His research interests include the experience and context of psychological distress (particularly in psychosis), the experience of 'loss of control', and the meaning of family and peer relationships in coping with distress and facilitating wellbeing.

Antonia Lyons is an Associate Professor in the School of Psychology at Massey University, Wellington, New Zealand. Her research focuses on issues around gender, health and identity, particularly the social contexts of behaviours related to health and wellbeing. She has just completed a three-year study into young people's drinking cultures and social technologies. Antonia is a co-author (with Kerry Chamberlain) of the text *Health Psychology: A Critical Introduction* (Cambridge University Press) and is currently a co-editor of the journal *Qualitative Research in Psychology*, an Associate Editor for *Health Psychology Review* and on the editorial boards of the *Journal of Health Psychology* and *Psychology and Health*.

Michael Murray is Professor of Social and Health Psychology at Keele University, UK. He is interested in developing critical psychological approaches to the study of health, illness and ageing. He has written or edited several books including *Qualitative Health Psychology* (with Kerry Chamberlain, Sage) and *Critical Health Psychology* (Palgrave Macmillan).

Janette Perz is Associate Professor in the Centre for Health Research at the University of Western Sydney, Australia. Her research is in the field of reproductive and sexual health with a particular focus on gendered experiences, subjectivity and identity, including sexual experiences of people facing cancer; changes to fertility after cancer; pre-menstrual syndrome (PMS) in heterosexual and lesbian relationships; sexual wellbeing and reproductive needs in CALD populations.

Helena Priest is a Senior Lecturer at Keele University and Research Director on the Universities of Staffordshire and Keele Doctorate in Clinical Psychology Programme, UK. She is a qualitative researcher with interests in the psychological aspects of care delivery, the mental health needs of people with intellectual disabilities, and interprofessional learning and working.

Damien Riggs is an Australian Research Council Future Fellow and Senior Lecturer in social work at Flinders University, where he teaches in the areas of gender/sexuality, family studies and mental health. He is the author of over

100 publications in these areas, including (with Victoria Clarke, Sonja Ellis and Elizabeth Peel) *Lesbian, Gay, Bisexual, Trans and Queer Psychology: An Introduction* (Cambridge University Press), which won the 2013 British Psychological Society prize for best textbook.

Poul Rohleder is Reader in Psychology at Anglia Ruskin University, Cambridge, UK. He is a registered clinical psychologist and a qualitative and mixed-methods researcher, with particular interests in psychosocial and public health aspects of HIV and sexual health. He is the author of *Critical Issues in Clinical and Health Psychology* (Sage).

Charlotte Smith is a PhD student and graduate teaching assistant at the department of psychology, Anglia Ruskin University, Cambridge, UK. Her main research interest is in the psychosocial issues faced by women living with HIV in the UK. Specifically, within a mixed-methods doctorate she is exploring the process through which women disclose a positive HIV status to an intimate partner.

Anneke Sools is Assistant Professor in narrative psychology at the University of Twente, The Netherlands, and researcher at the Dutch Lifestory Lab (www.utwente.nl/lifestorylab). She is co-founder of the Dutch Network for Narrative Research. Her main research interests are narrative futuring in relation to resilience and wellbeing, and the qualitative therapy process research of web-based treatments.

Wendy Stainton Rogers is Professor Emerita of Health Psychology at the Open University and the current Chairperson of the International Society of Critical Health Psychology. Her research interests are in understanding health inequalities. Her expertise is in qualitative research methods, with her particular speciality being Q methodology. She is the co-editor of *The SAGE Handbook of Qualitative Research in Psychology* (Sage) and author of *Social Psychology: Experimental and Critical Approaches* (McGraw-Hill).

Leslie Swartz is a Professor of Psychology at Stellenbosch University, South Africa. He has a long-standing interest in language issues in psychological research and practice, in public mental health and in disability studies. His current work focusses on issues of formal and informal care in low-resource contexts, and on research capacity development in disability-related work in Africa.

Gareth Terry is a Research Associate at the Open University, UK. His research interests are broadly located around understanding and theorizing the social construction of masculine identities. He is currently involved in research projects in the areas of young men's masculine identity formation, domestic violence prevention, heterosexual consent practices, body hair-removal practices and men's health decision-making. He has methodological interests in thematic analysis and qualitative survey design.

Gareth Treharne is a Senior Lecturer in the Department of Psychology at the University of Otago, Aotearoa/New Zealand. His research focuses on the experiences of people living with chronic illnesses such as rheumatoid arthritis and the role of societal perceptions of chronic illnesses. He applies phenomenological, discursive, participatory and correlational methodologies in his research, and he has a particular interest in the use of the 'think aloud' method to unpack the process of questionnaire completion. He also has an interest in use of the autoethnographic process to investigate the outsider–insider interface and personal reflexivity of researchers and health-care practitioners.

Alison Tweed is Clinical Director and Principal Lecturer on the Universities of Staffordshire and Keele Doctorate in Clinical Psychology Programme, UK. She is a clinical psychologist and qualitative researcher with research interests in the fields of medical psychology, particularly chronic illness, psychotherapy processes and clinical psychology training.

Jane Ussher is Professor of Women's Health Psychology in the Centre for Health Research at the University of Western Sydney, Australia. She is editor of the Routledge *Women and Psychology* book series and author of a number of books, including *The Psychology of the Female Body*; *Women's Madness: Misogyny or Mental Illness?*; *Fantasies of Femininity: Reframing the Boundaries of Sex*; *Managing the Monstrous Feminine: Regulating the Reproductive Body*; and *The Madness of Women: Myth and Experience*. Her current research includes couple interventions for PMS, the sexual health of refugee migrant women, sexuality and fertility after cancer, and GLBTI experiences of cancer.

Cathy Vaughan is a Lecturer and researcher based in the Melbourne School of Population and Global Health at the University of Melbourne, Australia. She has a particular research interest in the process and impacts of participatory and visual research methodologies. Her current research projects focus on sexual and reproductive health, disability inclusive development, migrant health and young people's health in contexts of rapid social change in Asia and the Pacific.

Kerryellen Vroman is an Associate Professor at the University of New Hampshire, Durham, USA. Much of Dr Vroman's research programme utilizes mixed-methods designs with a specific interest in personal projects analysis. Her areas of research include affective and social factors that influence adaptation to illness, therapeutic interactions among health-care providers and care recipients, and mental health and wellbeing among youth and young adults.

Chris Walton is a Lecturer in Social Psychology at Lancaster University, UK. His research interests are primarily focused on institutional practices involving people with learning disabilities, the application of qualitative research methods to those practices and the translation of policy into everyday practice.

Introduction: Qualitative Research in Clinical and Health Psychology

Poul Rohleder and Antonia C. Lyons

About the book

Qualitative research methods in psychology have in the past held a marginalized position, viewed as a 'soft' method of research compared to the 'hard' scientific, experimental approach to developing psychology knowledge. In recent decades this has changed, however, and there is increased recognition of the importance of qualitative research in understanding human behaviour and psychological experiences. Rather than conceptualizing quantitative versus qualitative methods in terms of 'hard' science versus 'soft' science, there is an increasing acknowledgement that we need various approaches for fully understanding complex psychological phenomena. Qualitative approaches do not need to be set in opposition to quantitative approaches as they ask different, and frequently complementary, questions (Lyons, 2011).

Without going into a long history of the use of qualitative methods in psychology (interested readers may want to refer to Willig & Stainton Rogers, 2008), it is worth noting that much of the engagement with qualitative research methods has tended to be in certain sub-disciplines of psychology (such as social psychology) rather than others (such as cognitive psychology). Health psychology and clinical psychology, as the sub-disciplines in psychology concerned with issues of physical and mental ill-health and wellbeing, have traditionally tended to aim for alignment with medicine (a field that arguably provides the most powerful knowledge and set of practices). This has led to the use of statistical and/or experimental research methods, to provide credible knowledge that is taken seriously by professionals working in the health and medicine fields. Yet qualitative research across various disciplines has gained ground as a way of understanding the experiences, perspectives and contexts of ill-health and wellbeing from the viewpoint of the 'patient', and the various meanings associated with the psychosocial determinants of ill-health and its consequences.

Qualitative research remains the 'poor relation' in health psychology (Chamberlain, 2013) and clinical psychology research. This may be partially due to the fact that the field can be confusing, with different methods developed in different disciplines and from different research traditions, sometimes drawing on quite different ideas of science (Polkinghorne, 2005). Additionally, health and clinical psychology courses often do not provide strong training programmes in qualitative research or the use of qualitative methods (Chamberlain, 2013). Another major issue has been a broader lack of understanding regarding the rigour of qualitative approaches and alternative quality criteria that may need to be employed in assessing the value of specific qualitative approaches (Lyons, 2011). Nevertheless, the wealth of health and clinical psychology research described in this book, employing a range of qualitative research approaches, really does highlight its 'coming of age' in these fields. We hope that this book will demonstrate how valuable qualitative research approaches can be within clinical and health psychology, and how forcefully they can contribute to our understanding and knowledge.

The aim of this edited text is to focus on the contributions that the different qualitative methodologies and methods can make to issues of physical and mental health. We refer to many of the chapters in this book as 'methods' chapters, although we acknowledge that some of them are more than methods and provide a methodology. This distinction will become clear throughout Part I of the book (see the subsequent outline of the book's structure).

The book includes contributions from authors from a variety of countries (e.g. the United Kingdom, New Zealand, Australia, South Africa), and also from those who have conducted research in different parts of the world (e.g. India), providing a highly valuable international perspective. The book will not only introduce students and practitioners to the various methods, but will also provide illustrative examples and 'how-to' guides, drawing from contributors' own research projects that involve issues related to physical and mental health. Readers will be able to see how these methods are applied to these areas and, more importantly, what sorts of knowledge are created with these methods. For example, in clinical psychology, qualitative research works well for answering research questions such as:

- What are young clients' emotional investments in counselling?
- What are the personal meanings of the experience of addiction?
- How do interactions between carers and people with intellectual disabilities occur in practice?
- What are the experiences of users of mental health services?

And in health psychology, qualitative research enables researchers to explore questions such as:

- What are sexual health professionals' understandings of factors that undermine sexual health and wellbeing?
- How do people with end-stage renal disease experience the transition to dialysis?

■ What are women's constructions of negative pre-menstrual change?

■ What do young people living in a high HIV-prevalence area think are the most important influences on their health?

This book is suitable for psychology students at both undergraduate and post-graduate levels. However, although specifically referring to health psychology and clinical psychology, it is also relevant for undergraduate and postgraduate students in related fields who want to include qualitative methods in their research. Students of psychiatry, behavioural medicine and nursing will find this book directly relevant, focusing as it does on physical and mental health. Students from other related health and social care disciplines, such as social work, physiotherapy and occupational therapy, who are specifically interested in working in mental health or rehabilitation services will also find the book useful.

Thinking about qualitative research in clinical and health psychology

It is important to understand that research – all research – is never straightforward. Experienced and sophisticated researchers know that the processes involved in research are 'messy', and these processes are more messy than the various chapters in this book might suggest (although the authors do try to be up front about some of these less-discussed aspects of doing research). Some methods are more prescriptive than others, but, given that qualitative research is involved with 'real-world' issues and frequently takes place in 'real-world' settings (as opposed to observations within a laboratory, for example), there is always a need to consider the unexpected, the phenomena that cannot be controlled for, and the many emerging problems and difficulties.

Many of the research issues covered in this book apply to all research, not merely qualitative research. For example, all research needs to have a strong conceptual and theoretical argument, clear research aims, a study design that is consistent with the aims and epistemological positioning of the research, and methods and analytical strategies that are appropriate and coherent within the project. Issues such as evaluation vary in their criteria across different forms of research approaches. Ethical issues also vary considerably across different qualitative projects depending on study design and methods. The care and attention that researchers pay to these broader issues will make for stronger and more robust research projects, and we strongly advise new and emerging researchers to take the time to consider them within their own research frameworks.

While this book employs specific examples from completed research, every project is different. Thus, the issues and methods covered in the book must be adapted (with careful consideration) to the developing research topic or project. Readers may also be unsure as to what method may be best for their

Table 1.1   Questions regarding research assumptions

Key questions	Range of considerations	
	From	*To*
What is your view on the nature of the research?	Neutral and technical	Critical and controversial
What is your positioning relative to the participants?	Distant and objective	Intimate and involved
What is the direction of your 'gaze'?	Outward towards others	Inward and self-reflective
What is the purpose of your research?	Private and professional	Useful for participants
Who is the intended audience of your research project?	Academics and clinicians	Participants and communities
What is your political positioning?	Neutral	Explicitly political
How do you see the researcher's and participants' agency in the research?	Passive	Engaged in praxis (making a difference)

Source: Based on Marshall & Rossman (2011); Brantlinger (1997).

project, or how best to adapt the issues and methods to their own work. There are a number of crucial assumptions that researchers make in qualitative (and quantitative) research that need to be considered when making decisions about your own project (Marshall & Rossman, 2011; Brantlinger, 1997). We have summarized these in Table 1.1. Research and its subsequent methods vary according to where the research is located and the assumptions that are made. These are often not explained or even considered in any detail. Explicit consideration of these kinds of assumptions, and how they are grounded in the conceptual framework of the research, will help strengthen the arguments of the research project and, importantly, will boost its integrity (Marshall & Rossman, 2011).

The methods chapters in this book take different perspectives, all of which are informed by various epistemological and theoretical frameworks. They all make assumptions along the dimensions shown in Table 1.1 and the authors help to make these explicit. Some qualitative methods aim for 'making a difference' and have a clear political orientation, and here participants are sometimes asked to assist with the research design and also data-collection processes. The aims and positionings of the methodology influence the research *from the outset*. We hope that this book will help to reinforce the importance of these notions.

Synopsis of the book

This book is divided into four broad sections.

Part I deals with conceptual and theoretical issues relevant to qualitative research. It includes five chapters that deal with the important topics of epistemology (Chapter 2), key ethical concerns (Chapter 3), considering the role of culture and language in qualitative research (Chapter 4), strategies for ensuring quality in qualitative research (Chapter 5) and different approaches to collecting data (Chapter 6). All these topics are very broad and there is much that can be considered and discussed. Thus, these chapters can only provide a brief introduction and an outline of key considerations, and students who are embarking on their first qualitative project are encouraged to do further reading. To assist in this, each chapter has a list of recommended further reading.

Each of the remaining 11 chapters covers a particular qualitative method. These are by no means exhaustive, but they are methods that have been the most frequently used, or are considered especially relevant, in clinical and health psychology. For each of these methods chapters, the authors provide an introduction, historical background regarding the method, the theoretical or conceptual framework involved, how the method has been used (or could be used) in clinical and health psychology, a worked example or step-by-step guide, a relevant example of research using the method and finally a list of further reading.

We have made a necessarily simplistic division in grouping these methods along the lines of whether each may be more useful for understanding individual experiences or understanding social processes. This was one way for us to organize and structure the book, but it is important to note here that a method's being listed under one section does not mean that it is not relevant for the other. For example, narrative research (Chapter 9) is included in Part II (Exploring Individual Worlds), as it is a method that is often used for understanding individual autobiographical stories, although it can be (and is) also used for understanding 'social' phenomena and stories.

Part II includes five methods that are particularly useful for exploring 'individual worlds'; that is, for exploring the experiences and meanings of individuals. The methods introduced here are thematic analysis (Chapter 7), grounded theory (Chapter 8), narrative research (Chapter 9), phenomenological approaches (Chapter 10) and psychoanalytically informed research (Chapter 11). All these chapters (and those in Parts III and IV) draw on research examples to illustrate the method itself and the processes involved. Some make use of examples from health psychology, while others employ research examples from clinical psychology, but all chapters incorporate discussion of uses within both sub-disciplines.

Part III includes four methods that are often used for understanding 'social worlds'. The first two chapters are concerned with social worlds as experienced or constructed through language and verbal interaction; namely, conversation analysis (Chapter 12) and discourse analysis (Chapter 13). The other two are methods more concerned with group behaviour and group processes; namely, ethnography (Chapter 14) and participatory action research (Chapter 15).

There is an increasing recognition that research in psychology may benefit from drawing on a variety of sources of data to understand complex phenomena. Qualitative methods can be particularly useful for understanding and exploring that complexity, but they have also been employed in combination with quantitative methods to allow researchers to gain a broad and varied understanding of the phenomena under study. The final section, *Part IV*, comprises two chapters that explore how qualitative and quantitative data can be combined. Chapter 16 covers Q methodology, which is predominantly a qualitative method but can generate data that can be used to conduct some quantitative analysis (it could also have fitted into either of Parts I and II, depending on how it is used, highlighting the somewhat artificial nature of these distinctions). The final chapter (Chapter 17) explicitly discusses different approaches for mixing qualitative and quantitative methods in research projects.

Qualitative research can reveal people's complex and situated behaviours, practices and experiences. As health and clinical psychology researchers, we need to continue to strive for the development of creative ways to tap into people's experiential lives and social worlds. We hope that this book will assist you in undertaking coherent, rigorous and informative research that will help develop our understanding and knowledge base in rich, relevant and insightful ways.

References

Brantlinger, E. (1997). Using ideology: Cases of nonrecognition of the politics of research and practice in special education. *Review of Educational Research*, 67(4), 425–459.

Chamberlain, K. (2013). What is the subject matter of health psychology? *European Health Psychologist*, December, 1–4.

Lyons, A.C. (2011). Editorial: Advancing and extending qualitative research in health psychology. *Health Psychology Review*, 5(1), 1–8.

Marshall, C. & Rossman, G.B. (2011). *Designing Qualitative Research* (5th ed.). Los Angeles, CA: Sage.

Polkinghorne, D.E. (2005). Language and meaning: Data collection in qualitative research. *Journal of Counseling Psychology*, 52(2), 137–145.

Willig, C. & Stainton Rogers, W. (eds) (2008). *Handbook of Qualitative Research Methods in Psychology*. London: Sage.

PART I Issues in Qualitative Research

Epistemology and Qualitative Research

Kerry Chamberlain

2

When we undertake research, we inevitably make assumptions. In fact, we cannot conduct research without making assumptions – about the best way to conduct an interview, the theoretical framing of the methodology we will use, the nature of the issue we are investigating. For example, when setting out to investigate how people experience depression, we need to decide how we will proceed. Even the way our question is framed – in this case, in terms of people's experience – implies assumptions: that people have experiences, that they can report on them (perhaps accurately?), that they will disclose them to the researcher, that researchers will understand what is reported and so on. Although these assumptions are important, they are generally given minimal attention in reporting research, and in many cases are taken for granted by researchers and given limited consideration in planning research.

Our research assumptions are important, not only because they drive our research agendas but also because they determine the directions, practices and findings of our research (Carter & Little, 2007). It may not seem obvious, but how we conduct our research determines what we find – our methods determine our findings. As Radley et al. (2010:36) state, 'the data – or what can be made of them – are tied up with the means of producing them'. Data do not exist independently of the ways of collecting them. Many psychologists act and argue as though this was so, because they take epistemological issues for granted and do not examine or reflect on their underlying assumptions. Rather, they treat these assumptions as common sense, as not requiring further examination or explication. Pascale (2011:4) notes how social science students are likely to be well trained in data collection and analysis but to 'inherit broad epistemological assumptions that render core aspects of inquiry a matter of common sense'.

More importantly, how methods work and what they can accomplish – the data that get collected and interpreted – are determined strongly by the assumptions we make about the nature of the world and how it can be investigated. We can illustrate this with our example of depression. When we ask people who have experienced depression to inform us about that experience (through questionnaires or interviews), do we consider that they are providing us with the 'truth' about that experience? This is a difficult issue. On the surface, of course we assume that our research participants will seek to inform us as accurately as they are able what it was like to feel depressed and how that affected them. However, are they able to provide an objective and truthful account of their experience, or will they offer a more constructed, partial and uneven account of what they understand has happened and how it has affected them? If we assume the former, we might also be concerned about whether their accounts are coloured by them complying with what they think we want to know, thus introducing assumptions of 'bias' and 'demand characteristics'. In this case, our underlying assumptions are likely to be that there is a reality, independent of the research, which can be revealed through their responses, and is open to being uncovered by researchers through a robust, rigorous research process. In doing so, we would seek to minimize demand characteristics and bias. Alternatively, if we assume the latter, we might consider that participants will do their best to provide a sound account of their experience, but that any account they give will inevitably be limited, partial and created within the context of the research. In this case, our underlying assumptions are likely to be that participants are constructing an account of their experience, for a range of reasons: to make sense of their experience, to present themselves as moral and responsible persons and so on. We might also assume that participants cannot provide an accurate, objective account of their experience, and that their accounts – their possibilities for speaking – are constrained by their backgrounds, culture, setting or location. We might also consider that people speaking about experiences of depression can challenge, rework or subvert common understandings of who a person with depression may be. These two approaches to research are premised on very different sets of assumptions about how research can and should proceed.

Researching assumptions

The most fundamental assumptions for research are those made about the nature of the world and how we can investigate it (research it) successfully. These issues are usually referred to respectively as ontology (assumptions about the nature of the world) and epistemology (assumptions about how the world can be investigated). This chapter discusses these assumptions, what they are, why they are important and how they shape our research, as well as considering some of the important debates in the field. It specifically focuses on qualitative research practice, illustrating the discussion with examples to show how these assumptions function and shape our research. Before going into this, some prior issues need comment.

First, issues of ontology and epistemology are closely tied up in what counts as knowledge within the discipline. As Pascale (2011:4) notes:

> Ontologies are theories about the nature of existence. Ontological assumptions are extremely powerful, not just because they shape what

counts as valid knowledge, but because they do so in ways that are not explicit and therefore not accountable, and not even easily open to doubt.

Hence, ontological assumptions about the world allow certain forms of knowledge, especially knowledge gained through (scientific) research, to be accepted readily and other forms to be dismissed. Epistemological assumptions are similarly bound up with knowledge claims. As Pascale (2011:4) also comments, epistemology

> concerns the nature, sources, and limits of knowledge. As such, it regards issues of belief – assertions and propositions about how the world can be apprehended. How can we produce knowledge about the social world? Under what conditions can we know what we know? Epistemology can be understood as a *justificatory account* of the scientific production of knowledge.

Hence, it is important to remember as we go forward that our assumptions, and their associated ideologies and values, are enormously influential in shaping what we do and the knowledge that we produce. Furthermore, this is also bound up with ethics, politics and power (see Flyvbjerg, 2001; Pascale, 2011), although consideration of these issues is beyond the scope of this chapter.

A related issue concerns limitations on what is counted as 'proper' knowledge. Kempner et al. (Kempner, 2005; Kempner et al., 2011) discuss forbidden knowledge in research: knowledge that is not sought in research because of the perceived constraints that it may be too sensitive, dangerous or inappropriate. They suggest that such constraints operate in two forms. Formal constraints – imposed by government regulations, professional bodies or publication outlets, such as around stem cell research or that funded by cigarette manufacturers – limit knowledge, although these constraints are generally open and recognizable, and are usually the topic of public discussion and debate. Informal constraints also operate, those tacitly agreed but unspoken rules and boundaries on what should and should not be studied. Kempner et al. suggest that these constraints are discipline specific, culturally ingrained and resistant to change, offering limited opportunities to assess their effects. We know that clinical psychology and health psychology have formal constraints on what they study (e.g. through ethics), but do they also have informal constraints on knowledge production? Here, we need to consider such factors as the ideological bases of the discipline and – more relevant to the present discussion – barriers to publication imposed by considerations of what constitutes 'proper' research and 'proper' knowledge. Such constraints are tacitly sustained by a strong emphasis on empirical research and 'evidence', defined in particular ways, as well as by publishing conventions invoking word limits and specific formats. These barriers can make qualitative research more difficult to publish and for it to be accepted and considered as 'proper' knowledge.

We also need to acknowledge that making sense of ontological and episte-mological issues is difficult. Different scholars offer differing accounts and cat-egorizations of these, and there is considerable debate and disagreement on how they are best understood and invoked. One way forward is proposed by Becker (1993), who argues that these issues have troubled us for over 2000 years without solutions and will continue to do so, and therefore we should simply leave them to people who adopt 'philosophical and methodological worry as a profession' (1993:226), philosophers of science. That may be suf-ficient if we seek to undertake quantitative research, as the underlying assump-tions in that arena are widely agreed, frequently taken for granted and pre-sumed as the 'natural' state of the world, and research proceeds without much reference to them, particularly in psychology. However, when we move into qualitative research, we enter territories substantially less well agreed and for-mulated, and debate about such things as objectivism and constructionism, realism and relativism continues to thrive and divide, largely because they are so fundamentally important for research practice. So in the qualitative arena, we need to make sense of where we stand on these philosophical matters if we are to undertake sound, rigorous and defensible research. Furthermore, we should also keep in mind that the assumptions we make are just that – assump-tions, positions to work from; they do not identify any truth claims about the nature of the world. As Blaikie (2004a:768) notes, debates about 'ontological and epistemological claims cannot be settled by empirical enquiry'.

The diversity of positions on these philosophical issues, and the potential for confusion, are readily evident in even a cursory examination of the litera-ture. For example, Guba and Lincoln (1994) proposed four different para-digms underlying qualitative research (positivism, postpositivism, critical the-ory et al. and constructivism). Paradigms as used here are 'the basic belief sys-tem or worldview that guides the investigator, not only in choices of method but in ontologically and epistemologically fundamental ways' (1994:105) and are differentiated by their ontological, epistemological and methodological assumptions. This does provide a framework for research, but one with sub-stantial difficulties, with one paradigm (postpositivism) being a limited modi-fication of another (positivism) and another (critical theory et al.) being con-sidered as a combination of different paradigms. Madill and Gough (2008) also drew on the concept of paradigm to locate qualitative research within psychological science. They reviewed social science research and suggested that five paradigms could be identified: positivism, postpositivism, pragma-tism, advocacy/participatory and social constructivism. Madill and Gough also noted how the concept of paradigm differed considerably, using Morgan's (2007) classification of paradigmatic views as based on shared beliefs of researchers in a particular field, on epistemological stances or on more global worldviews including values, ethics and ways of thinking. To complicate the notion of paradigm further, Johnson et al. (2007) proposed another view, arguing that quantitative, qualitative and mixed methods research could be considered as different paradigms. The point of this is not to establish how paradigms may be useful for systematizing differing assumptions underlying research, but to demonstrate how terminology changes, in definition, scope and usage, from one text to the next, which can be very confusing for researchers trying to locate a place to stand.

This can also be demonstrated from another direction. Pistrang and Barker (2012) argue that the philosophical background to qualitative research is marked by two dichotomies. The first is between positivism and naturalistic inquiry, the latter referring to 'exploring and understanding the phenomenon in question' and 'concerned more with inner experience than with observable behaviour' and with 'words rather than numbers' (2012:7). The second is between realism and constructionism, where constructionism assumes 'that there is no objective reality independent of human thought' and research participants and researchers 'make their own constructions that cannot be independently verified because there is no reality against which to verify them' (2012:7–8). While these arguments may seem reasonable on first glance, they are confusing and unhelpful in practice. First, all researchers, including those espousing positivist positions, are concerned to explore and understand 'the phenomenon in question', although they may have a variety of ways for doing that and different assumptions about what constitutes knowledge. Second, many would argue that Pistrang and Barker confuse and conflate epistemological assumptions with ontological ones when they contrast realism with constructionism (Crotty, 1998; Maxwell, 2011). Third, there is considerable debate about the issue of relativism within social constructionism (e.g. Elder-Vass, 2012; Maxwell, 2011; Nightingale & Cromby, 1999). This is, of course, just another illustration of the potential confusions in terminology and debate that await the social science researcher seeking to make sense of philosophical matters for qualitative research (for more, see Blaikie, 2004b).

Moving forward: Making sense of assumptions

So how can we move forward? Quantitative researchers have an easier path here, as they can simply follow the 'received view' of positivism as the basis of 'scientific research', get on with their research and evade these philosophical debates. Qualitative researchers do not have it so easy, as they are required to warrant their findings, not only through their methods but also through their methodologies and underpinning philosophical stances. Therefore, they need to have engaged with these issues and have a defined and argued position on them. Accordingly, let us start with some clarification of the distinction between the core philosophical underpinnings of research, ontology and epistemology. Table 2.1 sets these out, providing a brief definition of each and some differing positions illustrated using anorexia.

However, this is slippery stuff. Although we may distinguish between ontology and epistemology at the definitional level, this is much more difficult once we try to describe and exemplify it. For instance, exemplifying these issues

Table 2.1   Ontology and epistemology

Issue	Positions	Examples
Ontology: Assumptions about the nature of the world and the phenomena in it.	There is a real material world...	Anorexia exists...
	...that can be examined and researched; it has objective existence.	...as a real entity.
	...but it can only be partially apprehended through our sensory processes.	...but we have difficulty apprehending it objectively and completely.
	...that is created through our interactions with it.	...as a set of meanings negotiated between people in interaction.
	There is no real material world; the world is created by us.	...as a shared understanding.
Epistemology: Assumptions about how we can learn about the world, investigate issues and gain knowledge.	The meaning of the world resides...	Anorexia may be investigated...
	... in the objects of the world, which can be investigated objectively; knowledge is objective and provides truthful information about the world.	...objectively and understood lawfully; we can gather factual information about it that is independent of the researcher.
	...in the interaction between investigators and objects of the world; there is no absolute truth; knowledge is constructed for particular purposes.	...with findings about it being constructions that are historically, socially and culturally shaped.
	...in the observer; knowledge is created by the observer and is independent of the objects in the world.	...subjectively; we can only gather shared understandings about it.

with anorexia can be problematic, as even the disciplinary perspective from which we approach anorexia can produce a difference. As a clinical psychologist, we may see this as a 'disorder' and consider questions around treatment. As a health psychologist, we may see this more as a health issue and raise questions around health outcomes and behaviour change. As a critical clinical or health psychologist, we may see this more as an issue of power and query who benefits from the situation. Furthermore, it is exceedingly difficult to discuss ontology and epistemology separately because they are inevitably intertwined; as soon as we start discussing one, we slide into the other and vice versa (Crotty, 1998). To progress this, let us ignore ontology for the moment and consider epistemology. We return to ontological issues later in discussing pragmatism and critical realism.

As noted above, epistemological assumptions drive research practice and the generation of knowledge. Carter and Little (2007:1319) argue that 'epistemology is inescapable' and that reflexive researchers actively engage with epistemological assumptions, whereas non-reflexive researchers adopt them implicitly, since it is impossible to engage in research 'without at least tacit assumptions about what knowledge is and how it is constructed'. Hence, researchers need to be critical and reflexive about their research practice, and that includes having an informed understanding of epistemological assumptions. Very helpful for this is the categorization of epistemological stances proposed by Crotty (1998). In doing this, Crotty makes two important distinctions. First, he distinguishes between four levels, or elements, of research: epistemology, theoretical perspective, methodology and method. Second, he distinguishes three epistemological stances: objectivism, social constructionism and subjectivism. We will discuss these epistemological stances first and return to the four research levels later. Together, these provide a strong framework for conceptualizing qualitative research.

Epistemological stances, for Crotty (1998), are distinguished in terms of where meaning resides. Table 2.2 outlines the three stances from this perspective.

We can illustrate these stances using illness, particularly a contestable illness like chronic fatigue syndrome (CFS). Researchers adopting an objectivist (positivist) stance would be likely to consider CFS to be a real biological illness, a disease (although problematically so, since its existence is contested) with associated symptoms, and seek to explore its diagnosis, treatment and precipitating and causal factors (e.g. Whiting et al., 2001). Researchers adopting this stance often seek to discriminate between 'objective' scientific meanings and 'subjective' and biased meanings, thereby privileging scientific understandings over people's experiences and personal understandings.

Researchers adopting a social constructionist stance would consider CFS to be a constructed entity whose meaning(s) would depend on who is constructing it and for what purpose. These researchers would be more likely to explore the experience of the illness and its implications for the family (see e.g. Crix et al., 2012) or citizenship (see e.g. Brown et al., 2011). In this perspective, 'scientific' findings have no better claim as knowledge than other forms; scientific

Table 2.2   Epistemological stances

Objectivism (Positivism)	Constructionism (Social constructionism)	Subjectivism
Meaning (and meaningful reality) exists apart from any consciousness (in the absence of an observer); meaning resides in the objects of the world, which can be investigated objectively; knowledge is objective and provides truthful information about the world.	Meaning arrives out of our engagements with the objects in the world; meaning requires a mind and it resides in the interaction between investigators and the objects of the world; there is no absolute truth; knowledge is constructed for particular purposes.	Meaning is imposed on objects by observers; meaning therefore resides in the observer; knowledge is created by the observer and is independent of the objects in the world.

Source: After Crotty (1998).

knowledge is treated as a construction like all other constructions of knowledge. Claims to objectivity, and to other matters of science such as validity, reliability and generalizability, may be dismissed once knowledge is assumed as constructed, for particular purposes, in particular places and at particular times.

Researchers adopting a subjectivist stance would consider CFS to be a creation of the observer, making meaning out of their own observations. It is difficult to find exemplars of research from this perspective, since the assumptive base involved is that humans form meaning out of their own consciousness and independently of the objects in the world. However, people are always engaged with their world in some form and are intentional beings; as such, they cannot avoid making sense *with* the objects in the world rather than independently of them. It has been suggested that research taking an extreme postmodern perspective, or engaging in methods like auto-ethnography, could invoke subjectivist epistemology, although when we seek exemplars (e.g. Birk, 2013) the account often looks much more constructionist than subjectivist, invoking theoretical concepts to interrogate and interpret data. In practice, most qualitative research involves a social constructionist stance, although some positivist qualitative research can be found. Given that, subjectivism will not be discussed further in this chapter.

However, we should note that Crotty's view on epistemology would be debated and challenged by many theorists. Almost all scholars, Crotty included, agree that considerable variation exists within these epistemological stances. For example, many researchers have discussed different versions of social constructionism (e.g. Danziger, 1997; Nightingale & Cromby, 1999; Stam, 2001, 2002). We have insufficient space to discuss these epistemological debates; rather, this chapter offers an account of epistemological matters that can provide a foundation for psychology researchers engaging in qualitative research. Nevertheless, some important issues surrounding epistemology remain that need addressing, three in particular.

Three further epistemological issues

First, many feminist scholars argue for a feminist epistemology, or, rather, for various feminist epistemologies. Schwandt (2007a), for example, identifies three contrasted forms of feminist epistemology: feminist empiricism, feminist standpoint epistemology and feminist postmodernism. When we look into these positions more critically, we find that they do involve assumptive positionings about the world and objects of study, but their framing is often quite broad and not focused specifically on epistemological matters, similar to the paradigmatic perspectives discussed earlier. If we consider the differing feminist epistemological positions identified by Schwandt (and others) and ask where meaning resides – Crotty's determining question for separating epistemological stances – then we find that there is, in the way these various forms are labelled, discussed and debated, some overlap with objectivist and social constructionist positions as presented by Crotty. For example, Anderson's comment that feminist epistemology 'investigates the influence of *socially constructed conceptions and norms of gender and gender-specific interests and experiences* on the production of knowledge' (2009:54, italics in original) implies a strongly social constructionist version, although this would be contested by many empiricist and some standpoint feminists. This provides a further example of the complexity of epistemological discussions and how researchers may be confused by terminology. Because the language is slippery, almost any assumptive position backgrounding research can be argued into something like an epistemology. Crotty avoids these debates by placing feminism as a theoretical perspective for research, rather than an epistemology. From that viewpoint, feminist approaches theorize and frame both assumptions of how the world works and the methodologies for investigating it. Underlying that, Crotty would argue, feminist positions on epistemology can be subsumed into one or other of the three epistemological perspectives he identifies (although he also offers a thorough discussion of the complexities invoked by such positioning; see Crotty, 1998:160–82). This is a convenient and tidy solution for researchers grappling with epistemology, but also a contested one. There is no doubt that the activities of feminist scholars and researchers have changed the ways in which research is conceptualized and conducted and have created important new knowledge. However, the issue of whether there is a distinctive feminist epistemology, in the tightly defined way we are using it here, is more contentious. Feminist researchers have a particular perspective on research, which is based epistemologically and framed theoretically, and is consequently influential on methodology and participant relationships. Holding Crotty's four-level framework for research in view allows for a functional and organized perspective on these matters, and for consideration of epistemological matters in research without precluding us from engaging with ongoing epistemological debates.

The second issue concerns the epistemology of phenomenology. The study of experience is a major endeavour in qualitative psychological research, and many researchers use some form of phenomenology to investigate it. The question then arises: What is an appropriate epistemology for phenomenological research? Willig (2012) recently discussed epistemological bases for qualitative research, proposing that such research generates three different types of knowledge: realist knowledge, phenomenological knowledge and social constructionist knowledge. We are familiar with the first and last of these from our discussions above. However, is there a separable phenomenological knowledge and, by implication, a distinctive phenomenological epistemology? The argument in favour is based on the premise that phenomenological research seeks 'knowledge of the quality and texture of the participant's experience' (Willig, 2012:11). This is contrasted with realist knowledge, 'valid and reliable knowledge about a social or psychological phenomenon that exists independently of the researcher's awareness of it' (2012:11), and with social constructionist knowledge, concerned with 'how they [people] construct versions of reality through the use of language' (2012:12). Phenomenology itself has many different theoretical (and methodological) framings (Langdridge, 2007); some of these appear to consider the knowledge gained as having objectivist tenets (e.g. Sousa, in press), but most would see phenomenal knowledge as constructionist in nature (e.g. Clegg, 2012). If we hold to Crotty's (1998) proposal to differentiate epistemologies by where meaning resides, then we would argue that there is no need for a unique epistemology for phenomenology, and that it is better to consider phenomenology as providing particular theoretical framings and methodological approaches for conducting research, rather than as constituting a distinct epistemological stance.

The third issue concerns the recent rise of mixed-methods research – research using combinations of quantitative and qualitative methodologies – and its epistemological foundations (see O'Cathain, 2010). Qualitative and quantitative research into a phenomenon will ask different questions and use different methods, and this raises queries about the epistemological underpinnings implicated therein. The proponents of mixed-methods research argue for yet another epistemology, pragmatism. So do we need to include pragmatist epistemology in our categorization of epistemologies? Pragmatism is a philosophical tradition, or 'philosophical movement' (McCaslin, 2008), with a long history of debate and contestation, making it difficult to offer any precise clarification of the pragmatist stance. Vannini, for instance, distinguishes between forms of classical pragmatism and more contemporary critical pragmatism, in which 'critical pragmatists strongly emphasize the emancipatory, polemical, and transformative potential of pragmatist philosophy and social theory and research as well as the polemical and even activist role of the citizen-scholar' (2008:160). This is essentially a generic critical position, applicable to all research approaches, and does not help much with regard to epistemological considerations. Others propose that pragmatism is not 'epistemologically centred' (McCaslin, 2008:674) and that ontological concerns are more fundamental for pragmatism (McCaslin, 2008; O'Cathain, 2010). They argue that practical consequences are 'the central criteria of knowledge' for pragmatism (McCaslin, 2008:674). The emphasis on ontological considerations of realism would seem to locate pragmatism in a position similar to critical realism, discussed later in the chapter. Hence, while both epistemological and ontological claims are made within the pragmatist perspective, it is clear that the arguments go well beyond these and treat pragmatism as a 'philosophical movement' (McCaslin, 2008). Once again, if we return to Crotty's core question – where does meaning reside? – it becomes clear that some accounts of pragmatism accept it as having an epistemological base effectively similar to social constructionism, seeing knowledge as provisional and relative (e.g. Yardley & Bishop, 2008; Vannini, 2008), while others argue for a dismissal of epistemological relevance (e.g. McCaslin, 2008). However, most accounts invoke pragmatism as a wider philosophical stance and do not allow it to be located comfortably within Crotty's standpoint. This does not mean that the 'paradigm clash' in mixing methodologies can be avoided, although pragmatism provides some arguments for working around it. Nevertheless, some suggest that this is simply an evasion; Lincoln (2010:7), for example, argues that 'the pragmatism claimed for some mixed-methods theorists rests at the enacted level only. The mixed-methods pragmatists tell us nothing about their ontology or epistemology or axiological position.' Once again, we are enmeshed in a substantial debate that serves to complicate the way forward in understanding the epistemological underpinning of research. For mixed-methods research, we do not need a further epistemology if we conduct the quantitative and qualitative research components from objectivist and social constructionist stances respectively, and recognize that insights gained from these different methods will not necessarily converge (Yardley & Bishop, 2008).

Social constructionism

The major epistemological stance assumed by researchers conducting qualitative research is social constructionism. This is not essential (since epistemological stances are assumptions about knowledge that cannot be independently verified) and some conduct qualitative research from an objectivist stance (e.g. Audrey, 2011). However, it is more common to see qualitative research that assumes a realist ontological position alongside a constructionist epistemological position (e.g. Jobling, 2014).

So what is social constructionism? As noted above, it is an epistemological stance that assumes that meaning arises from our engagements with objects in the world, that it resides in the interaction between investigators and objects and that knowledge is constructed through those interactions for particular purposes. There are many versions of social constructionism and considerable contestation around its delineation (see Elder-Vass, 2012), making it difficult to offer a definitive account of the approach. The explanation offered here draws heavily from Crotty (1998) and arises from attempting to simplify and systematize broad, differing epistemological stances. Gergen and Gergen (2008:817) note that 'social construction typically refers to a tradition of scholarship that traces the origin of knowledge and meaning and the nature of reality to processes generated within human relationships'. Certainly, a key tenet of social constructionism is that interactions determine knowledge.

Social constructionism offers a significant challenge to objectivist notions, by rejecting assumptions that knowledge is fixed and determinate and that lawful causal relationships can be determined. Rather, social constructionists argue that knowledge is formed in context, that it is provisional and that it is inevitably located socially, historically and culturally. Hence, social constructionism challenges the essentialism that lies at the core of objectivism – that objects exist in ways that can be known independently of the knower. In psychology, an objectivist view is widespread and taken for granted; many would not understand why anyone would critique the idea that people have measurable amounts of intelligence or self-esteem. Under constructionist assumptions, such objects are always constructed, by someone, for some purpose, in some context. When people give accounts, they do so to an audience – they construct different accounts for researchers than for friends, for friends than for family. Our participant with anorexia might give the researcher an account that is constructed to present herself as a worthy, moral person facing adversity, but to friends she may give an account of a normal, albeit thin, person, and to family she may offer an account of victimization and oppression. In these ways her situation and standing will be contextually and interactionally created, or constructed.

Understandings, and knowledge, are also culturally and historically contextual, and another key tenet of social constructionism is that knowledge is historically, socially and culturally located. For instance, we do not expect people living before the widespread availability and use of the internet, and other forms of social media, to have the same understandings and expectations of psychological matters as do 'digital natives'. Considerable effort has gone into using these new technologies to provide behaviour change methods (e.g. Civljak et al., 2010) and forms of therapeutic help (e.g. Kazdin & Rabbitt, 2013), simultaneously changing their use and their meaning. Changes to the Diagnostic and Statistical Manual of Mental Disorders (DSM), and critical challenges to those changes, have systematically reconstructed what we understand as a disorder over time (e.g. Kirschner, 2013). Social constructionists argue that, within our social cultures, nothing remains stable and, consequently, neither can knowledge. It makes considerable sense, therefore, to adopt a constructionist stance towards knowledge generation and to recognize that what we find only holds for here and for now.

So, in one sense, social constructionism is a reaction to objectivism and denies an objectivist view of the world. However, this critical view on objectivism, that things in the world have no single objective meaning, opens social constructionism to charges of relativism – if nothing can be considered 'real' and meaning is formed only in the interaction between subjects and objects, then there can be as many meanings as there are people interacting with objects. As Moghaddam (2005:315) puts it: 'relativism is the Archilles' heel of social constructionism'. We turn to this debate later in this chapter.

Three further constructionist issues

First, many writers use the term constructivism, rather than constructionism, in discussing epistemological issues. For many (e.g. Guba & Lincoln, 1994), these terms have exactly the same meaning. In psychology, however, because cognitive psychologists (who are mainly objectivist) use the term 'constructivist' to describe processes, as in memory, but with objectivist connotations, the term 'constructionism' has come to be used more specifically to designate an epistemological stance. Schwandt (2007b:39–40) distinguishes these two strands:

> One strand, known as radical constructivism or psychological constructivism, focuses more on the individual knower and acts of cognition …
> A second strand of constructivism focuses more on social process and interaction and is generally known as social constructionism.

For psychologists undertaking constructionist research, the descriptor 'social constructionism' will provide a generally unambiguous statement of their epistemological positioning and allow them to avoid the cognitivist flavour of constructivism.

The second issue concerns the meaning of social as a prefix for constructionism. Does this imply that only 'social' objects, like anorexia, extraversion and stigma, are the objects of construction? Some (e.g. Blaikie, 2007) argue this to be the case, suggesting that physical objects, like trampolines and tranquillizers, have a material reality and cannot be socially constructed in the way that non-material, culturally created objects, like tranquillity and tension, may be. We can quickly put this argument to rest: if we adopt a social constructionist epistemology, then everything in the world, material or non-material, is socially constructed. At least, this is the position that most social constructionists would adopt, arguing, as Crotty (1998:55) does, that 'The "social" in social construction is about the mode of meaning generation and not about the kind of object that has meanings.' Put simply, the meaning of a tree is as socially constructed as the meaning of a trait.

The third issue is more complicated and troublesome; namely, how we should deal with relativism, Moghaddam's 'Achilles' heel of social constructionism'. This is frequently referred to as the realism–relativism debate. Indeed, some (e.g. Guba & Lincoln, 1994) contrast social constructionism with realism, but this erroneously confounds epistemology with ontology. Critical researchers seek to eschew extreme versions of relativism and argue that a 'real' world exists, one containing poverty, disparity, stigma, happiness and other aspects of material existence. We can overcome this debate by assuming a position that 'to say that reality is socially constructed is not to say that it is not real. ... constructionism in epistemology is perfectly compatible with a realism in ontology' (Crotty, 1998:63). This is about returning to onto-logical matters – the nature of the world – as they underlie epistemology: how can the world be investigated, how is knowledge generated? Researchers fre-quently take up this position, adopting a social constructionist epistemological stance with a critical realist ontological stance. But *critical* realism? This can be understood as assuming an ontological reality, although one that can be known only imperfectly through our sensory capacities as social beings (see Elger, 2010). Knowledge, in this view, is considered partial and subject to revision and change. However, we should not take this to mean that any particular con-struction is arbitrary, as good or useful as any other – the strident case for rel-ativism, as Smith (2006) terms it. Smith contrasts this with the reasonable case for relativism, based on how understandings of the 'real' have changed over time, and can only be examined through specific discourses. Hence, although interpretations may be relativist, in the research context we must accept that researchers will strive to be rigorous in data collection, analysis and interpre-tation, and accept that they will seek to offer interpretations and insights that are better than arbitrary – the best possible interpretations they can make. This works to rebut the strident case for relativism. Although this provides a solu-tion to the realist–relativist debate, we should acknowledge that this consti-tutes another contested arena, and that debates around realism and critical realism are another hotbed of debate, with contested views abounding.

Conducting research

Let us now return to Crotty's (1998) four elements of research and consider implications arising from structuring the research process in this way. Crotty proposes that four questions determine the 'basic elements of any research process' (1998:2). These questions can be stated as:

- What *methods* will we use to collect our research data?
- What *methodology* frames this choice and use of particular methods?
- What *theoretical perspective* underlies this methodology?
- What *epistemology* informs this theoretical perspective?

The first requires little discussion. Psychology researchers understand methods very well and, in fact, have been criticized for being overly concerned with method (Danziger, 1990). In qualitative research, the interview in all of its forms is easily the most commonly used method, often employed creatively in conjunction with material objects, photo and video elicitation, graphic elicita-tion and mapping processes (see Chapter 6).

Methodology is more problematic and many researchers, and some research texts, confuse and elide methods and methodologies. Perhaps this is not surprising, as this area, like epistemology, is replete with differing definitions and conceptualizations. Essentially, a methodology is the framework underlying the plan of action for conducting the research, informing the methods and what they are intended to produce as data, and how the analysis of data will be approached. A useful definition is offered by Schwandt (2007c:194), proposing that methodology

> involves analysis of the assumptions, principles, and procedures in a particular approach to inquiry (that, in turn, governs the use of particular methods). Methodologies explicate and define (a) the kinds of problems that are worth investigating, (b) what comprises a researchable problem, testable hypothesis, and so on, (c) how to frame a problem in such a way that it can be investigated using particular designs and procedures, (d) how to understand what constitutes a legitimate and warranted explanation, (e) how to judge matters of generalizability, (f) how to select or develop appropriate means of generating data, and (g) how to develop the logic linking problem–data generation–analysis–argument.

Methodologies are therefore those frameworks for research – ethnography, narrative inquiry, critical discourse analysis, grounded theory – that tie together planning, identification of appropriate methods, data collection and analysis into a coherent whole. Note that methodology 'governs the use of methods', but is separate from them. For example, a researcher may use interviews as a method, but why and how interviews are used will differ according to the methodology: interviews for narrative methodology will be different to interviews for grounded theory or ethnography.

Lying behind methodology is the next level, the theoretical perspective for our research. But what do we mean by theoretical perspective? It is important to note that this does not mean the theories or theoretical concepts driving the subject matter or topic of research. For instance, in researching dying, we might consider theoretical issues of hope, resignation, anxiety or life review. However, this is not the theoretical thinking that informs our methodology. That refers to the way in which the methodology is understood and the theoretical ideas in which it is rooted. For instance, phenomenology incorporates a range of theoretical ideas that inform how phenomenological methodology is approached and utilized: the methodology adopted, be it descriptive, hermeneutic, interpretative or critical narrative phenomenology, will differ according to which theoretical perspective on phenomenology is utilized (see Langdridge, 2007). Earlier in this chapter it was argued that feminism was best considered a theoretical perspective informing methodological approaches, with different theoretical understandings of feminism associated with different methodological approaches. Discursive research provides a range of methodological approaches, including discursive psychology, Foucauldian discourse analysis and critical discourse analysis, all with differing theoretical underpinnings that shape how they function methodologically. Hence, it is incumbent on researchers to understand how the methodology they adopt is theoretically shaped and framed.

Behind theoretical perspectives lie the epistemological assumptions underpinning research. These have already been discussed, and the argument made that these are fundamental drivers of the research process, determining what counts as knowledge. Thus, it is equally incumbent on researchers to understand the epistemological assumptions framing their research.

Identifying these four elements of research helps clarify the different aspects of the research endeavour and its underpinnings. These elements operate at different levels; methodologies are not methods, nor are they epistemologies – they are all differing components of the research agenda, albeit associated, connected and mutually informing. Equally important is that these four elements must be appropriately aligned if the research is to have coherence. For example, a social constructionist epistemology can inform a discursive theoretical perspective, which sustains the choice of discourse analytical methodology, and the use of interviews or focus groups as methods. Also aligned would be social constructionism with symbolic interactionism, theoretically informing ethnography as a methodology and participant observation as a method. However, it makes little sense to invoke social constructionism and a theoretical perspective of phenomenology, and then to move to use experimental research methodology and measurement and statistical analysis as methods; the disjunctures here will be obvious. Similarly, objectivist epistemology, with positivism as a theoretical perspective, cannot be coherently located with narrative methodology and life history interviews as method.

In this discussion, we have largely ignored one important aspect of the research process, ontology (see Table 2.1). Where do ontological considerations fit? Once again, we find that this philosophical concept, like others we have considered, generates substantial debate and disagreement about its nature and function. Also, as argued previously, ontology and epistemology are inevitably intertwined and difficult to discuss independently. As Crotty argues, 'ontological issues and epistemological issues arise together. Given that state of affairs, it seems we can deal with the ontological issues as they emerge without expanding our [four element] schema to include ontology' (1998:11). This is not to say that ontological issues should be dismissed or ignored, and it recognizes that ontological matters are crucial, particularly in relation to some substantial debates in the field, especially around realism.

Concluding comments

This chapter has sought to provide a pathway through the difficult terrain of the philosophy of science that underpins research, with a specific focus on qualitative research. It has presented a particular version of these issues and, necessarily, given the space available, oversimplified the terrain and minimized the debate. On the other hand, it has endeavoured to provide a clear framework, largely adopted from the position established by Crotty (1998), for understanding and considering the fundamental assumptions that underlie all research. It has emphasized social constructionism as the major epistemological stance for qualitative research. Throughout, the chapter has argued for achieving conceptual clarity over engaging in depth with the nuanced debates and contestations in this arena, so that researchers unfamiliar with these issues and seeking to establish a perspective for their own research activities can forge pathways forward and conduct coherent, reflexively driven qualitative research. In doing so, it has also attempted to point to significant areas of debate and to provide a starting point for those interested in pursuing such debates further. Above all, it has been argued that qualitative researchers must understand these issues; they must be able to defend the ontological and epistemological assumptions underlying their research, and their theoretical and methodological choices for conducting it. These assumptions and choices should not be tacit.

Further reading

Crotty, M. (1998). *The Foundations of Social Research*. Thousand Oaks, CA: Sage.
  Michael Crotty's book remains one the clearest presentations on these issues, which is why the ideas presented there are featured so strongly in this chapter. The book will extend and clarify many of the debates discussed here.
Elder-Vass, D. (2012). *The Reality of Social Construction*. Cambridge: Cambridge University Press.
  A detailed consideration of social constructionism, and the arguments and debates surrounding it, with particular treatment given to reconciling the relationship between realism and social constructionism.
Pascale, C.-M. (2011). *Cartographies of Knowledge: Exploring Qualitative Epistemologies*. Thousand Oaks, CA: Sage.
  A readable but more deeply philosophical treatment of epistemology, which extends many of the issues and arguments touched on in this chapter.

References

Anderson, E. (2009). Feminist epistemology: An interpretation and a defense. *Hypatia*, *10*(3), 50–84.
Audrey, S. (2011). Qualitative research in evidence-based medicine: Improving decision-making and participation in randomized controlled trials of cancer treatments. *Palliative Medicine*, *25*(8), 758–765.
Becker, H.S. (1993). Theory: The necessary evil. In D.J. Flinders & G.E. Mills (eds), *Theory and Concepts in Qualitative Research: Perspectives from the Field* (pp. 218–229). New York: Teachers College Press.
Birk, L. (2013). Erasure of the credible subject: An autoethnographic account of chronic pain. *Cultural Studies ↔ Critical Methodologies*, *13*, 390–399.

Blaikie, N. (2004a). Ontology, ontological. In M.S. Lewis-Beck, A. Bryman & T.F. Liao (eds), *The SAGE Encyclopedia of Social Science Research Methods* (p. 768). Thousand Oaks, CA: Sage.

Blaikie, N. (2004b). Epistemology. In M.S. Lewis-Beck, A. Bryman & T.F. Liao (eds), *The SAGE Encyclopedia of Social Science Research Methods* (pp. 310–311). Thousand Oaks, CA: Sage.

Blaikie, N. (2007). *Approaches to Social Enquiry* (2nd edn). Cambridge: Polity Press.

Brown, P., Morello-Frosch, R. & Zavestoski, S. (eds). (2011). *Contested Illnesses: Citizens, Science, and Health Social Movements*. Los Angeles: University of California Press.

Carter, S.M. & Little, M. (2007). Justifying knowledge, justifying method, taking action: Epistemologies, methodologies, and methods in qualitative research. *Qualitative Health Research*, 17(10), 1316–1328.

Civljak, M., Sheikh, A., Stead, L.F. & Car, J. (2010). Internet-based interventions for smoking cessation. *Cochrane Database of Systematic Reviews*, 9, CD007078.

Clegg, J.W. (2012). The importance of feeling awkward: A dialogical narrative phenomenology of socially awkward situations. *Qualitative Research in Psychology*, 9(3), 262–278.

Crix, D., Stedmon, J., Smart, C. & Dallos, R. (2012). Knowing 'ME' knowing you: The discursive negotiation of contested illness within a family. *Journal of Depression and Anxiety*, 1, 119.

Crotty, M. (1998). *The Foundations of Social Research*. Thousand Oaks, CA: Sage.

Danziger, K. (1990). *Constructing the Subject: Historical Origins of Psychological Research*. New York: Cambridge University Press.

Danziger, K. (1997). The varieties of social construction. *Theory & Psychology*, 7(3), 399–416.

Elder-Vass, D. (2012). *The Reality of Social Constructionism*. Cambridge: Cambridge University Press.

Elger, T. (2010). Critical realism. In A.J. Mills, G. Durepos & E. Wiebe (eds), *Encyclopedia of Case Study Research* (pp. 254–258). Thousand Oaks, CA: Sage.

Flyvbjerg, B. (2001). *Making Social Science Matter*. Cambridge: Cambridge University Press.

Gergen, K. & Gergen, M. (2008). Social constructionism. In L. Given (ed.), *The SAGE Encyclopedia of Qualitative Research Methods* (pp. 817–821). Thousand Oaks, CA: Sage.

Guba, E. & Lincoln, Y.S. (1994). Competing paradigms in qualitative research. In N.K. Denzin & Y.S. Lincoln (eds), *Handbook of Qualitative Research* (pp. 105–117). Thousand Oaks, CA: Sage.

Jobling, H. (2014). Using ethnography to explore causality in mental health policy and practice. *Qualitative Social Work*, 13(1), 49–68.

Johnson, R.B., Onwuegbuzie, A.J. & Turner, L.A. (2007). Toward a definition of mixed methods research. *Journal of Mixed Methods Research*, 1(2), 112–133.

Kazdin, A.E. & Rabbitt, S.M. (2013). Novel models for delivering mental health services and reducing the burdens of mental illness. *Clinical Psychological Science*, 1(2), 170–191.

Kempner, J. (2005). Forbidden knowledge. *Science*, 307(5711), 854.

Kempner, J., Merz, J.F. & Bosk, C.L. (2011). Forbidden knowledge: Public controversy and the production of nonknowledge. *Sociological Forum*, 26(3), 475–500.

Kirschner, S. (2013). Diagnosis and its discontents: Critical perspectives on psychiatric nosology and the DSM. *Feminism & Psychology*, *23*(1), 10–28.

Langdridge, D. (2007). *Phenomenological Psychology: Theory, Research and Method.* Harlow: Pearson.

Lincoln, Y.S. (2010). 'What a long, strange trip it's been…': Twenty-five years of qualitative and new paradigm research. *Qualitative Inquiry*, *16*(1), 3–9.

Madill, A. & Gough, B. (2008). Qualitative research and its place in psychological science. *Psychological Methods*, *13*(3), 254–271.

Maxwell, J.A. (2011). Epistemological heuristics for qualitative research. In H. Soini, E.-L. Kronqvist & G.L. Huber (eds) *Epistemologies for Qualitative Research* (Qualitative Psychology Nexus, vol. 8; pp. 9–27). Tübingen: Center for Qualitative Psychology.

McCaslin, M. (2008). Pragmatism. In L.M. Given (ed.), *The SAGE Encyclopedia of Qualitative Research Methods* (pp. 672–676). Thousand Oaks, CA: Sage.

Moghaddam, F. (2005). *Great Ideas in Psychology*. Oxford: Oneworld Publications.

Morgan, D.L. (2007). Paradigms lost and pragmatism regained: Methodological implications of combining qualitative and quantitative methods. *Journal of Mixed Methods Research*, *1*, 48–76.

Nightingale, D. & Cromby, J. (eds). (1999). *Social Constructionist Psychology: A Critical Analysis of Theory and Practice.* Buckingham: Open University Press.

O'Cathain, A. (2010). Mixed methods involving qualitative research. In I. Bourgeault, R. Dingwall & R. De Vries (eds), *The SAGE Handbook of Qualitative Methods in Health Research* (pp. 575–589). London: Sage.

Pascale, C.-M. (2011). *Cartographies of Knowledge: Exploring Qualitative Epistemologies.* Thousand Oaks, CA: Sage.

Pistrang, N. & Barker, C. (2012). Varieties of qualitative research: A pragmatic approach to selecting methods. In H. Cooper, P. Camic, D. Long, A. Panter, D. Rindskopf & K. Sher (eds), *APA Handbook of Research Methods in Psychology* (vol. 2; pp. 5–18). Washington, DC: American Psychological Association.

Radley, A., Chamberlain, K., Hodgetts, D., Stolte, O. & Groot, S. (2010). From means to occasion: Walking in the life of homeless people. *Visual Studies*, *25*(1), 36–45.

Schwandt, T.A. (2007a). Feminist epistemologies. In T.A. Schwandt (ed.), *The SAGE Dictionary of Qualitative Inquiry* (3rd edn; pp. 111–112). Thousand Oaks, CA: Sage.

Schwandt, T.A. (2007b). Constructivism. In T.A. Schwandt (ed.), *The SAGE Dictionary of Qualitative Inquiry* (3rd edn; pp. 38–42). Thousand Oaks, CA: Sage.

Schwandt, T.A. (2007c). Methodology. In T.A. Schwandt (ed.), *The SAGE Dictionary of Qualitative Inquiry* (3rd edn; pp. 194–196). Thousand Oaks, CA: Sage.

Smith, M. (2006). Relativism. In V. Jupp (ed.), *The SAGE Dictionary of Social Research Methods* (pp. 261–263). London: Sage.

Sousa, D. (2014). Validation in qualitative research: General aspects and specificities of the descriptive phenomenological method. *Qualitative Research in Psychology*, *11*(2), 211–227.

Stam, H.J. (2001). Introduction: Social constructionism and its critics. *Theory & Psychology*, *11*(3), 291–296.

Stam, H.J. (2002). Introduction: Varieties of social constructionism and the rituals of critique. *Theory & Psychology*, *12*(5), 571–576.

Vannini, P. (2008). Critical pragmatism. In L.M. Given (ed.), *The SAGE Encyclopedia of Qualitative Research Methods* (pp. 160–164). Thousand Oaks, CA: Sage.

Whiting, P., Bagnall, A., Sowden, A., Cornell, J., Mulrow, C. & Ramirez, G. (2001). Interventions for the treatment and management of chronic fatigue syndrome: A systematic review. *Journal of the American Medical Association*, *286*(11), 1360–1368.

Willig, C. (2012). Perspectives on the epistemological bases for qualitative research. In H. Cooper, P. Camic, D. Long, A.T. Panter, D. Rindskopf & K. Sher (eds), *APA Handbook of Research Methods in Psychology: Vol. 1. Foundations, Planning, Measures, and Psychometrics* (pp. 5–21). Washington, DC: American Psychological Association.

Yardley, L. & Bishop, F. (2008). Mixing qualitative and quantitative methods: A pragmatic approach. In C. Willig & W. Stainton Rogers (eds), *The SAGE Handbook of Qualitative Research in Psychology* (pp. 352–372). London: Sage.

Ethical Issues

Poul Rohleder and Charlotte Smith

3

In qualitative research, the aim is often to explore in-depth participants' subjective lived experiences or perspectives on personal and social phenomena. In clinical psychology and health psychology, this often involves the exploration of personal human experience in relation to suffering, disability, pain and distress. Qualitative research in these sub-disciplines of psychology may also focus on 'positive' aspects such as coping, resilience and wellbeing. Nevertheless, it typically invites the participant to share their intimate, personal experience. As a result, there are significant ethical issues to consider. In this chapter, we will discuss some key ethical considerations, including informed consent, confidentiality and anonymity, the consequences of research and ownership of data, and the role of the researcher and the participant. We will refer primarily to the interview in our discussion of ethics, as that is often adopted as the key method for collecting data in qualitative research. However, the ethical issues discussed are generally relevant for all forms of data collection.

A brief history of ethics in psychological research

The concept of a code of ethics is rooted in Greek philosophy (Pettifor, 1996). Kant proposed the thesis that human beings, through a process of logical reasoning, could come up with a unified set of rules of moral conduct to be practised; the definition of today's ethics. The importance of having an ethical code became evident after the Second World War following the atrocities committed by the Nazis (Hazelgrove, 2002), including experiments that were conducted on humans in the pursuit of 'racial purity' (Bogod, 2004). This research was not guided by any moral compass and was incredibly harmful to participants, causing profound short- and long-term suffering and resulting in many deaths (for examples see Bogod, 2004). At this point there was consensus among the scientific community regarding the urgency to introduce a formal code of ethics in science, and the Nuremberg code (1947, as cited by Hazelgrove, 2002) followed. This formed the basis of future medical and scientific research ethics.

A code of ethics in psychological science is relatively new (Pettifor, 1996). In 1948 a code of ethics specific to psychology professionals was initiated (Korkut, 2010), when Hobbs (1948) expressed dissatisfaction regarding the applicability of medical ethical guidelines in guiding the ethical practice of psychological researchers and practitioners. He argued that there are unique sets of specific ethical challenges to psychologists that are not covered in codes of medical practice. In 1947, the American Psychological Association (APA) endorsed a psychology ethics board (Hobbs, 1948) and in 1953 the APA drew up the first code of ethics.

The national psychological societies of various countries have codes of ethics to which their members are required to adhere. We looked through the code of ethics of the American Psychological Association, the Australian Psychological Society, the British Psychological Society, the Canadian Psychological Association, the New Zealand Psychological Society and the Psychological Society of South Africa. Central to all of these codes is the requirement to treat participants in psychological interventions and research with respect and dignity. Furthermore, informed consent and the right to confidentiality are key ethical concerns.

National research bodies have codes of ethical practice that include similar principles. For example, the Economic and Social Research Council (ESRC) in the United Kingdom lists six key principles for good ethical research (see Box 3.1). Psychological research should adhere to both the professional body's code of ethics and specific ethical research principles.

It is important to acknowledge that ethical guidelines are continuously changing as the field and practice of research change and new technologies are used. An example is the rapid increase in internet-based research, which prompts new ethical considerations (as discussed in the British Psychological Society's [2013] publication of ethical guidelines for 'internet-mediated' research).

BOX 3.1   The six key principles of the ESRC's Framework for Research Ethics

1. Research should be conducted in a manner that ensures quality, integrity and transparency.
2. All those involved in research (staff and participants) should be fully informed about the aims, methods and purpose of the research and what their participation involves (including possible risks).
3. The anonymity of research participants and the confidentiality of information provided must be respected.
4. Research participation should be voluntary.
5. Research should ensure the avoidance of harm to participants and researchers.
6. Research should be conducted independently, with any conflicts of interest explicitly stated.

Source: ESRC (2012:2–3)

Core ethical considerations in qualitative research in psychology

Brinkmann and Kvale (2008) argue that the core fields of ethics in research – consent, confidentiality, the consequence of research and the competency and role of the researcher – are not issues that can be fully addressed and settled in any standardized way prior to the start of any research endeavour. Rather, they view these core fields as 'fields of uncertainty' (2008:265), describing them as issues that need to be reflected on continually and addressed throughout the research process. Thus, this involves more than merely answering a series of ethical tickboxes, but rather a continuing ethical stance and thoughtfulness about the researcher's own practice and the whole research endeavour. Ethics is not specific to the start of research, and ethical consideration does not stop once ethical approval is granted. Ethical concerns are ongoing and require constant consideration.

Many readers of this book will be familiar with these core ethical principles as applied to research generally, so we focus our discussion here to the sorts of ethical considerations that may be important when conducting qualitative research in clinical and health psychology. Box 3.2 on pg. 39 provides a summary of key points and considerations. As discussed in Chapter 6, a variety of methods are used for collecting data in qualitative research. It is beyond the scope of this chapter to consider all aspects of ethics related to each method of data collection, thus we use the interview as an illustrative example of a dominant method.

Informed consent

Informed consent involves asking people to take part voluntarily in research after they have been fully informed about the purpose and design of the research study, and the consequences of their voluntary participation. That participation remains voluntary throughout the duration of the study, so participants have the right to withdraw at any time. In interviews, this is typically achieved through a process of briefing the potential participant prior to an interview and debriefing them afterwards. Beforehand, the participant should be informed about the aim and purpose of the research and what they should expect, as well as how the information they give will be treated (not only in terms of confidentiality and who will have access to it, but also how it will be analysed and reported on). Consent is typically sought and recorded at the start of the interview. At the end, participants should be debriefed, offering them an opportunity to reflect on their experience of participating and raising any questions about what the researcher will do with the data. Here the participant still has the right to withdraw.

Informed consent is thus often viewed as an agreement prior to the start of participation, which is then reviewed at the end. What occurs during the research process is sometimes not adequately considered. Hollway and

Jefferson (2000), in writing about their psychoanalytically informed free association narrative interview, argue that it is impossible for the researcher to inform the potential participants accurately about how the interview will be subjectively experienced. They argue that often participants give their 'informed consent' based on their previous understanding and assumptions of what an interview will be like; perhaps a formal question-and-answer–type interview. Thus, informed consent cannot be considered in terms of a once-off cognitive decision process, but rather as a 'continuing emotional awareness that characterises every interaction' (2000:88). Informed consent is a continuous process, informed by the emotional experience of the interview. While Hollway and Jefferson write in terms of their particular psychoanalytically informed approach to interviewing, this is equally true of the semi-structured interviews often used in qualitative research, where the agenda evolves as the interview progresses, following the nuances of the narrative given by the participant. This is not about deception, but rather about the participant and the researcher not fully *knowing* what the interview will be like until they are actually experiencing the interview. For example, qualitative research in clinical and health psychology often aims to explore the lived experience of people who are undergoing various physical and mental health difficulties. The participant and the researcher may have a sense of what sorts of things might be discussed, but, in line with the nature of exploration, unexpected factors may frequently emerge or be revealed during the course of the interview. Furthermore, researchers sometimes have to weigh up how much information to give about the interview beforehand, particularly if what is being sought is participants' spontaneous thoughts, where leading the participant in how they 'should' respond may be detrimental to the aims of the research. Enough information needs to be given to ensure that participants are not deceived, but still allow for spontaneity. Thus, careful attention should be given to the participant's willingness to continue participating as the interview (or whatever their participation involves) progresses.

In situations where there is a clear research participant (such as an interview), gaining consent is relatively straightforward (although see later in this chapter). However, in other methods where more than one individual is participating, consent needs to be gained from various individuals, whether they are actively or passively involved in the study (there is a discussion of this in Chapter 14 in relation to ethnographic research). Drawing from their example of participatory action research (see Chapter 15), Khanlou and Peter (2005) suggest that pre-data-gathering information meetings are a useful means by which the aims and purpose of the study can be communicated and discussed and any questions that the various participants may have raised and answered.

In clinical and health psychology, the issue of who has capacity to consent often arises; for example, in the case of participants with learning disabilities, or older adults with dementia, or young children. Here, researchers should consult with relevant laws and guidelines (such as the Mental Capacity Act [2005] in the United Kingdom). In institutional settings, consent (or permission) may be required from more than merely the immediate potential participants. For example, Heggestad et al. (2013) provide an overview of these issues as practically encountered within their own qualitative study among adults living with dementia in a health-care setting. The protocol used by these researchers involved first discerning the patients' ability to give informed consent. Consent was gained from a close relation where it was deemed inappropriate to seek informed consent from an individual due to their limited capacities. The participant was not recruited for the research if consent was not provided after this stage. The nurse in charge of the unit was informed, and had approved, of such procedures.

As discussed by Heggestad et al. (2013), assessing whether a participant with disabilities is able to give informed consent is an issue in and of itself. A method often used by health and clinical psychologists to guide a decision is employing standardized psychological tests that are quantitatively scored. However, as Heggesad et al. (2013) highlight, it is important to give thought to the weaknesses of this approach for each particular sample under study, and to consider the possibility of drawing on diverse sources of information. In their own study, Heggestad et al. (2013) discussed the weaknesses of using neuropsychological tests with dementia patients to discern their capabilities. While these appear to offer an internally valid measure of cognitive functioning and to possess good psychometric properties, their value when applied in the real-world setting for this purpose was questionable, because the degree of awareness of dementia patients varies over time. For this reason, the researchers opted to utilize the lived and extensive knowledge of the head nurse as their main method for informing their decisions about informed consent.

Aside from capacity to consent, consideration also needs to be given to potential implicit coercion. For example, as Thompson and Russo (2012) observe, requests to interview patients in health-care settings (or other institutions) as potential research participants may compromise participation as voluntary, since patients may be influenced in deciding to participate out of a need to interact with others or provide relief from boredom. It may be that patients feel like they *should* consent if they want to be considered a 'good' patient. It is often the practice to provide participants with a monetary incentive for their participation. A guiding principle is that this should be a nominal amount to reimburse the participant for their time and effort (including travel costs), but not be a big amount that could be regarded as potentially coercive. However, when research is conducted with participants who are vulnerable and may be living in situations of relative deprivation, any monetary incentive could potentially be coercive (Ensign, 2003). Critical researchers in clinical and health psychology, who tend to favour qualitative research methods, are often concerned with issues of power in relation to health and ill-health. Power dynamics exist in the research endeavour, with the researcher at times being in a position of relative power to the participant. Students can make use of supervision to reflect on possible power dynamics.

Issues of consent also arise when the internet is used as a source of data for qualitative studies (see Eysenbach & Till, 2001; British Psychological Society, 2013). Internet sites such as blogs or discussion boards may provide access to unique, publicly available narrative accounts of users' experiences; for instance, experiences of living with a particular health problem. Informed consent is not generally viewed as being required on the basis that the information (data) is publicly available; it has already been shared. However, there is some debate about whether such discussion forums are viewed by those posting to them as semi-private or not; people may post items that are intended for a particular audience and have not considered these as being used for research. The issues at play relate to undisclosed observation for research purposes (British Psychological Society, 2013). Eysenbach and Till (2001) suggest that in these cases ethical consideration should be given to whether sites are 'private' or 'public', and so whether the research, or the presence of the researcher, is intrusive and potentially harmful. Another method for making a decision could be to use the 'ethic of reciprocity', in which researchers put themselves in the data-maker's shoes when discerning what is appropriate (Honderich, 1995, as cited by McKee, 2013). In situations in which an online forum or discussion space is set up for the purposes of research, all the necessary information needed to facilitate informed consent can be provided and built in as part of the online registration process of potential participants (see for example Flicker and colleagues' [2004] development of an online forum as part of a youth-focused health research study). However, consideration needs to be given to how this information is presented so as to ensure as far as possible that the participant is engaging with the information; for example, not using information pages that are lengthy and overly detailed, which may encourage readers to skim read over them or to skip them and click on to the next page (see British Psychological Society, 2013).

Anonymity is another key issue associated with using material from the internet for a research investigation. As McKee (2013) points out, if online information is included, unaltered, within a research publication there is a potential risk to the anonymity of the 'now participant'. This is because the original data is uniquely in the public domain and thus accessible to the public via a search engine as well as being available within the research dataset. Using information from social network site profiles, for example (one of the predominant sources of internet data at present), leaves the participant vulnerable to being identified (McKee, 2013), potentially revealing their name, age, location, image and occupation. This is particularly an issue where the data has been interpreted deeply. Simply transforming the same content into the researcher's own words can mitigate this risk (McKee, 2013).

Confidentiality and anonymity

Confidentiality and anonymity are two key concerns often expressed by potential participants, who have numerous motivations for taking part in interviews.

In our experience, one such motivation is the recognized opportunity for them to 'tell someone their story', in a way that may lead to possible positive changes but will not expose them to the responses and potential judgements of others. The primary way in which this is achieved is to disseminate any data anonymously; that is, in a way that will not identify who the participant is. This may be done through the use of pseudonyms or numbering the various participants, and also by changing all potentially identifying features in a transcript or image (or whatever the source of data is), such as place names, people's names, workplaces and so on.

Limits to confidentiality need careful consideration and discussion with potential participants. This may be a particularly salient issue in clinical and health psychology research; for example, if a participant reveals a situation of risk during the interviews, such as suicidal intentions or incidents of child abuse. Thus, particularly with sensitive topics involving vulnerabilities, both researcher and participant need to be clear about breaking confidentiality when safeguarding issues arise. Another situation that can occur is obtaining information that implicates the participant in illegal activity (for example, taking illegal drugs). It would be important to seek the advice of ethical review boards in such instances, as the data collected may implicate participants or other people and could be regarded as potential evidence if any police or legal investigation should be conducted.

Another limitation to confidentiality may arise when a participant may be easily identifiable when reporting results – for example, as a result of them having a rare condition, working in a unique setting or having a unique role within an organization that is the study location. This may arise particularly in the case of small sample numbers, which is often the case in qualitative research. Also, an organization in which the study is being conducted may request a feedback report of the results. Care needs to be taken that participants (whether staff or service users of the organization) are not easily identifiable. In qualitative research, quotes are often used as illustrative data of reported findings, so members of the organization may be able to identify colleagues on the basis of what is said and how. Consent could be sought from participants with regard to what quotes may or may not be used in reporting results (for example, as in Donnison et al.'s [2009] study on community mental health teams). Thus, as with informed consent, issues of confidentiality are considerations that need to be held in mind at all stages of research, not only during the process of gaining ethical approval. Any issues that arise need to be clearly discussed with participants.

The consequences of research

Some ethical principles are core to all types of research in all disciplines; for example, ensuring that research does not involve a risk of harm to participant and researcher. Numerous psychological studies have been conducted in the past that have been considered as inflicting harm on participants (for example,

Milgram's experiments on social obedience). In clinical and health psychology, consideration needs to be given to issues of protecting participants from harm, as the topic of study is often emotive or even emotionally painful (for example, ill-health or trauma). Care needs to be taken to respect participants' privacy and dignity, and thus research should avoid questioning that is too unnecessarily intrusive. It is important to consider the 'vulnerability' of the participants and the 'sensitive' nature of particular topics, but, as Thompson and Chambers (2012) point out, the use of such terms may risk participants in clinical and health research being disempowered, as they are treated in a potentially paternalistic way. Participants should retain the autonomy to decide what they wish to participate in and what they wish to share in the interview. An interview may result in some experience of distress in participants as they talk about emotionally painful things, but this does not equate with the study being *harmful*, if the participants consent to take part and see the study as worthwhile (e.g. Graham et al., 2007). Nevertheless, consideration needs to be given to how such distress is managed during the interview and afterwards (Haverkamp, 2005). This may raise dilemmas for health psychologists, particularly clinical psychologists, in relation to negotiating the role of researcher and clinician/therapist (see later in this chapter).

While issues of potential harm often revolve around the participants, they are also important for the researchers involved. For example, one of us (PR) recalls conducting a series of interviews with HIV-positive women living in a deprived area of South Africa, about their experiences of being the stigmatized 'other' (see Rohleder & Gibson, 2006). Some of these interviews were conducted with the aid of an interpreter. Some of the participants spoke of incredible social hardships and the impact that HIV has had on them as women. The interviews were often very emotive. All participants were given the opportunity to stop the interviews if they wanted, but most welcomed the opportunity to tell their story. However, this did take its toll, particularly for the interpreter, who herself was living with HIV. During one particularly emotive interview, some time was taken to debrief after the interview so that the interpreter could discuss the impact on her. The voluntary nature of her participation also needed to be ensured. Novice researchers may find themselves affected by the emotional nature of the topics being explored, and students can use supervision as an important space for exploring their emotional reaction to the research (Davison, 2004).

The British Psychological Society's (BPS, 2009) code of ethics also advises psychologists to notify research participants about evidence obtained during research that indicates the presence of a physical or psychological problem of which the participant is unaware, if the participant's not knowing of this may cause them harm. The BPS goes on to caution researchers about giving advice or discussing outcomes; rather, they should arrange appropriate assistance.

The consequence of research does not only involve issues of risk. Typically, research involves the dissemination of results, usually in the form of publishing findings in journal articles. In qualitative research, this often involves a process of *interpretation* of the qualitative data. Researchers work with the data that are gathered and frequently are required to interpret their meaning; see, for example, the process of interpretation in phenomenological analysis (Chapter 10) or psychoanalytically informed research (Chapter 11). Such interpretations may have ethical consequences (see Willig, 2012). This may be unintentional, but may be received as potentially harmful when interpretations are made about groups of participants. For example, Crossley's (2004) interpretation of published autobiographical and fictional texts as data to understand potential motivations for 'barebacking' (sex without a condom in the context of HIV risk) was met with significant critique by HIV researchers and the lesbian and gay academic community for the method of identifying data, and for her interpretations, which were argued potentially to infringe on the rights and dignity of the participants to whom she referred (gay men who take part in 'barebacking') and which related to 'communities and practices that are easily stigmatized' (Barker et al., 2007). As Willig (2012) points out, it is often the interpretation of data (or the consequences of research) that has the more lasting effect.

Willig (2012) offers three strategies that researchers can use to address ethical concerns in their interpretations:

1. Approaching the interpretation of data with the research questions in mind and 'being modest about what the research can reveal' (2012:56).
2. Always considering the participant's voice, which may include consulting them about the findings being produced.
3. Being open to alternative ways of interpreting the data.

Also helpful is to keep in mind strategies for ensuring quality and validity in qualitative research (see Chapter 5).

Furthermore, the publishing of results has many benefits for the researcher and the broader academic community, but does not always have a direct benefit to research participants. As Sieber points out, often a cited 'benefit' of research is that it will be of broader benefit to society or the population group, but this is frequently 'based on the vague hope that all research is bound to help – somehow' (1992:101). Greater emphasis is placed on *real* impact by more and more funding bodies, as researchers are tasked with showing how a research project will benefit more than merely the academic community. Potential difficulties also arise around the ownership of data. For example, methods for data collection are frequently used that are produced by the participants, such as diaries, drawings or photographs (see Chapter 6). It needs to be made clear who has ownership of these data and how they can or cannot be used. For example, Castleden and colleagues (2008) outline the steps taken to ensure that ethical concerns were addressed when using Photovoice (photographs taken by participants as data) in their community-based research. What they did was to ensure that participants were adequately trained and informed about issues of privacy and consent with regard to who and what they were photographing, and that a release agreement was drawn up with regard to how the photographs would be used and published. Chapter 15 discusses the use of Photovoice as a technique for participatory action research. In cases where information available on the internet is used as data, consideration needs to be given to ownership. Although the data may be 'publicly' available (see the earlier discussion), the content of the webpages may be copyrighted to the web hosting company or the website author (British Psychological Society, 2013).

Researchers are increasingly encouraged to archive data for future use by other researchers. This has raised considerable debate about the ethical dilemmas that this may pose for qualitative research (Parry & Mauthner, 2004). The archiving and sharing of qualitative data, which may often involve transcribed material, may compromise confidentiality and anonymity, particularly when the data involve others' sensitive, intimate and personal accounts. Ensuring the confidentiality and anonymity of participants in quantitative data is relatively unproblematic given that the data are often reduced to numbers. Qualitative data include significantly more detail.

Thus, in considering potential ethical dilemmas involving the consequences of research, it is clear that ethical concerns are not only considered at the start of research, when getting ethical approval. Some very careful reflections may be required after data have been collected.

The role of the researcher and the participant

General ethical principles for all types of research apply to qualitative research too, such as the integrity and honesty of the researcher, the professionalism and scientific rigour of the research, and declaration of any conflicts of interest related to funding or the aims of the research. Issues connected with differences in power also need to be considered (as in, for example, the issues of paying participants, discussed earlier). One particular issue regarding the role of the researcher that is important to take into account when researching 'sensitive' topics concerns the tensions for the researcher of remaining in their role of *researcher*, rather than non-researcher. Thompson and Russo (2012), when referring to qualitative research in clinical psychology, highlight the potential dilemmas that arise when the researcher is also a practitioner. Obvious dilemmas include the potential dual roles of the researcher-clinician, as in when a psychologist may conduct research with patients with whom they have worked clinically. They refer more specifically to the researcher needing to be mindful of not adopting a therapeutic role within a qualitative research interview. This may pose some difficulty when qualitative interviews may involve some element of therapeutic communication skills, particularly when it involves sensitive topics. A therapeutic stance to listening and questioning may be useful in creating rapport and managing emotions in the interview, but, as Thompson and Russo argue, it may potentially 'place implicit pressure on privacy boundaries' (2012:35), encouraging the participant to reveal more than

---

BOX 3.2   Considerations for ensuring ethical research

Informed consent
- Provide clear information about the aims, purpose and methods of research, and what participation will involve.
- Take care to avoid explicit and implicit pressures on participants to consent, and ensure that participation is always voluntary.
- Ensure that participants have the capacity to consent, and if not that appropriate ethical approval and consent from key parties have been sought.
- Ensure that participation remains voluntary during the course of the interview (or other methods of data collection), being mindful of any implicit pressures participants may feel about completing.

Confidentiality and anonymity
- Discuss with participants how confidentiality and their anonymity will be ensured through all stages of the research process, and discuss any limits to confidentiality.
- Be mindful of participants' right to privacy, and any implicit pressure placed on them to share more than what they would otherwise wish to.

The consequences of research
- Ensure avoidance of harm to participants and researchers, including paying attention to the emotional impact on research staff and the ways in which the research is disseminated.

The role of the researcher and the participant
- Ensure awareness of the dual roles, adhering to the mandate given as researcher, ensuring that clinical roles are not transgressed.

---

they perhaps would otherwise choose to do. This should be balanced against respecting participants' rights to autonomy and their right to withdraw. However, dilemmas may also arise when a participant becomes distressed during the interview. In some cases, Haverkamp (2005) argues that it may become important for the clinician not only to stop the interview, but to abandon the researcher role and take on the non-researcher role in order to respond to the potential risk.

Taking account of ethics in writing up research

Students and novice researchers often think that ethical considerations require most attention at the study proposal and ethical approval stage. When it comes to writing up results, many might think that all that is required is a brief mention of how key ethical issues were considered at the planning stage. For example, one may write that ethical approval was granted and describe how consent was gained and how confidentiality and anonymity were assured.

However, the importance of detailing how issues of ethics were considered at all stages of the research process (including writing up) should not be underestimated and should form part of the researcher's reflective process for ensuring quality in qualitative research (see Chapter 5). When it comes to publishing journal articles, word limitations mean that often authors offer a token description of ethical issues, but in theses or research reports these can be considered more fully.

Concluding comments

We have argued in this chapter that ethical considerations are not an issue only for the start of a project, when seeking ethical approval, but require ongoing consideration throughout the research process and afterwards. This reflects Brinkmann and Kvale's notion that the core fields of ethics in research are 'fields of uncertainty' (2008:265). Certainty is not achieved when ethical approval is granted, as issues may arise that create uncertainty and they need to be considered and reviewed. For students, the supervision process should provide a necessary space in which any such uncertainties can be discussed and thought about. For all researchers, seeking the advice of ethical review boards may be important.

Further reading

Brinkmann, S. & Kvale, S. (2008). Ethics in qualitative psychological research. In C. Willig & W. Stainton Rogers (eds), *The Sage Handbook of Qualitative Research in Psychology* (pp. 263–279). London: Sage.

British Psychological Society (2013). *Ethics Guidelines for Internet-Mediated Research*. Leicester: British Psychological Society.

Thompson, A.R. & Russo, K. (2012). Ethical dilemmas for clinical psychologists in conducting qualitative research. *Qualitative Research in Psychology*, 9, 32–46.

References

Barker, M., Hagger-Johnson, G., Hegarty, P., Hutchison, C. & Riggs, D.W. (2007). Responses from the Lesbian & Gay Psychology Section to Crossley's 'Making sense of "barebacking".' *British Journal of Social Psychology*, 46(3), 667–677.

Bogod, D. (2004). The Nazi hypothermia experiments: Forbidden data? *Anesthesia*, 59, 1155–1159.

Brinkmann, S. & Kvale, S. (2008). Ethics in qualitative psychological research. In C. Willig & W. Stainton Rogers (eds), *The Sage Handbook of Qualitative Research in Psychology* (pp. 263–279). London: Sage.

British Psychological Society (2009). *Code of Ethics and Conduct*. Leicester: British Psychological Society.

British Psychological Society (2013). *Ethics Guidelines for Internet-Mediated Research*. Leicester: British Psychological Society.

Castleden, H., Garvin, T. & First Nation, H. (2008). Modifying photovoice for community-based participatory indigenous research. *Social Science & Medicine*, 66(6), 1393–1405.

Crossley, M.L. (2004). Making sense of 'barebacking': Gay men's narratives, unsafe sex and the 'resistance habitus'. *British Journal of Social Psychology*, 43, 225–244.

Davison, J. (2004). Dilemmas in research: Issues of vulnerability and disempowerment for the social worker/researcher. *Journal of Social Work Practice*, 18, 379–393.

Donnison, J., Thompson, A.R. & Turpin, G. (2009). A qualitative study of the conceptual models employed by community mental health team staff. *International Journal of Mental Health Nursing*, 18, 310–317.

Economic and Social Research Council (ESRC) (2012). *ESRC Framework for Research Ethics (FRE) 2010 updated September 2012*. London: ESRC. http://www.esrc.ac.uk/about-esrc/information/research-ethics.aspx, accessed 1 May 2014.

Ensign, J. (2003). Ethical issues in qualitative health research with homeless youths. *Journal of Advanced Nursing*, 43(1), 43–50.

Eysenbach, G. & Till, J.E. (2001). Ethical issues in qualitative research on internet communities. *British Medical Journal*, 323, 1103–1105.

Flicker, S., Haans, D. & Skinner, H. (2004). Ethical dilemmas in research on internet communities. *Qualitative Health Research*, 14(1), 124–134.

Graham, J., Grewal, I. & Lewis, J. (2007). *Ethics in Social Research: The Views of Research Participants*. London: NatCen.

Haverkamp, B.E. (2005). Ethical perspectives on qualitative research in applied psychology. *Journal of Counseling Psychology*, 52(2), 146–155.

Hazelgrove, J. (2002). The old faith and the new science: The Nuremberg code and human experimentation ethics in Britain. *Society for the Social History of Medicine*, 15, 1945–1973.

Heggestad, A.K.T., Nortvedt, P. & Slettebo, A. (2013). The importance of moral sensitivity when including persons with dementia in qualitative research. *Nursing Ethics*, 20(1), 30–40.

Hobbs, N. (1948). The development of a code of ethical standards for psychology. *The American Psychologist*, 3(3), 80–84.

Hollway, W. & Jefferson, T. (2000). *Doing Qualitative Research Differently: Free Association, Narrative and the Interview Method*. London: Sage.

Khanlou, N. & Peter, E. (2005). Participatory action research: Considerations for ethical review. *Social Science & Medicine*, 60(10), 2333–2340.

Korkut, Y. (2010). Developing a national code of ethics in psychology in Turkey: Balancing international ethical systems guides with a nation's unique culture. *Ethics & Behavior*, 20, 288–296.

McKee, R. (2013). Ethical issues in using social media for health and healthcare research. *Health Policy*, 110, 298–301.

Parry, O. & Mauthner, N.S. (2004). Whose data are they anyway? Practical, legal and ethical issues in archiving qualitative research data. *Sociology*, 38(1), 139–152.

Pettifor, J.L. (1996). Ethics: Virtue and politics in the science and practice of psychology. *Canadian Psychology*, 37, 1–12.

Rohleder, P. & Gibson, K. (2006). 'We are not fresh': HIV-positive women talk of their experience of living with their spoiled identity. *South African Journal of Psychology*, 36(1), 25–44.

Sieber, J.E. (1992). *Planning Ethically Responsible Research: A Guide for Students and Institutional Review Boards*. Newbury Park, CA: Sage.

Thompson, A.R. & Chambers, E. (2012). Ethical issues in qualitative mental health research. In D. Harper & A.R. Thompson (eds), *Qualitative Research Methods in Mental Health and Psychotherapy* (pp. 23–37). Chichester: John Wiley & Sons.

Thompson, A.R. & Russo, K. (2012). Ethical dilemmas for clinical psychologists in conducting qualitative research. *Qualitative Research in Psychology*, 9, 32–46.

Willig, C. (2012). *Qualitative Interpretation and Analysis in Psychology*. Maidenhead: Open University Press.

Thinking about Culture and Language in Psychological Research and Practice

4

Leslie Swartz

Most of what psychologists know about the world comes from research and theories developed in high-income countries, chiefly in North America and Europe. Even within these countries it is often easier for psychologists to research people who speak the same languages that they themselves speak (with the result that there is a bias in psychological research as a whole towards studying people who are English-speaking) and who come from similar social and educational backgrounds. The fact is, however, that most people in the world do not live in high-income countries, most do not speak English or other European languages and most live in poverty. Within high-income countries themselves, furthermore, widespread migration is leading to much greater diversity of populations and a plurality of ways of living and views of the world. The issues at stake here for clinical and health psychology are not merely those of a diversifying world, but also the impacts on people of the perception of diversity. In Europe, for example, the perception that there is a threat to western values and lifestyles from an increase in the number of people who adhere to Islam has consequences for the fabric of society and for people's mental health.

These changes are occurring in a context of very rapid technological change. In an increasingly interconnected world, technology is disrupting much of what used to be taken for granted about the role of physical distance in separating people from one another. Mobile phones are increasingly being used to deliver health-care messages (Van Heerden et al., 2012) and though there are many reasons to celebrate the potential for the internet to revolutionize the way psychologists do their work and reach new populations (Kazdin & Blase, 2011; Norris et al., 2013), there is also reason for caution, as we are not yet quite sure of what new technologies can or cannot do to change people's lives and their health (Tomlinson et al., 2013).

Different ways of viewing diversity

These technological changes interconnect with developments in how psychologists view human diversity. Historically, attempts to position psychology as a science alongside medical sciences and 'hard' sciences like physics have been associated with an attempt to discover the universal features of human behaviour, an approach known as 'universalism' (Swartz, 1998). This approach to the acquisition of knowledge about the world has led to the development of standard instruments of measurement that are translated into many languages and used across a wide range of contexts, with the assumption that if we measure correctly, we will be able to find similar or the same patterns of human emotion and behaviour in people who on the surface seem very different from one another. In the field of mental health, for example, the DSM-5 (American Psychiatric Association, 2013), together with its predecessors, is a manual for diagnosing mental disorders throughout the world, leading to the possibility of comparing the rates of what is viewed as a single disorder – schizophrenia, say, in different countries. The DSM approach, resting as it does on universalist ideas, would argue that though there may be differences in presentation and symptoms across cultures and contexts, and differences in some local treatments and in the course of disorders, the underlying disorders are essentially the same. This universalist view of disorders is closely associated with the widespread belief that as cognitive scientists learn more about the brain and the human body, we will come to understand human behaviour more and more in terms of a universal underlying set of physical characteristics and processes.

Human emotion and behaviour are, however, more complex than this, something that more sophisticated proponents of a universalist approach would agree. Those who subscribe to what may be termed a more 'relativist' (Swartz, 1998) approach to understanding human diversity in psychology point out that all behaviour occurs in and is shaped by context. In the field of mental health, for example, some behaviour that may appear to be a sign of mental disorder to outsiders may be viewed by cultural insiders as part of a process of becoming an indigenous healer or shaman (Kakar, 1991). Relativists argue that it is not possible to understand people and their behaviour without understanding the context within which people live their lives, and many will use ethnographic approaches (see Chapter 14) to try to develop a more nuanced sense of the local meanings of behaviour. This approach within psychology has provided us with many detailed accounts of local worlds and practices, and it resists easy large-scale comparisons across cultures.

The process of studying human diversity, however, is never value free. There are those who would argue, for example (sometimes without providing detailed evidence for this argument), that a major driving factor behind the search for universals of mental disorders is the quest for financial gain on the part of pharmaceutical companies (Summerfield, 2012). Others would point out that some relativist approaches to understanding mental disorders resonate with and reinforce essentially racist ideas about the 'otherness' of people with different social and cultural backgrounds from those in high-income countries in the West. In what has become a classic of social theory, Said (1979) showed how the idea of the East (the Orient) as 'other' has been reproduced by western anthropologists and other social scientists not only as a way of producing images of others as different but also, often implicitly, as a way of delineating boundaries between a valued 'western' culture and the rest of the world. What Said (1979) would have described as 'Orientalist' ideas may contribute in some degree to what contemporary scholars have called the myth of 'the clash of civilizations' (Bottici & Challand, 2013) – the view that current geopolitical conflicts, and terrorism in particular, can be ascribed to a clash between an enlightened and liberal view of the world on the part of the West, and more totalitarian views coming from the 'East'. In some ways, the perception that there are radically different worlds and worldviews, and that the differences among these worldviews create a basis for conflict, can be seen as a contemporary version of an old evolutionist view of cultural difference (Swartz, 1998). In this view, western culture is seen as the pinnacle of human civilization and other, more 'primitive' cultures are in the process of evolving to this western ideal. Ideologies such as this, linked as they are to a crude social take on Darwin's theories of evolutionism, were used to provide pseudo-scientific support for genocide under Nazism, which saw part of its role as protecting the developed nations and people from contamination both by racial or culturally inferior groups such as Jews and gypsies and by inferior versions of human beings within dominant groups, such as people with disabilities and homosexuals (Evans, 2010; Lifton, 2000).

These questions are complex and cannot be dealt with fully here. They may also, to some readers of a text on methods in psychology, seem somewhat out of place. The key point is that we cannot separate thinking about methods in psychology from thinking about the broader politics of what we do, and about the political role of psychology as a discipline. The feminist disability studies scholar Rosemarie Garland-Thomson cleverly entitled a recent book *Staring: How We Look* (Garland-Thomson, 2009). Her title has a double meaning for scholars in disability studies and in other fields: we should understand how different people and groups 'look' or appear to outsiders, but we must also understand what is at stake in the ways all of us 'look' at others – how we construct our own understandings and images of others.

But who is the 'other' and who is the 'we'? In a rapidly changing and very unequal world, identities are shifting and creolizing (Kirmayer, 2006; Swartz, 2008) and technology is also altering ideas about the boundaries of what it means to be human (Swartz & Watermeyer, 2008; Turkle, 2012). Old ideas about boundaries between cultures and communities – especially geographical boundaries – are being broken down (Rohleder et al., 2008). As an academic psychologist based in South Africa, for example, I may feel myself to have more in common with an academic psychologist based in India than with many people who live very close to my own home. Because I use technology –

notably computers, mobile phones and the internet – every day, I can also come to feel that part of me (part of my mind, part of who I am) resides in technology (Turkle, 1995). As the world changes, and it changes all the time, psychologists must rethink their assumptions about people and the differences between them all the time.

Thinking about language and language diversity

One of the key media through which psychologists do their work is that of language. Much if not most of what we know about people we find out by asking them questions, or listening to their talk. In a very simplistic view, language is no more than a set of labels for things out there in the 'real world'. But language is much more than this – it is a medium through which we constitute our ideas and constructions of the world and reality. Experiments in social psychology have shown how apparently very minor cues in language can dramatically change our perceptions of events as well as our memories of events (for an entertaining overview of how subliminal, including linguistic, cues affect emotion and behaviour, see Alter, 2013). This raises important questions for how people who speak different languages experience emotion and relationships. In some African languages, for example, it is common (and polite) to call all people of a similar age 'sister' or 'brother', and to call older people 'mother' or 'father'. Does this affect social relationships? Things become even more complex when non-standard terms are placed in a cross-cultural context. For example, the *Oxford Advanced Learners' Dictionary* defines a 'cousin brother' as 'a male cousin of your own generation', stating that this is Indian English and informal usage. In some African contexts, a cousin-brother refers more specifically to a cousin with whom a person grew up as part of the same household or linked households. In Yiddish, a 'machatenesta' is the mother of your child's spouse – there is no specific word for this in English (people tend to use the generic 'my in-laws' to refer to relatives of a spouse or sometimes a child's spouse). All these terms both reflect and constitute how we experience relationships.

The complexity increases still more when we start trying to translate terms for emotions. In many languages there is no single or uncontested word for depression or anxiety, and psychologists have long been interested in the extent to which this implies that the emotional experience associated with depression is experienced in the same way across different cultural contexts (Swartz, 1998). Obeyesekere (1986), for example, has argued that not only are some of the affects associated with depression in the West, such as feeling hopelessness and resignation, not experienced negatively within a Buddhist Sri Lankan context, but the terms used to describe these experiences do not share negative associations. Bilinguals or multilinguals, furthermore, may experience different emotions for apparently the same affect translated into the different languages they speak, and may use different aspects of their native languages to describe different feelings (Pavlenko, 2006). In African and other contexts, multilingualism and its attendant switches in codes and registers are the norm among large numbers of people (Heugh, 2013), leading to a situation in which many people do not identify as having a primary or single first language. The study of language and emotion, then, becomes the study of how people marshal different linguistic resources in different contexts. It is also the case that languages change and develop all the time, so people's experiences and their language use also change. Within migrant families, different members of the same household may use language slightly differently and attach slightly different emotional resonances and meanings to the same words.

In summary, though language is central to much of what psychologists do, thinking about language is never a simple matter. The points made here are, of necessity, very preliminary and rather superficial, but the key issue to remember is that translation and interpretation across contexts are never simple matters to be dismissed as a methodological footnote.

Putting culture and language to work: Translation and interpretation in psychological research

Though cultural and language issues are relevant to all psychological research, much of such research does not focus specifically on these issues as areas of study. The rest of this chapter will concentrate on some practical issues associated with translation and interpretation in psychological research, and will also give an example of how researching language issues can open up a way of exploring other issues in psychology.

There are different conventions for how the terms 'translation' and 'interpretation' are used. In this chapter, 'translation' will refer to the translation of texts and psychological instruments, whereas 'interpretation' refers to the use of interpreters in interaction between two or more people (mediation of language in person-to person interactions).

Translating texts and instruments

In a landmark paper published over 40 years ago but still widely used and cited, Brislin (1970) suggested a straightforward method for the translation of psychological instruments and texts. He noted that it is not sufficient simply to translate from one language into another; back-translation is far preferable. If, for example, we would like to translate an English psychological instrument into Yoruba, a back-translation approach would be to employ a Yoruba/English bilingual person to translate the instrument. Then a second Yoruba/English bilingual, who has not seen the original English version, back-translates the Yoruba version into English. The new English version is compared with the original and changes made where there are differences, often using a committee of bilinguals to discuss the inconsistencies and suggest the best way forward. Ideally, translation, back-translation and the use of a committee of experts may be a recursive process, with the instrument going through a number of iterations.

In practice, it is rare for all bilinguals and native speakers to agree easily on either translations and back-translations, and there are many possible permutations of the translation–back-translation paradigm. For example, in some contexts it may make sense to start two translation processes of the same instrument simultaneously but independently and then later to compare the results of both processes. There may be reasons to select for different characteristics of translators and back-translators, because different people use and engage with language in different ways, depending on issues such as gender, age and where the translators and back-translators live. As a rule of thumb, and given what we know about the fluidity and constitutive nature of language, it is worth recognizing that there will probably be no single ideal translation of any psychological instrument. It makes sense, where this is possible, to have translators and back-translators who are as similar as possible to the people for whom the psychological instrument is intended. Say, for example, that a psychological instrument is to be used in a rural South African context where some people follow the *hlonipa* custom. *Hlonipa* refers to a set of linguistic practices whereby, among other things, married women may not use the name of their husbands in speech but must use circumlocution to refer to their husbands. If a psychological instrument is to be employed in this context, it does not make sense for the translators all to be urban men unfamiliar with the *hlonipa* customs. However, an instrument designed for urban men would have to take into account their linguistic context, their use of language and their patterns of code-switching. In all languages a variety of registers and metaphors are employed and these need to be considered. This is the case as much in English as in other languages – in English as used in the United States, for example, the sentence 'I feel blue' is commonly understood to be roughly equivalent to 'I feel sad' and, indeed, the term 'blue' for 'sad' is used in some depression inventories. Nevertheless, there are many first-language English speakers around the world who neither use the term 'blue' as roughly synonymous with 'sad' nor recognize this usage. For them, an item such as 'I feel blue' would be meaningless or bizarre, though it would be appropriate in many US contexts.

A complex issue at the heart of translation practices, no matter how carefully they are engaged with, is expertise. I have suggested earlier that an important source of expertise is insider knowledge on behalf of people who are as close as possible to the population being studied. Insiders without any training in thinking about issues of language, however, may find it difficult to talk about issues of language in abstract terms and may experience discussions about the words they have chosen as critical of their linguistic abilities (Drennan et al., 1991). It may be useful to have both linguistic insiders as well as people who have studied language issues on any translation team. Issues of power and authority among people who are regarded as cultural insiders and those regarded as experts on language will need to be carefully thought about and managed. Even within the context of qualitative research (the focus of this volume), psychological instruments, questionnaires and interview schedules may be used and need to be translated. A common mistake when these research tools are translated and back-translated is to assume that people with professional knowledge in psychology may make the best translators and back-translators, when in fact the opposite may the case. The problem here is that people familiar with psychology, in their processes of translation and back-translation, may consciously or unconsciously apply their knowledge of psychology to the translation process. They may, for example, read a poorly translated item on a psychological scale but be able to divine to what the translation probably referred, as they are familiar with the field. Many people to whom the scale will be administered may not be able to make this leap and will simply not understand the item.

There are, in summary, no easy steps to translation and back-translation. This is a complex process and is necessarily tentative and imperfect. Too often, translations of instruments are dealt with in large studies with a footnote, or with the blanket claim that Brislin's method has been applied. This does no justice to Brislin's contribution to the field, and studies that give due attention to the challenges, difficulties and successes of translation of texts and instruments have much to offer the field of psychology. In research budgets, the costs, in terms of both time and money, of translation processes are commonly underestimated. It is easy to obtain a quick, cheap translation of anything, but research based on poorly translated tools is not good research (Kagee et al., 2013).

One issue that is commonly overlooked is that of where and how translation occurs in different phases of the research process. It is often the case that researchers will train fieldworkers to conduct research (including qualitative interviews) in a language that the researchers themselves do not speak. Ideally, the recordings of these interviews should be transcribed in the language in which they were made (that is, a direct verbatim transcription of what was said in the interview), these transcriptions checked, and then translations made and checked using the techniques described above. This is extremely time consuming and costly, and it is often left to bilingual transcribers simply to listen to recordings and then to transcribe them directly into the language spoken by researchers, leaving the door open to errors. The problem here, of course, is that the researcher has no way of assessing the accuracy of texts that have been simultaneously translated and transcribed, as they cannot check against the original recordings. At the very least, a check should be made on a sample of text to ascertain the overall skill level of translation and transcription. This is not ideal, but it is often easy to gain a reasonable impression of which translator/transcribers experience more difficulty than others with this extremely complex and demanding task.

Interpreting processes and practices

Every challenge associated with the translation of texts and instruments applies to interpretation during person-to-person encounters. Interpreting, though, involves the layer of managing interpersonal processes and adds a layer of complexity. The field of interpreting has professionalized dramatically over recent decades and it is widely recognized that interpreting is highly skilled work (Bot, 2005). In many contexts, however, especially in lower-income contexts, there are no formally trained interpreters and various arrangements for interpreting are made, ranging from the use of family members to interpret for patients in health-care settings to developing a cadre of what are termed 'community interpreters' (Hale, 2011), community members who work, remunerated or otherwise, to interpret within their contexts.

The field of interpreting in psychological research and practice is extremely varied and complex (see, for example, Swartz, 1998; Tribe & Lane, 2009) and it is not possible to do justice to the whole field here. There are, however, some key points that always need to be taken into account when working with interpreters, which are very briefly outlined here.

A triangular relationship

As soon as an interpreter is present in any encounter, even when the interpreter is at the other end of a telephone and not physically present, what may originally have been conceived of as a relationship between two people – in this case, the researcher and the person with whom the researcher wishes to communicate – becomes a relationship among three people. Where there are three people, alliances may develop between two of the three, as anybody who has been in a three-person interaction will know; triangular communication and relationships are commonly difficult to manage (Swartz, 1998). Because the interpreter is the only person able to understand both the researcher and the person with whom the researcher is trying to communicate, it is most likely that alliances will be formed between the interpreter and one of the other parties. This possibility needs to be thought about in context, planned for and discussed with the interpreter in advance.

Multiple understandings of roles

Only somebody very naïve about language could expect that an interpreter will be able to act simply as a translation machine, a black box through which words in one language are simply translated into words of another language. It is important for both the researcher and the interpreter to have thought about the possible roles the interpreter may take, from advocate for the patient, to cultural broker, to junior member of the psychology team. There are many terms for interpreter roles, but the key issue here is that the researcher and the interpreter should have developed a common understanding of what the role of the interpreter should be in a particular context. This is crucial in particular where researchers are interested in emotional and mental health issues. We know, for example, that psychological researchers are commonly interested not only in what people say but in how they say things. An interpreter working with a researcher interested in such issues must be aware that it will be considered appropriate by the researcher for the interpreter to comment on the way people talk, and not merely to translate words for their content.

Trust, ethics and politeness

Any interpreted interview should be introduced to the person being interviewed by the interpreter, who should explain what the roles will be, who is in charge of the interview and what its goals are. It can be upsetting and intimidating for somebody being interviewed through an interpreter suddenly to have to listen to a discussion between the researcher and the interpreter in a language the person does not understand. Much of how the interview proceeds will depend on the quality of the relationship between the psychologist and the interpreter, and the degree of trust between them. At worst, an interpreted interview can develop into a power struggle between the psychologist and the interpreter, with the person being interviewed a cipher in this struggle. Politeness and consideration for all parties are important; it is remarkable how often basic rules of politeness (such as the rule of not talking about someone in the third person in a language they do not understand) can become violated when psychologist and interpreter have not prepared properly for the interview and want to get it over with as soon as possible. Issues of confidentiality are also important, and it is crucial that interpreters are informed about confidentiality rules in psychological research and practice.

Prepare, discuss, debrief

Interpreting is a necessary part of much psychological research and related practices will and must differ in different contexts. At the heart of successfully interpreted interviews, however, is preparation for the interviews by psychologists and interpreters, open and frank discussions between interpreters and psychologists, and debriefing after each session. Interpreting practices can too often be rendered invisible, as the later example will show, but it is only through continually keeping in focus the complexity both linguistically and interpersonally of what is at stake in interpreted interviews that the best work can be done.

Beyond the triangle: A broader context

Interpreting in psychological research commonly takes place in contexts that go beyond the individual psychologist attempting to communicate with the individual research participant. Even apparently small-scale interventions, such as the translation of one psychological instrument, will have political dimensions and may evoke intergroup feelings and tensions that could affect the job of translation (Drennan et al., 1991). Similarly, training of professionals or research assistants in something that may appear politically neutral, such as good communication skills, may raise fundamental issues about how people from different groups see the world, and the danger of the inappropriate imposition of one group's set of values on the practices of another (Blatt et al., 2009).

Much psychological research is conducted in group settings or in the context of community work and other larger-scale engagements, and may even be about large-scale public or political events and processes (see, for example, Krog et al., 2009). All of the principles mentioned earlier apply in these challenging contexts, but there are a few added considerations. In larger-scale work one is probably dealing with multiple linguistic repertoires and with participants who have varying understandings of the language(s) the psychological researchers speak. Particularly where the research is conducted with people of relatively lower social status than the researchers, differing access on the part of participants to understanding the researchers directly may set up dynamics of power and competition among participants. If this issue is not properly managed, participants who are able to communicate directly with the researchers may dominate the conversations and may also act as gatekeepers between the researchers and the research participants, with the researchers being unable to assess the accuracy of the translations that participants make of the contributions of other participants. For these reasons, and taking into account the reality that many people have access to a range of linguistic repertoires, it is useful, with the aid of an interpreter, to discuss this issue with participants up front. Researchers do not want to get into the absurd situation in which people who are able to communicate directly with them with ease are prohibited from doing so, but it is important that everyone present should understand all that is said, so there must still be time for interpreting to take place. In a context within which the researchers have prepared well for the linguistic complexity of a group or community situation, the varying linguistic repertoires and discussions among participants about how best to translate terms and concepts can lead to a positive atmosphere for discussion. All participants and the researchers become involved together in a process of trying to understand one another and what is being said, and this can be both a pleasant and an illuminating experience for all concerned.

Increasingly, as research is conducted using newer information and communication technologies, these principles can be applied to conversations among groups and people who are not physically in the same place, making use of both the spoken and the written word, commonly with varying degrees of literacy on the part of participants. More research is needed to record and explore the issues in these complex but fascinating new relationships, and the central principles, as in one-to-one interpreted interviews, are prior preparation; naming and discussing the language issues up front; a thoughtful and flexible approach to the issue of language as it develops in the interaction itself; good recording of all that takes place (in written and oral form, and noting where possible visual aspects of interaction such as gesture and use of the body to communicate); and careful debriefing. The possibilities here for the development of new knowledge are exciting, and an advantage throughout of the researchers not being able to understand everyone without help is that they can position themselves as curious and wanting to know and understand more. This acknowledgement of the limitations of the researchers' linguistic repertoires, especially in larger-scale community or group research, can, if properly handled, help invert power hierarchies and position community or group members as insider experts assisting the researchers to understand things better. This is precisely what good psychological researchers want, especially when applying qualitative methods.

Concluding comments: Researching language practices as a gateway to exploring a range of psychological questions

It is not possible to do justice to the many issues associated with thinking about culture and language in psychological research and practice in the space of a few thousand words. Thinking about these issues is essential, nevertheless, and is endlessly fascinating for those interested in psychological processes.

As part of a larger study on language and interpreting practices in mental health care in South Africa, a research team of which I am a part (Smith et al., 2013) interviewed cleaners who performed informal interpreting duties in a large psychiatric hospital. From previous research (Hagan et al., 2013; Kilian et al., 2010), our team knew that most of the interpreting conducted in local psychiatric hospitals was undertaken by informal or lay interpreters, many of whom were not fully conversant in English, which has obvious implications for the quality of the interpretations undertaken. We were interested in how different groups of informal, lay interpreters experienced their informal interpreting work, and one of the groups was cleaners called on to provide interpreting services on an ad hoc basis. These cleaners had no training in health care or interpreting, which was not seen as part of their formal duties. We approached all the cleaners in the hospital who we knew to perform these duties, and they were all eager to talk with us. It was important in setting up our interviews with them to make it clear that we were not interested in judging the quality of their interpreting work (which some of them feared) and that we were not part of the management of the hospital. These were low-level employees in a hierarchical organization (the hospital) and it was ethically important to take due account of their structural vulnerability in the hospital context. Because we had learned from previous research that these cleaners were utilized as informal interpreters, we did not use interpreters for our interactions with them, and it was important to handle with sensitivity the fact that some of them were not fully fluent in English.

We had thought that our discussions with them would be purely about informal interpreting, but we learned much more. When given the opportunity to talk about language and interpreting issues with an interested outsider, the interpreters discussed a wide range of factors. The cleaners regarded themselves as an important part of the health-care team, providing much of the care for patients. We as the research team realized as a result of this study that though we had been studying language practices for some years, we had overlooked some very simple facts of mental health care in this context and probably in many others. Patients often spend longer with cleaners and people not formally seen as part of the health-care team than with any health-care professionals, such as psychologists, nurses and doctors. We realized that ignoring what cleaners do in terms of patient care is tantamount to ignoring much of the experience of patients in care situations. In this regard, our study opens up new areas for research on the management of emotion in mental health care, analogous to the work of Ward and McMurray (2011) in the United Kingdom. These authors found that receptionists in general practices do much of the work surrounding the emotions of patients in a context within which they, like the interpreters in South Africa, are not seen as part of the formal health-care system. Penn and Watermeyer (2012), similarly, show how informal interpreters in contexts such as HIV care in South Africa perform a multitude of informal and unrecognized roles, roles that can easily be hidden if due attention is not given to issues of the culture of the health system and language.

This brief example highlights an important principle in thinking about language barriers in psychological research, a point that has been made repeatedly in various ways throughout this chapter. Although the issue of a psychological researcher not being able to understand the languages of research participants is one of language barriers, thinking about these barriers and trying to deal with them may actually lay bare precisely some of the research issues themselves. When we think carefully about language, we think also about power, about meaning and about relationships, and we learn something about people's emotional lives and investments in cultural and identity issues. We learn about people's positioning in institutions and about their cultural practices. The issues of language and cultural differences in psychological research are issues not to be 'solved' or 'overcome'. On the contrary, if we engage with them thoughtfully, they can tell us a great deal about whichever psychological issues we are exploring.

Further reading

There are many useful writings on issues of language and culture in psychological research, and the following books and articles provide more background:

Baraldi, C. & Gavioli, L. (eds). (2012). *Coordinating Participation in Dialogue Interpreting*. Amsterdam: John Benjamins.

Durrheim, K., Mtose, X. & Brown, L. (2011). *Race Troubles: Race, Identity and Inequality in Post-apartheid South Africa*. Lanham, MD: Lexington Books.

Krog, A., Mpolweni, N. & Ratele, K. (2009). *There Was This Goat: Investigating the Truth Commission Testimony of Notrose Nobomvu Konile*. Pietermaritzburg: University of KwaZulu Natal Press.

Smith, J., Swartz, L., Kilian, S. & Chiliza, B. (2013). Mediating words, mediating worlds: Interpreting as hidden care work in a South African psychiatric institution. *Transcultural Psychiatry*, *50*, 493–514.

Stigler, J.W., Schweder, R.A. & Herdt, G. (eds). (1990). *Cultural Psychology: Essays on Comparative Human Development*. Cambridge: Cambridge University Press.

Swartz, L. (1998). *Culture and Mental Health: A Southern African View*. Cape Town: Oxford University Press.

References

Alter, A. (2013). *Drunk Tank Pink: And Other Unexpected Forces That Shape How We Think, Feel, and Behave*. New York: Penguin.

American Psychiatric Association (APA). (2013). *Diagnostic and Statistical Manual of Mental Disorders (5th edn; DSM-5)*. Washington, DC: APA.

Blatt, B., Kallenberg, G., Lang, F., Mahoney, P., Patterson, J., Dugan, B. & Sun, S. (2009). Found in translation: Exporting patient-centered communication and small group teaching skills to China. *Medical Education Online*, *14*, 6. doi:10.3885/meo.2009.T0000136.

Bot, H. (2005). *Dialogue Interpreting in Mental Health Care*. Amsterdam: Rodopi.

Bottici, C. & Challand, B. (2013). *The Myth of the Clash of Civilizations*. London: Routledge.

Brislin, R.W. (1970). Back-translation for cross-cultural research. *Journal of Cross-Cultural Psychology*, *1*(3), 185–216.

Drennan, G., Levett, A. & Swartz, L. (1991). Hidden dimensions of power and resistance in the translation process: A South African study. *Culture, Medicine and Psychiatry*, *15*, 361–381.

Evans, S. (2010). *Hitler's Forgotten Victims: The Holocaust and the Disabled*. London: History Press.

Garland-Thomson, R. (2009). *Staring: How We Look*. New York: Oxford University Press.

Hagan, S., Swartz, L., Kilian, S., Chiliza, B., Bisogno, P. & Joska, J. (2013). The accuracy of interpreting key psychiatric terms by ad hoc interpreters at a South African psychiatric hospital. *African Journal of Psychiatry*, *16*, 424–429.

Hale, S.B. (2011). The positive side of community interpreting: An Australian case study. *Interpreting*, *13*(2), 234–248.

Heugh, K. (2013). Multilingual education in Africa. In C. Chapelle (ed.), *The Encyclopedia of Applied Linguistics*. doi: 10.1002/9781405198431.wbeal0782.

Kagee, A., Tsai, A.C., Lund, C. & Tomlinson, M. (2013). Screening for common mental disorders in low resource settings: Reasons for caution and a way forward. *International Health*, *5*(1), 11–14.

Kakar, S. (1991). *Shamans, Mystics and Doctors: A Psychological Inquiry into India and Its Healing Traditions*. Chicago, IL: Chicago University Press.

Kazdin, A.E. & Blase, S.L. (2011). Rebooting psychotherapy research and practice to reduce the burden of mental illness. *Perspectives on Psychological Science*, *6*, 21–37. doi:10.1177/1745691610393527.

Kilian, S., Swartz, L. & Joska, J. (2010). Linguistic competence of interpreters in a South African psychiatric hospital. *Psychiatric Services*, *61*, 310–312.

Kirmayer, L.J. (2006). Culture and psychotherapy in a creolizing world. *Transcultural Psychiatry*, *43*(2), 163–168.

Krog, A., Mpolweni, N. & Ratele, K. (2009). *There Was This Goat: Investigating the Truth Commission Testimony of Notrose Nobomvu Konile*. Pietermaritzburg: University of KwaZulu Natal Press.

Lifton, R.J. (2000). *The Nazi Doctors: Medical Killing and the Psychology of Genocide*. New York: Basic Books.

Norris, L., Swartz, L. & Tomlinson, M. (2013). Mobile phone technology for improved mental health care in South Africa: Possibilities and challenges. *South African Journal of Psychology*, *43*, 377–386.

Obeyesekere, G. (1986). Depression, Buddhism, and the work of culture in Sri Lanka. In A. Kleinman and B. Good (eds.), *Culture and Depression: Studies in the Anthropology and Cross-Cultural Psychiatry of Affect and Disorder* (pp. 134–152). Berkeley: University of California Press.

Pavlenko, A. (2006). *Emotions and Multilingualism*. Cambridge: Cambridge University Press.

Penn, C. & Watermeyer, J. (2012). When asides become central: Small talk and big talk in interpreted health interactions. *Patient Education and Counseling*, *88*, 391–398.

Rohleder, P., Swartz, L., Bozalek, V. & Leibowitz, B. (2008). 'Communities isn't just about trees and shops': Students from two South African universities engage in dialogue about 'community' and 'community work'. *Journal of Community and Applied Social Psychology*, *18*(3), 253–267.

Said, E. (1979). *Orientalism*. New York: Vintage.

Smith, J., Swartz, L., Kilian, S. & Chiliza, B. (2013). Mediating words, mediating worlds: Interpreting as hidden care work in a South African psychiatric institution. *Transcultural Psychiatry*, *50*, 493–514.

Summerfield, D. (2012). Afterword: Against 'global mental health'. *Transcultural Psychiatry*, *49*(3–4), 519.

Swartz, L. (1998). *Culture and Mental Health: A Southern African View*. Cape Town: Oxford University Press.

Swartz, L. (2008). Globalisation and mental health: Changing views of culture and society. *Global Social Policy*, *8*, 304–308.

Swartz, L. & Watermeyer, B. (2008). Cyborg anxiety: Oscar Pistorius and the boundaries of what it means to be human. *Disability in Society*, *23*, 187–190.

Tomlinson, M., Rotheram-Borus, M.J., Swartz, L. & Tsai, A.C. (2013). Scaling up mHealth: Where is the evidence? *PLoS Medicine*, *10*(2): e1001382. doi:10.1371/journal.pmed.1001382.

Tribe, R. & Lane, P. (2009). Working with interpreters across language and culture in mental health. *Journal of Mental Health*, *18*(3), 233–241.

Turkle, S. (1995). *Life on the Screen*. New York: Simon and Schuster.

Turkle, S. (2012). *Alone Together: Why We Expect More from Technology and Less from Each Other*. New York: Basic Books.

Van Heerden, A., Tomlinson, M. & Swartz, L. (2012). Point of care in your pocket: Policy recommendations for the field of mHealth. *Bulletin of the World Health Organization*, *90*, 393–394. doi:10.2471/BLT.11.099788.

Ward, J. & McMurray, R. (2011). The unspoken work of general practitioner receptionists: A re-examination of emotion management in primary care. *Social Science and Medicine*, *72*, 1583–1587.

Ensuring Quality in Qualitative Research

Gareth J. Treharne and Damien W. Riggs

5

Introduction: What does quality mean in qualitative research?

> Why should qualitative researchers care about quality criteria? Which quality criteria apply to the qualitative research that you are doing or reading?

In this chapter we outline some of the ways in which quality can be achieved when conducting qualitative research and how quality can be demonstrated in qualitative research outputs (particularly articles and dissertations/theses). We make use of a binary distinction by categorizing some research as qualitative and other research as quantitative. We acknowledge the limitation of this qualitative–quantitative binary, and we go some way towards redressing that limitation in our section on triangulation, in which we talk about how quality can be enhanced by comparing various forms of data.

We draw on a range of systems of quality criteria that have been put forward for qualitative research in recent decades. In each of these systems different terminologies are created, extended or reconstituted. The most highly cited system of quality criteria for qualitative research is that developed by Guba, Lincoln and colleagues (Guba, 1981; Lincoln, 1995; Lincoln & Guba, 1985; Lincoln et al., 2011). They continue to advocate for five key concepts that can be used to assess the quality of qualitative research: credibility, transferability, dependability, confirmability and authenticity, which are described in Box 5.1.

This chapter is split into four sections. We start by outlining the concept of transparency as an overarching way of thinking about quality in research. We then detail three additional facets of quality for qualitative research: personal reflexivity and end-user involvement; the transferability of findings; and triangulation of data sources (Box 5.2). Throughout this chapter we also attend to how facets of quality for qualitative research diverge from markers of quality for quantitative research. We contend that these facets of quality

---

BOX 5.1   Guba and Lincoln's concepts for defining and investigating quality in qualitative research

Concept	Definition and approaches to investigation
Credibility	Do participants or members of the community being researched feel that the findings represent their experience? Activities that make it more likely that research will produce credible findings include prolonged engagement with participants; negative (divergent) case analysis; and triangulation (of sources and researchers). Member checking and peer debriefing with other researchers can be used to investigate credibility.
Transferability	Are the findings applicable in other contexts? Providing a rich description of participants' responses (and the researcher's interpretations) makes transferability easier to evaluate. Naturalistic generalization occurs when the findings are in harmony with the experiences of the individual evaluating the research, and thus appear transferable in the eyes of the reader.
Dependability	Would similar findings be produced if someone else also undertook the research? Triangulation across researchers can be used to investigate dependability. Auditing can also be carried out to allow another researcher to follow the audit trail (ideally) generated by the original researcher.
Confirmability	Are the findings a product of participants' responses and not the researcher's 'biases, motivations, interests, or perspectives' (Lincoln & Guba, 1985:290)? Auditing can be used to evaluate the confirmability of findings. A more transparent report of the findings (with signposted reflexivity) makes confirmability easier to evaluate.
Authenticity	Does the research represent a fair range of differing viewpoints on the topic? Do the findings have transformative potential? Is there community consensus that the findings are 'useful and [have] meaning (especially meaning for action and further steps)' (Lincoln et al., 2011:116)? Member checking can be used to inquire about apparent authenticity with participants or other members of the community in question, sometimes known as 'end-users'. These individuals might include practitioners who would potentially change their practice based on the findings.

for qualitative research raise the bar of what might be expected of all research and of all researchers.

Transparency of research outputs

Due to constraints of communication, it is never possible to be fully transparent when describing research. The word limits that journals have for articles

---

BOX 5.2   Facets of enacting and demonstrating quality in qualitative research covered in this chapter

Quality facets	Questions for researchers
Universal for all research	
Transparency	How clear is the report on the research?
	Could another researcher attempt to replicate your methods?
	Can the reader grasp how your data support your findings and conclusions?
Specific to qualitative research	
Personal reflexivity and end-user	How aware are you, the researcher, of your influence on the research?
involvement	How can you go about recording the development of your study from initial idea to final conclusions?
	How much are members of the community being researched truly involved in the research?
	Are they consulted at the time of the initial idea and at every stage of the research beyond that?
The transferability of findings	How likely is it that the findings transfer to other community members?
	Is there something about the participants/data that suggests that people from another community or different location may have a different perspective?
	How useful is the study for informing what can be done in psychological practice?
Triangulation	Is more than one kind or source of data used in order to question whether the findings transfer across contexts, researchers etc.?
	Are there convergences, complementarities or divergences in the narratives produced by the different sources of data (Erzerberger & Prein, 1997)?

---

and universities have for dissertations/theses place an extra pressure when doing qualitative research. Nonetheless, transparency is a worthy goal of any research output. Elliott et al. (1999) argue that ensuring transparency across all sections of a research output is a subtle process of forming a rationale, selecting a method and explaining the findings. Yardley (2000) also emphasizes the importance of transparency in demonstrating a matching of the research questions, the methods, the findings and the epistemology (see Chapter 2) and how the researcher(s) addressed reflexivity (which we cover in the next section).

Tong et al. (2007) published a set of criteria termed 'COnsolidated criteria for REporting Qualitative research' (COREQ) with the aim of producing a transparent universal system of quality criteria for qualitative research to match similar systems for the evaluation of randomized controlled trials. The COREQ checklist does not apply equally to all qualitative methods given its inclusion of concepts specific to grounded theory, such as data saturation (for further details on grounded theory, see Chapter 8). The COREQ checklist also implies that qualitative studies only involve one-on-one interviews or focus groups with adult participants who are intellectually and cognitively normative and where everyone speaks the same language (see Chapter 4 for issues regarding language, translation and cross-cultural research). Assessing quality criteria for qualitative research against a checklist constrains the methods of data collection and diversity within and across the qualitative approaches discussed throughout this book, and can inhibit transparency by closing down discussion of anything outside the checklist. Seale (1999) explained that qualitative research involves 'craft skills' that researchers develop and apply flexibly to fit their research questions rather than to fit a checklist. Two important craft skills are the ability to think reflexively and the process of consulting end-users.

Ensuring quality through personal reflexivity and end-user involvement

How is the research shaped by the researcher? How is the research shaped and received by the people who are investigated in the research?

Personal reflexivity involves the researcher looking inwards to see how they themselves have informed the research. In contrast, end-user involvement is about looking outwards to others by consulting members of the community being researched during the planning, actualization and/or dissemination of the study. Both of these considerations are ongoing challenges that are ideally started before the research protocol is anticipated (Finlay, 2002). The dual processes of personal reflexivity and end-user involvement draw attention to 'who speaks, for whom, to whom, for what purposes' (Lincoln, 1995:282).

Being a reflexive researcher involves taking a look at how your research is informed by your personal circumstances, privileges, facets of identity, experiences and location (Willig, 2013). However, being reflexive requires more than writing a shopping list of the personal characteristics that define researchers as an insider or outsider based on specific elements of your personal identity (Hellawell, 2006; Treharne, 2011). Instead, personal reflexivity involves an ongoing process of questioning the relevance of your identity in forming how the research proceeds.

Regular journaling of your reflections is one of the main ways of keeping records of your research project. These records can then be used in what Guba, Lincoln and colleagues call an 'audit' (see Guba, 1981, and Box 5.1).

Journaling comes naturally to some researchers (Hellawell, 2006), but is intellectually demanding for all researchers. Journaling may have more utility for certain qualitative approaches such as phenomenology, psychoanalytic research or participatory action research (see Chapters 10, 11 and 15; see also Finlay, 2002). The style and frequency of journaling are idiosyncratic and can vary depending on the aims of the research, the type of data you are using and the intended output (for instance, to facilitate writing a dissertation/thesis). A number of different writing formats can be used for journaling, including communications like emails, memos about realizations and narratives that might be considered more typical of a diary or novel (see Ellis, 1999, 2004; Sparkes, 2007). Some researchers may prefer audio recording their reflections (Lodge, 2001), particularly when in the field (for example, immediately after an interview, as long as there is nobody within earshot). Journaling can be informed by guidance on good record keeping for psychologists (Newton, 2008). A useful rule of thumb is only to journal things that you would be happy to be seen publicly, particularly by any individuals informing the journal entry. This suggestion may sound constraining, but it can help hone your reflexive thinking and ethical practice.

One of the biggest challenges of using your personal reflexivity productively when undertaking qualitative research is finding the right balance between self-insight and not forgetting to look outwards to others. Being reflexive by drawing on your personal characteristics can be differentiated from what is called epistemological or methodological reflexivity, which involves the researcher questioning how the methods they selected have informed (and limited) what could be found (Willig, 2013:55–56). One limitation of much research in psychology is the artificial separation of the researchers from the community with whom (or traditionally, on whom) the research has been carried out, who are increasingly being referred to as end-users because in the end they are the ones who will make use of the research or may potentially be affected by it.

Seale noted that 'the social research community is no different from the rest of society in its divisions of status and power, acting at times to oppress and silence particular groups' (1999:471). Even in qualitative research it is relatively rare to consult end-users beyond their involvement as sources of data. This lack of end-user consultation is problematic on occasions such as when the research is debated in the media and causes distress for some members of the community when no one from the community has been consulted (e.g. Treharne et al., 2011).

One way of fostering end-user involvement is to include end-user perspectives and expertise from the start of a project. Hewlett et al. (2006) devised a way of developing research partnerships between rheumatology patients and researchers. Three of these authors are rheumatology patients who have been involved in numerous research projects and coordinate local teams of patients who contribute to research projects. Hewlett et al. propose a model to facilitate end-user consultation that goes beyond what Guba, Lincoln and

---

BOX 5.3   A summary of Hewlett et al.'s (2006) 'first' model for facilitating inclusion of end-users' input into research

F   Facilitate inclusion and contribution of end-users in the research process by setting up pragmatic protocols for meetings between researchers and end-users (e.g. having a suitable venue, covering travel expenses). Reinforce a collaborative attitude by offering substantive roles and acknowledgement.

I   Identify relevant research projects and potential end-user partners by matching the end-users' personal experience, interests and expertise (and availability).

R   Respect the end-users' contribution by treating them like any other (volunteer) researcher. Consider providing things like honorary contracts and supporting conference attendance. Imagine how different conferences would be with a 50–50 mix of researchers and end-users.

S   Support communication and a practical working environment by ensuring access to email facilities, providing a buddy with more experience in the role, offering office space, if possible, and discussing timelines for input into the project (e.g. rather than sending out documents at the last minute).

T   Train end-users to have the required knowledge for their role in the same way that training is provided for other researchers (the continuing professional development model). Identify training needs early and facilitate access to seminars, courses etc. Discuss use of plain language and develop tools like glossaries that allow researchers and end-users to move closer to a shared language.

---

colleagues call 'member checking' (see Box 5.1). Hewlett et al.'s model focuses on pragmatic considerations and reaching a common language (Box 5.3). This example shows how end-user involvement can be achieved and can balance the more internal focus of reflexivity, but often starts to resemble participatory action research (see Chapter 15). A more moderate form of consultation is always achievable and can enrich qualitative research when the topic is outside the realm of personal experience of the researchers (for example, see Smith et al., 2013).

Ensuring quality through thinking about the transferability of findings

> Is generalization possible or desired in qualitative research and how does that relate to data gathering? How far might qualitative findings transfer beyond the sources of data included in the study?

Once the qualitative data are collected and the analysis is complete, what might be said of the findings beyond the sample in a specific qualitative study? Two alternatives to statistical generalization that can be applied to qualitative research are analytical generalization and case-to-case transfer generalization (Firestone, 1993; Lincoln & Guba, 1985; Polit & Beck, 2010). Analytical generalization is the process of generalizing from some data to an extant theory rather than generalizing from some data to the population, as is attempted in statistical generalization. Firestone (1993) argued that analytical generalization can be applied to theory-driven qualitative research, where the researchers analyse the qualitative data to answer a specific research question (see Chapter 7). In this way, researchers can test whether the theory holds under certain 'scope conditions' (Firestone, 1993:17). For example, in McGavock and Treharne's (2011) study, the common-sense model of illness perceptions was used as the theoretical framework and the qualitative findings support the scope condition of young, 'healthy' adults talking about chronic illness in ways that matched the common-sense model.

Analytical generalization can also be examined for inductive qualitative research when a data-driven theme is composed that provides evidence for a theory that was not the starting point of the research, but is found post hoc to have parallels with the theory. For example, the phenomenological study by Hale et al. (2006) focused on appearance issues among women with lupus, a chronic autoimmune disease that causes widespread rashes, fatigue, arthritis and a host of other symptoms (Lupus UK, 2013). Participants described the social visibility of their changed body and how they attempted to manage that visibility using cosmetics, clothing or social withdrawal. These findings were not being tested deductively against a theory, but they can be analytically generalized to Goffman's (1963) theory of bodily stigma and Bury's (1982) theory of chronic illness as biographical disruption; Hale et al. provided evidence that lupus is a scope condition for these two theories.

Case-to-case transfer generalization is particularly relevant to qualitative research (Firestone, 1993; Lincoln et al., 2011; see Box 5.1). Transferability is judged by the reader of the research output; for example, in Hale et al.'s (2006) study, do the results convince or resonate with readers who have lupus? Or their loved ones? Or the health-care professionals who provide their care? Or you, who may not have heard of lupus before reading this example? Thinking about case-to-case transfer generalization allows researchers to ponder on whether, for example, replicating the study with women with lupus in other cities or other countries would provide useful additional data. Is there some gap in what Lincoln and Guba (1985) call the 'similarity' of participants that limits the case-to-case transfer? For example, there may be a gap in 'similarity' between Hale et al.'s participants and women with lupus whose cultural practices include clothing that veils the face. Thinking about scope conditions such as culture can thus be more useful than worrying about statistical generalization, which has little if any relevance in qualitative research.

The key question about what might be done with any research findings, particularly qualitative findings, was explicated by Lincoln et al.: 'Are these findings sufficiently authentic (isomorphic to some reality, trustworthy, related to the way others construct their social worlds) that I may trust myself in *acting on their implications?*' (2011:120, emphasis added). Practising clinical and health psychologists can ask themselves: Will I change my practice based on this piece of qualitative research? Polit and Beck argue that 'Many leaders in qualitative research have begun to note the importance of addressing generalization, to ensure that insights from qualitative inquiry are recognized as important sources of *evidence for practice*' (2010:1451). The alternatives to statistical generalization discussed in this section provide a pragmatic way forward for practitioners working in clinical and health psychology. Triangulation is another important pragmatic tool.

Ensuring quality through triangulation

> How can the analysis of qualitative and quantitative data be combined? How does the use of multiple sources of data improve the accessibility and impact of research findings?

The practice of triangulation has been advocated as a way of ensuring the quality of qualitative research in clinical and health psychology. Farmer et al. noted that 'there has been a tremendous surge in the level of interest in triangulation within the realm of public health and health promotion' (2006:377). Based on the work of Erzberger and Prein (1997), the primary purpose of triangulation can be thought of as comparing different types or sources of data to explore convergences, complementarities and dissonances, terms that are defined in Box 5.4.

BOX 5.4   A summary of Erzerberger and Prein's (1997) key aspects of triangulation

Aspect	Application process
Convergence	Differing data sources (e.g. focus groups, interviews, media data) produce similar findings on the same issue, and thus one relatively consistent narrative about the issue under examination.
Complementarity	Differing data sources produce differing takes on the same issue because they construct the object of the focus in differing ways. This produces a range of narratives about the issue under examination.
Dissonance	Divergences between the findings of differing data sources are so great that they lead to challenging the original assumption, hypothesis or question about the issue under examination.

Triangulation is perhaps most strongly associated with mixed-methods research, in which a mixture of types of data are used within one study (see Chapter 17). The mixture of data used in triangulation does not only refer to the combination of some form of qualitative data with some form of quantitative data. However, when making use of qualitative and quantitative data, triangulation can enhance the quality of qualitative research when the combination serves a clear purpose, as in the case study later in this chapter.

Seale (1999) noted that triangulation tends to emphasize a realist epistemological approach to qualitative data analysis – 'that there is a world of events out there that is observable and independent of human consciousness' (Denzin & Lincoln, 2011:11; see also Chapter 2). The case example presented in the next section adopts a realist ontology/epistemology in that it treats the experiences of the population group as a reality that they were able to demonstrate in their responses. This kind of realist approach is often adopted when there is a clearly identified problem experienced by a particular population, and where the most appropriate response is to identify pragmatic solutions to address that problem, particularly for the individuals or groups most affected by it. Massey and Barreras (2013) argue that researchers who seek to target social change need to consider from the very beginning of their research how the various forms of data they collect and the findings they produce can make an impact on their target population or the issue at stake. In terms of quality in qualitative research, the desire for what Massey and Barreras term 'impact validity' may lead researchers to undertake their research within a realist ontology/epistemology with the aim of directly influencing those who may play a key role in creating social change (such as those working in public policy or practitioners such as clinical and health psychologists).

Case study: Triangulation in qualitative research with transgender individuals

This case study is an example of triangulation at the intersection of clinical and health psychology, and arose from the second author's private practice as a psychotherapist working with transgender clients in Adelaide, South Australia. Since 2008, the second author has worked with ten people who have self-identified as transgender, including approximately equal numbers of transgender men and transgender women, in addition to some transgender children. Of these people, some were undertaking hormone therapy (including hormone blockers for some of the children), but none had been through sex-affirming surgery. Many of the individuals had come for psychotherapy with the second author due to an expressed dissatisfaction with other mental health-care professionals they had seen previously (including counsellors, psychologists and psychiatrists) and they often spent considerable time in their early sessions expressing anger, disappointment and frustration about these previous experiences. In response to these views, and through consultation with transgender organizations in Australia, the second author embarked on a series of research projects that aimed to achieve a better understanding of the experiences of Australian transgender people in regard to health-care provision. The projects provide a worked example of triangulation by comparing multiple types of data and examining the convergences, complementarities and dissonances.

The first of the projects adopted the language of 'female assigned at birth' (FAAB), in response to concerns raised by transgender community members that the category 'transgender men' may not necessarily be inclusive of all men who are transmasculine. The data for this first project were collected in 2012 in the form of an online survey that included the collection of qualitative and quantitative data. A total of 78 people responded to the 80 questions in the survey, which addressed issues such as experiences with a range of non-surgical health-care providers, mental health-care professionals, surgeons and hospital staff, in addition to questions covering individual demographics and experiences within both gender-related communities as well as the broader community. Questions included forced response items (i.e. yes or no responses in regard to having accessed a range of services), Likert scale responses (e.g. ratings of satisfaction, perceived support and discrimination) and open-ended responses (e.g. asking participants to write about their experiences with differing professionals). Findings from this survey are reported in full elsewhere (Riggs & Due, 2013).

The second project followed the design of the first and focused on the experiences of transgender women. The term 'transgender women' was adopted instead of 'male assigned at birth', as community members indicated that the latter was less commonly used and that the former was most likely to be considered acceptable by a wide variety of people. The survey was almost identical to that administered in the first project. This survey was conducted in 2013 and 109 people responded. For the purposes of the present chapter the two samples have been combined to allow for an exploration of convergences, complementarities and dissonances between the two cohorts regarding experiences with mental health-care professionals specifically.

In terms of combining the two samples, and while cognizant of the problems with attributing categories to samples who have self-identified in diverse ways, we treat the two samples as discrete groups and we utilize the language of FAAB to refer to the first sample outlined above and MAAB to refer to the second sample. We do this because, as the results demonstrate, the issue at stake is not potentially how the participants identified themselves (as transgender men or women, or simply as men or women, or as genderqueer as was the case for some participants), but rather how the clinicians with whom they engaged viewed them.

Point of triangulation I: Quantitative findings

Participants in both of the surveys responded to three questions asking whether or not they had accessed either a counsellor, psychologist or psychiatrist in regard to their gender identity, and then were asked to rate their experience with each professional (if they had accessed them) on a rating scale where 1=very negative, 2=negative, 3=neither negative nor positive, 4=positive and 5=very positive. In the first study, 51% of the people FAAB had accessed a counsellor, 48% had accessed a psychologist and 65% had accessed a psychiatrist. Numbers were higher in the second study in regard to people MAAB accessing mental health-care professionals, with 72% having accessed a counsellor, 78% having accessed a psychologist and 82% having accessed a psychiatrist. Rates of access were not mutually exclusive, with many participants accessing two or all three of the mental health-care professional categories.

Participants classified in this chapter as FAAB reported significantly higher satisfaction with counsellors, psychologists and psychiatrists than those classified as MAAB, with the mean for participants MAAB being close to 'positive' across the three mental health-care professional groups, and the mean for participants FAAB being close to negative for counsellors and psychologists, and close to neutral for psychiatrists. These differences all remained after controlling for age, which was required because the participants FAAB were significantly younger than the participants MAAB and younger participants across both samples were more satisfied all three groups of mental health-care professionals. What precisely these differences mean can best be understood, however, by looking closely at what participants had to say about their experiences.

Point of triangulation 2: Open-ended responses

Participants who stated that they had accessed a counsellor, psychologist or psychiatrist in regard to their gender identity were asked to provide comments about their experience (see Box 5.5). In examining these responses, the differences identified by the statistical analysis were evident in the comments, such that younger respondents made more negative comments in general than did older respondents. This was also true in regard to assigned sex, with participants MAAB making more positive comments than did participants FAAB.

In an attempt at further explaining the differences between participants in terms of experiences with mental health-care professionals and the variables of assigned sex and age, it was hypothesized that having had surgery may also be related to outcomes. Given that gatekeeping was a concern for many of the participants (in addition to participants in previous research; Speer & Parsons, 2006), those who had 'passed through the gate' and undertaken their desired surgery or surgeries were hypothesized to have been in general more positive about mental health-care professionals than those who were still in the process of negotiating with professionals to secure their support for surgery. However, surgery status was not associated with experiences with any of the mental health-care professional groups, even when controlling for age or assigned sex.

BOX 5.5 Examples of participants' comments about mental health-care professionals from Riggs and Due (2013 and unpublished data)

Participants FAAB	Participants MAAB
Experiences with counsellors	
Younger participants (n=6 negative and 2 positive comments) There is a lack of basic understanding needed to tackle trans issues. It took me two full paid sessions just to explain it to her. Educating my counsellor about gender was not only really annoying but a waste of my sessions.	*Younger participants (n=4 negative and 2 positive comments)* The counsellor was freaked out and more or less told me I was mad. The answer provided by the counsellor was to remain distracted from my desire to become a woman.
Older participants (n=4 positive and 2 negative comments) She was totally affirming and supportive. Counselling helped me get through the attempt to get a diagnosis of GID, which was stressful and traumatic.	*Older participants (n=8 positive and 3 negative comments)* A counsellor is in my opinion a vital part of the transitioning process and mine made everything else bearable. The right counsellor who is across trans issues makes the world of difference.
Experiences with psychologists	
Younger participants (n=6 negative and 1 positive comment) My psychologist didn't take my decision to transition seriously enough, held me back heaps, was not trans aware whatsoever. Having to educate a professional who does not understand gender issues can lead to a sense of feeling unheard and that can have carry-on blocking effects to the effectiveness of treatments.	*Younger participants (n=4 negative and 2 positive comments)* The psychologist I was forced to see was awful. Lack of definite information, inefficient, caused lengthy delays in treatment.
Older participants (n=2 positive and 0 negative comments) Was very helpful and allowed me to look at the concerns from different angles. Again minimal knowledge, but asked lots of open-ended questions and came on the journey of understanding with me.	*Older participants (n=6 positive and 2 negative comments)* He made me feel like a person and understood how I was feeling and empathised with me which gave value to my life and made me feel that my life was worthwhile not a failure. Was very helpful in encouraging me to come to terms with myself, was quite good at dealing with the lack of adequate information available to them, and was very good in empowering me to deal with an abusive relationship.
Experiences with psychiatrists	
Younger participants (n=5 negative and 1 positive comment) My experience was rather traumatic and I was constantly subjected to ridicule and had to work hard to prove myself as trans. He ritualistically talked about my body in ways that was shaming, and treated my chronic pain as psychosomatic.	*Younger participants (n=3 negative and 1 positive comment)* The guy was a complete moron, seriously how many years and how much money spent for these quacks to hang a shingle and practice psychiatry. Horrible gender stereotyping. Offensive descriptive language. Inappropriate questioning and details asked for. Offensive assumptions such as variant sexuality.
Older Participants (n=5 positive and 2 negative comments) She was professional, helpful, and knowledgeable. My psychiatrist was a caring, humane practitioner.	*Older Participants (n=6 positive and 2 negative comments)* He was thorough, kindly, and very good at getting me to discuss all aspects of my life. Very knowledgeable and professional.

Conclusions from the triangulation case study

The findings presented in this case study expand knowledge of Australian transgender people's interactions with counsellors, psychologists and psychiatrists, and provide an indication of the role of two factors that may shape such experiences. The findings also offer dissonance in terms of refuting the phenomenon that appeared in the second author's clinical practice; namely, that surgery may play a role in predicting experiences. Whether or not this dissonance holds true beyond this sample is an important question for future research.

Importantly, while this case study offers an example of triangulation directly related to clinical practice, this is not the only approach suited to examining transgender people's experiences with health-care providers. Critical discursive analyses of how discrimination occurs within the talk of service providers (see Speer & Parsons, 2006, for an example of this), as well as critical analyses of the role of the mental health-care professions in creating and perpetrating stigma towards transgender people, are vital. Such accounts locate the findings identified in this chapter in a broader social context, and do not simply answer the question of what is happening, but also address why it happens and how. Importantly, such analyses also engage in triangulation by utilizing a range of sources from which to map out the discursive terrain of mental health discourse about transgender people (see Lane, 2012).

To conclude, triangulation, regardless of the epistemological orientation that underpins it, offers a concrete approach to ensuring quality in qualitative research. Although triangulation may include quantitative and clinical data, this does not undermine the centrality of the qualitative data, nor does it suggest that qualitative data can only be interpreted through supplementary quantitative analysis. Rather, it suggests that if qualitative researchers seek to ensure that their research has real-world impact, finding multiple ways to tell the story is important. Crystallization is an alternative term for triangulation that is based on the nature of crystals as more multifaceted in shape than triangles; the metaphor is that crystals grow and have many different shapes that provide multiple lenses on data when looked through from different vantage points (Denzin, 2012).

Approaching a topic from a range of vantage points not only demonstrates the quality of the research, but also provides multiple entry points for policymakers, practitioners and other end-users to engage with the findings. Throughout this book a range of forms of qualitative data are described; triangulation can make use of all forms of data and is not limited to examining the combination of qualitative and quantitative data. Life histories, diaries, photographs, newspapers, online forums and so on all provide multiple vantage points from different qualitative methods and approaches. Triangulation is one formal way of combining those vantage points to provide greater quality not in the form of an absolute check, but as an opening-up of dialogue about the convergences, complementarities and dissonances. That some forms of data may be more accessible than others across a range of settings illustrates the point that in order for research to have an impact, it must not only tell a story, it must also tell it in ways of which multiple audiences can make sense. Triangulation, in addition to being a mode of quality assurance, is thus also a way of ensuring that research is accessible to as broad a range of audiences as possible.

Concluding comments

In this chapter we structured our discussion around four broad facets of enacting and demonstrating quality in qualitative research. We emphasized transparency as an overarching facet that is important in demonstrating quality in research outputs, particularly the articles and dissertations/theses written by qualitative researchers. Transparency can be seen as the culmination of enacting the three other facets of quality that we have outlined:

1. Being transparent about working with your personal reflexivity and involving end-users. How will you handle personal and methodological reflexivity? Will you make use of journaling or another form of record keeping? How might you involve end-users in your research process other than as people who can provide you with data?
2. Being transparent in your thinking about the transferability of findings. What kind of generalization claims do you hope to make?
3. Using triangulation to explore convergences, complementarities and dissonances within your research and beyond. Will you use more than one type or source of data in your research? How will the nature of your data come to bear on your analysis and the impact of your research?

These three facets of quality are potentially relevant to all qualitative research in clinical and health psychology, although the facets can be enacted and emphasized in different ways across the various approaches to qualitative research described throughout this book. There cannot be a perfect checklist for calculating the quality of all qualitative research, although some authors will continue to propose such checklists even though the concept of quality is as flexible as truths generated by qualitative psychological research. Thinking about how you might address each facet can be useful preparation before embarking on a study and when preparing the final report, as it can help you avoid the pitfalls that qualitative researchers can encounter when attempting to carry out quality research that has a positive impact on the readers/examiners and more broadly on the community of end-users.

Acknowledgements

We begin by acknowledging that respectively we live on the lands of the Ngāi Tahu iwi of Te Wai Pounamu (the South Island of Aotearoa/New

Zealand) and the Kaurna people of the Adelaide plains. We thank Elizabeth Hale and Clemence Due for their input into the research examples discussed in this chapter. The research reported in the triangulation case study was supported by a Faculty of Social and Behavioural Science Grant. Thanks also go to the Zoe Belle Gender Centre and A Gender Agenda for supporting that research.

Further reading

Clarke, V., Ellis, S.J., Peel, E. & Riggs, D.W. (2010). *Lesbian, Gay, Bisexual, Trans and Queer Psychology: An Introduction*. Leiden: Cambridge University Press.

Ellingson, L.L. (2008). *Engaging Crystallization in Qualitative Research: An Introduction*. Thousand Oaks, CA: Sage.

Finlay, L. & Gough, B. (eds). (2003). *Reflexivity: A Practical Guide for Researchers in Health and Social Science*. Oxford: Blackwell.

Hesse-Biber, S. (2012). Feminist approaches to triangulation: Uncovering subjugated knowledge and fostering social change in mixed methods research. *Journal of Mixed Methods Research*, 6, 137–146.

References

Bury, M. (1982). Chronic illness as biographical disruption. *Sociology of Health & Illness*, 4, 167–182.

Denzin, N.K. (2012). Triangulation 2.0. *Journal of Mixed Methods Research*, 6, 80–88.

Denzin, N.K. & Lincoln, Y.S. (2011). Introduction: The discipline and practice of qualitative research. In N.K. Denzin & Y.S. Lincoln (eds), *The Sage Handbook of Qualitative Research* (4th edn; pp. 1–19). Thousand Oaks, CA: Sage.

Elliott, R., Fischer, C.T. & Rennie, D.L. (1999). Evolving guidelines for publication of qualitative research studies in psychology and related fields. *British Journal of Clinical Psychology*, 38, 215–229.

Ellis, C. (1999). He[art]ful autoethnography. *Qualitative Health Research*, 9, 669–683.

Ellis, C. (2004). *The Ethnographic I: A Methodological Novel about Autoethnography*. Walnut Creek, CA: AltaMira Press.

Erzberger, C. & Prein, G. (1997). Triangulation: Validity and empirically-based hypothesis construction. *Quality and Quantity*, 31, 141–154.

Farmer, T., Robinson, K., Elliot, S.J. & Eyles, J. (2006). Developing and implementing a triangulation protocol for qualitative health research. *Qualitative Health Research*, 16, 277–294.

Finlay, L. (2002). 'Outing' the researcher: The provenance, process, and practice of reflexivity. *Qualitative Health Research*, 12, 531–545.

Firestone, W.A. (1993). Alternative arguments for generalizing from data as applied to qualitative research. *Educational Researcher*, 22, 16–23.

Goffman, E. (1963). *Stigma: Notes on the Management of Spoiled Identity*. Englewood Cliffs, NJ: Prentice-Hall.

Guba, E.G. (1981). Criteria for assessing trustworthiness of naturalistic enquiries. *Educational Communication and Technology Journal*, 29, 75–91.

Hale, E.D., Treharne, G.J., Norton, Y., Lyons, A.C., Douglas, K.M.J., Erb, N. & Kitas, G. D. (2006). 'Concealing the evidence': The importance of appearance concerns for patients with systemic lupus erythematosus. *Lupus*, 15, 532–540.

Hellawell, D. (2006). Inside–out: Analysis of the insider–outsider concept as a heuristic device to develop reflexivity in students doing qualitative research. *Teaching in Higher Education*, 11, 483–494.

Hewlett, S., De Wit, M., Richards, P., Quest, E., Hughes, R., Heiberg, T. & Kirwan, J. (2006). Patients and professionals as research partners: Challenges, practicalities, and benefits. *Arthritis Care & Research*, 55, 676–680.

Lane, R. (2012). Paradigm and power shifts in the gender clinic. In L. Manderson (ed.), *Technologies of Sexuality, Identity, and Sexual Health* (pp. 203–230). London: Routledge.

Lincoln, Y.S. (1995). Emerging criteria for quality in qualitative and interpretive research. *Qualitative Inquiry*, 1, 275–289.

Lincoln, Y.S. & Guba, E. (1985). *Naturalistic Enquiry*. Beverly Hills, CA: Sage.

Lincoln, Y.S., Lynham, S.A. & Guba, E.G. (2011). Paradigmatic controversies, contradictions, and emerging confluences, revisited. In N.K. Denzin & Y.S. Lincoln (eds), *The Sage Handbook of Qualitative Research* (4th edn; pp. 97–128). Thousand Oaks, CA: Sage.

Lodge, D. (2001). *Thinks* ... London: Random House.

Lupus UK. (2013). *What Is Lupus? The Symptoms*. http://www.lupusuk.org.uk/what-is-lupus/the-symptoms, accessed 22 November 2013.

Massey, S.G. & Barreras, E. (2013). Introducing 'impact validity'. *Journal of Social Issues*, 69, 615–632.

McGavock, Z.C. & Treharne, G.J. (2011). Young adults' beliefs about people living with HIV/AIDS and rheumatoid arthritis: Thematic analysis of a think-aloud questionnaire investigation. *New Zealand Journal of Psychology*, 40, 71–78.

Newton, S. (2008). *Record Keeping: Guidance on Good Practice*. Leicester: Division of Clinical Psychology (of the British Psychological Society).

Polit, D.F. & Beck, C.T. (2010). Generalization in quantitative and qualitative research: Myths and strategies. *International Journal of Nursing Studies*, 47, 1451–1458.

Riggs, D.W. & Due, C. (2013). Mapping the health experiences of Australians who were female assigned at birth but who now identify with a different gender identity. *Lambda Nordica*, 19, 54–76.

Seale, C. (1999). Quality in qualitative research. *Qualitative Inquiry*, 5, 465–478.

Smith, C.M., Hale L.A., Mulligan, H.F. & Treharne, G.J. (2013). Participant perceptions of a novel physiotherapy approach ('Blue Prescription') for increasing levels of physical activity in people with multiple sclerosis: A qualitative study following intervention. *Disability and Rehabilitation*, 35, 1174–1181.

Sparkes, A.C. (2007). Embodiment, academics, and the audit culture: A story seeking consideration. *Qualitative Research*, 7, 521–550.

Speer, S.A. & Parsons, C. (2006). Gatekeeping gender: Some features of the use of hypothetical questions in the psychiatric assessment of transsexual patients. *Discourse and Society*, 17, 785–812.

Tong, A., Sinasbury, P. & Craig, J. (2007). Consolidated criteria for reporting qualitative research (COREQ): A 32-item checklist for interviews and focus groups. *International Journal for Quality in Health Care*, 19, 349–357.

Treharne, G.J. (2011). Questioning sex/gender and sexuality: Reflections on recruitment and stratification. *Gay and Lesbian Issues and Psychology Review*, 7, 132–154.

Treharne, G.J., Brickell, C. & Chinn, A. (2011). Surveying 'non-heterosexual orientation': The problems of unstratefied sampling, non-inclusive categorizations, and implied causality. Commentary on Wells, McGee, and Beautrais (2011). *Archives of Sexual Behavior*, 40, 663–665.

Willig, C. (2013). *Introducing Qualitative Research in Psychology* (3rd edn). Maidenhead: McGraw-Hill International.

Yardley, L. (2000). Dilemmas in qualitative health research. *Psychology and Health*, 15, 215–228.

Approaches to Collecting Data

Antonia C. Lyons

6

Qualitative research is diverse, covering a range of different qualitative approaches that come from different traditions (as you will see throughout this book). These diverse approaches seek to answer different kinds of research questions and employ different analytical tools in doing so. They also collect different kinds of data, which they do in different ways. Specific qualitative methods have developed in different disciplines, come from different traditions and are based on different ideas of science, so any form of data collection will be informed by these positions (Polkinghorne, 2005). This chapter cannot do justice to the vast array of approaches to data collection that qualitative researchers have used, so it aims to outline some key issues involved in making decisions about ways to collect data, as well as providing brief overviews of some main data-collection approaches that are relevant for clinical and health psychology.

The term 'data collection' implies a relatively straightforward process that involves a researcher going out into the world to gather up bits of information (data) to provide evidence for whatever is being investigated. It also implies that these data exist independently of the researcher, although in many research situations data are 'produced' through research processes rather than simply 'collected' (Polkinghorne, 2005). Undertaking interviews, for example, provides a unique dialogue that is produced by the interviewer and the participant together. Many forms of quantitative data are similarly 'produced' (survey data do not exist independently of the researcher, but are brought into being through the generation of responses to a questionnaire). As researchers, we collect, generate and produce qualitative data within the context of a research project to address particular research questions. Being able to address those questions successfully depends a great deal on ensuring that the methods employed and the ways in which the data are collected are consistent with the assumptions and positioning of the research project. Indeed, where and how we obtain our data 'determine the data that we produce, the meanings that we craft from those data, and the knowledge claims that we make' (Suzuki et al., 2007:296).

Self-awareness and reflexivity are particularly important in qualitative research, as the researcher is often the main instrument throughout the data-collection, analysis and interpretation processes (Onwuegbuzie et al., 2010). Your values, positions, personal experiences and so on have an impact on what you choose to study, how you choose to study it, how you analyse it and what you choose to report (Suzuki et al., 2007; Yin, 2011). Being self-aware is also important in considerations of ethical issues that arise in collecting qualitative data (see Chapter 3), including relationships with participants, the ways in which the research questions are conceptualized, who is included in the research and has their voice heard (and who does not), for whom the research is beneficial and so on (Suzuki et al., 2007). In this chapter I begin by considering some key issues involved in making decisions about how best to collect data within a research project, including when and how to make these decisions, who to include as participants and how they should be selected. I then consider some main approaches to collecting qualitative data.

Making decisions about data collection

Beginning researchers frequently select a topic and start by making decisions about methods and the ways in which they will collect their data. However, this is not the place to begin a research project. If data-collection decisions are driving the project it can lead to all sorts of problems further down the track. Many research projects flounder (or fall over) because people start at what appears to be the beginning (collecting data), only to find that their data are unanalysable (Greig et al., 2013) because they have not been collected in a way that enables the research question to be answered, or because the data do not address the research question at all. Deciding on methods prior to developing a solid research question is setting a project up for failure (Hays & Singh, 2012).

Importantly, whatever approach you take to data collection, it must be able to answer the research question. The research question must be clear and well defined at the outset. It should be well justified with a strong rationale based on relevant previous literature and theoretical frameworks. It may become more specific and detailed through the process of collecting data, but if the research question is vague or poorly defined at the start it will impinge on all aspects of the research project (Frith & Gleeson, 2012). You should also think carefully about the assumptions that underpin your research question, in terms of what kinds of knowledge it seeks to produce (see Chapter 2) and how it constructs the key concepts of the research (Frith & Gleeson, 2012). Researchers make a number of assumptions throughout any research project; these should be reflected on throughout the design of the project, as they shape (implicitly or explicitly) how methods and approaches to data collection are conceived and implemented throughout the study (Marshall & Rossman, 2011; see Chapters 1 and 2).

Thus, choosing what data-collection approach to take is not a simple or a neutral task, and it makes no sense to consider data-collection methods separately from research methodologies, because 'the actions involved in collecting data take on very different meanings from the standpoint of different methodologies and when the epistemological underpinnings of research are examined' (Frith & Gleeson, 2012:59). Methodology guides decisions about what kind of data are relevant, useful and ideal. For example, conversation analysis frequently employs naturally occurring talk as data (see Chapter 12) and ethnography primarily employs observation (see Chapter 14). So once the conceptual framing, methodology, aims and research questions are clearly outlined, it is time to start thinking about particular data-collection approaches that will generate data that fit with the epistemological assumptions (Frith & Gleeson, 2012). We will keep returning to this point throughout this chapter.

Making decisions about participants

Your research topic will obviously guide your decisions about who would be the best participants to include in your research study. Some studies have research questions that do not require participants, such as analyses of media or textbook representations (e.g. Gough, 2007; Niland & Lyons, 2011), although most research in clinical and health psychology does involve participants. Whatever approach you take, you need to think about what it means for participants, what demands it places on them, whether they have the necessary abilities and skills to be involved with the approach, and whether engaging in the research makes sense to them (see Frith & Gleeson, 2012, for a fuller discussion of these issues). If you are conducting research with children or young people, you need to ensure that your data-collection approaches engage them and use forms of communication that are useful for eliciting their voices (e.g. see McIntosh & Stephens, 2012). If participants are willing to share in the aims of a research project, find their participation meaningful and engage with the data-collection approach, the data generated and the research itself should be rich, relevant and beneficial for all involved.

Researchers must also decide on the appropriate number of participants to include. This causes much concern among beginning researchers, who are worried that small numbers of participants will not be enough. The main question here is: 'Enough for what?' The ideal sample size will depend on the research question and methodology: gaining in-depth information from one individual case may be sufficient to address the research question. In quantitative research it is common to refer to the term *sampling* to describe how participants are selected, although this implies that they are sampled from a given population and have been chosen so that findings can be applied back to that population (Polkinghorne, 2005). Thus, *selection* of participants might be a better term to use in qualitative research, which usually does not have such a goal. Most often, qualitative research seeks to answer research questions that involve gaining insights into the meanings of some phenomenon (rather than generalizing from a set of people to show averages of experience; Polkinghorne, 2005). There are different ways to select participants,

Table 6.1   Sampling strategies for selecting participants

Strategy	Selecting participants
Purposive sampling	For their relevance to the study/topic
Maximum variation sampling	For their divergence in relation to the topic (to explore both variations and commonalities)
Homogeneous sampling	For their similarity in relation to the topic
Typical sampling	For whom the topic is typical
Deviant sampling	Who are extremely different in relation to the topic (to explore the boundaries of difference)
Critical case sampling	For whom the topic is particularly intense or irregular
Criterion sampling	Who meet some important pre-determined criteria
Convenience sampling	Based on ease of access and availability
Snowball sampling	Who then go on to nominate other potential participants

Source: Based on Polkinghorne (2005); Petty et al. (2012).

as outlined in Table 6.1. Convenience sampling is common, as it involves finding people who are available and easy to access, but is not always the best approach. The approach employed for participant selection needs to fit with the research framework and research questions, and be justifiable (Polkinghorne, 2005).

Data-collection approaches

In this section I provide an overview of data-collection approaches employed by qualitative social science researchers; namely, talking to people (in interviews and groups), observing people and their environments, collecting documents and artefacts, and using social networking technology. Some of these approaches have a longer history than others, and some have been used more frequently than others in clinical and health psychology. Some will fit nicely as ways to collect data for a particular research project, while others will not. It all depends on the research framework, methodology and aims. These approaches do not need to be used on their own – quite often a unique and insightful study will combine one or two (or three) of these approaches – but again, this will only work if such combinations make sense within the conceptual framing and methodology of the research. New technologies offer novel ways to gather data for research projects. The internet is a daily feature of many people's everyday lives in the Western world, so I have considered it within each of the specific approaches where relevant. The virtual environment provides both strengths and weaknesses for data collection – and their relevance will also depend on the research project. In addition, I consider new digital technologies, such as social networking and smartphones, and their potential for data collection.

Talking to people individually

Undertaking individual interviews with participants is the most widely used form of qualitative data collection in psychology. Entire textbooks have been written on interviewing (e.g. Kvale, 1996; Seidman, 2006; Kvale & Brinkmann, 2009). Researchers use interviews to try to obtain detailed accounts from participants about the topic under investigation. They have been popular for good reason: they enable specific and direct questions to be asked of participants, further areas can be explored as they arise, they are relatively quick and do not take a lot of participants' time and they are also relatively cheap. Interviews are frequently used to gain fuller insight into what a particular experience is like for a person (such as living with depression or chronic illness) and how they make sense of that experience (Seidman, 2006). Importantly, they provide a person's *description* of that experience – not the experience itself. How much insight you might gain via an interview will depend on the verbal ability of participants to explain their experiences fluently and clearly.

Interviews are a co-construction between the interviewer and the participant. This is why some qualitative researchers use the term 'accounts' to refer to qualitative data gathered through talk with participants (Polkinghorne, 2005). According to Kvale, the interview is a 'professional conversation' (1996:5) and a 'construction site of knowledge' (1996:2). It is led by the interviewer and involves give-and-take conversation guided by the researcher to produce the information required for the research project (Polkinghorne, 2005). The type, focus and content of the interview will vary depending on your research project and research question. Decisions about structure, purpose, depth, tone and emotional focus all need to be made in line with the research project (Suzuki et al., 2007).

Interviews vary in terms of how structured they are based on their purpose and aim. Structured interviews are highly organized, follow a consistent and pre-established process and have a set of standard questions that the interviewer asks. Semi-structured interviews are more open without a pre-determined sequence of questions, but with a protocol that serves as a guide and provides a reminder of the topics to be covered (Hays & Singh, 2012). Unstructured interviews, as the name implies, have little or no structure and the participant talks freely with only some follow-ups and prompts; these occur commonly as part of a participant observation (Hays & Singh, 2012). More open, conversational styles of interview would be appropriate for research that is exploratory, such as obtaining life history narratives (see Chapters 9 and 11 for more about interview styles in narrative and psychoanalytic research approaches), whereas more structured styles of interview are driven by the researcher's agenda and may be more about hypothesis testing (Howitt, 2013).

Qualitative psychology research projects frequently use a one-off interview, although, depending on the research topic and focus of investigation, this may not be the best approach to produce highly relevant and useful data. It takes time to build rapport with participants, and if the aim is to get rich and full descriptions of participants' experiences, then a series of interviews might be worth considering (Polkinghorne, 2005). Thus, rapport could be built in the first interview, while subsequent ones could be more focused and enable greater elicitation of accounts. The time between interviews enables the participant (and researcher) to think about the topic in more depth, and also allows the researcher to consider previous information further and what might be useful to clarify or expand on.

The interviewer's presence, characteristics and ways in which they listen and respond within the conversation are an integral part of the conversation, and indeed of the participant's account (Polkinghorne, 2005). This is particularly so in face-to-face interviews. Telephone interviews are often employed when face-to-face interviews are not feasible, and increasingly email and other online forms of communication are used to conduct interviews with participants at a distance or for ease of participation. Most of these approaches mean that non-verbal communication is not available to the interviewer (with the exception of online video interviews, via software such as Skype), so these cues are not available to help guide the flow of the interview. Not seeing each other also introduces a level of anonymity into the interview, which may hinder aspects such as rapport building, but, depending on the topic and the interview format, could also promote participants' intimacy, honesty and disclosure (Suzuki et al., 2007). Anonymity may render participants much more willing to talk, especially if the topic is highly sensitive or if the participant is acutely anxious, shy or does not want people to see them. It might also reduce power imbalances between the researcher and the participant, decreasing real or perceived differences in identities and status (Robinson, 2001).

There are many benefits to employing online interviews. They enable access to participants who would otherwise not take part in a study due to their location (e.g. people in hospital or in prison) and circumstances (e.g. new parents, people with certain disabilities; see Bowker & Tuffin, 2004). They also enable great reach to participants across a wide range of settings and geographical locations (Robinson, 2001), meaning that a sample can quite literally be global (Marshall & Rossman, 2011). If the interaction is typed, an accurate transcript is immediately provided. Interviews over email can be highly convenient for participants, who can respond in a time frame that suits them (Hays & Singh, 2012). Email interviews are asynchronous in that the participant and interviewer do not need to be available at the same time, in contrast to synchronous interviewing, which takes place online in real time and with the expectation of a reasonably rapid interaction (such as via instant messaging). Many of the main principles of sampling, recruitment and interviewing apply to the online context (Hays & Singh, 2012), although there are also unique practical, conceptual and ethical issues (see Evans et al., 2008; Kazmer & Xie, 2008).

Interviews involve power dynamics that influence the data that are produced, as well as the interpretations that researchers make of the data (Suzuki et al., 2007). Researchers lead the conversations with participants and set the boundaries and framework of the ensuing discussion. Power imbalances may mean that participants are unwilling or unable to challenge such boundaries, or the focus of the discussion. Within clinical and counselling psychology, it is important for researchers to be very clear about their researcher role and the purpose of the interview as a data-collection tool for a research project; it is never appropriate for the researcher to shift into a therapist or clinician role (Polkinghorne, 2005; Suzuki et al., 2007; see also Chapter 3).

Interviews have been critiqued as the automatic go-to method of choice for qualitative psychology research (Potter & Hepburn, 2005). As they are very much like natural conversations, they can be conducted thoughtlessly, superficially and in an untheorized way (Marshall & Rossman, 2011). Undertaking an interview is a process that requires planning beforehand and consideration afterwards (Howitt, 2013). Potter and Hepburn (2005) outline a number of problems with the ways in which interviews have been conducted, transcribed, analysed and reported in psychology, and conclude that interviews are very hard to do well. Interviewing well is a skill that is learned over time and conducting excellent interviews is a deceptively difficult thing to do, not at all like our routine daily talk (Hermanowicz, 2002). Some strategies and considerations on how interviewers can conduct great interviews are provided in Box 6.1.

Talking to people in groups

Interviewing participants within groups is an approach derived from business and marketing disciplines and was originally termed 'focus' groups because participants are there to engage in a discussion with a clear focus. Group discussions have been increasingly used in social science research and can include people who are unknown to each other, or who are very close friends or relatives. What is appropriate will depend on the research questions and research methodology. Usually group participants share a common experience or have some kind of similarity (Hays & Singh, 2012). Group discussions can be particularly beneficial to see social processes in action: for example, how groups of friends socially co-construct together their views, opinions and beliefs about a particular topic.

Onwuegbuzie and colleagues (2010) summarize a range of key benefits of discussion groups, noting that they are economical; can involve greater number of participants than interviews; provide data from a social environment; capture interaction between people; and create an atmosphere in which a range of responses can occur. On the other hand, participants could feel pressure to align with what is being said in the group and feel reluctant to put forward views that oppose the majority of the group (Hays & Singh, 2012). Conversation and talk within groups tend to be somewhat chaotic: people talk over the top of each other, interrupt each other, finish each other's sentences and sometimes have two or three mini-conversations going on at once. For many research projects this kind of talk is highly informative as it captures

---

BOX 6.1   Conducting great interviews

What makes an outstanding interview? Great interviews are richly detailed. According to Hermanowicz (2002), to obtain such rich detail interviewers should let go of social norms or rules that might constrain the nature of an interview and be more forward, candid and adventuresome. He outlines 25 key issues that will help interviewers undertake great interviews with participants, rather than merely average or good ones. If a researcher wants to undertake a great interview, they should:

1. Converse
2. Listen
3. Explore what's important to the participant
4. Probe
5. Remain quiet at times
6. Persist
7. Play the innocent sometimes
8. Make sure the interview isn't too short, or too long
9. Word questions clearly
10. Have a structure with well-sequenced questions
11. Divide the conversation into topical stages
12. Be balanced – have easy as well as difficult, sensitive and unflattering questions
13. Be candid
14. Preserve the integrity of the interview: have a sense of equality but remain in charge
15. Show respect
16. Embody detached (quiet) concern: participants are not casual friends or acquaintances
17. Test your questions beforehand
18. Rehearse (know your questions)
19. Avoid interviewing people you know
20. Start strong: have a good introduction
21. End positively: include some concluding questions
22. Write field notes afterwards: thoughts, impressions, hints, ideas that arose
23. Record the interview
24. Do face-to-face interviews
25. Practise, practise, practise

Source: Hermanowicz, J.C. (2002). The great interview: 25 strategies for studying people in bed. *Qualitative Sociology, 25*(4), 479–499.

---

group interaction in action, including processes such as how people are cut off, or allowed to speak, which may be a key factor of interest in a research project (e.g. see Chapter 12).

The size of the group fully depends on the research project itself. Groups that are large (between 8 and 12 participants) enable a greater number of participants to be involved, but may make it difficult for everyone to have a say.

BOX 6.2 Transcribing

What is transcription? What gets transcribed?
Transcription is not a simple, neutral or technical task, but involves judgement and interpretation (Marshall & Rossman, 2011). Whenever oral talk is transcribed into written text, it loses much of the information and nuance (Polkinghorne, 2005). Facial expressions, gestures, coughs, sneezes, laughs, pacing, tone and non-verbal communication are frequently not included in transcripts. The importance of these nuanced and more detailed forms of interaction and meaning-making depend fully on your research project, framework and the specific research questions you have developed. Your methodology will guide you as to how much detail you should include in your transcription, from minute detail regarding every noise, length of pauses, intakes of breath and so on (e.g. for projects employing conversation analysis – see Chapter 12 for an example of a detailed transcription) through to less detailed transcripts of the speech uttered (e.g. for some kinds of thematic analysis).

Who should transcribe?
As far as possible you should do your own transcribing, because turning talk into text requires the interpretation of meaning, and as the researcher you are the best person to make these intepretations. The rigour of the transcript, and consequently the data, is determined largely by the transcriber (Hays & Singh, 2012). Saldana (2011) argues that transcribing your own work provides you with the opportunity to become fully intimate with the data. Transcription can also be viewed as a preliminary stage of analysis as you get familiar with the data and start to think about it analytically.

A good discussion group is run by a facilitator who is skilled at enabling the flow of conversation while encouraging reticent participants to engage in the conversation and managing dominant, persuasive or charismatic participants (Suzuki et al., 2007). Thus, the quality of the group discussion and the data generated will depend heavily on the skills of the facilitator. Both interviews and group discussions are usually recorded (audio or video recorded) so that the talk can be transcribed into text, producing qualitative data. Box 6.2 outlines some key issues to consider around transcription.

Data can also be collected from discussion groups within an online environment. These can be advantageous, as their anonymity can increase the trust and the amount that participants are willing to share. They also can reach people who share a common experience, or a phenomenon, that might be rare or is difficult to discuss in a group of people face to face (Hays & Singh, 2012). Accessing and recruiting participants from discussion groups require the permission of group moderators or website administrators, as does any form of web-based recruitment advertising for participants (Evans et al., 2008). Greater numbers of participants can take part more easily in online focus groups. Hays and Singh (2012) argue that they are most effective when the group is naturally occurring; that is, they are already online as a group discussing a particular topic, phenomenon or experience, such as a discussion board or chat room. There are unique ethical considerations that arise in conducting online interviews and focus groups, not least of which are issues around informed consent.

Observing people and their environments

Observation is fundamental to all qualitative research (Marshall & Rossman, 2011). The collection and use of observational data have traditionally been employed more widely in sociology and anthropology than in psychology, especially as the primary source of data. Observations involve collecting data through recording what is seen (and heard) by the researcher, and their goal is to capture behaviour, actions and interactions within a naturalistic context (Saldana, 2011). The focus and extent of the observations, and their length, depend on the research framework and aims. Observations might usefully be employed in conjunction with other forms of data: for example, interview data could be supplemented by written observations about the participants involved (e.g. clothing, behaviours, expressions etc.) and their surroundings (e.g. photos, books, pictures; Polkinghorne, 2005). The quality of the data gathered depends a great deal on the skill of the observer. Choosing what to observe is key to this type of data collection. Selecting certain objects, events or people for observation and disregarding others are important decisions made by researchers and highlight the importance of reflexivity throughout the data-collection process. These decisions are not made objectively (Suzuki et al., 2007) but are informed by the research project, the design, researcher characteristics, values and abilities, as well as pragmatic considerations regarding access and availability.

Participant observation was developed primarily in cultural anthropology and qualitative sociology (Marshall & Rossman, 2011) and unfortunately has been frequently neglected in qualitative psychology research (Howitt, 2013). It involves the researcher being involved in the social world of interest, to begin to experience social life in a way that is similar to participants – so in this sense the researcher is a participant but also an observer (see also Chapter 14 on ethnography). The extent of researcher participation will depend on the project, but it can range from being relatively non-involved, observing like a 'fly on the wall', through to complete participation involving living and working within the culture, group or community under study to obtain deep experiential knowledge (Saldana, 2011). In conducting participant observation, researchers make field notes that are taken during the observational period and continually expanded and developed after the observation to provide a detailed written record of the field activities (Hays & Singh, 2012). As well as field notes, data might also be captured through other methods such as audio and video recordings (Petty et al., 2012).

The key aim of some research projects is to obtain naturalistic data, particularly talk – that is, talk between people that is naturally occurring in everyday life. For example, researchers using conversation analysis (and sometimes discourse analysis) emphasize the importance of using naturally occurring talk-in-interaction, such as telephone conversations, discussions between doctors and patients, family interactions at the dinner table and so on (Hugh-Jones & Gibson, 2012). Lively debate has arisen over the value of naturalistic talk as opposed to that generated in interview settings. Employing naturalistic data aims to avoid active researcher involvement in the talk (see Potter & Hepburn, 2005), although even with naturalistic data the researcher makes decisions about what to record and when to record it (Hugh-Jones & Gibson, 2012).

Observations can also be conducted in an online environment. Observing and collecting data from existing online material such as newsgroups, discussion boards, online communities and listservs might be highly relevant. Researchers may choose to observe asynchronous electronic data, such as websites, news sites, bulletin boards and emails, or synchronous electronic data that occur online in real time, such as chat rooms and instant messaging (Suzuki et al., 2007; Onwuegbuzie et al., 2010). However, this raises unique ethical issues, such as whether something that is produced online for a particular purpose (e.g. contributing to a discussion forum) can be employed for a different purpose (as research data; see also Chapter 3).

Collecting and using documents and artefacts

The use of documents and artefacts in data collection involves 'physical data', also termed material culture (Suzuki et al., 2007). Collecting this kind of data has been used most frequently in biographies, ethnographies and case studies to provide historical insight, although they are increasingly being used alongside other forms of data collection in psychology to gain greater insight or depth into a phenomenon or topic. Records are forms of official material such as bank statements, death and marriage certificates, driving licences and other government information, whereas documents can be public (newspapers, magazines, reports) or personal (letters, diaries, journals; Suzuki et al., 2007). Artefacts are another form of material culture and include films, photographs, videos, drawings, paintings, media representations and electronic visual data (Suzuki et al., 2007). Whatever their background and purpose, all kinds of material 'texts' require interpretation on the part of the researcher as their meaning is not transparent, and they have little meaning outside the context in which they were created (Suzuki et al., 2007). In addition, collecting documents and artefacts can be extremely time consuming as they can be available in abundance. Researchers need to think carefully about which deserve their attention (Yin, 2011).

We can distinguish between materials that existed prior to the research project and those that are generated or produced as part of the research project. The use of visual data has become increasingly argued for and employed within psychology research (see Reavey, 2011). Visual methods allow participants to express their views, experiences or understandings in deeper, and non-verbal, ways (Hays & Singh, 2012). Scholars have argued that visual culture is an integral part of contemporary western life (Jenks, 1995). Images are 'everywhere' (Pink, 2007) and their meanings are made by viewers at particular times and places (Rose, 2005). Visual images and other visual forms are evocative and can be profoundly moving (Marshall & Rossmann, 2011). Photographs enable a way of accessing and grounding people's accounts in concrete experiences, and both existing photographs and those produced for a research project can help with a focus on particular experiences, especially concerning lived, embodied events (Del Busso, 2011). Photovoice is a participatory data-collection method in which participants take photographs and describe them from their own perspectives, providing a personal description of their experiences, community or life (Wang et al., 2000) to promote dialogue about it and mobilize change (Wang & Burris, 1997). Chapter 15 provides a more detailed discussion of Photovoice as a data-collection strategy.

Asking participants to write or record diaries to produce data is another approach that may be valuable, particularly if you are interested in experiences and reflections over time. These can be unobtrusive, provide more depth and understanding, access participants' lived experience and enable access to changes over a period of time (Hays & Singh, 2012). Diaries could be written, typed, shared online with the researcher, or could be in the form of audio or video recordings (in this way they are not dependent on participants' writing skills). Many blogs (weblogs) and online life journals can be considered a popular form of diary, involving self-reporting and self-reflection (Kaun, 2010). These include a series of entries written by a single author and a set of chronologically ordered archives, and thus enable examination of social processes over time (Hookway, 2008). Blogs are publically available, unobtrusive and inexpensive, and have been described as naturalistic data in textual form (Hookway, 2008). Vlogs (videologs) are essentially the same but with videos rather than text (Hays & Singh, 2012).

Drawing is another way in which to generate data. While initially used as a valuable way to obtain data from children, drawing can be employed effectively with adults as well, for example to explore the ways in which they understand illness conditions to provide rich insights into how people make sense of their world (e.g. Guillemin, 2004). Asking participants to select material objects from their lives to share with the researcher within the context of an in-depth interview can also enhance, extend and elaborate the interviewing process and the insight (and interpretation) gained (Sheridan & Chamberlain, 2011). Participants' stories can be enhanced by the material objects (such as photographs, clothing, journals and home videos) that they have selected as highly relevant to them and the topic under investigation. These items can increase the depth of the narrative and can also act in powerful ways to change the shape and direction of the interview and the relationships between the participant and the researcher (Sheridan & Chamberlain, 2011). Meanings are not inherent in the object but in the ways in which people make sense with it (Radley & Taylor, 2003).

Digital culture provides further possibilities for accessing documented information. Facebook pages, for example, provide a unique autobiographical account of a person through their posted photos, comments, status updates, group memberships, links to other sites and also what might be excluded (Saldana, 2011). Within the online world images are also central; one of the key features of Facebook is the uploading and sharing of digital photos. There are over 250 billion photos uploaded onto this site and approximately 350 million photos are added daily (Smith, 2014). Texts and tweets also provide a history of people's communication and sharing of information.

Social networking and new technologies

Rapidly evolving digital media technologies may be beneficial as ways to collect data, particularly social networking technologies such as Facebook, Myspace, Twitter, YouTube, Flickr and so on (Onwuegbuzie et al., 2010). As many young people spend a lot of their time with new technologies, this may be a good way to engage them in research participation (Greig et al., 2013). For example, webcams and self-cams could be employed by participants to provide regular information in a fun and easy manner. YouTube is a video-sharing tool by which users can upload, share and comment on video clips, and it can be employed as an exclusive way to share such material within groups (Onwuegbuzie et al., 2010). There are many photo-sharing (e.g. Flickr) or content-sharing (e.g. Pinterest) networks that could also be harnessed by qualitative researchers in diverse ways. Interviews can be used alongside data from social networking sites. For example, 'go-along interviews' involve researchers interviewing participants talking about their social networking activities, and also filming or screen-recording these (e.g. Niland et al., 2014). In addition blogging and vlogging have a great deal of potential for data collection, as they can be public or private and require little technical expertise (Hookway, 2008).

Smartphones provide an array of different kinds of digital data. Most have geolocation technology and apps that enable geographical information to be shared in different ways (e.g. status updates in Facebook regarding where you currently are). These technologies enable geographical data to be collected and may be beneficial in enhancing researchers' understandings of particular phenomena to extend to geographical and spatial contexts (Onwuegbuzie et al., 2010). Smartphones are increasingly used by researchers in conducting research projects. Van Doorn (2013) provides an engaging account of how smartphones can facilitate many research activities, such as using maps to find locations, recording talk or field notes, taking videos, texting participants, replying to participant emails and so on. However, he also argues that the technologically mediated nature of all of these actions and interactions can shape the way in which researchers are involved in the research project and that they have implications for research processes, knowledge production and the intimacies and boundaries of research relationships.

There are unique ethical issues involved in collecting data via new digital technologies. Importantly, there is a digital divide between people who can afford and have access to these technologies and those who do not. It is not quite as straightforward as this either, as although people might have access to the internet (via school, libraries or even computers at home), this is not the same as being connected many hours a day via PDAs (personal digital assistants such as iPods and iPads) or smartphones. While researchers may be tempted to use new digital technologies to collect data because they seem novel or cool, such choices must be made cautiously. As noted, the best guide in choosing which data-collection method to employ is considering which would enable you to understand your topic of inquiry as fully as possible, in a way that addresses the research questions and is consistent with your conceptual framework (Hays & Singh, 2012). Researchers must ask themselves whether this is the *best way* to capture, elicit and gain understanding and insight into the research topic.

Further considerations

Multimodal and multisensory research

People's lived experiences are multimodal and multisensory (Del Busso, 2011) and much of the qualitative research in psychology has tended to emphasize talk and text over other modes and senses, such as feeling, emotion, sight, sound, smell, touch and taste. Senses are powerful:

> particular smells can force us to instantly recall people or moments in our lives; touch can invoke strong memories and feelings; sounds, such as music, can take us back decades in time; and taste induces a spectrum of embodied reactions from sheer pleasure to strong disgust. (Harris & Guillemin, 2012:690)

Psychology researchers' reluctance to explore and engage in qualitative research that is multimodal and multisensory may be partially explained by the difficulty of analysing and interpreting material that has multiple meanings and involves interpretations that are not always fixed (Reavey & Johnson, 2008; Reavey, 2011). Yet multimodal approaches may be highly appropriate for experiential issues in clinical and health psychology, including those around embodiment, experiences of physical and mental health, and illness and health care. How might research projects be designed so that they include a greater consideration of multisensory data? The interview itself can be considered a multisensory event (Pink, 2009). Harris and Guillemin (2012) argue that developing and employing sensory awareness in interviewing can enrich data, providing insight into healthcare and illness experiences that cannot be articulated in any other way, either because they are too sensitive or too difficult to describe. Sensory awareness involves acknowledging the importance of the senses in the research project, developing skills to tune into the senses and integrating senses into the analysis. Employing material objects can also expand a research project to include expression and meaning that are multisensorial and multidimensional; for example, the touch involved in handling and passing photographs, the smell of objects, the feel of clothing (Sheridan & Chamberlain, 2011; Pink, 2008).

Methodolatry

Polkinghorne has pointed out that qualitative research and methods have expanded considerably in the past 40 years, but alongside their acceptability has come a kind of rule setting and 'textbookification' of the 'right' way to do things (2005:137). This can limit creativity, innovation and generating new ways to collect data and produce knowledge. Methodolatry is the term given to 'the privileging of methodological concerns over other considerations' (Chamberlain, 2000:286). An over-concern with methodology, and a reification of methods, can lead to a focus on description over interpretation, considerations of method rather than meaning, and a shift away from the theoretical frameworks that inform research questions and enable them to be addressed in appropriate and insightful ways (Chamberlain, 2000). Onwuegbuzie et al. argue that we are entering a time when qualitative researchers can move towards a period of 'methodological innovation' and 'go beyond traditional ways of collecting primary and reflexive data' (2010:721). Psychology researchers have not been very creative when it comes to data collection, but no data-collection approach or method should be fixed and inflexible, and often the most successful research projects are those that have allowed for openness, flexibility, development and creativity (Frith & Gleeson, 2012). Rigidity around data-collection techniques will not help researchers identify methods that fit best with their research aims and questions. In addition, research design is a creative and iterative process, so it will ideally grow and change over time (Frith & Gleeson, 2012). The use of a combination of records, documents, artefacts and interviews may provide more nuanced, in-depth and full insight into a topic – something that a researcher may only realize well into the research project. The use of multiple and various data-collection approaches may also be suitable to employ with vulnerable populations, as 'they support participant expression and encourage diverse perspectives' (Walsh et al., 2010:192).

Concluding comments

Research is an iterative process, and collecting data is not an independent stage of a research project. It is accompanied continually by analysis: for example, deciding when to probe for more detail in an interview context, when to change focus during observations, and if and when to alter your original research design or conceptualization or research questions. All of these are analytical choices (Yin, 2011). Thus, you should continually think about, assess and revise your approach to data collection to ensure that your research project demonstrates integrity and quality (Hays & Singh, 2012). Doing research produces knowledge through the intentional choices that we make as researchers, from selecting the topic, to the approach, to the decisions about ways to obtain, produce and generate data. How effective, useful, insightful and beneficial this knowledge will be depends on the coherence and consistency of the research project as a whole, including the approach taken to data collection.

Further reading

Hays, D.G. & Singh, A.A. (2012). *Qualitative Inquiry in Clinical and Educational Settings*. New York: Guildford Press.
Polkinghorne, D.E. (2005). Language and meaning: Data collection in qualitative research. *Journal of Counseling Psychology*, 52(2), 137–145.

References

Bowker, N. & Tuffin, K. (2004). Using the online medium for discursive research about people with disabilities. *Social Science Computer Review*, 22(2), 228–241.
Chamberlain, K. (2000). Methodolatry and qualitative health research. *Journal of Health Psychology*, 5(3), 285–296.
Del Busso, L. (2011). Using photographs to explore the embodiment of pleasure in everyday life. In P. Reavey (ed.), *Visual Methods in Psychology: Using and Interpreting Images in Qualitative Research* (pp. 43–54). Hove: Psychology Press.
Evans, A., Elford, J. & Wiggins, D. (2008). Using the Internet for qualitative research. In C. Willig & W. Stainton Rogers (eds), *The Sage Handbook of Qualitative Research in Psychology* (pp. 315–333). London: Sage.
Frith, H. & Gleeson, K. (2012). Qualitative data collection: Asking the right questions. In D. Harper & A.R. Thompson (eds), *Qualitative Research Methods in Mental Health and Psychotherapy: A Guide for Students and Practitioners* (pp. 55–68). Chichester: John Wiley & Sons.
Gough, B. (2007). 'Real men don't diet': An analysis of contemporary newspaper representations of men, food and health. *Social Science and Medicine*, 64(2), 326–337.
Greig, A., Taylor, J. & MacKay, T. (2013). *Doing Research with Children: A Practical Guide* (3rd edn). Los Angeles, CA: Sage.
Guillemin, M. (2004). Understanding illness: Using drawings as a research method. *Qualitative Health Research*, 14(2), 272–289.
Harris, A. & Guillemin, M. (2012). Developing sensory awareness in qualitative interviewing: A portal into the otherwise unexplored. *Qualitative Health Research*, 22(5), 689–699.
Hays, D.G. & Singh, A.A. (2012). *Qualitative Inquiry in Clinical and Educational Settings*. New York: Guildford Press.
Hermanowicz, J.C. (2002). The great interview: 25 strategies for studying people in bed. *Qualitative Sociology*, 25(4), 479–499.

Hookway, N. (2008). 'Entering the blogosphere': Some strategies for using blogs in social research. *Qualitative Research*, 8(1), 91–113.

Howitt, D. (2013). *Introduction to Qualitative Methods in Psychology* (2nd edn). Harlow: Pearson.

Hugh-Jones, S. & Gibson, S. (2012). Collecting your data. In C. Sullivan, S. Gibson & S. Riley (eds), *Doing Your Qualitative Psychology Project* (pp. 101–126). London: Sage.

Jenks, C. (1995). The centrality of the eye in Western culture: An introduction. In C. Jenks (ed.), *Visual Culture* (pp. 1–25). London: Routledge.

Kaun, A. (2010). Open-ended online diaries: Capturing life as it is narrated. *Journal of Qualitative Methods*, 9(2), 36–48.

Kazmer, M.M. & Xie, B. (2008). Qualitative interviewing in internet studies: Playing with the media, playing with the method. *Information Communication and Society*, 11(2), 257–278.

Kvale, S. (1996). *Interviews*. Thousand Oaks, CA: Sage.

Kvale, S. & Brinkmann, S. (2009). *InterViews: Learning the Craft of Qualitative Research Interviewing* (2nd edn). Thousand Oaks, CA: Sage.

Marshall, C. & Rossman, G.B. (2011). *Designing Qualitative Research* (5th edn). Los Angeles, CA: Sage.

McIntosh, C. & Stephens, C. (2012). A storybook method for exploring young children's views of illness causality in relation to the familial context. *Early Child Development and Care*, 182(1), 23–33.

Niland, P. & Lyons, A.C. (2011). Uncertainty in medicine: Meanings of menopause and hormone replacement therapy in medical textbooks. *Social Science and Medicine*, 73, 1238–1245.

Niland, P., Lyons, A.C., Goodwin, I. & Hutton, F. (2014). 'See it doesn't look pretty does it?' Young adults' airbrushed drinking practices on Facebook. *Psychology and Health*. Advance online. doi: 10.1080/08870446.2014.893345.

Onwuegbuzie, A.J., Leech, N.L. & Collins, K.M.T. (2010). Innovative data collection strategies in qualitative research. *Qualitative Report*, 15(3), 696–726.

Petty, N.J., Thomson, O.P. & Stew, G. (2012). Ready for a paradigm shift? Part 2: Introducing qualitative research methodologies and methods. *Manual Therapy*, 17(5), 378–384.

Pink, S. (2007). *Doing Visual Ethnography* (2nd edn). London: Sage.

Pink, S. (2008). Mobilising visual ethnography: Making routes, making place and making images. *Forum: Qualitative Social Research*, 9, article 36.

Pink, S. (2009). *Doing Sensory Ethnography*. London: Sage.

Polkinghorne, D.E. (2005). Language and meaning: Data collection in qualitative research. *Journal of Counseling Psychology*, 52(2), 137–145.

Potter, J. & Hepburn, A. (2005). Qualitative interviews in psychology: Problems and possibilities. *Qualitative Research in Psychology*, 2, 1–27.

Radley, A. & Taylor, D. (2003). Remembering one's stay in hospital: A study in photography, recovery and forgetting. *Health*, 7(2), 129–159.

Reavey, P. (2011). The return to experience: Psychology and the visual. In P. Reavey (ed.), *Visual Methods in Psychology: Using and Interpreting Images in Qualitative Research* (pp. 1–13). Hove: Psychology Press.

Reavey, P. & Johnson, K. (2008). Visual approaches: Using and interpreting images. In W. Stainton Rogers & C. Willig (eds), *The Sage Handbook of Qualitative Research in Psychology* (pp. 296–314). London: Sage.

Robinson, K.M. (2001). Unsolicited narratives from the internet: A rich source of qualitative data. *Qualitative Health Research*, *11*(5), 706–714.

Rose, G. (2005). Visual methodologies. In G. Griffin (ed.), *Research Methods for English Studies* (pp. 67–90). Edinburgh: Edinburgh University Press.

Saldana, J. (2011). *Fundamentals of Qualitative Research*. Oxford: Oxford University Press.

Seidman, I. (2006). *Interviewing as Qualitative Research: A Guide for Researchers in Education and the Social Sciences* (3rd edn). New York: Teachers College Press.

Sheridan, J. & Chamberlain, K. (2011). The power of things. *Qualitative Research in Psychology*, *8*(4), 315–332.

Smith, C. (2014). By the numbers: 75 amazing Facebook user statistics (updated January 2014). http://expandedramblings.com/index.php/by-the-numbers-17-amazing-facebook-stats/#.Uu4Dl3nlfwI, accessed 1 May 2014.

Suzuki, L.A., Ahluwalia, M.K., Arora, A.K. & Mattis, J.S. (2007). The pond you fish in determines the fish you catch: Exploring strategies for qualitative data collection. *Counseling Psychologist*, *35*(2), 295–327.

van Doorn, N. (2013). Assembling the affective field: How smartphone technology impacts ethnographic research practice. *Qualitative Inquiry*, *19*(5), 385–396.

Walsh, C.A., Rutherford, G. & Kuzmak, N. (2010). Engaging women who are homeless in community-based research using emerging qualitative data collection techniques. *International Journal of Multiple Research Approaches*, *4*(3).

Wang, C. & Burris, M.A. (1997). Photovoice: Concept, methodology, and use for participatory needs assessment. *Health Education and Behavior*, *24*(3), 369–387.

Wang, C.C., Cash, J.L. & Powers, L.S. (2000). Who knows the streets as well as the homeless? Promoting personal and community action through photovoice. *Health Promotion Practice*, *1*, 81–89.

Yin, R.K. (2011). *Qualitative Research from Start to Finish*. New York: Guildford Press.

PART II

Qualitative Methods: Exploring Individual Worlds

Thematic Analysis

*Virginia Braun, Victoria Clarke and
Gareth Terry*

7

Thematic analysis (TA) is a method for identifying, analysing and interpreting patterned meanings or 'themes' in qualitative data. In this chapter we outline our approach to TA (Braun & Clarke, 2006, 2012, 2013) and demonstrate its core processes of coding and theme development using worked examples from our study of sexual health professionals' views on impediments to sexual health in Aotearoa/New Zealand (A/NZ; Terry et al., 2012). First we consider the historical development of TA and the proliferation of different approaches to it, then we outline the hallmarks of *our* approach to TA: its unique status as a method, rather than a method*ology*, and its theoretical flexibility.

Historical background

Attempts to formalize and systematize analytical procedures for qualitative research started to appear in the late 1960s and early 1970s. Around this time 'thematic analysis' emerged, although the term described very different things. It was used interchangeably with 'content analysis' (Christ, 1970); it described particular forms of both quantitative (Woodrum, 1984) and interpretative (Baxter, 1991) content analysis; it referred to a quantitative scoring system for measuring cognitive complexity (Winter & McClelland, 1978); and it named a method for analysing the evolution of scientific ideas (Holton, 1973). Some early forms of TA (e.g. Benner, 1985; Dapkus, 1985) are recognizable as *something* akin to TA in the contemporary context. For example, Dapkus's (1985:409) research on human experiences of time involved the systematic analysis of interview data to identify 'common themes, which were then compiled into a category system designed to begin the task of describing' this experience.

It was not until the 1990s that *procedures* for TA as a qualitative method began to be discussed. US psychotherapist Jodi Aronson (1994), for example, briefly outlined procedures for the TA of transcripts of ethnographic interviews and therapy sessions. Her six-step version focused on 'identifiable themes and patterns of living and/or behavior' (1994:para 3). In its early development, TA was often discussed as a phenomenological method (e.g.

Benner, 1985). This common linking of TA with phenomenology continues – health researcher Helen Joffe (2011), for example, argues that TA fits well with the assumptions of social phenomenology (see also Guest et al., 2012), but TA is not only a phenomenological method.

Nowadays, two broad approaches to TA predominate, a 'small q' and a 'Big Q' (Kidder & Fine, 1987) version:

■ Many versions of TA can be categorized as 'small q' because they retain a foothold in quantitative (post)positivist research (e.g. Boyatzis, 1998; Guest et al., 2012; Joffe, 2011). These various approaches typically involve the use of a structured 'codebook', where researchers, after familiarizing themselves with their data, develop a coding framework, which is then applied to the entire dataset. They retain a concern for positivist conceptions of 'reliability' and advocate the use of multiple independent coders and the calculation of inter-rater reliability scores to determine the 'accuracy' of coding.

■ The 'Big Q' approach that we favour operates within a qualitative paradigm (Kidder & Fine, 1987). It is characterized by theoretical flexibility and organic processes of coding and theme development (Braun & Clarke, 2006, 2012, 2013).

This small q/Big Q distinction is significant, as it is underpinned by very different conceptualizations of knowledge, research and the researcher. In small q TA, the researcher is like an archaeologist digging through soil to discover buried treasures. Analysis is a process of *discovering* themes that already exist within a dataset. In Big Q TA, the researcher is like a sculptor, chipping away at a block of marble. The sculpture is the product of an interaction between the sculptor, their skills and the raw materials. Similarly, analysis is a creative process, the analysis a result of engagement between the dataset and the researcher's interpretative and analytical skills.

Theoretical and conceptual framework

The hallmark of our approach to TA (which we will simply call TA) is its flexibility, which stems from the fact that TA is only a method, not a methodology. Most other approaches to qualitative analysis *are* methodologies – they provide a theoretically informed framework for collecting *and* analysing qualitative data. TA, by contrast, only specifies analytical procedures, centred on coding and theme development. This means that it can be used to address most types of qualitative research question, ranging from questions about individual lived experience through to those about the social construction of meaning (see Table 7.1 on pg. 98); analyse most types of qualitative data (from qualitative interviews to secondary sources); analyse data generated by both homogeneous and heterogeneous samples (although some degree of homogeneity in sampling aids pattern identification in small projects); and analyse both smaller and larger datasets.

One criticism sometimes levelled at TA is that it is an 'unsophisticated' method that simply aims to *describe* or *summarize* patterns in data. TA is also often assumed to be an atheoretical or essentialist method. These critiques reflect a fundamental misunderstanding of TA and equate theoretical flexibility with an absence of theory – and, therefore, an absence of analytical sophistication. This is not the case. When using TA, the researcher should begin by answering some important questions:

- What broad *ontological* and *epistemological* frameworks will underpin my use of TA (for example, realism, critical realism, relativism, [post]positivism, contextualism, constructionism; see Chapter 2)?
- What specific *theories* will guide my use of TA (for example, phenomenology, poststructuralism and so on)?
- Will I use TA *inductively* or *deductively*? In other words, will my coding and analysis start 'bottom up' from the data (inductive TA) or 'top down' from prior theory (deductive TA)? Pure induction is never possible, because our standpoints and ontological, epistemological and theoretical frameworks always shape how we read and interpret data, but we can aim to ground our analytical observations in the data rather than in prior theory. Deductive TA can range from coding data for evidence of particular theories or concepts to using existing theories and concepts to deepen our interpretation of data.
- Will I code *semantic* (overt) meaning or *latent* (covert) meaning?

In practice, relativist/critical realist, constructionist, deductive and latent approaches tend to cluster together, as do realist, essentialist, inductive and semantic approaches – although analysis often combines elements of inductive/deductive and semantic/latent coding. What is crucial is a good fit between your research question, theoretical assumptions and approach to TA. For some research projects, such as evaluating an intervention or service, the form of TA that best fits your aims will probably be a descriptive overview of the semantic content of the data. Other research questions may require a more interrogative approach, such as that taken in our analysis of sexual health in A/NZ (introduced in Box 7.1). The important point is that TA is not merely one thing. There are many different ways in which TA can be applied, and TA can be just as 'sophisticated' (or not) as methods with inbuilt theoretical assumptions.

The need to determine your particular version of TA – by answering the questions just outlined – draws attention to the *active* role of the researcher in performing analysis. Making choices deliberatively can help you appreciate the way in which theoretical and methodological assumptions inform qualitative analysis. Good TA requires reflexivity (Finlay & Gough, 2003), a turning back on ourselves and questioning the assumptions we make in coding and analysing data in particular ways.

Uses for clinical and health psychology

TA has been associated with clinical and health research from the start and offers an excellent tool for such research. TA's inherent flexibility means that it can be used across the spectrum of clinical and health research, from more mainstream approaches (concerned with individual views and experiences) to more critical approaches (concerned with the social construction of meaning). Constructionist/critical versions of TA fit well with the assumptions and values of critical (health/clinical) psychology; essentialist and contextualist versions of TA are compatible with more experiential qualitative research (Clarke & Braun, 2014).

A wide range of different 'types' of research question can be answered using TA. Table 7.1 provides a typology of research questions for clinical and health

Table 7.1   A typology of research questions suitable for TA studies

Type of research question	*Examples of studies*
Experiences – research questions focused on individual lived experiences of particular health/ clinical conditions, interventions and so on.	Experiences of practising mindfulness in the context of living with bipolar disorder (Chadwick et al., 2011). Women's lived experiences of chemotherapy-induced hair loss (Frith et al., 2007).
Understandings and perceptions – research questions focused on how particular groups (of patients, professionals) view a particular health/clinical condition, intervention and so on.	Patients', parents' and clinicians' views on difficulties relating to emotions and emotional processing in anorexia (Kyriacou et al., 2009). Service users' perspectives on the use of weekly vs intensive-format cognitive behavioural therapy for the treatment of obsessive-compulsive disorder (Bevan et al., 2010).
Influencing factors – research questions that explore the individual and social factors that underpin particular health/clinical phenomena.	Exploring how fears related to HIV/AIDS affect women's use and health workers' provision of maternity services in Kenya (Turana et al., 2008). Exploring structural impediments to sexual health in New Zealand (Terry et al., 2012).
Practices/accounts of practices – research questions that explore the things people do in the world and/or how people make sense of the things they do in the world.	Negotiations of sleeping practices in same-sex couples (Kirkman, 2010). Exploring clinical psychologists' use of psychological case formulation in multidisciplinary teamwork (Christofides et al., 2012).
Construction – research questions focused on the role of language (or 'discourse') in constituting particular versions of 'reality'.	National identity explanations of New Zealand's poor sexual health statistics (Braun, 2008). Constructions of gay men's health in health literature (Aguinaldo, 2008).

research (based on Braun & Clarke, 2013), with examples of published TA studies. The divisions in this typology are somewhat idealized – in practice, the different types blur together and studies can address more than one type of question. For example, in experiential qualitative health or clinical research, the research question commonly addresses a combination of lived experiences and perceptions of a particular phenomenon.

A step by step guide to doing TA

In TA, as in most qualitative approaches, you learn best by doing, but you need to know what you *should* be doing when using our six-phase process for systematically identifying patterning across the dataset (Braun & Clarke, 2006, 2012, 2013). We provide illustrative examples from our project on sexual health in A/NZ (introduced in Box 7.1) to show you key features of TA at different stages of analysis.

It is useful to note two things. First, although we map out the analytical process phase by phase, in reality TA is a fluid and recursive, rather than strictly linear, process, meaning that you will probably need to move back and forth between phases. As you get more experienced, or when working with smaller datasets, you may even blur some phases together. Second, we describe the process as if you were coding the data manually, rather than using one of the various computer programs now available for assisting in qualitative data analysis (collectively referred to as CAQDAS; see Silver & Fielding, 2008). If you use a CAQDAS program, the basic process remains the same, but the mechanics change.

BOX 7.1   Key informants' views on sexual health in A/NZ

In A/NZ, there is no coordinated, national sexual health-prevention strategy or practice and sexual health statistics present a fairly depressing picture: rates of common sexually transmitted infections (STIs) like chlamydia are high by worldwide standards, and often rising. Given this, we wanted to understand sociocultural factors that work to undermine sexual wellbeing. As part of the larger project (see also Braun, 2008, 2013), we interviewed 32 key informants (KIs) – people with professional expertise in the area of sexual health and sexual health promotion – to identify what they saw as impediments to sexual health in A/NZ. As we were interested in developing a policy-relevant analysis, we started the analysis using a primarily semantic-level, descriptive form of TA, within a (critical) realist framework (Braun & Clarke, 2006). This analysis, grounded in the KIs' words, identified several structural-level impediments to sexual health. Moving then to a more interpretative and latent form of TA allowed us to explore some of the conceptual ideas underpinning the KIs' accounts. Combining these levels of insight, we were able to make some clear recommendations for improving sexual health promotion in A/NZ (see Terry et al., 2012).

Phase I: Familiarization with the data

The first phase of TA is one common to most qualitative analysis: a process of immersion through reading, and then re-reading, the entire dataset. The point of this phase is twofold: to really get to *know* what is in the data, the actual semantic meanings expressed, through an immersion in the content; and to start your *analytical* engagement with the data, by reading the data *as data* and starting to note potential points of analytical interest. The first of these is easy: you read and simply absorb the content of the data. The second involves a switch from consumption to engagement and it can be tricky to see data in this way, especially for topics where the data contain many common-sense ideas. Essentially, as an analyst, you are seeking a dual position of immersion and distance. Distance from the data is what gives you your 'analytical eye' and allows you to interrogate the data for things like the logic frameworks, assumptions or rationales that underpin its content and to identify the 'bigger-picture' commonalities that might unite seemingly disparate data content. The extent to which your analytical focus is semantic or latent will determine how you engage in this, but essentially, treating data as data means not taking the data for granted and asking questions about what ideas and assumptions they contain and what that might mean.

In our initial readings of the KI interviews, we picked up a consistent sense of frustration in the data, which was both expressly articulated and under-pinned the views expressed. There was variation in what KIs identified as frus-trating sexual health efforts (for example, government not prioritizing sexual health, a lack of funding for adequate sexual health promotion in schools or parental conservatism hindering open discussion of sexuality in the home), but familiarization, with immersion and distancing, allowed us to see frustration as a 'bigger issue' – a focus that we developed into the final analysis.

What 'familiarization' involves at a *practical* level is reading the data and making notes when something of interest occurs to you. These notes can be understood as casual observations about the data, rather than as systematic codes, so think of them as personal aids to memory, reminders of potential analytical insights or things you might come back to during coding and later analysis. If you are struggling to 'treat data as data', do not stress about it too much; the next phase – coding – will help. This phase is not one to spend too much time on: once you feel that you are deeply familiar with the dataset's content, and you are starting to treat the data analytically, move on to coding.

Phase 2: Coding the data

Coding is a systematic and thorough process whereby codes are derived from the entire dataset. A code is effectively a succinct label (a word or a short phrase) that captures a key analytical idea in the data and conveys this to the researcher. A good code should convey the key idea in the data without the researcher needing to see the data themselves. In our study, the code 'school sexuality education as inadequate' is a good code, because it tells us about both the focus of that data segment (sexuality education) and the participant's position on it (critical). In contrast, the phrase 'sexuality education (sex ed)' would be a bad code, as it only conveys the focus, and we would need to go back to the actual data to see *what* the participant had to say about the sexuality education.

Codes can range from the *descriptive*, where they summarize the semantic content of the data excerpt, to more *interpretative*, where they indicate an analytical, interpretative insight on the part of the researcher. In our example (see Table 7.2), the code 'sex ed focuses on dangers of sex' is descriptive, because it summarizes the content of what the KI is saying. The code 'communication as important for sexual health' is interpretative, because it describes an assumption underpinning what the KI says about sexuality education.

Practically, coding typically involves writing the code on the transcript, next to the relevant text (see Table 7.2), but there are other ways to do this, such as electronically or using CAQDAS. In TA, you code the entire dataset, but you do not need to code *all* the data, just the parts potentially relevant to answering your research question. This is crucial, otherwise you could be coding for ever. However, do remember that in TA your research question can evolve, and coding itself often informs the refining and shaping of the research question(s). So interpret your research question broadly and code inclusively. You want your codes to capture both the diversity of perspectives evident in the dataset and the patterning of meaning (Braun & Clarke, 2012). The other important

Table 7.2 An excerpt of coded data from one KI interview

Extract	Codes
KI6: y'know we focus so much on STIs and the and the unwanted pregnancies and what's bad and dangerous and wrong about young people having sex too early and all those sorts of things but I actually think promoting sexual health is about actually um creating an environment where young people are safe to explore and discuss and talk about and ask about all of those sorts of things in as broad a sense as they need to really (VB: mhm) yeah and having people around them that they're able to do that with so great relationships with family members and other people in their community and their peers and everybody else broad huge definition	Negative rather than positive focus on sexual health (SH)/sex education (sex ed) Sex ed focuses on dangers of sex School sex ed as inadequate Focus on STIs and pregnancy – symptoms rather than source Protectionism and young people Ideals of 'SH community' versus parents/schools and so on Environment Communication as important for SH Sex(uality) as broad 'Holistic' approach to SH Communication and relationships more important than 'information' Support structures Family as important to overall impact of SH messages SH as broad

thing to remember is that even once you have completed data familiarization, coding takes you to a different, deeper level of engagement with the data and your analytical insight develops. You will start to see things in the later data items that you might not have seen – or coded for – in earlier ones, and so your coding is likely to evolve to reflect this. This means that ideally you need to do at least two rounds of coding, or at a minimum go back and recode earlier data items, to ensure thoroughness and consistency.

Once you are satisfied that the coding has been thorough and consistent, and that it addresses your research question, you do two forms of compilation: of the codes generated, so that you end up with a long list of all the codes in the dataset; and of the associated extracts of data, so that you end up with a file of data that relates to each code. Both are important for the next phase of analysis, which is generating themes.

Phase 3: Searching for themes

This phase shifts your analytical focus from codes to themes. A theme generally identifies a broader level of meaning than a code. This means that many different codes are typically clustered together to create each potential theme, although a really rich and complex code may also be 'promoted' to a theme. At the start of theme identification it is best to think of your themes as *candidate* themes, as the analysis is all very provisional. Analysis is an organic process and your themes *will* evolve. So do not get too attached to the analytical ideas at the start, as you may need to discard some of them.

In practice, the first part of this process involves initially identifying clusters of similar meaning across your codes. First, look at the list of codes compiled at the end of the previous phase and see if you can identify any potential patterns of meaning by clustering similar codes together. Throughout this and subsequent analytical phases, keep three questions in mind (Clarke et al., 2014):

- Is this candidate theme centrally relevant to answering my research question? With many potential themes in data, the ones you identify should individually, and collectively, offer the fullest account of the data that answers your question.
- Is this candidate theme evident across more than one or two of my data items? TA is concerned with *patterned* meaning, so it is important that themes are evident *across* different data items. However, frequency is not the sole criterion for determining themes – themes may sometimes be *important* to your research question, even if only evident across a few data items (Braun & Clarke, 2006; Buetow, 2010).
- Can I easily identify a central organizing concept for each candidate theme? A central organizing concept is a clear core idea or concept that underpins a theme: the essence of what the theme is all about (Braun & Clarke, 2013). Identifying these for each theme ensures that themes are internally coherent and distinct from each other.

Good themes do not overlap; however, they should *relate* to each other to produce a coherent analysis. You can conceptualize your themes as the pieces of a puzzle that combine to create a clear image of your data (Braun & Clarke, 2012). This means that even at the early stages of theme development, it is important to think about the relationship between themes and the overall story that your analysis will tell.

After coding our sexual health data, a research question along the lines of 'What societal, systemic or structural factors affect sexual health in A/NZ?' seemed to capture clusters of patterned meaning across the codes. Codes clustered into a number of relevant candidate themes, including 'sexual conservatism' in A/NZ; inadequacy of A/NZ's school-based sexuality education; and the family as integral to sexuality learning. Table 7.3 provides an example of these candidate themes with a selection of associated codes.

Before moving on to the next 'review' phase, you want to have mapped out the candidate themes – perhaps using a visual mapping tool like a thematic map (see Figure 7.1 on pg. 105) or a table (see Frith & Gleeson, 2004) – and collated all the coded data extracts relevant to each candidate theme.

Table 7.3 Three candidate themes and selected associated codes

'Sexual conservatism' in the A/NZ context	A/NZ's school-based sexuality education as inadequate	The family as integral to sexuality learning
Fear of teenage sexuality Not being able to talk openly about sex with young people 'We' don't talk openly about sex – generally Focus on STIs and pregnancy – symptoms rather than source Limited public discussion about sexuality-related issues Limited financial investment in SH campaigns Parents not giving children in-depth sex ed Lack of government commitment to comprehensive SH promotion Government not funding 'comprehensive' sex ed	Focus on STIs/pregnancy Needs holistic approach Focus on STIs and pregnancy – symptoms rather than source 'Best practice' models being ignored in policy and practice Limited school hours devoted to sex ed Teachers lack training to make up 'home deficit' in sex ed Schools 'outsourcing' sex ed No consistent curriculum – government not funding 'comprehensive' sex ed	Importance of communication Family/peers etc. key to successful SH Majority of young people don't need front-line help Parents struggle to talk to children about sex Parents not giving children in-depth sex ed Healthy family relationships can often make up for poor school sex ed Family as important to overall impact of SH messages

Phase 4: Reviewing themes

This phase of TA is about two things: quality control by checking that the candidate themes are a good fit with the coded data; shaping up the themes so that they describe the full story of the relevant data. It involves first checking back to the coded data and developing the story of each theme through that. Second, it involves checking back to the entire dataset, to ensure that the candidate themes reflect meaning across that whole dataset. Reviewing ensures that coding has not missed crucial data, that developments in analytical thinking still reflect the dataset well and that the analysis is thorough and a meaningful account of the data. Through this review process your developing TA may be tweaked, it may be entirely discarded, or something in between. Candidate themes may be split into more than one theme; they may be combined to form a new theme; or they may be rejected as themes. And remember, as TA is not only about reporting patterns but patterns that are meaningful for *answering your research question*, that research question needs to remain at the forefront of your mind during the process.

Questions that may help in the revision and development of candidate themes include (Braun & Clarke, 2012):

- Is this a theme? (It could be just a code.) And if it is:
- What is the nature of this theme? (Does it tell me something useful about the dataset and my research question?)
- What are the boundaries of this theme? (What does it include and exclude?)
- Are there enough (meaningful) data to support this theme? (Is the theme 'thin' or 'thick'?)
- Are the data too diverse and wide-ranging? (Does the theme lack coherence?)

Keeping in mind the idea of a central organizing concept, introduced earlier in this chapter, can facilitate theme development and revision. If you can identify the central organizing concept for each theme, it is relatively easy to determine whether some aspect of the data is part of a theme or not. However, remember also to keep an open mind and not to set a rigid structure for your themes too early. This phase of TA, and TA overall, often involves a recursive process of review and revision in the shaping of the themes. In our sexual health data, we made a number of changes when reviewing our candidate themes and the developing analysis is illustrated in the thematic map in Figure 7.1. A thematic map provides a really useful tool in developing TA. It is particularly helpful in determining the *relationships* between themes and for shaping an overall structure and organization for the analysis. In our review, for instance, we identified that much of the data related to 'the family as integral to sexuality learning' (see Table 7.3) actually evoked a conservative family environment and so fit with the central organizing concept of the 'sexual

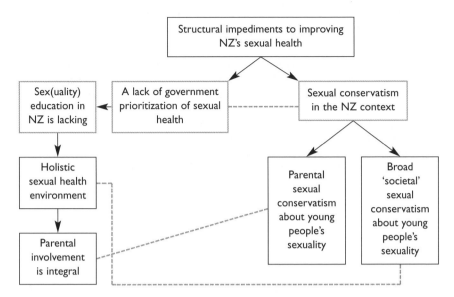

Figure 7.1 A first thematic map of our candidate themes

conservatism' candidate theme. We then developed 'the family as integral' as a *sub-theme* of sexual conservatism. Whether or not a theme contains one or more sub-themes is a key question to consider in the review phase. A sub-theme sits within a theme, sharing a central organizing concept but highlighting a particular aspect of the data and the theme (Braun & Clarke, 2013). If you have an element of a theme that is particularly salient and offers information that you want to highlight in answering your research question, identifying it as a sub-theme can be useful.

Our advice, however, is to use sub-themes judiciously – with many sub-themes the analysis risks becoming disjointed and underdeveloped. This raises a broader question of how many themes are appropriate in TA. The answer depends on the focus of the analysis and the length of the report, but we offer two to six as a good range to work within (Braun & Clarke, 2013), keeping in mind the balance between data and analysis (discussed later in this chapter). The more themes you have, the fewer sub-themes you will have the space to develop.

Phase 5: Defining and naming themes

This phase involves developing the overall analysis through a detailed analysis of the data in each theme, which refines each theme's focus and scope and determines the 'story' of the data. A helpful exercise, which tests your conceptual and analytical clarity, is to write a definition for each theme. A 'theme definition' can be conceptualized as an extended central organizing concept, extended because it highlights the analytical interpretation of the data as well

---

BOX 7.2   An example theme definition

The theme 'sexual conservatism in the A/NZ context' captures the ways in which KIs portrayed New Zealanders, and A/NZ society as a whole, as inherently sexually conservative. They felt that this sexual conservatism was a particular feature of A/NZ, and of being a NZer, and that it manifested itself as a discomfort around sex and sexuality and an unwillingness to discuss sex and sexual matters openly. They argued that this occurred at both the interpersonal and societal levels and made difficult any societal discussion about STI rates and other sexuality-related issues, such as (school-based) sexuality education. It was also seen to underpin a lack of government initiative around sexual health.

---

as describing the key concept encapsulated in the theme. Box 7.2 provides an example of a theme definition from our sexual health study.

In this phase, you need to finalize the data extracts that you will present or analyse in the final report (Phase 6 discusses how data can be used in TA). You want extracts that provide vivid, compelling examples that clearly capture and demonstrate the analytical points you will make. As TA reports patterned meaning from across a dataset, it is good practice to draw on extracts from *across* the dataset. Simply quoting the same data item over and over again – even if it demonstrates the ideas very clearly – can undermine the apparent validity of your analysis by suggesting that your themes are idiosyncratic to that data item, rather than being derived from across the dataset (see later in this chapter).

This is the point at which you also finalize the *story* of the analysis – the analytical narrative that surrounds the data excerpts and tells the reader what you think is going on in the data, why this is important for your research question and why the reader should care about it (this phase blurs with Phase 6, as writing is an integral part of doing TA). Remember, data do *not* 'speak for themselves' – analysis involves the interpretation of data, and the development of a narrative that provides the reader with an account of what is contained in the data and what that means for the focus of the study. In an analysis, you would typically want to have *at least* as much narrative surrounding your data extracts as data.

Finally, you need to identify the *name* you will give each theme (and sub-theme) – while this might sound like a trivial concern, the names are important. A good name will signal the focus of the theme *and* its analytical scope or content. Theme names should be informative to a reader without them reading the analysis. In our sexual health study, the theme name 'sexual conservatism in the New Zealand context' (see Table 7.3) both identifies the topical focus of the theme – that participants felt that New Zealand's high STI rates reflected a sexually conservative context – and our interpretative take on it – that sexual health in A/NZ appears to be understood within a framework of a particular 'New Zealand character' or 'national identity', with implications for sexual health promotion (see Braun, 2008; Terry et al., 2012).

Phase 6: Producing the report

The name of the last phase is slightly misleading, as it suggests that all the writing happens at this point. TA, like most qualitative research, is *saturated* with writing. You simply cannot *do* TA without writing down the analytical ideas into some draft analytical narrative. The reason we name this as a separate phase is to emphasize the importance of the final refinement of the analytical narrative, and the weaving together of data extracts, analytical narrative and (in most cases) discussion of the existing scholarly literature. This last point is important and so 'writing up' involves the production of two things: a polished *analysis*, which is your telling of what is in the data, and why that is interesting and/or significant, *and* which 'answers' your research question; and a polished *report*, which explains, locates and contextualizes *your* analysis in relation to existing theory and research.

There are two basic ways in which you can use data excerpts in 'writing up' your TA – illustratively or analytically – which may sometimes be combined. If you treat the data illustratively, the excerpts are used as illustrative examples within an otherwise seamless analytical narrative; you could remove the extracts and the analysis would still make sense. If you treat the data analytically, your analytical narrative actually comments on particular features or aspects in each excerpt; you could not remove the extracts from the analytical narrative, as they are enmeshed (see Braun & Clarke, 2013). We illustrate this in Box 7.3 by quoting an extract from our published analysis of the sexual health data (Terry et al., 2012), which starts with an illustrative treatment of the data, then moves (in the final paragraph) to an analytical treatment, where we critically interrogate some of the latent assumptions and ideas contained in the specific excerpt.

TA as an organic and reflexive process

It should be evident that the process of TA is far from a rigid or mechanical application of a set of processes or formulae to data in order to extract answers. Instead, like Big Q qualitative research in general, it is an organic and fluid, yet systematic, process and it requires an engaged, intuitive and reflexive researcher (Finlay & Gough, 2003) who considers the ways in which they are *part of* the analysis. This makes TA a personal, and sometimes even emotional, experience. Reflecting as you go along on the analytical process, and your insights, influences and assumptions, can be a useful exercise. In Box 7.4, Gareth briefly reflects on his experiences of doing TA with the sexual health data.

BOX 7.3 An example of data treated illustratively and then analytically

Despite noting that New Zealand does not have the same political climate as the USA, with its powerful religious conservative base (Scheepers et al., 2002), key informants suggested 'New Zealanders' struggled with talk about sex and sexual problems (see also Braun, 2008). This was not simply about sexual communication between sexual partners; it was also identified with regard to a 'societal debate' about sexual health:

> I think in lots of ways in New Zealand we like to think that we're quite liberal and there's lots of healthy discussion about most things, but when it comes to stuff around sexuality, sexual health we're actually really quite conservative in a lot of ways, particularly around talking openly about specific stuff. (KI1, Sexual Health Educator)

This unwillingness to enter into a broad discussion about New Zealand's STI problems was identified as particularly evident in relation to young people's sexuality:

> Our society, it's kind of 'discomforted' with the whole thing of pleasure and positive aspects of sexuality, particularly with teenagers and younger [...] I don't think we are entirely comfortable with teenagers having sex. (KI3, Sexuality Educator)

The portrayal of a particular 'New Zealand identity' (Braun, 2008) was important to understanding this conservatism. References to 'our society' and 'in New Zealand' gave some coherence to the KIs' account of 'how' and 'why' sexual health is the way it is, in New Zealand, providing a useful rhetorical base from which they could explain the resistances to change that they identified. Williams and Davidson (2004) portrayed a similar reluctance to discuss adolescent sexual health issue[s] within the Australian context, also constructing this as a nation-wide issue.

Source: Terry et al. (2012:323), reproduced here with kind permission from Springer Science+Business Media B.V.

Doing TA well

Many clinical and health researchers are doing TA – and some are doing it badly. Table 7.4 provides a quick checklist to ensure that both the *process* of TA, and the *analysis* you produce, are thorough, plausible and of high quality. We advise using this to guide and evaluate your TA process *and* outcome. Given the various problems that we see with TA (e.g. in supervising students, in reviewing manuscripts), we also emphasize the following:

■   When presenting an analysis, try to ensure a balance of at least 50:50 data:analytical narrative (point 10), or even 40:60, so that you tell *your story of the data* and do not merely present a collection of data extracts.

> ### BOX 7.4   Reflections on doing TA (by Gareth Terry)
>
> The dataset for the sexual health project had already gone through a round of coding when I came on board, but the research question was still open. In order to develop my own take on the data, I took the time to read through clean (non-coded) transcripts in detail, taking notes as I went. Because we intended undertaking a primarily semantic and descriptive TA, by the end of this stage I had a strong sense of the key aspects of the KIs' arguments. I was already starting to 'filter out' the information irrelevant to a research question related to 'impediments to sexual health'. With the insights gained through familiarization, coding was a straightforward and enjoyable process. I was able easily to identify key patterns in the KIs' arguments as related to structural and societal issues, and refine the focus of the research question around these aspects. This meant I could quickly determine whether data were pertinent to the research question, and thus needed to be coded. Following coding, I went back to the codes previously generated; the similarities and differences provided another layer to the developing analysis, and offered both a reinforcement of, and challenge to, the coding I had developed, which ensured a richer, deeper account of the data. I needed a reflexive stance throughout the interpretative process, as the KIs' arguments resonated strongly with my own position on sexual health promotion. This raised two challenges for the analysis: to ensure that it remained grounded firmly in the KIs' perspectives, without appearing just to reflect my interpretation; to ensure that the views that resonated so closely with mine were interrogated and unpacked just as much as those that clashed with mine.

- Make sure that you actually tell the reader what sense *you* make of the data and how the data *answer* your research question (point 9). This means that you need to present an *analysis* of the data – a narrative that goes *beyond* what has been said in the data. Instead of paraphrasing the data, make sure that you tell the reader what is interesting about them and why they are relevant for answering your research question (point 7).
- Make sure that you are *explicit* about what approach(es) you have taken (point 12) and, crucially, that the language and claims you make about the data are consistent with the approach(es) to TA that you say you have taken (points 13 and 14).
- Own your active role in developing the analysis and do not treat themes as something that merely *emerged* from the data (point 15). To claim that themes 'emerged' suggests that you opened your data box and they simply climbed out. Rather, you work to identify salient patterns through the knowledge and perspectives that you bring to the data; you select and develop the themes, they do not exist prior to your analytical work.

Example of a health-focused thematic analysis

We conclude by summarizing the findings of the study that we used in our worked example, the analysis of interviews with 32 KIs working in the field of

Table 7.4 15-point checklist for a good TA

Process	No.	Criteria
Transcription	1	The data have been transcribed to an appropriate level of detail and the transcripts have been checked against the tapes for 'accuracy'
Coding	2	Each data item has been given equal attention in the coding process
	3	Themes have not been generated from a few vivid examples (an anecdotal approach), but instead the coding process has been thorough, inclusive and comprehensive
	4	All relevant extracts for each theme have been collated
	5	Themes have been checked against each other and back to the original data set
	6	Themes are internally coherent, consistent and distinctive
Analysis	7	Data have been analysed – interpreted, made sense of – rather than merely paraphrased or described
	8	Analysis and data match each other – the extracts illustrate the analytical claims
	9	Analysis tells a convincing and well-organized story about the data and topic
	10	A good balance between analytical narrative and illustrative extracts is provided
Overall	11	Enough time has been allocated to complete all phases of the analysis adequately, without rushing a phase or giving it a light once-over
Written report	12	The assumptions about, and specific approach to, thematic analysis are clearly explicated
	13	There is a good fit between what you claim you do and what you show you have done – i.e. described method and reported analysis are consistent
	14	The language and concepts used in the report are consistent with the epistemological position of the analysis
	15	The researcher is positioned as *active* in the research process; themes do not simply 'emerge'

Source: Braun & Clarke (2006:96), reproduced here with permission from Taylor & Francis.

sexual health in A/NZ (Terry et al., 2012; see Box 7.1). TA, with coding at both the semantic and the latent levels, produced themes that cohered tightly around two key central organizing concepts: a gap between sexual health 'best practice' (often described in reference to research and practice in other more 'successful' countries) and the actual practices found within A/NZ; and the fact that real sexual health promotion in A/NZ was restricted by significant structural and social forces. The two most consistently recurring impediments identified were a lack of government prioritization in the area of sexual health and a 'sexually conservative culture' within A/NZ that inhibited the necessary changes being made.

Moving to a more interpretative level of analysis, we suggested that the KIs' version of events constructed an 'us' versus 'them' view of the situation in A/NZ, which set up the situation as a battle. This evidenced a lack of effective communication between the 'sides' in sexual health investment and provision, and we suggested the need for effective dialogue between people working at the front line of sexual health and those engaging in policy formation, if the sexual health situation in A/NZ is significantly to improve. We identified three key areas for dialogue and action:

- The need for government to provide fuller official explanations for A/NZ's high STI rates that go beyond brief press releases. Public engagement by government would signal sexual health as a priority and as something that should be publicly discussed.
- Finding appropriate ways to access both protective and problematic features of various cultural groups' approaches to STI prevention, rather than treating issues like 'sexual conservatism' as a blanket concept and/or only emphasizing the negative aspects of it.
- Recognizing the role that general practitioners currently have in offering both STI treatment and prevention and highlighting the importance of their experiences and training needs.

The status quo does not appear to be improving sexual health, with prior research (e.g. Jackson, 2004) providing evidence for a *lack* of improvement. This bolsters our argument for orchestrated efforts to create dialogue and change, especially given the context in which a culture of sexual conservatism – whether real or perceived – is seen naturally to impede sexual health efforts.

Further reading

Our original article on TA: Braun, V. & Clarke, V. (2006). Using thematic analysis in psychology. *Qualitative Research in Psychology, 3*(2), 77–101.
A chapter providing more detailed worked examples: Braun, V. & Clarke, V. (2012). Thematic analysis. In H. Cooper (ed.), *Handbook of Research Methods in Psychology. Vol. 2: Research Designs* (pp. 57–71). Washington, DC: APA Books.
A book explaining TA (and qualitative research) in much more detail: Braun, V. & Clarke, V. (2013). *Successful Qualitative Research: A Practical Guide for Beginners.* London: Sage.
The companion website for the book, which contains datasets for practise TA: www.sagepub.co.uk/braunandclarke
Our thematic analysis website, which includes FAQs: www.psych.auckland.ac.nz/ thematicanalysis

References

Aguinaldo, J.P. (2008). The social construction of gay oppression as a determinant of gay men's health: 'Homophobia is killing us'. *Critical Public Health*, *18*(1), 87–96.

Aronson, J. (1994). A pragmatic view of thematic analysis. *The Qualitative Report*, *2*(1). http://www.nova.edu/ssss/QR/BackIssues/QR2-1/aronson.html, accessed 1 May 2014.

Baxter, L.A. (1991) Content analysis. In B.M. Montgomery & S. Duck (eds), *Studying Interpersonal Interaction* (pp. 239–254). New York: Guilford Press.

Benner, P. (1985). Quality of life: A phenomenological perspective on explanation, prediction, and understanding in nursing science. *Advances in Nursing Science*, *8*(1), 1–14.

Bevan, A., Oldfield, V.B. & Salkovskis, P.M. (2010) A qualitative study of the acceptability of an intensive format for the delivery of cognitive-behavioural therapy for obsessive-compulsive disorder. *British Journal of Clinical Psychology*, *49*(2), 173–191.

Boyatzis, R.E. (1998). *Transforming Qualitative Information: Thematic Analysis and Code Development*. Thousand Oaks, CA: Sage.

Braun, V. (2008). "She'll be right"? National identity explanations for poor sexual health statistics in Aotearoa/New Zealand. *Social Science & Medicine*, *67*(11), 1817–1825.

Braun, V. (2013). 'Proper sex without annoying things': Anti-condom discourse and the nature of (hetero)sex. *Sexualities*, *16*(3–4), 361–382.

Braun, V. & Clarke, V. (2006). Using thematic analysis in psychology. *Qualitative Research in Psychology*, *3*(2), 77–101.

Braun, V. & Clarke, V. (2012). Thematic analysis. In H. Cooper (ed.), *APA Handbook of Research Methods in Psychology. Vol. 2: Research Designs* (pp. 57–71). Washington, DC: APA Books.

Braun, V. & Clarke, V. (2013). *Successful Qualitative Research: A Practical Guide for Beginners*. London: Sage.

Buetow, S. (2010). Thematic analysis and its reconceptualization as 'saliency analysis'. *Journal of Health Service Research & Policy*, *15*(2), 123–125.

Chadwick, P., Kaur, H., Swelam, M., Ross, S. & Ellett, L. (2011). Experience of mindfulness in people with bipolar disorder: A qualitative study. *Psychotherapy Research*, *21*(3), 277–285. doi: 10.1080/10503307.2011.565487.

Christ, T. (1970). A thematic analysis of the American business creed. *Social Forces*, *49*(2), 239–245.

Christofides, S., Johnson, L. & Musa, M. (2012). 'Chipping in': Clinical psychologists' descriptions of their use of formulation in multidisciplinary team working. *Psychology and Psychotherapy: Theory, Research and Practice*, *85*(4), 424–435.

Clarke, V. & Braun, V. (2014). Thematic analysis. In T. Teo (ed.), *Encyclopaedia of Critical Psychology* (pp. 1947–1952). New York: Springer.

Clarke, V., Braun, V. & Rance, N. (2014). How to use thematic analysis with interview data (process research). In A. Vossler & N. Moller (eds), *The Counselling and Psychotherapy Research Handbook*. London: Sage.

Dapkus, M.A. (1985). A thematic analysis of the experience of time. *Personality Processes and Individual Differences*, *49*(2), 408–419.

Finlay, L. & Gough, B. (eds). (2003). *Reflexivity: A Practical Guide for Researchers in Health and Social Sciences*. Oxford: Blackwell Science.

Frith, H. & Gleeson, K. (2004). Clothing and embodiment: Men managing body image and appearance. *Psychology of Men & Masculinity*, *5*(1), 40–48.

Frith, H., Harcourt, D. & Fussell, A. (2007). Anticipating an altered appearance: Women undergoing chemotherapy treatment for breast cancer. *European Journal of Oncology Nursing*, *11*, 385–391.

Guest, G., MacQueen, K.M. & Namey, E.E. (2012). *Applied Thematic Analysis*. Thousand Oaks, CA: Sage.

Holton, G.J. (1973). *Thematic Origins of Scientific Thought: Kepler to Einstein*. Cambridge, MA: Harvard University Press.

Jackson, S. (2004). Identifying future research needs for the promotion of young people's sexual health in New Zealand. *Social Policy Journal of New Zealand*, 21, 123–136.

Joffe, H. (2011). Thematic analysis. In D. Harper & A.R. Thompson (eds), *Qualitative Methods in Mental Health and Psychotherapy: A Guide for Students and Practitioners* (pp. 209–223). Chichester: John Wiley & Sons.

Kidder, L.H. & Fine, M. (1987). Qualitative and quantitative methods: When stories converge. In M.M. Mark & L. Shotland (eds), *New Directions in Program Evaluation* (pp. 57–75). San Francisco, CA: Jossey-Bass.

Kirkman, A. (2010). 'My bed or our bed?' Gendered negotiations in the sleep of same-sex couples. *Sociological Research Online*, *15*(2). http://www.socresonline. org.uk/15/2/5.html, accessed 1 May 2014.

Kyriacou, O., Easter, A. & Tchanturia, K. (2009). Comparing views of patients, parents and clinicians on emotions in anorexia: A qualitative study. *Journal of Health Psychology*, *14*(7), 843–854.

Scheepers, P., Te Grotenhuis, M. & Van Der Slik, F. (2002). Education, religiosity and moral attitudes: Explaining cross-national effect differences. *Sociology of Religion*, *63*(2), 157–176. doi: 10.2307/3712563.

Silver, C. & Fielding, N. (2008). Using computer packages in qualitative research. In C. Willig & W. Stainton Rogers (eds), *The Sage Handbook of Qualitative Research in Psychology* (pp. 334–351). Los Angeles, CA: Sage.

Terry, G., Braun, V. & Farvid, P. (2012). Structural impediments to sexual health in New Zealand: Key informant perspectives. *Sexuality Research and Social Policy*, *9*(4), 317–326.

Turana, J.M., Miller, S., Bukusic, E.A., Sanded, J. & Cohen, C.R. (2008). HIV/AIDS and maternity care in Kenya: How fears of stigma and discrimination affect uptake and provision of labor and delivery services. *AIDS Care*, *20*(8), 938–945.

Williams, H. & Davidson, S. (2004). Improving adolescent sexual and reproductive health. A view from Australia: Learning from world's best practice. *Sexual Health*, *1*(2), 95–105.

Winter, D.G. & McClelland, D.C. (1978). Thematic analysis: An empirically derived measure of the effects of liberal arts education. *Journal of Educational Psychology*, *70*(1), 8–16.

Woodrum, E. (1984). Mainstreaming 'content analysis' in social science: Methodological advantages, obstacles, and solutions. *Social Science Research*, *13*, 1–19.

Grounded Theory

Alison Tweed and Helena Priest

8

Grounded theory (GT) is one of the longest-established approaches to dealing with qualitative data, having been conceived in the 1960s and popularized in the 1970s, and for some considerable time it was seen as the market leader in qualitative research (McLeod, 2001; Payne, 2007). With its origins in sociology and used extensively within the social sciences, GT was not, however, widely adopted by psychology until the early 1990s. Since then, as demonstrated through the publication of books such as this one, new qualitative research methods and strategies have been developed, creating many opportunities for qualitative researchers to select, adapt and combine approaches. Nonetheless, GT remains popular within applied psychology and other professional spheres such as education, nursing and health care. One of the reasons for its continued popularity is that there is a set of explicit guidelines to follow; additionally, there are numerous published studies within health and clinical psychology that can be used as exemplars of the approach, some of which we consider later in the chapter.

Grounded theory is an appropriate methodology for exploring topics about which little is known or for which no adequate theory currently exists. Therefore, a broad, open-ended, action-oriented research question is generated as a starting point, although this is often refined and becomes more specific as the research progresses (Payne, 2007). The fundamental aims of grounded theory are to move beyond general description and, by uncovering the basic social and psychological processes that underpin human behaviour, to construct theory about issues of importance in people's lives (Cresswell, 2007; McLeod, 2001; Mills et al., 2006). In achieving these aims, GT can be viewed from two interrelated perspectives: as a method of analysis of qualitative data; and as a type of theory or general explanation produced from the analysis of such data (Henwood & Pidgeon, 2012). In other words, it is both a specific technique and a general approach for exploring and making sense of the world. In this chapter, we aim to present the broad principles and procedures of GT and to illustrate these with reference to published studies and illustrative case material, in which GT is applied to data from a study about people's experiences of receiving treatment for chronic kidney disease.

Historical background

Grounded theory was developed in the 1960s by Barney Glaser and Anselm Strauss, two sociologists undertaking ethnographic fieldwork around the experiences and processes of dying in hospital, a taboo topic at the time. Dissatisfied with the dominant experimental/quantitative methods in understanding and explaining human experience, they proposed a method for close examination of data that could move beyond description and into explanation and theory (Payne, 2007). Their seminal text, in which the research methodology they had devised was formally explained, was published in 1967 (Glaser & Strauss, 1967). The two authors subsequently came to disagree about the nature and procedures of grounded theory, with Glaser considering Strauss's approach too structured and prescriptive, simply a matter of following procedures in order to 'force' theory from the data. For Glaser, analysis was more a matter of patience and waiting for creative insights to emerge (Cresswell, 2007; McLeod, 2001). Strauss later collaborated with Corbin (1990, 1994, 1998) in producing a more widely used general introduction to GT that also included a set of procedural rules (McLeod, 2001). More recently, challenges to this structured, objective and perhaps even positivist approach to GT have been made, exemplified by the work of Charmaz (1995, 2006) in her 'constructivist grounded theory'. This version of GT emphasizes the interpretation of diverse social worlds and multiple realities (Cresswell, 2007). As such, it has flexible guidelines and takes into account the researcher's subjective view, rather than aiming for a more objective reality, leading to a theory that 'is situated in time, place, culture and situation' (Charmaz, 2006:131). However, it has been criticized for not providing steps to guide the researcher and thus being challenging to apply (Hunter et al., 2011).

Since its early origins, many researchers have drawn on grounded theory principles, and several different manifestations are evident within the published literature, including modified or *abbreviated* versions. Willig (2008) describes abbreviated grounded theory as limited to analysing the original data only and not seeking out new informants or new data to broaden and refine the emerging theory. The extent to which these reduced versions can truly generate theory is debatable, although they do offer a useful starting point – especially, perhaps, for the novice researcher. Ultimately, however, to arrive at any kind of theory the key components must be established: a central phenomenon, context, conditions, strategies and consequences (Cresswell, 2007).

Theoretical framework

As noted, GT was conceived by sociologists and has links both to *ethnography* (the study of a cultural group, often through extensive and intensive participant observation of the group in its natural environment; see Chapter 14) and to *symbolic interactionism*. Strauss in particular was interested in symbolic interactionism, which emerged in the United States in the 1920s and 1930s, and in which reality is seen as a meaningful social interaction with others. People interact with others, therefore, based on a shared social understanding of reality rather than on any objective reality.

To a large extent, Charmaz's (1995, 2006) constructivist GT echoes this notion. *Social constructivism* is a worldview in which people develop subjective, varied and multiple meanings of their experiences (see Chapter 2). Thus, constructivist GT emphasizes the subjective interrelationship between the researcher and the participant, as well as the co-construction of meaning (Mills et al., 2006). The goal of constructivist GT, therefore, is to draw on participants' views as they have been formed through social interactions with others. This contrasts to more *objectivist* versions of GT (e.g. Glaser, 1992), in which an external, knowable reality is assumed to exist and GT methods provide a means by which this reality can be discovered. In this approach, the role of social context and the interaction between researcher and participant is minimized. While it may seem that these are dichotomous positions, the theoretical and epistemological underpinnings of different versions of GT tend to run on a continuum between objectivist and constructivist poles (for a review, see Madill et al., 2000) and there remains a core of similarity in approach and analytical process, emphasizing collaboration and co-construction and drawing on a wide range of data sources. The researcher's choice will be guided by their epistemological position, the aims of the particular study and its research questions. Hunter et al. (2011) provide a clear account of evaluating and choosing between the different approaches.

Uses for clinical and health psychology

Grounded theory has been successfully used to study topics within many professional contexts, including nursing, management, education and social work, as well as clinical and health psychology. Table 8.1 includes studies from the clinical and health psychology fields, while the illustrative example that follows is drawn from the health psychology arena.

Doing GT research: Outline of the method

Types of data

As noted, GT is an approach and a method for the analysis of data, rather than being overly concerned with the type of data or the way in which that data is collected. It is therefore suitable for analysing data gathered from a range of sources, including individual interviews, focus group interviews, observational studies where field notes or other forms of recording are made, documents, images and artefacts (see Chapter 6 on techniques for collecting data). For

Table 8.1 Clinical and health psychology studies using grounded theory

Author(s) and date	Title	Journal	Aims, data and findings
Crossley, J. & Salter, D. (2005)	A question of finding harmony: A grounded theory study of clinical psychologists' experience of addressing spiritual beliefs in therapy.	*Psychology and Psychotherapy: Theory, Research and Practice,* 78(3), 295–313.	This study aimed to produce a theory of how clinical psychologists understand and address spirituality within therapy. Data were gathered from eight interviews and two core categories were developed: *spirituality as an elusive concept* and *finding harmony with spiritual beliefs,* although the authors acknowledge that it was difficult to construct a coherent concept of spirituality.
Abba, N., Chadwick, P. & Stevenson, C. (2008)	Responding mindfully to distressing psychosis: A grounded theory analysis.	*Psychotherapy Research,* 18(1), 77–87.	This study aimed to produce a theory of the core psychological process involved in responding mindfully to distressing psychotic sensations. Sixteen interviews were conducted with participants who had completed a mindfulness group. The theory produced represented the process as comprising three stages: *centring in awareness of psychosis; allowing voices, thoughts and images to come and go without reacting or struggle; and reclaiming power through acceptance of psychosis and the self.*
Homewood, E., Tweed, A., Cree, M. & Crossley, J. (2009)	Becoming occluded: The transition of motherhood of women with post-natal depression.	*Qualitative Research in Psychology,* 6(4), 313–329.	This study aimed to produce a psychological theory and process of the transition to motherhood of nine women diagnosed with postnatal depression. The core category was termed *Becoming Occluded* and represented mothers' attempts to sustain their infants in the context of distress and difficult emotions.
Knott, V., Turnbull, D., Olver, I. & Winefield, A. (2012)	A grounded theory approach to understand the cancer-coping process.	*British Journal of Health Psychology,* 17(3), 551–564.	The authors interviewed 20 cancer patients on their experience of communication about their condition. Using Glaser's GT method, three models were developed from the analysis including patient's evaluation of quality of care, cancer-coping processes and distress. The study aimed to move away from individualistic conceptualizations of cancer experiences to one encompassing the social context.

many novice researchers, data acquired from semi-structured interviews tends to be the form of choice. Where data is collected in this way, questions are kept deliberately broad and general. In the illustrative example that follows we use diary entries rather than interview data, but the key principles are the same.

The excerpt of data in Box 8.1 is part of a diary entry from Linda, a 62-year-old kidney patient with end-stage renal disease (ESRD). This is a life-threatening condition whereby a person's kidneys are functioning so poorly (or not at all) that they are unable to remove sufficient waste or excess water from the body. At this stage, the individual will require a form of renal replacement therapy: either kidney dialysis or a transplant. Linda was due to commence dialysis renal replacement therapy as part of a planned procedure and of the two dialysis options available to her (haemodialysis, blood cleaning through a machine; or peritoneal dialysis, where fluid is passed into the body cavity to remove toxins), she had opted for peritoneal dialysis. Linda had

---

BOX 8.1   Excerpt from Linda's diary

August
I am itching everywhere, even in my head! I have never had to cope in my life with anything like this. It is far worse than pain as at least you can take a painkiller for that. This itching is really awful I feel like screaming and screaming. It gets me occasionally in the day but it really gets going in the evening and gets worse and worse.

At this moment, I must admit to feeling at rock bottom and wishing I was out of it all. I really do! I started my CAPD [continuous ambulatory peritoneal dialysis] training on Monday and that frightened me out of my wits. I feel that I have come to the end of ever having control of my body and any say in the future of my life. I know I ought not to feel so but I am afraid I do. I have had my op now and resent the intrusion of the tube so much.

Writing all this down is as usual helping me to calm down. It is a long time since I felt so much anger, helplessness and frustration. I dread everything now to do with my body and my treatment.

September
I do have some hates about dialysis and maybe it will help if I write them down:

1.   Having to remember the sequence of things
2.   Seeing the tube
3.   Changing the dressing as then I see the exit site
4.   Wearing a dressing all the time as the sticky tape makes me itch
5.   Not being able to have a proper bath with lots of water
6.   Constipation and fat tummy!

Now they are listed and although I seem to be negative I am positive at times. I think I ought to set myself goals. My first one could be going on holiday. Well I feel better now, hopefully I can get some sleep.

spontaneously kept a diary about her health condition and treatment for many months and had shared her diary notes with the researcher (AT) to assist in the preparation of information materials for pre-dialysis patients. She gave permission for these entries to be used for teaching and publication purposes (see Chapter 3 for discussion of the ethical consideration with regard to the use of personal data) and she also assisted AT in the development of a more formal GT study with pre-dialysis patients in the hospital unit. The extract in Box 8.1 captures the point of commencing treatment. The research question asked of the data is: 'How do people with ESRD experience the transition to dialysis?'

Position of the researcher

In GT, the researcher should have no pre-conceived ideas to prove or disprove and so has to be sensitive to multiple possible meanings of the data (McLeod, 2001). The researcher's task is to explore the stories that people tell about an area of interest that they have in common with the researcher (Mills et al., 2006) and this relies on full immersion in the data. Immersion involves listening to or reading the data closely on multiple occasions to absorb as much as possible the content, meaning and nuances of the material. To some extent, collaborative working with other researchers is downplayed to allow an individual researcher to immerse themselves in the data.

When using Linda's diary material it is important to read and re-read the extracts: to start to document ideas, emergent thoughts and patterns as part of the *audit trail* for the research process. These initial notes will evolve into *memos* (see later in this chapter), a critical aspect of the GT process. In addition, researchers need to consider their own part in the research process: their prior understanding of the area, what they hope to achieve from the research and their epistemological position. This is often referred to as *foregrounding*. Understanding epistemology is something with which many novice researchers struggle, but it essentially refers to how individuals acquire and understand knowledge about the world; in summary: 'How do we know what we know?' In interpreting Linda's diary data, the GT researcher (AT) adopted an epistemological approach of critical realism, partway along the continuum between more positivistic and more constructivist versions of GT. Critical realism assumes the existence of a reality, but only one that is approximately known and that as such can be modified by social interactions, culture and time (for a review, see Madill et al., 2000). She had worked as a clinical psychologist with kidney patients over many years in a hospital setting, so was familiar with the treatment procedures and their psychological sequelae (see the next section).

Use of prior knowledge

There is a potential dilemma within GT concerning how much the researcher should use their prior knowledge and the available literature about their chosen topic to inform the GT analytical process. Ideally, when planning a GT study, the researcher does not attempt to review the available literature before collecting data, in order to approach the topic and participants with an open mind and sensitivity. The literature is searched and reviewed after the grounded theory has been produced, and compared with developing categories and theory in order to examine to what extent the new theory has supported, deviated from or extended existing knowledge. In reality, it would be unusual if a researcher had no knowledge of the literature around their topic of interest, so the extent to which this naïve approach is possible is questionable. As a reasonable compromise, most GT researchers will carry out some preliminary searching and reviewing of the literature to ensure that the topic of interest is indeed lacking in exploration and theory development and warrants the GT approach (Payne, 2007; Willig, 2008). Indeed, while working up a research proposal for external scrutiny, awareness of the scope of existing knowledge on the topic would be expected by peer reviewers and ethics panels. This preliminary review also enables the researcher to be aware of and make explicit their own influence and pre-conceived ideas that they might be in danger of imposing on the data, and to take steps to limit this as far as possible.

Returning to the illustrative example, the GT researcher's experience of working clinically with kidney patients and extensive knowledge of the literature and evidence base will no doubt influence her approach to Linda's diary excerpt. Her knowledge and experience suggest that many people commencing dialysis find the process difficult and challenging and she is not surprised to see a similar process for Linda. However, it is important for her to remain open to new insights or elements within Linda's data; and not to bypass sections that are difficult to interpret and understand, but to make use of supervisory and reflexive processes to challenge her assumptions about the data. For example, because her clinical work is principally with those who are experiencing extreme distress in relation to dialysis treatment, she is less likely to work with those who successfully manage the transition and so may assume that all transitions are fraught and distressing. This may mean that she misses the more positive or optimistic aspects of the data.

The supervisory and reflective processes can include keeping a reflective diary to note thoughts and feelings about working with the data and to discuss these within research supervision to see how they might be influencing the analysis. Another example is to involve others in the analysis of excerpts of the data so that any differences in interpretation can be highlighted or challenged. See Chapter 5 for further discussion about reflexivity and ensuring quality.

Recruiting participants

Where face-to-face data is collected from participants (rather than from documents or images, for example), all participants must have experienced the process, action or interaction of interest, therefore sampling is *purposive* – deliberately targeting individuals whose individual characteristics and experiences can best inform the developing theory. Recruitment can include people who exemplify different facets of the area of interest or who have different experiences and perspectives. For example, as we are interested in studying transitions to dialysis treatments we will seek out those people who are at that particular stage of the kidney disease process. Purposive sampling can also allow the researcher to seek out *deviant or negative cases*, representing people who might offer a challenge to the developing insights and theory. In the illustrative example, this may include people who are on planned renal replacement therapy trajectories (such as Linda), as well as those who have experienced acute kidney failure and so have received no medical pre-planning.

In purposive sampling, all the participants may be chosen before data collection commences (as in abbreviated GT) or, as is more usual, they may be recruited gradually as the research progresses and after tentative codes or categories have been produced, in order to target specific individuals, groups or data that can best clarify questions and expand or test the developing theory. This is a process known as *theoretical sampling* and it can continue until *saturation* has been reached. Saturation is the point at which the researcher ceases to gain any new insights or ideas from the data being collected (McLeod, 2001) and does not expect that seeking out new participants or data would produce any further significant insights. At this point, data collection ends. GT researchers, therefore, do not usually state explicitly the number of participants that they will recruit to their study from the outset, although they may give a potential range based on their experience, expectations and knowledge of similar published studies. It is of note that abbreviated versions of GT generally work with the original data alone and do not engage with theoretical sampling. The extent to which such versions can ever achieve saturation is therefore debatable.

Procedure

Unlike many other forms of qualitative research, data collection and analysis in grounded theory are synchronized. The first set of data collected is analysed and then used to sensitize the researcher to what needs to be addressed in the next piece of data collection. Over the years, different terms have been used by GT for the analytical stages that can cause confusion to new researchers. Birks and Mills (2011:90) provide a very helpful table of GT terminology to help navigate this process.

Analysis takes the form of a series of coding stages. *Open coding* begins with breaking the data down into small segments as a way of deconstructing the material. It is up to the individual researcher to decide on the size and nature of a segment. It could be a single word, but is more likely to be a phrase, sentence, line or even paragraph of transcribed text; line-by-line coding is commonly used as it is helpful for analysing in-depth interviews of the type likely to be obtained in clinical or health psychology research. Taking each segment in turn, the researcher asks 'What does this mean?' and 'What else could it mean?' and then gives each segment an appropriate code label that captures its meaning. The label may be a word or phrase taken directly from the data (known as *in vivo* coding) or it may be the researcher's own imposed word or phrase. The aim is to generate and record as many code labels as possible to explain each data segment. As coding progresses within and across datasets, the researcher will notice that the same code labels are applied repeatedly and that, eventually, few or no new codes are needed.

Tweed and Charmaz (2012) and Charmaz (2011) advocate labelling codes with *gerunds* rather than with topic or theme words. A gerund is the use of a verb as a noun (that is, in its -ing form), as in 'It's not the *winning* but the *taking* part that counts'. Using gerunds makes it easier to reveal links, processes and relationships between data rather than separating them into discrete units, as is likely to happen when using topic or theme labels. The example in Box 8.2 highlights initial open coding, principally using gerunds for Linda's diary excerpt. The data has been broken into *meaning units*, each representing a distinct thought, idea or statement, instead of breaking the data down into words, lines or paragraphs. Code names are a combination of words imposed by the GT researcher as well as *in vivo* codes arising directly from the excerpt. Initial open coding provides a good opportunity to question personal assumptions about the data and to highlight areas for further exploration or analysis (see the notes to Box 8.2).

Once the first dataset has been open coded, the next stage of analysis is *focused or selective coding*. Here, larger segments of data are coded using more abstract or theoretical code names, which involves a decision-making process to select those initial open codes that appear most relevant to the research question. By undertaking focused or selective coding, the GT researcher explores possible relationships between the initial codes, and generates broader-focused codes or categories that contain a number of individual but closely related items. Categories are then given their own label, which may be new or taken from one of the original code labels. Strauss and Corbin (1998) use a different term for focused coding, called *axial* coding. Axial coding is a structured process for highlighting relationships between codes and categories, and uses a model for coding that involves looking for conditions, context, action and consequences within the data.

During focused or selective coding, it would be usual to gather more data through theoretical sampling in order to refine, elaborate and test out ideas presenting from the emerging categories. Box 8.3 highlights the focused coding of Linda's diary excerpt. Here, potential category names are elicited, including *Losing physical and psychological autonomy*, *Experiencing physical manifestations of illness* and *Reclaiming physical and psychological autonomy*. These may encompass potentially lower-order codes such as *Using coping strategies*, a possible sub-category of *Reclaiming physical and psychological autonomy*. At this point, potential category names may be long, somewhat unwieldy and not fully defined. Further coding, data gathering and memo writing help refine and shape categories during this process.

BOX 8.2   Open coding of Linda excerpt

August

Experiencing global symptoms   ***Extending coping abilities**
I am itching everywhere, even in my head!//   I have never had to cope in my life with anything like this.//

Making comparisons to other symptoms   **Having means of symptom control**
It is far worse than pain//   as at least you can take a painkiller for that.// This itching is

Suffering unbearable symptoms   **Increasing intensity of symptoms over the day**
really awful I feel like screaming and screaming.//   It gets me occasionally in the day but it really gets going in the evening and gets worse and worse.//

                 Feeling at rock bottom   ****Wanting isolation/suicide?**
At this moment, I must admit to feeling at rock bottom// and wishing I was out of it all. I really do!//

                 Fearing new treatment regimen
I started my CAPD training on Monday and that frightened me out of my wits.//

                                         Losing control of body
I feel that I have come to the end of ever having control of my body//

          Losing autonomy   **Fearing own emotional response**
and any say in the future of my life.// I know I ought not to feel so but I am afraid I do.//

                 Resenting physical intrusion
I have had my op now and resent the intrusion of the tube so much.//

                 Using strategy to calm self
Writing all this down is as usual helping me to calm down.//

                 Comparing emotional states to the past
It is a long time since I felt so much anger, helplessness and frustration.//

                 Experiencing all-consuming dread
I dread everything now to do with my body and my treatment.//

September

                 Using strategy to express emotional state
I do have some hates about dialysis and maybe it will help if I write them down://

          Having to remember sequence of treatment
  1.   Having to remember the sequence of things
          Experiencing physical manifestation of illness
  2.   Seeing the tube
  3.   Changing the dressing as then I see the exit site
  4.   Wearing a dressing all the time as the sticky tape makes me itch
  5.   Not being able to have a proper bath with lots of water
  6.   Constipation and fat tummy!//

                 Using strategy to enhance positivity
Now they are listed and although I seem to be negative I am positive at times.//

                 Setting goals
I think I ought to set myself goals. My first one could be going on holiday.//

  Feeling better   **Hoping for rest (physical and psychological)**
Well I feel better now,// hopefully I can get some sleep.

Notes: * 'Coping' is a psychological term and may be pre-emptive. Try not to assume that these are coping strategies but gather more evidence.
** Statement potentially needs greater investigation. Does this relate to a wish for isolation or a wish for death?

BOX 8.3   Focused coding of Linda excerpt

August

Suffering unbearable symptoms

I am itching everywhere, even in my head!// I have never had to cope in my life with anything like this.// It is far worse than pain// as at least you can take a painkiller for that.// This itching is really awful I feel like screaming and screaming.// It gets me occasionally in the day but it really gets going in the evening and gets worse and worse.//

Fear driving wish for escape

Losing physical and psychological autonomy

At this moment, I must admit to feeling at rock bottom// and wishing I was out of it all. I really do!// I started my CAPD training on Monday and that frightened me out of my wits.// I feel that I have come to the end of ever having control of my body// and any say in the future of my life.// I know I ought not to feel so but I am afraid I do.// I have had my op now and resent the intrusion of the tube so much.//

Experiencing all-consuming dread

Writing all this down is as usual helping me to calm down.// It is a long time since I felt so much anger, helplessness and frustration.// I dread everything now to do with my body and my treatment.//

Using coping strategies

September

I do have some hates about dialysis and maybe it will help if I write them down://

Experiencing physical manifestation of illness

1. Having to remember the sequence of things
2. Seeing the tube
3. Changing the dressing as then I see the exit site
4. Wearing a dressing all the time as the sticky tape makes me itch
5. Not being able to have a proper bath with lots of water
6. Constipation and fat tummy!//

Reclaiming physical and psychological autonomy

Now they are listed and although I seem to be negative I am positive at times.// I think I ought to set myself goals. My first one could be going on holiday.// Well I feel better now,// hopefully I can get some sleep.

Throughout these stages the researcher uses a *constant comparison* technique, cycling back and forth in the data to examine new codes and categories in relation to previously identified concepts, incidents and cases, and to determine where they might fit into the evolving analysis (Gordon-Finlayson, 2010). This makes GT a non-linear process, in which the emerging theory can be refined based on new material or perspectives. Codes and categories are thus revised and relabelled as required. These processes are greatly aided by *theoretical sensitivity* and *memo writing*. Theoretical sensitivity involves looking at the data and emerging analysis from new and different perspectives.

Memos are an essential record of the researcher's thoughts and reflections on the data and analysis as they go along, and they serve as an audit trail of these processes and the decisions taken. They may take the form of written notes, notes made on a voice recorder or sketch diagrams, and they can also be made using computer software such as NVivo™. Memos are likely to change in nature as the analysis proceeds, with early memos being 'partial, tentative and exploratory', while later memos are likely to be more precise and sophisticated (Tweed & Charmaz, 2012:140). According to Gordon-Finlayson, it is through memo writing, and not simply through coding, that 'the interpretative and theory generation processes happen' and where the 'final theory starts to take shape' (2010:165).

Box 8.4 highlights a tentative memo on the category *Reclaiming physical and psychological autonomy* from Linda's diary excerpt. Here, the category is defined and any gaps or further ideas to be explored are developed through the narrative. Linkages and relationships are made with other tentative categories, sub-categories and codes, and exemplar quotes are highlighted as a way

---

BOX 8.4   Example memo

Reclaiming physical and psychological autonomy
Reclaiming physical and psychological autonomy appears to be a transformative process commencing at around the time of starting dialysis treatment. Regaining physical autonomy relates to having greater control over bodily processes and reducing disease symptomatology through managing the new treatment regimen. This is not always a straightforward process and is potentially fraught with setbacks both in relation to problems with the treatment itself (e.g. infections, medication issues) and with *managing* the treatment. This category may be mediated by whether treatment is pre-planned or not, and it will be important to gather data from someone who did not go through a planned pre-treatment schedule. Further research may elucidate whether this process is also similar to other chronic conditions.

Reclaiming psychological autonomy involves gaining greater control over mood, fear, anger and memory (e.g. 'having to remember the sequence of things'). Levels of psychological distress appear to be at their peak in the last stages pre-dialysis and in the initial stages of treatment. At times, psychological distress can seem uncontrollable (e.g. 'I know I ought not to feel so but I am afraid I do'). Small steps, such as goal setting, are taken to start to regain autonomy. Personally, I am surprised by the amount of optimism present in people's accounts and this challenges my assumptions about psychological distress being all-consuming. Perhaps this reflects my fears about chronic illness and my own wellbeing.

Example quotes from participants include Ben: '[I]t's not going to mess my life about any more than I have to. Really trying to keep it at bay. It's there but push it in the corner'; and Gail: 'Then you just tell yourself, well you know you've got to deal with it, so you've got to make the best of what you've got.'

Related categories: *Using coping strategies* and *Losing physical and psychological autonomy*.

of keeping track of relevant data. Memos play a vital role in the final writing-up of the analysis and enable the GT researcher to keep track of the emerging grounded theory from inception to conclusion.

The final stage of analysis is when the relationship between categories is identified in a process known as *theoretical coding*. From theoretical coding, the GT researcher can develop a *storyline* (Birks & Mills, 2011; Strauss & Corbin, 1998). A storyline is a narrative description of the theoretical framework derived from the analysis and aims to provide a coherent account of the grounded theory produced. One aspect of developing the storyline involves identifying a more abstract *core category* around which all categories derived so far can be organized, and which has major explanatory power and links to existing theory (Glaser, 1992; Payne, 2007). Using the constant comparative method enhances goodness of fit between the original data and the core category. Once data saturation has been reached (that is, when no new insights are deemed possible), then data collection ends. The final task is to develop a theory that encompasses the core category and other important components of the analysis. The type of theory developed will differ according to epistemological position, but data should be re-conceptualized, understood and interpreted in *abstract* terms. From a more positivist position, the resulting theory may claim the predictive and explanatory power of a process or core category within a known phenomenon. From a more constructivist position, theory development involves the understanding of patterns, relationships and processes, and the acceptance of multiple realities (Charmaz, 2006; Tweed & Charmaz, 2012).

Box 8.5 shows an advanced memo, highlighting a tentative core category and storyline based on the analysis of Linda's diary excerpt and other data from kidney patients commencing dialysis treatment. The category of *Reclaiming physical and psychological autonomy* has been promoted as both the core category and the basic social-psychological process through which an individual manages the transition to dialysis treatment and beyond. Another GT researcher could well have selected an alternative core category and process based on their analysis of the data, but this illustrates the interpretative and analytical approach to GT. There are no right and wrong answers here: the trajectory of the analysis is shaped by personal, contextual and interpretative factors. It does not mean that GT lacks credibility or coherence – quite the opposite: it can produce an understanding of a phenomenon that is highly meaningful.

In summary, then, for data analysis in GT open coding enables categories of information to be identified; focused or selective coding allows for these categories to be interconnected; and theoretical coding enables a story to be built by connecting categories, ending with theory. However, it is important to bear in mind that the skilled GT researcher is not simply applying a formula; rather, the formula enables the analysis but is not the analysis itself (Gordon-Finlayson, 2010). Figure 8.1 on pg. 128 provides a visual representation of the GT process. The bottom of the pyramid represents the large amount of raw data typically produced during data collection about the phenomenon of interest.

BOX 8.5   Core category and storyline

Reclaiming physical and psychological autonomy
Reclaiming physical and psychological autonomy provides a core, overarching frame-work for the data collected and is the process by which kidney patients manage the transition to dialysis treatment. Pre-dialysis is predominated by wide-ranging negative symptomatology, heightened anxiety, dread and fear of the unknown. The commence-ment of dialysis treatment marks a change-point whereby these negative symptoms can potentially be more effectively managed, but also where patients can start to look ahead again in order to regain an element of prior functioning and quality of life. However, *reclaiming* is not a passive process of waiting for improvement, but an active process of seeking and claiming back autonomy and independence of the body's con-trol and one's affect, memory and optimism. These patients are not victims, but man-agers of adversity with a will to do more than survive: to reclaim their bodies and minds in order to make the most of life.

    Reclaiming shares many parallels with existing research, including the theme of *Maintaining lifestyle*, derived from the systematic and thematic review of 18 qualitative studies investigating the treatment decision-making of patients with chronic kidney disease (Morton et al., 2010). Similarly, Mitchell et al. (2009) highlighted *Cognitive style* as a key theme in their qualitative analysis of 10 kidney patients' experiences of dialy-sis. This encompassed positive re-appraisal, optimism and developing realistic expecta-tions as elements, and shares many similarities with the sub-categories of *Reclaiming*. It is anticipated that *Reclaiming* may be a similar process for other kidney patients mak-ing the transition to dialysis, as well as for patients with other chronic diseases requir-ing long-term treatment.

Initial, selective and focused coding reduces the raw data into packaged ele-ments consisting of codes and categories. These become increasingly abstract and conceptual. At the same time, theoretical sampling and constant compar-ative analysis enable the GT researcher to move back and forth within the data to refine and focus the analytical process. Theoretical coding denotes the final stage of analysis and the development of the core category. Throughout the process, memoing links one analytical stage to the next, acting as the metaphorical mortar holding the building blocks of the pyramid together.

Writing up

The aim in writing up a GT report is to produce an account of the substantive theory that has been produced from the data analysed, often accompanied by an explanatory diagram. The report can follow a standard format, including sections on background to the topic, rationale for studying it, research ques-tion, participants, tools, procedure, results and links/extensions to existing knowledge. Enough detail needs to be provided so that the reader can follow all the steps and decisions taken, and the report needs to be illustrated with ver-batim extracts from interview transcripts or other data such as observational

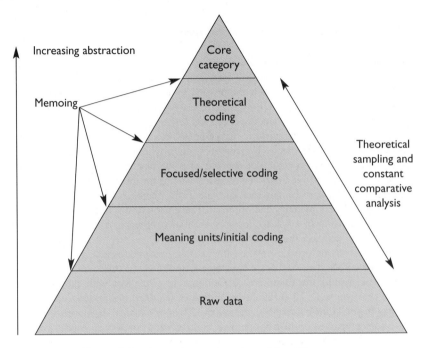

Figure 8.1   A visual representation of the GT process

notes. The researcher may also choose to include extracts of memos and other notes illustrating the analytical process.

Quality control

The key test of the adequacy of the theory is *goodness of fit*: in other words, it must be meaningful to people with an interest in the topic explored (for example, clinical or health psychologists). Quality checking in GT may be somewhat different from other methods because of its focus on individual rather than collaborative working. Thus, strategies such as member checks may be less relevant. Equally, respondent validation (for example, by seeking verification of the theory from the participants who contributed to it) may merely produce more data rather than establishing the credibility of the researcher's perspective (Payne, 2007). Both Charmaz (2006) and Madill et al. (2000) have provided useful information on enhancing the quality of GT studies. Charmaz presents the concepts of *Credibility*, *Originality*, *Resonance* and *Usefulness* as markers of quality, while Madill et al. use a number of quality criteria to evaluate a GT study within different epistemological positions. Their conclusion is that researchers must be clear about their epistemological position and be consistent with this in their methods of analysis. Any quality criteria used must therefore also be consistent with the stated epistemological position, rather than being employed as a box-ticking exercise. Regardless of the position taken, it is important that a GT project is undertaken rigorously and there is a clear audit trail of research decision-making (see Chapter 5 for various strategies for ensuring quality).

Challenges of GT

While GT may initially seem attractive to novice researchers because of the ready availability of 'how-to' guides, it is important to be aware of the many challenges, not least in ensuring consistency between the theoretical and epistemological framing of the study and the form of GT employed. There are many decisions for the researcher to make, such as whether or not to transcribe interview data; what counts as a data segment; who to approach to expand the emerging theory; when saturation has been achieved and data collection can end; and when the theory is adequately developed and detailed. No manual will fully answer these questions for the researcher and it is only by doing GT that a researcher will become fully appreciative of the interpretative and creative process involved.

Concluding comments

As has been seen from this chapter, GT is a rigorous, creative and flexible approach to deriving new meanings and understandings from qualitative data. The challenge for the GT researcher is to move beyond the descriptive to produce meaning and understanding that are abstract and theoretical. While GT by its very definition is grounded in the data, it should not be limited by it. At times, the GT process can feel overwhelming, confusing and complex, yet it is important to persist, to immerse oneself in the process in order to achieve the outcome and end-point. Using Linda's diary material, the GT analysis helped elucidate a process of reclaiming autonomy in spite of chronic illness and treatment; an optimistic, hopeful and restorative process that other kidney patients and health professionals can find beneficial. We hope that this chapter also serves a similar function and enables you to embark on a successful GT journey.

Glossary of terms used in grounded theory

Axial coding	Axial coding takes place after open coding and is a structured process for putting data back together and highlighting relationships between codes and categories. It uses a model for coding that involves looking for conditions, context, action and consequences within the data.

Constant comparison	An analytical process that involves the researcher repeatedly going back into their data to compare elements within it. For example, codes are compared with categories, other codes and new data to look for similarities and differences.
Core category	A central category or phenomenon, around which all categories derived so far can be organized, and which has major explanatory power and links to existing theory.
Focused/selective coding	This form of coding follows open coding and involves selecting those open codes that have most relevance to the research area and using them to group larger amounts of data. Focused/selective codes tend to be more abstract and conceptual than open codes with greater descriptive or explanatory power.
Foregrounding	This includes the influences, hopes, expectations and position of the researcher(s) in relation to the research area, method or epistemology. Providing this information may enable the reader to understand how the researcher has approached and analysed the data.
Gerund	The use of a verb as a noun. Using gerunds makes it easier to reveal links between data.
Meaning unit	A meaning unit represents a distinct thought, idea or statement within the data. It can be of varying lengths, from a word or phrase to a paragraph, and will depend on the level of detail the researcher is looking for and what is being conveyed.
Memo	An analytical process whereby the researcher produces a parallel set of notes to the data containing theoretical ideas, reflections and links between data in order to aid the process of analysis and writing-up.
Open coding	An initial form of coding whereby data meaning units are identified and given a name (either descriptive, *in vivo* or abstract).
Purposive sampling	A process of seeking out and selecting new data or participants in order to inform, refine or elaborate the emerging grounded theory.
Saturation	A point within the data-collection and analysis process where no further insights or development of the grounded theory can be gained.
Storyline	A brief, narrative description of the theoretical framework derived from the analysis that aims to provide a coherent account of the grounded theory produced.

Theoretical sampling	A process of sampling new data or seeking new participants to help develop the theoretical categories of the GT.
Theoretical sensitivity	Looking at the data and emerging analysis from new and different perspectives in order to pull out meaning and relevance. It involves using the researcher's prior knowledge and understanding, but also what has been learned during the research process itself.

Further reading

Bryant, A. & Charmaz, K. (2007) *The SAGE Handbook of Grounded Theory*. London: Sage.

Charmaz, K. (2006) *Constructing Grounded Theory*. London: Sage.

Strauss, A.L. & Corbin, J. (1998) *Basics of Qualitative Research: Grounded Theory Procedures and Techniques* (2nd edn). Thousand Oaks, CA: Sage.

References

Abba, N., Chadwick, P. & Stevenson, C. (2008). Responding mindfully to distressing psychosis: A grounded theory analysis. *Psychotherapy Research*, *18*(1), 77–87.

Birks, M. & Mills, J. (2011). *Grounded Theory: A Practical Guide*. London: Sage.

Charmaz, K. (1995). Grounded theory. In J.A. Smith, R. Harré & L.Van Langenhove (eds), *Rethinking Methods in Psychology* (pp. 27–49). London: Sage.

Charmaz, K. (2006). *Constructing Grounded Theory*. London: Sage.

Charmaz, K. (2011). Grounded theory methods in social justice research. In N.K. Denzin & Y.S. Lincoln (eds), *The SAGE Handbook of Qualitative Research* (4th edn). Thousand Oaks, CA: Sage.

Cresswell, J. (2007). *Qualitative Inquiry and Research Design: Choosing among Five Approaches* (2nd edn). Thousand Oaks, CA: Sage.

Crossley, J. & Salter, D. (2005). A question of finding harmony: A grounded theory study of clinical psychologists' experience of addressing spiritual beliefs in therapy. *Psychotherapy Research*, *18*(1), 77–87.

Glaser, B.G. (1992). *Basics of Grounded Theory Analysis*. Mill Valley, CA: Sociology Press.

Glaser, B.G. & Strauss, A.L. (1967) *The Discovery of Grounded Theory*. Chicago, IL: Aldine.

Gordon-Finlayson, A. (2010). Grounded theory. In M. Forrester (ed.). *Doing Qualitative Research in Psychology: A Practical Guide* (pp. 154–176). London: Sage.

Henwood, K. & Pidgeon, N. (2012). Grounded theory. In G.M. Breakwell, J.A. Smith & D.B. Wright (eds), *Research Methods in Psychology* (pp. 461–484). London: Sage.

Homewood, E., Tweed, A., Cree, M. & Crossley, J. (2009) Becoming occluded: The transition of motherhood of women with post-natal depression. *Qualitative Research in Psychology*, 6(4), 313–329.

Hunter, A., Murphy, K., Grealish, A., Casey, D. & Keady, J. (2011). Navigating the grounded theory terrain. Part 1. *Nurse Researcher*, 18(4), 6–10.

Knott, V., Turnbull, D., Olver, I. & Winefield, A. (2012) A grounded theory approach to understand the cancer-coping process. *British Journal of Health Psychology*, 17(3), 551–564.

Madill, A., Jordan, A. & Shirley, C. (2000) Objectivity and reliability in qualitative analysis: Realist, contextualist and radical constructivist epistemologies. *British Journal of Psychology*, 91, 1–20.

McLeod, J. (2001). *Qualitative Research in Counselling and Psychotherapy*. London: Sage.

Mills, J., Bonner, A. & Francis, K. (2006). The development of constructivist grounded theory. *Journal of Qualitative Methods*, 5(1), 25–35.

Mitchell, A., Farrand, P., James, H., Luke, R., Purtell, R. & Wyatt, K. (2009) Patients' experience of transition onto haemodialysis: A qualitative study. *Journal of Renal Care*, 35(2), 99–107.

Morton, R.L., Tong, A., Howard, K., Snelling, P. & Webster, A.C. (2010) The views of patients and carers in treatment decision making for chronic kidney disease: Systematic review and thematic analysis of qualitative studies. *British Medical Journal*, 340(112), 1–10.

Payne, S. (2007). Grounded theory. In E. Lyons & A. Coyle (eds), *Analysing Qualitative Data in Psychology* (pp. 65–86). London: Sage.

Strauss, A.L. & Corbin, J. (1990). *Basics of Qualitative Research: Grounded Theory Procedures and Techniques*. Newbury Park, CA: Sage.

Strauss, A.L. & Corbin, J. (1994). Grounded theory methodology: An overview. In N.K. Denzin & Y.S. Lincoln (eds), *Handbook of Qualitative Research* (pp. 273–285). Thousand Oaks, CA: Sage.

Strauss, A.L. & Corbin, J. (1998). *Basics of Qualitative Research: Grounded Theory Procedures and Techniques* (2nd edn). Thousand Oaks, CA: Sage.

Tweed, A. & Charmaz, K. (2012). Grounded theory methods for mental health practitioners. In D. Harper & A.R. Thompson (eds), *Qualitative Research in Mental Health and Psychotherapy* (pp. 131–146). Chichester: Wiley-Blackwell.

Willig, C. (2008). *Introducing Qualitative Research in Psychology* (2nd edn). Maidenhead: McGraw Hill/Open University Press.

Narrative Research

Michael Murray and Anneke Sools

9

Narrative psychology is concerned with how human beings make sense of the world in storied form. More specifically, it is concerned with the structure, content and function of the stories we tell in everyday social interaction. It accepts that we live in a storied world and that we interpret the actions of others and ourselves through the stories we exchange. Through narrative we not only shape the world and ourselves, they are shaped for us through narrative.

After the initial burst of enthusiasm in the 1980s about the study of narrative within psychology (e.g. Bruner, 1986; Mishler, 1986; Polkinghorne, 1988; Sarbin, 1986a), interest in this approach within qualitative psychology has faltered somewhat, not least because of the multiple forms that narratives can take and also the many ways in which they can be analysed. However, across the other social sciences where there is less anxiety about methodological certainty, there has continued to be a growth of interest and the development of interdisciplinary forums. This is illustrated in the establishment of journals (e.g. *Narrative Inquiry*; *Narrative Works*), the organization of conferences (e.g. *Narrative Matters*) and the publication of guides to narrative analysis (e.g. Andrews et al., 2013; Bold, 2012; De Fina & Georgakopoulou, 2012). To the novice researcher this rapid growth of research can sometimes seem confusing.

The aim of this chapter is to introduce some of the key theoretical issues and ways of collecting and analysing narratives. At the outset, we should offer a caveat that we are not being prescriptive but rather offering suggestions on how to proceed. It is our contention that the study of narrative offers great potential in understanding everyday lives. However, while we offer a guide, the challenge is to maintain that creative flair in interpretation that enables you to see the world in a different way rather than imposing standard frameworks on it.

Historical background

Narrative psychology has its philosophical roots in hermeneutics stretching back at least to Dilthey and more recently to Gadamer and Ricoeur. Of particular note is the work of Paul Ricoeur (e.g. 1984), who placed narrative at the centre of his phenomenology. He argued that since we live in a temporal world, we need some means to bring order to what would seem to be chaotic. Narrative is that means of bringing order to this constantly changing flux. However, as Ricoeur emphasized, this capacity to emplot is not always easy, especially after traumatic events. It is these 'capacities and incapacities that make human beings acting and suffering beings' (Ricoeur, 1997:xxxix). After crisis, we struggle to make narrative sense of our world and to move on or continue to experience distress and disorientation.

Interest in the study of narrative within psychology can be traced back to its earliest development as a discipline in the nineteenth century. Wilhelm Wundt, who is often termed the father of experimental psychology, also had considerable interest in the role of myths and legends in everyday life (Murray, 2002). Around the same time, William James (1893), in his discussion of the nature of thinking, explicitly referred to its narrative form:

> to say that all human thinking is essentially of two kinds – reasoning on the one hand and narrative, descriptive, contemplative on the other – is to say what every reader's experience will corroborate.

Moving into the twentieth century, Frederick Bartlett (1932) emphasized the importance of narrative as a means of organizing our memory. While several psychologists continued this interest in narrative, the experimental emphasis within psychology pushed the study of narrative to the sidelines. However, with the turn to language and the increasing interest in qualitative research in the 1980s, there was something of a rebirth of interest in the study of narrative within psychology. At that time a number of social/personality psychologists began to explore the potential of the concept for both understanding and investigating human identity.

One of the earliest was Dan McAdams (1993), who argued that we are narrative-making beings and that we create our identities though narrative. He began his book with a useful summary of his approach:

> If you want to know me, then you must know my story, for my story defines who I am. And if I want to know myself, to gain insight into the meaning of my own life, then I, too, must come to know my own story. (1993:11)

Thus, it is through narrative that we define ourselves both to ourselves and to others.

At this time Jerome Bruner (1986) developed James's (1893) argument that human beings have two ways of thinking: the scientific and the narrative. While the former conceived of thinking as a form of information processing, which has become the dominant approach within cognitive psychology, the latter narrative approach is more concerned with meaning-making. This meaning-making is a socially shared process through which we collectively create our understanding of the world.

In the same year, Ted Sarbin (1986a) published his collection of essays on narrative psychology. In his own contribution, Sarbin (1986b) argued that psychology has been dominated by a machine metaphor with its fascination with the measurement of variables. Sarbin argued for narrative as a more dynamic metaphor for understanding the way in which human beings made sense of the world. For Sarbin, human beings are best considered as narrative beings, in the sense that we bring order to our phenomenological worlds through the development of narrative plots. In that sense, we see the world through narratives and act accordingly.

Also in 1986 Elliott Mishler published his work on interviews as a method of social research. At that time the qualitative turn within psychology was in its early days and Mishler was concerned that analysts were ignoring the meaning-making person through decomposing interview transcripts into a series of themes or discourses. He argued that interviewers often disrupt the narrative accounts provided by interviewees and then either ignore them or decompose them through the process of coding in the analysis of interview transcripts.

Not surprisingly, narrative psychologists have drawn on classic literary work on narrative. Within the psychoanalytic tradition, Peter Brooks wrote that 'the structure of literature is in some sense the structure of mind' (1994:24) and noted that Freud had accepted that poets and philosophers had anticipated all that he had to say. Brooks placed narrative at the centre of psychoanalysis and argued that people who come to the therapist do so 'precisely because of the weakness of the narrative discourses that they present: the incoherence, inconsistency, and lack of explanatory force in the way they tell their lives' (1994:47).

In the 1990s, other social psychologists turned to the ideas of Ricoeur. Of note is Mark Freeman (1993), who studied under Ricoeur in Chicago. He developed these ideas in his wonderful book on *Rewriting the Self* to argue that narrative should be at the centre of a psychology concerned with understanding the 'living, loving, suffering, dying' person. He argued for the ontological significance of narrative: 'the very act of making sense of ourselves and others, [which] is only possible through the fabric of narrative itself' (1993:21). Narrative is not something apart from ourselves but is intimately involved in the process of constructing our selves and the world around us.

In recent years, interest in narrative psychology had continued to grow, although to a lesser extent than some other qualitative approaches whose growth has been facilitated by the development of methodological guides with often limited reference to the theoretical bases of particular approaches. Narrative psychology emphasizes the theoretical underpinnings of its approach and its concern not only with detailing individual experience but also with exploring the character of social and cultural narratives and how these interpenetrate (Murray, 1999, 2000).

Theoretical or conceptual framework

Human beings develop narratives as a means of making sense of the world. In developing narrative accounts, we assume that human beings have a certain degree of agency and can take action to change their circumstances. As such, the narrative approach has certain similarities with attribution theory, which posited that in trying to make sense of our world we make causal inferences about the actions of others. These others are considered intentional beings to whom the perceiver can attribute not only causality but responsibility for their actions. Indeed, in one of his early studies (Heider & Simmel, 1944), Heider explored the accounts that people gave when presented with a series of pictograms and invited to describe them. The accounts that his participants gave were comparable with short narratives that not only provided narrative causal attributions (e.g. the queen died of grief after the king died) but other narrative details. However, narrative psychology goes further than looking for causal inferences to explore other dimensions of narrative and how these are constructed through language in particular social and cultural contexts.

Narrative psychology has been especially concerned with the structure and content of narrative accounts. In looking at structure, it has drawn on ideas from the humanities and other human sciences. The pentad developed by Kenneth Burke (1952), and introduced to narrative psychology by Jerome Bruner (1986), offers a good starting point. According to this model, narrative can be considered according to the act or the detail of what happened; the agent or the central character of the characters involved; the scene or the background to the action; the agency that is concerned with the structure of the action; and the purpose of the action. We will take up this model in our discussion of narrative analysis.

Recently, a continuum between big and small stories has been introduced in narrative inquiry (Georgakopoulou, 2006; Bamberg, 2006) and in narrative health research (Sools, 2012). A small-story approach directs attention to the 'other stories' that easily disappear from view. They consist of fragmented, everyday pieces of ongoing conversation, messy stories that are not fully fledged, which might be especially prevalent in times of illness. Sools and Schuhmann (2014) have argued that a small-story approach allows for the inclusion in mental health care and counselling of people who do not have the necessary reflexive capacities to tell big stories, as well as the inclusion of stories that do not display the features of big stories.

Narrative psychology has also been concerned with the overall tone of the narrative account. This approach was developed by McAdams, who noted that 'while some life stories exude optimism and trust, others are couched in the language of mistrust and resignation' (1993:47). This is somewhat similar to the suggestion by Gergen and Gergen (1986) that narrative structure can be organized depending on its overall trajectory as regressive, stable or progressive. Frank (1995) proposed three comparable narrative structures that function to give meaning to health and illness: the chaos narrative, the stable narrative and the restitution narrative. Similarly, Murray (2002) organized personal narrative accounts of cancer in terms of death, fighting and rebirth and noted the similarity of this trinity with the classic literary narrative forms of tragedy, comedy and romance.

Narratives develop in interpersonal and social contexts. Previously, Murray (2000) argued for the need to be explicit about the particular level of narrative analysis in the sense that we can talk about personal stories, interpersonal stories and societal stories. Stephens (2011) extended this approach to consider how through particular forms of narrative accounting people position themselves in different ways in different social contexts. Bamberg (1997) introduced the concept of 'narrative positioning', which connects the narrative with the social and moral context. Murray (2002) also considered the narrative structure of social representations and how personal narrative accounts interconnect with these social representations. Similarly, Hammack (2010) discussed the process of narrative engagement whereby in developing personal narratives we engage with broader sociocultural narratives. He describes how Palestinian youth engage with what he describes as a 'tragic master narrative of loss and dispossession' (2010:507). This master narrative is supported by the continuing presence of conflict, occupation and material disadvantage. Thus, narrative can be considered in terms of the person, the interpersonal context and the broader social situation. While they can be analysed separately, the challenge is to connect these different levels of analysis. In the analysis section we begin to explore this process.

Collecting narratives

We are born into a world of narratives, we live and share narratives throughout our lives and we are described in terms of narratives after we die. In view of this, it is not surprising that narrative psychologists have emphasized the many sources for narrative accounts. However, there remains a preference for the interview as a primary source of data. McAdams (1995) has provided a very detailed guide to obtaining life-story narratives. He suggests beginning the interview with some introductory remarks in which the interviewer invites the interviewee to tell the story of their life. Thus, the interviewee is deliberately invited to organize their account in a story format with 'characters, scenes, plots, and so forth' (1995:1). He even encourages the interviewee to consider their life story in the form of chapters. He also asks the interviewee to draw attention to critical events and to any challenges they may have faced in their lives. He concludes the interview by encouraging the interviewee to reflect on any underlying meaning or shape to their life story.

From the German biographic tradition, an approach has developed known as the biographic interview method (BIM) and subsequently the biographic narrative interview method (BNIM; Wengraf, 2001). This method is considered both sociobiographic and psychoanalytic, in the sense that in telling their stories people are influenced both by conscious concerns and by a range of unconscious cultural, societal and individual presuppositions and processes. The BNIM method suggests proceeding through three steps in conducting narrative interviews. The interviewer begins with a single narrative question (e.g. 'Please tell me the story of your life, all the events and experiences that have been important to you personally in life; begin wherever you want to begin, I won't interrupt, I'll just take some notes for afterwards'). Following this, the interviewer asks for more narrative detail about the various topics raised, sticking strictly to the sequence of topics and the words used. The interviewer can conclude with more non-narrative questions.

From the outset, narrative researchers have been sensitive about the context within which the interview is conducted. In his introduction to research interviewing, Mishler (1986) drew attention to the caveats identified by many early social researchers about the nature of the interview. For example, Schuman (1982) cautioned about the supposed transparency of surveys:

> too much can be inferred from answers taken at face value to questions of dubious merit ... all answers depend upon the way a question is formulated. Language is not a clean logical tool like mathematics that we can use with precision ... As if this complexity were not enough, our answers are also influenced by who asks the question. (1982:22)

It is for these reasons that narrative researchers are attentive to the conversational nature of storytelling. Rather than narrative interviews following a definite protocol, they should be considered an opportunity for storytelling. Riessman (2008) argues that since narratives come in many forms, it is the task of the researcher to provide an opportunity for the research participant to tell their story, which can occur when least expected. In that sense, she argues that the narrative researcher should follow more the guide of ethnography than the formal interview. This may require many meetings during which the researcher builds rapport with the interviewee and also relinquishes control and allows the participant to develop the direction of the narrative.

In addition, the discussion about big and small stories has reminded narrative researchers that people do not narrate long life histories in one interview but can focus on particular issues. Flick (2009) introduced the concept of episodic interviews as a strategy for handling this feature. Thus, the researcher can work with the participant to focus on particular issues and to place these within a larger framework.

Analysing narratives

The method proposed here consists of five parts, each divided in steps (see Box 9.1). The parts and steps in the analysis should be used flexibly and in an iterative process of going back and forth. Overall, the steps are designed as a bottom-up process that starts with the unique words of participants and gradually moves up to include wider contexts and become more theory driven. For each research project, the student has to decide how inclusive and complex the analysis needs to be and, accordingly, which of the parts and steps to include. The more inclusive the analysis, the more complexity can be addressed, but also the more time-consuming the analysis becomes. The less inclusive the analysis, the more cases can be analysed, which allows for developing narrative patterns and overarching findings, although some of the particularity of cases gets lost.

Because the parts build on each other, it is advisable always to start with Part I. This concerns a presentation of the case as a whole, which is a very useful first step to getting a sense of the whole before going into more detail. Also, Part I analysis provides context for the analysis in the subsequent parts. It is a form of narrative content analysis, which is the easiest to execute for beginning students. Part II combines content and structural analysis, and is still doable for beginning students, although this part requires more interpretative skills. Part III concerns interactional or dialogical narrative analysis, which is less commonly used and requires analytical tools similar to discourse analysis. However, it is not the power dynamics or discursive strategies as such that are topic of investigation, but how they contribute to the development of certain stories and not others. Part IV builds on the previous parts (especially Parts II and IV) and typically uses theory to put storyline patterns and interactional

---

BOX 9.1   Step-by-step guide to narrative analysis

Part	Step	
I. Introduction	1.	Formulate case title
	2.	Introduce case
II. Storyline analysis	3.	Formulate storyline title
	4.	Identify and describe storyline elements and breach
	5.	Write narrative summary of storyline
	6.	Draw conclusions regarding your research question based on steps 3–5 and discuss your findings
III. Interactional narrative analysis	7.	Positioning of storylines
	8.	Positioning of storytellers/listeners
	9.	Conclusion and discussion of what is at stake
IV. Contextual analysis	10.	Positioning of storylines in the wider social, societal and political context
	11.	Positioning of storytellers/listeners and interactional patterns in wider contexts
V. Comparative analysis of storylines, interactional patterns and/or contexts	12.	Make comparison of similarities and differences between cases

dynamics into a wider social, cultural and societal context. Part V involves comparative analysis, and is especially relevant when moving from single to multiple cases to find patterns across cases.

Step-by-step guide

Part I: Introduction

Step 1: Case title
Formulate a title to capture the case story as a whole, staying as close as possible to participants' own words. After reading the case several times, start by formulating a preliminary title, which you can revise during or after the analysis if necessary.

Step 2: Introduction
Introduce the case as a whole to readers who do not know it. Quotes can be used to substantiate your interpretation of the case: for example, by inserting sentences or words in quotation marks in the text. The quotes should be adequately chosen in such a way that the particularity of the case comes to the fore; the person and story comes to 'life'; and transparency is sufficient for readers to follow and criticize the interpretation.

Part II: Level 1 – Storyline analysis

Perform a storyline analysis using Burke's (1969[1945]) pentad of five storyline elements (agent, act, agency, scene, purpose) and a breach. The following modified version of the pentad (Sools, 2010) is particularly useful in the context of narrative analysis in health research. The pentad is described in more detail in Step 4.

Step 3: Storyline title
Formulate a title to capture the essence of the storyline, which can differ from the overall story of the case. It is possible to look for a storyline capturing the story as a whole, but also to identify multiple storylines.

Step 4: Identify and characterize the five storyline elements and the breach
Systematically identify all storyline elements, which might entail describing one or more missing elements. Missing elements or gaps in the story are as important as fully fledged storylines. In addition to identifying the elements, characterize each of them in such a way that insight is gained in the meaning-making of the particular case, and the particularity of the case comes adequately to the fore. The elements might be ambiguous and multiple. Although this method of analysis pushes the researcher to make a more or less coherent story, the aim is also to try to represent the multiplicity and ambiguity of the case. The setting, for instance, might have different qualities, such as 'dangerous terrain' and 'a

place where self-development is encouraged'. There might also be a change from a protected childhood in a small village 'where the neighbors keep an eye on you' to an 'adventurous life of travelling the globe' later on.

- **Agent/character: Who** is the main agent in the story? It is important to *characterize* this agent (the protagonist of the story) truly, not simply naming the protagonist and possible other characters in their relation to the agent: for example, 'mother', 'friend Amy' and so on. Instead, give a more elaborate interpretation, such as Lucy's 'mum with her always vivid imagination', who functioned as an inspiration to her while at the same time turning the child Lucy into a mature person looking after her 'crazy' mother. When the story lacks details regarding the main agent, so that the listener does not get a picture of them, address this lack of description.
- **Acts/events: What?** While acts denote what actions are typical and available to agents, events 'happen' to them. The act/event distinction allows for the analysis of how characters are positioned as active, in control or subjected to circumstances.
- **Means and/or helpers: With what/whom?** This element indicates persons or means that are helpful or hinder achieving the goals/intentions of the story. (Note that the term means/helpers is employed instead of agency, the term used by Burke, which has a different meaning in psychology and can therefore be a cause of confusion.)
- **Setting/scene: Where?** Some stories have clear or elaborate descriptions of physical environments such as schools, hospitals, houses and streets or geographical places such as cities, countries and continents, whereas other stories give minimal or no such spatial information. Settings can also take the form of psychological or emotional environments such as somewhere hostile or warm, or be characterized by adjectives such as supportive, educational or competitive. Finally, settings can be more psychological than physical, as in a story that has the form of an internal dialogue of the protagonist on what to do, what to think or what to feel.
- **Purpose, intention, desired or feared goal: What for?** Sometimes the purpose of the story is implicit rather than explicit. In health research, a desired end-state of wellbeing might be taken for granted and therefore not named explicitly, while ill people might not talk about undesired end-states such as an expected lack of healing.
- **Breach:** The breach refers to an imbalance between two storyline elements. A typical fairy tale, for example, is an imbalance between the purpose (fighting the evil stepmother queen) and the means (not having the courage and hope to stand up and fight for the good cause). The whole fairy tale is consequently motivated by the protagonist's quest to find courage and hope. Thus, the breach makes understandable what motivates the story and how the storyline elements are connected into a meaningful whole. The breach might be implicit, for instance when the means to the preferred goals are lacking or when no actions of the protagonist

are mentioned. This might indicate that the agent in the story does not feel able to reach their goals, or does not have access to resources, or has no idea (yet) on how to accomplish these goals.

The term 'breach' is more neutral and provides less confusion than the Burkean term 'trouble'. The essence of a breach is not necessarily the emergence of a problem in life (illness, for example), but rather a breach at story level, which entails a fracture with the unexpected, the canonical, the taken for granted. According to Bruner (1986), it is exactly these breaches that motivate storytelling in order to repair the breach. In addition, it is important to keep in mind that what constitutes the story breach should not be determined in an objective sense, but by paying close attention to subjective meaning-making. The onset of illness might objectively be considered a breach in normality (although for some people with chronic health problems illness is normality), but it also might function in the story as background for the sick person who is admitted to hospital and develops a romantic relationship with a hospital staff member. The story trouble then revolves around this relationship and the uncertainty of the ill person (character) about the mutuality of feelings and its potential permanence (purpose).

Step 5: Researcher's narrative summary

Write a summary of the storyline, which follows logically from the previous analysis (Step 3). Following logically means that no essential elements are missing and no new information is given. The summary follows the content, structure, perspective and wording of the case, while explicating the narrative causal connections made between the parts. It might be helpful to put together different pieces of verbatim excerpts from the interview, and then carefully edit them in such a way that the story logic becomes clear. In the following example, taken from an interview study in the Netherlands (Sools, 2013), the main storyline of a three-hour narrative BNIM interview on 'her story of becoming resilient' with a Dutch-Indonesian woman (Miepie, age 85) is summarized. Although this is a radical reduction of the richness of the interview, there is an important difference from a standard summary. Essential components of her narrative are preserved by keeping intact her *own wording* by using her own sentences as much as possible ('let's try and deal with that!') and piecing them together with words to clarify the *causal linkages* ('but'); the *order* of the interview is maintained (in this case chronologically, but this is not necessarily the case); and the change in *perspective* (from first-person I to 'we', to third-person 'some hungry guy', to second-person 'you', to first person again).

> **'I always took care of me and my own'**
> I was raised in relative abundance, which I accepted as taken-for-granted, but ended up with my neighbors in a dreadful camp situation where we had to protect each other. Once, some hungry guy nicked a bunch of bananas from the Japs, which resulted in withholding food for the entire

camp for three days. Well, let's try and deal with that! These things turn you into an adult for sure, learning how to take care of each other. Now, what has happened in the camps does not exist anymore. Talking about it does not help. You just need the will to (go on living). I am happy and grateful to be alive now.

Step 6: Conclusions and discussion

The conclusions drawn based on the storyline analysis depend on the research question (e.g. identity construction, the development of agency, assessment of quality of care, motives for therapy adherence). However, independent of the content of the conclusions, all conclusions need to be firmly grounded in the analysis yet generate insights that transcend previous descriptions (e.g. highlighting the role negotiation of a mother who seeks recognition for her role as co-professional in the hospital, based on expertise of her daughter's chronic illness). In addition, the conclusions need to do justice to the narrative character of the analysis by keeping intact the connection between parts and/or the sequentiality of how the story is told. Focusing on the connection and sequentiality prevents the story being fragmented into separate themes, which are interesting but not narrative analysis.

You can discuss your conclusions by putting them in a wider perspective and by providing possible explanations. In this step it is possible to use theory to draw conclusions moving beyond the actual text, but making sure that the conclusions are not assimilated by superimposing theoretical concepts while losing case particularity.

Part III: Interactional analysis

In this part, the question to be answered is what happens to storylines in interaction. This part is most obviously relevant in research designs in which storylines are brought into actual dialogue, such as interview studies. When the audience is less clearly visible in the data, in for instance online research where written stories are submitted without researcher interference in the course of writing (by posing questions, for instance), the anticipation of audience perceptions and responses becomes more difficult to analyse but no less interesting.

Step 7: Positioning of storyline

In this step, the focus is on how storylines are positioned by storytellers/listeners in the interaction. (It is important to keep in mind the distinction between characters who operate at story level [Part II], storytellers who operate at the interactional level [Part III] and the 'persons of flesh and blood' whom we can only know indirectly through the stories they tell and how they appear as characters in them.) Questions to be asked are, for example: Which storylines are presented as taken for granted? Which storylines are told using a lot of arguments and apparently need to be accounted for? Which storylines do storytellers identify with and consider important and desirable, and which do they distance themselves from or construct as undesirable? It is important to address all storylines identified in Part II systematically, if only to state that this particular storyline did not receive much attention. A more fine-grained analysis (see, for example, the precarious emergence of a healthy living storyline in an interview dominated by illness; Sools, 2012) might reveal whether partial or novel storylines are emerging and are carefully negotiated, but do not become substantiated and subsequently disappear; or are picked up, encouraged and grow into fully fledged storylines.

Step 8: Positioning of storytellers/listeners
This step is concerned with the question of power. What is the role of the participants in the conversation and, in particular, who determines which storylines become established/dominant/desired and which disappear or are disqualified in the course of the conversation?

Step 9: Conclusion and discussion
Steps 7 and 8 can result in a conclusion and discussion of what is at stake for storytellers that might explain their positioning of storylines and of themselves/others. This step anchors the interpretation in relevant psychological, emotional, physical, social or moral realities and requires creative imagination substantiated by theory and/or sound argumentation.

Part IV: Identifying and describing relevant larger contexts

The aim of this part is to gain more insight by placing the narrative within the relevant wider context of stories in which individual stories are embedded. Researchers use different terms to refer to the wider context such as master narratives, dominant narratives, canonical narratives or local moral contexts.

Step 10: Positioning of storylines in the wider social, societal and political context
This might entail providing contextual explanations for your findings and connecting them to the literature. While the previous part stays largely within an *emic* perspective (participant driven; that is, privileging the meaning made relevant by storytellers, looking over their shoulders/through their eyes), the fourth part moves to a more *etic* (researcher and theory-driven) perspective. At this point researchers can opt for a more or less critical perspective in which they identify or distance themselves in differing degrees with the meaning-making of participants.

Part V: Comparative analysis

By comparing differences and commonalities between storylines of particular cases, plot types can be identified. Both storyline and plot refer to 'how events are connected into a meaningful whole'. However, the term 'plot type' indicates a more general story pattern, while the term 'storyline' refers to the particular way of connecting events and articulating meaning with words specific to one participant. Commonalities between storylines at the level of the breach are key markers for identifying an over-arching plot. In addition to the construction of plot types, the comparative part can result in overarching conclusions about interactional patterns, local moral contexts, and conclusions about self and identity, which might result in theory building. Perhaps the best-known example of a plot type in narrative psychology is the redemptive self plot, described by Dan McAdams (2008:20):

> **The redemptive self**
> In the beginning, I learn that I am blessed, even as others suffer. When I am still very young, I come to believe in a set of simple core values to guide me through a dangerous life terrain. As I move forward in life, many bad things come my way – sin, sickness, abuse, addiction, injustice, poverty, stagnation. But bad things often lead to good outcomes – my suffering is redeemed. Redemption comes to me in the form of atonement, recovery, emancipation, enlightenment, upward social mobility, and/or the actualization of my good inner self. As the plot unfolds, I continue to grow and progress. I bear fruit; I give back; I offer a unique contribution. I will make a happy ending, even in a threatening world.

Similar to the narrative summary in Step 5, attention is paid to the particular wordings of the storytellers, but now, instead of the particularity of individual storytellers, representatives of a certain group are central (in this case older, generative, religiously oriented Americans). Because the plot is representative of many stories by different people of a certain group, the order, the clarification of narrative causality and the use of perspective are made more generic while retaining narrative quality. In fact, the sub-division of form (atonement, recovery, emancipation, enlightenment, upward social mobility and/or the actualization of my good inner self) represents sub-plots that are less generic than the redemptive self plot but are already abstracted from individual cases.

Example: Abdullah's story of healthy living

This example works through each of the parts of the analysis detailed above. The aim is to give the student confidence in developing an understanding of narrative.

Part I: Introduction

■ 'How a man who was never in school, ends up speaking as master'

The interview with a person whom we will call Abdullah was conducted by Anneke (the second author of this chapter) in the context of a health-promotion project in the Netherlands (Sools, 2012; Mens-Verhulst & Bavel, 2005) that focused on lower-educated elderly Dutch and Dutch-Moroccan men and women. Abdullah is a Moroccan immigrant man belonging to the Tamazigh ethnic group. He was born in a small village in Morocco and has been living in Rotterdam for 34 years. He is married, a father of eight and a grandfather of three, and suffers from various health complaints such as heavy bronchitis, blocked blood vessels, painful feet and diabetes. At the time of the interview Anneke was 27 years old, highly educated, without children and in good health. The interview can be characterized as a communal attempt to bridge different worlds of meaning, in response to the research question regarding what healthy living means to Abdullah. A plurality of meanings, embedded in a variety of intersecting and coalescing contexts, come to the fore, which are very different from the health-promotion narrative involving getting regular exercise, not smoking, not drinking alcohol and eating healthy food. The interview took place in a public setting chosen by Abdullah (educational centre), which turned out to be surprisingly suited to one of the major themes in the interview, 'learning', his symbol for healthy living. The title formulated above refers to this symbol and will be explained in Part II. Abdullah takes his interviewee role very seriously, considering that he talked to several Moroccan elderly, including an imam (Muslim priest), in preparation for the interview. More generally, he positions himself as a group representative who talks 'not only about myself, but about what we experienced with our parents'.

Part II: Storyline analysis

■ 'Searching for a way to see myself fit with the environment'

Setting
Two settings serve as contrasting spaces. The first setting is talked about in the past tense. It is a rural area in Morocco that is 'closer to nature', which 'made it easier to live a healthy life' thanks to a long tradition of knowledge passed on between generations. Time in this setting is cyclical, following the change of seasons and the day–night cycle. Time is also slow. The second setting in which the story takes place is the present, which is described as 'fashionable', favouring greediness, consumerism and materialism. Time here is fast. This world is continuously changing 'from fashion to fashion'. In the background a third setting plays a role: a supernatural world in which time is eternal, with continuity instead of change.

Agent/character(s)
Abdullah's grandfather, who 'lived for 105 years, who actually received not more than one injection from the physician', serves as a role model beyond his reach. This vital old man has the benefit of a traditional way of living, in contrast to a 'young man of 40 years who merely complains' about his constant pains. The protagonist is unfortunately more like this young man, as Abdullah

confesses, 'I am 53 years old, but my feet hurt all the time'. This ill protagonist does not see himself 'fit in the environment'. This present, fashionable environment is inhabited by greedy, materialistically oriented consumers, 'people who want to keep up with what is fashionable'. An identity more favourable to the protagonist comes to the fore in the form of a human being with a purpose, whose existence on earth 'has to mean something'. This is a morally responsible agent who 'has been given understanding' about 'the difference between dark and light'. At the same time, this character is very much aware of (his) existential boundaries and thus of his own relative agency.

Acts/events

When the grandfather was ill, others took care of him by 'rubbing his body with olive oil, keeping him warm with a little piece of cloth'. Getting well was a slow process of recovery; however, it was 'never a problem'. The young, suffering man is presented as someone without action possibilities other than complaining. The consumers at first sight seem to have more action possibilities, but their efforts to keep up with fashion are questioned as a form of undesired or unrealistic social comparison: 'people look at each other too much. People just want the same in their lives on earth, and that is not so. That is not so.' The desired action is *looking* at 'the time ... what they *do* themselves. Everybody should look at himself.' Abdullah daily evaluates 'all he contributed and accomplished, and all that he received instead of focusing on what you were unable to get'. So he advocates the importance of conscious action and gratitude, thus establishing a more mutual relationship with the environment than consumerist action aimed uni-directionally at getting desired things from the environment.

Means/helpers

While the grandfather had (unspecified, presumably female) relatives to take care of him, the main cause of the young man's illness is the lack of 'food/vegetables that are left intact in their own shape' (that is, not modified to change the outer appearance, with known origins and harvested in their right time). The consumerist people surrounding him are characterized as aiming too high for their own good: 'how can someone without degree, without a job, without money drive a car?' Their preoccupation with 'this one thing' (affording a car) keeps them unhealthy. Patience, a change of temporal perspective and an alternative moral compass help the protagonist to resist the temptations of 'fashion'. At the same time these means further emphasize the lack of person–environment fit. The protagonist derives his strengths from (knowledge of) the eternal life/time that provides a clear moral compass and strong motivation to carry on his difficult task.

Purpose

The initial desired goal to reach very old age in good health contrasts with the actual situation of living 'in constant pain' from a young age onwards.

Consequently, undesired goals dominate the story and provide insight into the many challenges the protagonist faces. The overall purpose of the story is the establishment of an appropriate fit between Abdullah and his environment, without losing one's self and one's sense of place in life.

Breach

Initially, the protagonist is placed in a setting where he no longer fits with current environmental demands, resulting in poor *health*. The breach arises when he fails or refuses simply to accept this state of affairs. Consequently, an imbalance emerges between the setting and characters: the protagonist (with his morals, ideals, knowledge, goals and capacities) does not fit with the fashionable urban environment. This results in a fixed situation, in which no healthy outcome seems possible and his patience is put to the test. While partly this breach is bridged, an imbalance (or perpetual challenge) remains as a result of a difference between a healthy *time* (on earth, defined by one's actions: for example, taking care of your body, your self and others) and a healthy *life* (perfect health in the afterlife, envisioned as 'paradise').

Conclusion about identity, agency and healthy living

The protagonist of the story is partly presented as a victim of changing circumstances, who is out of necessity cut off from his roots and consequently suffers from daily (physical) pains. At the same time, he is presented as a strong, patient man, who struggles and succeeds in maintaining his moral standards at the expense of his physical, social and mental health. While he is presented as a person endowed with moral awareness, responsibility and the capacity to spend his earthly time in a healthy way, there are no guarantees that this will result in a healthy life; certainly not on earth, but hopefully in the afterlife.

Part III: Interactional analysis

Abdullah considers himself an actively religious man and presupposes that Anneke is secular, evidenced by his attempts throughout the interview to explain what living a religious life means. This turns out to be central to how he gives meaning to healthy living or bettering his current unhealthy life. Relevant to the interactional accomplishment of this explanatory account is a distancing of Abdullah from 'well educated but stupid' people, because 'reading little books does not teach you about people'. In this way, Abdullah positions himself as wise in life instead of illiterate and 'stupid'. Over the course of the interview he comes to acknowledge himself as a 'master' teaching his well-educated listener about healthy living, without, however, being arrogant about it. It is more a silent recognition, spoken hardly audibly, by a modest man, in interaction with someone who takes the position of a student willing to learn from him. The dynamics of an older man talking to a younger woman support the student positioning of Anneke and the master positioning of Abdullah.

Part IV: Analysis of wider contexts

The interview took place in 2004, two years after the murder of the populist politician Pim Fortuyn, and around the time of the war in Iraq and the aftermath of 9/11, the terrorist attack on New York's World Trade Center in 2001. Muslims have been under heavy attack in Dutch public debate for years, even more so in the city of Rotterdam, where more than half of the population is from non-western origin, including a large Muslim population. Therefore, much is at stake for Abdullah when talking about healthy living in a religious way. On one occasion he remarks that it would be better to postpone the project to a later, less politicized time. This detracts attention from the timeless truths that he brings to the fore. What is at stake is finding an answer to the predicament of the Muslim migrant who finds himself unfit for a (post)modern world, while countering claims from a highly politicized world in which religious answers, particularly from Islam, are under suspicion. Critically reviewing his answer, one might question the idea to wait for a better, less politicized time. In the meantime, Abdullah's story offers a way of life that partly aligns with health-promotion discourse (taking care of self and body), but also stretches the individualized health discourse (Lupton, 1995) to include care for others and the social inclusion of migrants.

Review of example: What Abdullah's story says about healthy living

In the example we can see how narrative (storyline) analysis can contribute to health psychology knowledge in several ways. First, personal accounts become *contextualized*. Narrative analysis does not aim for generalizable conclusions, but, rather, aims for contextualized results that allow for improvements relevant to specific contexts. At the same time, stories are highly particular and universally recognizable. This quality of stories allows for the transference of insights to other situations, people and groups based on plausibility rather than numbers. For instance, by invoking the political and societal context, we may come to recognize and understand Abdullah's very personal experience of healthy living as exemplary for other male, migrant, older people's religious experiences. In addition, we might wonder how these identity positions (gender, citizenship status, age and religion) intersect to produce this specific story. Narrative analysis contributes to intersectional analyses by carefully analyzing how in a particular story axes of difference intersect. Moreover, by contextualizing personal stories, narrative research is a way of widening the scope of behavior-oriented health-promotion research to include other dimensions of human existence.

Second, narrative research makes visible and understandable how health-promotion discourse is *lived or contested* in actual practice. Conservatively used, health promoters might come to see new ways of implementing behavioural and cognitive changes that are more in line with service users' perceptions, needs and wishes. The content of the message does not change, but the form does in order to make health services more effective. The more radical option, however, is to use narrative analysis for countering existing health practices; for instance, by foregrounding the importance of immigrant rights, sense of belonging and so on as equally or more important than exercising programmes. In this way, participatory methods are used not only instrumentally, but also to influence the content and agenda of health-promotion programmes.

Third, similar to qualitative research in general, new meanings can be constructed due to a bottom-up analysis strategy that follows the participant perspective. Narrative qualitative research adds to this the concept of *story as meaningful whole*, and pays close attention to the *particular wording* of participants. Instead of looking for distinct (though sometimes related) and abstracted themes across cases, all parts of the story are considered in relationship to a whole. This holistic knowledge sensitizes health promoters to the existence of a meaningful whole ('grammars of motive') quite different from what they know. Actions and words previously misunderstood or overlooked can now be noticed and acknowledged as part of living healthily. In addition, holistic knowledge reminds health promoters to see the relationships between seemingly disparate actions and meanings. In Abdullah's case, this could be sensitivity to different temporal orderings involved in living healthily (in the afterlife) and spending healthy time (on earth), with accompanying dilemmas and actions. While aiming for a healthy life might seem to be an act of blasphemy or simply impossible for Abdullah, focusing on how to spend a healthy time does make sense.

Fourth, narrative analysis focuses attention on *health as dilemmatic practice* and the moral and emotional issues at stake for the healthy and the ill. As such, narrative analysis is offered as an alternative to a rational, behavourial health model (Kleinman & Seeman, 2000). In Abdullah's case, we learn how he tries to balance the demands of three different environments, times and actions. There is no easy solution or way out of his dilemma of fitting in; rather, we come a little closer to understanding the complexities of his situation.

Uses of narrative for clinical and health psychology

Narrative psychology has been used to explore the character of different health experiences and encounters. Although this chapter focuses on the analysis of narrative accounts, there has been a surge of recent interest in how narrative theory can be used to guide therapeutic interventions. White and Epston (1990) developed a form of psychotherapy known as narrative therapy. They argued that not only were certain stories at the basis of the problems people experience, it was through reworking these stories that people can develop new strategies for living. As they argue:

> Persons experience problems for which they frequently seek therapy, when the narratives in which they are 'storying' their experience, and/or

in which they are having their experience 'storied' by others, do not sufficiently represent their lived experience, and that in these circumstances there will be significant aspects of their lived experience that contradict these dominant narratives. (White & Epston, 1990:14)

James Pennebaker has promoted the health benefits of writing short narratives as a therapeutic tool. He and his colleagues (e.g. Pennebaker & Seagal, 1999) have shown that people who are provided with the opportunity to write about important personal experiences show improvements in physical and mental health. The initial research in this field has provoked a large amount of research to replicate and extend the findings, with greater and lesser success. Two examples are given in Table 9.1. The first, by Bernard et al. (2006), found that those clients who had the opportunity to write short narratives about their first psychotic episode showed less severity of post-traumatic stress disorder. The second, by Adler et al. (2013), found that clients who were given the opportunity to write personal narratives prior to and during psychotherapy were more likely to show sudden gains in that psychotherapy. Careful coding of the written narratives found that two narrative meaning-making processes – processing and coherence – were most predictive of benefits.

In the area of health psychology, narrative has been used as a means of promoting various health behavior changes. Two examples are given in Table 9.1. The first, by Janssen et al. (2012), was on the impact of narrative communication on sun-bed risk assessment. In this case, the narrative communication consisted of a personal testimonial about the risks of sun-bed usage. People who received this message were more likely to have imagination and feelings of cancer risk associated with sun-bed usage than those who received a more

Table 9.1 Narrative and clinical and health psychology

Researchers	Clients	Intervention	Impact
Bernard et al. (2006)	Receiving treatment for PTSD	Write about psychotic experience	Less severity of PTSD
Adler et al. (2013)	General psychotherapy	Write narrative accounts	More sudden gains in psychotherapy
Janssen et al. (2012)	Sun-bed use	Narrative and non-narrative health information about risks of sun-bed usage	Narrative communication promoted greater perceptions of cancer risk
McQueen et al. (2011)	African American women	Narrative and non-narrative information about breast cancer	Narrative information promoted more positive and negative affect

factual risk information message. The second study, by McQueen et al. (2011), explored the impact on a sample of African American women of viewing either a narrative message about breast cancer or a standard informational message. They found that the narrative message had both positive and negative effects on the women's attitudes to and beliefs about cancer.

Concluding comments

In this chapter we have summarized the background to the study of narrative in clinical and health psychology, proceeded to detail an approach to both collecting and analysing narratives, given an example of narrative analysis of a personal story derived from an interview study in the area of health promotion, and finished with a few examples of the use of narrative in different clinical and health settings. The storyline analysis that we detailed can be used with different kinds of data, narrative or otherwise. As we noted at the outset, these guidelines should not be used in a prescriptive manner, but are more an introductory guide to enable the researcher to begin to enter into the narratives and see how they are structured. As researchers gain in experience, they can bring in ideas from their wider reading to begin to interpret the particular narratives more forcefully and develop a more sophisticated understanding of them. The use of narrative in health settings is a new and exciting area that provides opportunities for both active clinicians and researchers.

Further reading

McAdams, D.P. (1993). *The Stories We Live By: Personal Myths and the Making of the Self*. New York: Guilford Press.

Mishler, E.G. (1986). *Research Interviewing: Context and Narrative*. Cambridge, MA: Harvard University Press.

Riessman, C.K. (2008). *Narrative Methods for the Human Sciences*. Thousand Oaks, CA: Sage.

References

Adler, J.M., Harmeling, L.H. & Walder-Biesanz, I. (2013). Narrative meaning making is associated with sudden gains in psychotherapy clients' mental health under routine clinical conditions. *Journal of Consulting and Clinical Psychology*, *81*, 839–845.

Andrews, M., Squire, C. & Tamboukou, M. (2013). *Doing Narrative Analysis*. London: Sage.

Bamberg, G.W. (1997). Positioning between structure and performance. *Journal of Narrative and Life History*, *7*, 335–342.

Bamberg, M. (2006). Stories: Big or small: Why do we care? *Narrative Inquiry*, *16*, 139–147.

Bartlett, F.C. (1932). *Remembering: A Study in Experimental and Social Psychology.* Cambridge: Cambridge University Press.

Bernard, M., Jackson, C. & Jones, C. (2006). Written emotional disclosure following first episode psychotic effects on symptoms of post-traumatic stress disorder. *British Journal of Clinical Psychology, 45,* 403–414.

Bold, C. (2012). *Using Narrative in Research.* London: Sage.

Brooks, P. (1994). *Psychoanalysis and Storytelling.* Oxford: Blackwell.

Bruner, J. (1986). *Actual Minds: Possible Worlds.* Cambridge, MA: Harvard University Press.

Burke, K. (1952). *A Rhetoric of Motives.* New York: Prentice Hall.

Burke, K. (1969[1945]). *A Grammar of Motives.* Berkeley: University of California Press.

De Fina, A. & Georgakopoulou, A. (2012). *Analyzing Narrative: Discourse and Sociolinguistic Perspectives.* Cambridge: Cambridge University Press.

Flick, U. (2009). *An Introduction to Qualitative Research* (4th edn). London: Sage.

Frank, A. (1995). *The Wounded Storyteller: Body, Illness and Ethics.* Chicago, IL: University of Chicago Press.

Freeman, M. (1993). *Rewriting the Self: History, Memory, Narrative.* London: Routledge.

Georgakopoulou, A. (2006). Thinking big about small stories in narrative and identity analysis. *Narrative Inquiry, 16,* 122–130.

Gergen, K.J. & Gergen, M. (1986). Narrative form and the construction of psychological science. In T.R. Sarbin (ed.), *Narrative Psychology: The Storied Nature of Human Conduct* (pp. 3–21). New York: Praeger.

Hammack, P.L. (2010). The cultural psychology of Palestinian youth: A narrative approach. *Culture & Psychology, 16,* 507–537.

Heider, F. & Simmel, M. (1944). An experimental study of apparent behavior. *American Journal of Psychology, 57,* 243–249.

James, W. (1893). *The Principles of Psychology.* New York: Dover.

Janssen, E., van Osch, L., de Vries, H. & Lechner, L. (2012). The influence of narrative risk communication on feelings of cancer risk. *British Journal of Health Psychology, 18,* 407–419.

Kleinman, A. & Seeman, D. (2000). Personal experience of illness. In G. Albrecht, R. Fitzpatrick & S.C. Scrimshaw (eds), *The Handbook of Social Studies in Health and Medicine* (pp. 230–242). Thousand Oaks, CA: Sage.

Lupton, D. (1995). *The Imperative of Health: Public Health and the Regulated Body.* London: Sage.

McAdams, D. (1993). *The Stories We Live By: Personal Myths and the Making of the Self.* New York: Guilford Press.

McAdams, D. (1995). *The Life Story Interview* (revd edn). Evanston, IL: Department of Psychology, Northwestern University.

McAdams, D. (2008). American Identity: The Redemptive Self. *The General Psychologist, 43*(1), 20–27.

McQueen, A., Kreuter, M.W., Kalesan, B. & Alcaraz, K.I. (2011). Understanding narrative effects: The impact of cancer survivor stories on message processing, attitudes and beliefs among African American women. *Health Psychology, 30,* 674–682.

Mens-Verhulst, J. van & Bavel, M. van (2005). Beyond the life style approach: The role of femininity codes in aspiring for healthy living. A comparison of Moroccan migrant and Dutch women in the Netherlands. Paper for the *Gender and Health* conference, Tallinn, 15 April.

Mishler, E. (1986). *Research Interviewing: Context and Narrative*. Cambridge, MA: Harvard University Press.

Murray, M. (1999). The storied nature of health and illness. In M. Murray & K. Chamberlain (eds.), *Qualitative Psychology: Theories and Methods* (pp. 47–63). London: Sage.

Murray, M. (2000). Levels of narrative analysis in health psychology. *Journal of Health Psychology*, 5, 337–348.

Murray, M. (2002). Connecting narrative and social representation theory in health research. *Social Science Information*, 41, 653–673.

Pennebaker, J.W. & Seagal, J.D. (1999). Forming a story: The health benefits of narrative. *Journal of Clinical Psychology*, 55, 1243–1254.

Polkinghorne, D.E. (1988). *Narrative Knowing and the Human Sciences*. Albany, NY: SUNY Press.

Ricoeur, P. (1984). *Time and Narrative*. Chicago, IL: University of Chicago Press.

Ricoeur, P. (1997). A response by Paul Ricoeur. In M. Joy (ed.), *Paul Ricoeur and Narrative: Context and Contestation* (pp. 1–12). Calgary: University of Calgary Press.

Riessman, C.K. (2008). *Narrative Methods for the Human Sciences*. Los Angeles, CA: Sage.

Sarbin, T.R. (ed) (1986a). *Narrative Psychology: The Storied Nature of Human Conduct*. New York: Praeger.

Sarbin, T.R. (1986b). The narrative as a root metaphor for psychology. In T.R. Sarbin (ed.), *Narrative Psychology: The Storied Nature of Human Conduct* (pp. 3–21). New York: Praeger.

Schuman, H. (1982). Artifacts are in the mind of the beholder. *American Sociologist*, 17, 21–28.

Sools, A. (2010). *De ontwikkeling van narratieve competentie: Bijdrage aan een onderzoeksmethodologie voor de bestudering van gezond leven [The Development of Narrative Competence: Towards a Research Methodology for the Study of Healthy Living]*. The Hague: Albani.

Sools, A. (2012). Narrative health research: Exploring big and small stories as analytical tools. *Health*, 17(1), 93–101.

Sools, A. (2013). 'There is a right time for every need and feeling': A narrative analysis of resilience processes. Paper presented at the *ARPH* conference, 1 February, Enschede.

Sools, A. & Schuhmann, C. (2014). Theorizing the narrative dimension of psychotherapy and counseling: A big and small story approach. *Journal of Contemporary Psychotherapy*. doi: 10.1007/s10879-014-9260-5 (online first).

Stephens, C. (2011) Narrative analysis in health psychology research: Personal, dialogical and social stories of health. *Health Psychology Review*, 5, 62–78.

Wengraf, T. (2001). *Qualitative Research Interviewing*. London: Sage.

White, M. & Epston, D. (1990). *Narrative Means to Therapeutic Ends*. London: Norton.

Phenomenological Psychology

Michael Larkin

10

Phenomenology is a philosophical domain concerned with understanding the meaning and quality of experience and existence. It might be helpful to think of it as a body of knowledge that is concerned with understanding the 'phenomenon of being human'. I am going to use the word phenomenology to refer to this 'body of knowledge' and to the philosophical dialogue that produces it. Sometimes phenomenology is used by psychologists as a noun that works as a substitute for 'subjective experience'; for example, 'What is the phenomenology of that cognitive process?' I will avoid that usage here, because it is confusing.

Phenomenological philosophers are often engaged in two parallel forms of inquiry. One of these is concerned with 'what' questions – for example, what is the nature of our being and what is the nature of our relationship to the world? The other form is concerned with matters of 'how' – that is, how can we best engage with and answer these questions?

Phenomenological psychology is a strand of psychology that is concerned with developing and applying the ideas generated by phenomenological philosophers in the psychological domain. It has tended to draw on both aspects of phenomenology; that is, both 'What is it like?' and 'How can we make sense of it?'. The former provides an epistemological focus which distinguishes phenomenological approaches from others, and the latter provides a conceptual and methodological repertoire from which researchers may draw.

Historical background

Phenomenology has a long-established relationship with psychology. Many of the concerns and curiosities of the major phenomenological philosophers are focused on issues that psychologists will recognize: how we recognize and employ objects and tools; how we perceive the world; how we relate to others; how our embodied state shapes our subjective experience; what matters to us and motivates us; what consciousness is. The work conducted and inspired by phenomenological philosophy's key figures (in chronological order, these are

155

Edmund Husserl, Martin Heidegger and Maurice Merleau-Ponty) addresses these questions at a conceptual level. However, there are complications. For the most part, phenomenological philosophy was not produced with psychologists' methodological requirements in mind. Sometimes it has been developed with the aim of shaping psychology's conceptual domain – certainly this is present in some of Husserl's work, and much of Merleau-Ponty's. However, phenomenological philosophy does not provide us with a single, coherent solution to the problems with which it engages. Instead, it presents us with a complex dialogue about these problems, and introduces us to a range of specialist concepts and methods for exploring them (more on this later in this chapter). Thankfully, there *are* many threads of work within the tradition of phenomenological philosophy that can be very helpful in this translational activity. A diverse range of writers (e.g. Edith Stein, Ludwig Binswanger, Alfred Shutz, Paul Ricoeur, Hubert Dreyfus, Don Ihde, Sean Gallagher) have produced work exploring various aspects of the more practical implications of phenomenological philosophy. Some of this translational work is broadly methodological (e.g. Ricoeur's work on interpretation) and some is implicitly psychological (e.g. Stein's work on empathy), but the task of elucidating the implications of phenomenological philosophy for psychological methods has largely been left to psychologists themselves.

As a consequence, the history of phenomenology's relationship with psychology can be characterized as a process of translation, adaptation and interpretation. In this chapter, I focus on some of the ways in which phenomenological philosophy has been translated, adapted and interpreted for use in recent *qualitative* psychological research, although it is worth noting that phenomenology has been influential on experimental psychology too (e.g. see Larkin et al., 2011).

Conceptual framework and implications for design

Phenomenological psychology is now a broad field and there are a number of established approaches to the research process (for a concise and insightful overview, see Finlay, 2009). What they tend to have in common is a primary concern with 'third-person' data. That is, the research strategies which they advocate do tend to assume that researchers will be interested in understanding *someone else's* experience; though this does not necessarily rule out the usefulness of one's own experiences, as a source of either reflection or interpretation. While the 'someone else' is typically a research participant, there have also been attempts to develop phenomenological analyses of other data sources (e.g. literary accounts). The experience of the participant is typically accessed via a verbal account, although sometimes this may be supplemented or enhanced through the use of other forms of data (e.g. visual expressions; researcher's reflections; written accounts). This would often take the form of an open-ended, semi-structured, one-to-one interview (or series of interviews) between the researcher and their respondents (e.g. see Kvale & Brinkmann, 2008).

The 'open-minded' stance of the researcher in this scenario is important. Researchers in phenomenological psychology tend to be interested in describing and understanding experiences and their contexts (i.e. processes, events and relationships in the 'lifeworld' of the person) from the *point of view* of the person experiencing them. This requires a willingness to take an 'inside perspective' and to set aside, as best one can, one's own preconceptions and values. Therefore, a unifying feature of phenomenological psychology is that it is concerned with understanding experiences as they present themselves to (or as they are rendered meaningful by) the person who is engaged in them.

Key concepts

Phenomenological writing is conceptually rich. Interested readers may wish to explore the opening chapters of books by Langdridge (2006) and Smith et al. (2009) before moving on to more primary sources. By way of introduction, however, here are three key 'bundles' of concepts which are important to most phenomenological work. As you will see, they have overlapping concerns.

Directedness, relatedness, intersubjectivity

One key concept, reflected in each of the terms 'directedness, relatedness and intersubjectivity' is concerned with capturing the relationship between person and world. It began its life as 'intentionality', in the foundational phenomenological work of Brentano and then Husserl. Intentionality describes a core quality of human consciousness, which can best be described as the 'aboutness' of our consciousness. Consciousness is consciousness *of* something. While the later phenomenologists (Heidegger and Merleau-Ponty) moved away from talking about consciousness per se, their writing retained a commitment to this aboutness – in the form of an interest in the 'directed' and 'related' aspects of human Being (e.g. see Larkin et al., 2011). Thus, when phenomenologists think of 'a person', they do not think of a discrete individual, with a pychological reality that is contained in an exclusively internal location (such as 'in the head'). Instead, they consider a *being-in-the-world*: someone who is always, inevitably, immersed in a network of relationships with objects, events, processes, environments and other people. These are 'things that matter' to the person (cares, concerns). When we use phenomenological psychology to explore a person's 'experience', we are not tapping directly into some sort of internal reality. Instead, we are exploring *their relationship to* the things which matter to them; or, to put it another way, we are interested in how the world takes on meaning through a person's engagement with it.

The lifeworld and its context

We can extend this a little further with the concept of the 'lifeworld' (for a more detailed introduction, see Ashworth, 2003). The lifeworld is the world as it appears from the perspective of a given person. Our lifeworlds overlap with one another at many points, but they also have a uniquely perspectival quality to them. For example, from my own stance, my lifeworld and my son's lifeworld contain many of the same 'objects of concern', but also some different ones. And in many profound ways, our respective views of these shared objects of concern differ greatly. Our experience of *time*, to take one example, means completely different things to each of us, although it exists as a real and significant thing for both of us.

There is a contextual dimension to this too – the lifeworld is embedded in the language and practices of our cultures. For phenomenological psychologists drawing primarily on the work of Husserl (e.g. Giorgi, 1995), the purpose of phenomenology is to *describe* the essential and abstractable features of a given experience. So in this instance, the specifics of context would have to be *transcended* by the researcher's analysis. However, for phenomenological psychologists drawing on the work of the more *interpretative* phase of phenomenology, as characterized by the hermeneutic phenomenology of Heidegger and Merleau-Ponty (e.g. Smith et al., 2009), context cannot be stripped. Instead, it is seen as a fundamental part of the lifeworld itself. In that instance, a successful analysis is *grounded* in context.

Situated embodiment

While Heidegger emphasizes the inevitable *worldliness* of our being (the sense in which it is inextricable from context: things, people, language and so on), Merleau-Ponty emphasizes the inevitably *embodied* aspects of our being. Thus, the perspectival quality of our relationship to the lifeworld – our 'situatedness' – is embodied. Merleau-Ponty argues that our existence as 'body-subjects' shapes our knowledge of the world. Phenomenological psychology is often attuned to this aspect of human existence, whether through data-collection methods that prompt reflection on embodied sensations, feelings, emotions and moods, or through analyses that attend closely to these features in participants' accounts (e.g. Boden & Eatough, 2014).

Uses for clinical and health psychology

Phenomenological research methods are widely used in applied psychology, particularly in health and clinical psychology. I have already mentioned in passing that one way of considering the differences *between* phenomenological approaches in psychology is to consider the distinctiveness of *descriptive* and *interpretative* approaches. These stances may often overlap (for instance, some approaches may take a 'both/and' position rather than an 'either/or' one). Certainly, both stances share a core concern with understanding the perspective of their respondents, and thus both provide – at a minimum – the option of 'giving voice' to a particular experience. Thus, many applied studies involve exploring other people's perspectives on important events (e.g. illnesses) and processes (e.g. interventions). Phenomenology provides researchers with a rich array of lenses through which to explore these perspectives, a way of 'seeing the world differently'.

Applied phenomenological research often reveals a gap between what is assumed (about a symptom or intervention, for example) and what meaning it actually has for the people concerned. Having opened up this 'gap', researchers working in the interpretative phenomenological tradition have the further option of developing a more explicit critique. This may be achieved through interpretations of language, narrative, metaphor, interpersonal context, or embodiment, but will retain a chain of connection to the participants' claims and concerns. In this respect, the interpretative phenomenological researcher uses experience as a *lever* for critique.

Phenomenological methods can be used to explore the meaning of any experience that is salient for the participant, in any situation where the participant is able to express those meanings. Thus, they work very well as exploratory methods in the early stage of research programs (for example, for theory development and hypothesis generation). They can also work well in helping to answer process questions arising from evaluative mixed-methods studies (for instance, while quantitative methods may be used to assess intervention outcomes, phenomenological methods may help us to understand processes and mechanisms, such as whether the intervention is acceptable, psychologically meaningful, personally sustainable and so on). As the point about critique should illustrate, they can be a useful way of exploring our assumptions about situations which have been studied extensively using more 'top-down' approaches, or exploring the experiential consequences of particular contexts (institutions, systems or relationships).

Introduction to interpretative phenomenological analysis

In the remainder of this chapter, I am going to present an example of a piece of research that applies one of the more interpretative approaches in phenomenological psychology (as above) to an exploration of the meaning of the experience of addiction, in the context of a 12-Step recovery programme (this account is developed from Larkin, 2001). Having presented the account, I will then describe the processes that produced it.

Interpretative phenomenological analysis (IPA; Smith et al., 2009) is an example of a phenomenological approach which has been used very widely in health (e.g. see Smith, 2011) and clinical (e.g. see Harper, 2012) psychology, and, increasingly, in psychology more generally (Hefferon & Gil-Rodriguez, 2011). IPA has an interpretative (aka hermeneutic) phenomenological epistemology. It also has a commitment to an idiographic level of analysis. Idiography indicates a focus on the *particular*, which here means both 'a particular experience in a particular context' and also that the reader should be given a sense of the individual voices within any analysis of a group's experiences.

In IPA research, we are interested in identifying what *matters* to participants, and then exploring what these things *mean* to participants, given their context and our own interest. The former is rather like 'mapping out' the life-world, while the latter is concerned with making sense of the terrain. Once we have developed a detailed, data-derived understanding of these things, we can organize and present an interpretative overview of our analytic work.

The subjective experience of loss of control

Context

This research took place at a privately run recovery centre for the treatment of people with addictive behaviour problems. The centre had outpatient psychiatric hospital status, its own dispensary, and a number of full-time nursing, counselling and administrative staff (for more details, see Larkin & Griffiths, 2002). Treatment at this centre was based on the 12-Step (or Minnesota) model, which is best known as the ethos of Alcoholics Anonymous (e.g. see Cain, 1991).

The model provides 12-Steppers with a specific understanding of addiction and of people who become 'addicts'. For example:

> Within the recovery centre, 'addiction' was understood generally as a pernicious disease. This disease was not restricted to substance use, and was understood to be inherent and genetic to 'addicts.' The disease is expressed as an unhealthy relationship with a reward-related behaviour, identifiable because they use it (or 'it uses them') as a means of avoiding or controlling deeper personal, emotional and relational problems. In this context, the experiences of 'addicts' were seen to be distinct from 'normal' experiences of risk-taking, of overindulgence, or of dependence behaviours. (Larkin & Griffiths, 2002:287)

Sample

The centre took self-referrals and health service referrals from GPs. At the time of the study, there were people residing in the centre seeking help for a range of chemical (e.g. alcohol, prescription drugs, illegal drugs) and behavioural (e.g. sex, gambling, eating disorders) difficulties, all of which were appetitive (Orford, 2002) and associated with a perceived lack of impulse control. Many of the patients were paying for their stay, and thus the sample was skewed towards the higher end of the socioeconomic spectrum, though not exclusively so.

Data collection

In this chapter, I will be reporting on some of the analytic outcomes from a series of open-ended, one-to-one interviews that I conducted with 13 of the patients. The interview schedule was concerned with exploring the person's understanding of their difficulties, and their experiences of the recovery process, and of the 12-Step programme. It was applied very flexibly, as is often

---

Box 10.1   Analytic structure

The subjective experience of loss of control
1. **Addiction as paradox**
    1a. Persisting long after the pleasure has gone.
    1b. Persisting even when the costs are clear.

2. **Acting without agency**

3. **Locked into a cyclical pattern**

---

the case in IPA research (see Smith et al., 2009), and the structure of each interview was largely determined by the concerns of the respondents.

Analysis
The complete analysis of these data is provided in Larkin (2001). For our purposes here, I have selected a single superordinate cluster, 'The subjective experience of loss of control', encompassing three major themes; see Box 10.1. I am presenting it *before* I describe the process of IPA work so that you can get a feel for the pitch and scope of this sort of work, and can then bring this understanding to your reading of a methodological account.

1. Addiction as paradox.
1a. Persisting long after the pleasure has gone.
1b. Persisting even when the costs are clear.

Addiction was clearly understood by the interview respondents as a paradoxical activity, and this paradox was experienced as a source of conflict. We might well expect this: it seems fundamental to the meaning of 'addiction' as a problem. However, it is interesting to explore the experiential meaning of this paradox.

Addiction was paradoxical for the respondents in one of two ways. Firstly, in some cases it was paradoxical because the participants found themselves engaging in their activities beyond the point at which they had once been pleasurable (that is, there was a *loss* of positive consequences). An extract from Frank's interview provides an example:

> I was in the office and I had been drinking– but I don't know why – I was very, very tired, and quite worried about one or two things [...] If I'm in good form, you can give me three bottles of whisky and hardly make me– you won't even know– well certainly on a bottle [...] You wouldn't know I'm pissed. Er and I just– I just felt myself going – I could feel myself going, and I said to my secretary, 'Get me in somewhere.'

> Then I think I passed out – I don't quite know what happened – and I
> found myself in here the next morning. And that's really the story of it–
> but I knew I– it was my final cry for help. I realised erm I couldn't cope
> any longer. [...] And realised I couldn't win it. I just wasn't winning it–
> just craving for it. (Frank)

Thus, in this example, Frank describes a point at which there appear to be no
remaining positive consequences to his drinking ('You wouldn't know I'm
pissed'), a point at which he is no longer able to disguise or control his drinking ('I could feel myself going') and a point at which he is 'just craving' alcohol. This craving, he subsequently reveals, has progressed despite the fact that
he actually 'didn't like the drink' any more.

Secondly, addiction was also seen to be paradoxical because, in other cases,
respondents had identified the negative consequences of their activities as having become unacceptably excessive, but had also found that they were unable
to give up their activities *despite* this insight. That is, the acquisition of clear
negative consequences was not sufficient to enable them to change their behaviours. An excerpt from George's transcript illustrates this:

> I started stopping drinking last year. Did it myself, went abroad, went to
> effectively a health farm, came out of that [...] I thought I'd sorted out
> most of the general problems I had – which were mainly financial, work
> etc. etc. [...] Sorted them all out. Thought everything was going
> absolutely fine – then relapsed completely, so I realised that there was
> something– there was something other than erm– there was something
> that I could– was obviously not capable of fixing myself without some
> form of help. (George)

Here, George describes his mystification on discovering that, despite attempting to take control of the situation and minimize the negative consequences of
his drinking (euphemistically described as 'general problems') in a rational
manner, he did not appear to be able to prevent himself from binge-drinking.

Both of these examples illustrate aspects of another of the primary phenomenological features of the addiction. This is what we might summarize as the
experience of an appetitive behaviour which is 'out of control'. That is, it is not
only paradoxical – it is also, in an important subjective sense, non-volitional.

2. Acting without agency

For the participants, the paradoxical element of addiction is connected to a
subjective experience of engagement in the activity as non-volitional. This is
unsurprising, and logical: otherwise, we might assume that one *would* simply
'stop'. Interestingly, in the respondents' accounts, agency for engagement in
the activity, and insight into its effects, are often denied or removed at some
point. Beyond such a point, the activity can then be understood and presented as 'addiction'. For example, Christopher had come to understand that, at

some point, his actions suddenly became 'out of control'. He described how this loss of control arose partly through an attempted return to moderate drinking, and partly how it was then amplified by his response to his girl-friend's disapproval:

> R: That [period of abstinence] lasted about 9 or 10 months and then I hit a downer erm for no particular reason– but I started going out with a girl– as far as I knew– that's not quite– having a bit of wine, with a huge amount of water – quite genuinely for the taste
> I: *Yeah*
> R: I think I was taking crack mixed with smack about 2 weeks later (LAUGHS)
> I: *Oh God! That's pretty rapid!*
> R: And then of course she booted me, which gave me the full excuse to really go to town. (Christopher)

We can see here that Christopher's shifts from sobriety into addiction are accompanied in his reconstruction by a subtle disappearance of agency. In the first shift – from drinking weakly-diluted wine to taking 'crack mixed with smack' – there is no rationalization at all. No decision is offered: the listener is simply asked to understand the story as a humorous case of the 'one thing led to another' narrative taken to its most extreme conclusion. In the second shift, there *is* a rationalization ('she booted me'), but this is used reflectively, as if to suggest that, at the time, Christopher had little choice but to respond by 'really going to town'. Agency evaporates under the microscope here, pre-cisely *because* addictive behaviours seem so paradoxical: how might one make sense of one's actions in such situations, unless one situates agency elsewhere?

In 12-Step, the real self and the addict self (or more simply, 'the addiction') are distinct. The addict self is powerful and appetitive. The real self is vulner-able when emotional, and vulnerable when complacent, and, thus, easily usurped. This dualism allows agency for paradoxical actions to be located out-side the person, either in a pathological 'other' (the powerful *inevitability* of the claim 'I was taking crack mixed with smack two weeks later' actually belongs to the implied 'addict' rather than to Christopher) or in the unstop-pable force of unwanted emotions ('she booted me'). In the participants' inter-views, non-volitional action is generally understood as emotional and/or pathological, rather than as contextual. Thus, the excerpt from Christopher provides examples of both types of non-volitional decision-making, and also of his retrospective recognition of it.

To expand further, descriptions of *emotional decisions* were utilized by respondents in ways that appeared to separate persons from their actions. Emotions are important objects of concern in most contexts, of course, and here they were clearly understood to be powerful forces (also see Rull, 2002). Relationships are also often implicated in *emotional decisions* across the inter-views. This is usually either because relationships are thought to be a source of 'difficult emotions' or because they are understood to require the 'open and authentic expression' of emotion. So, for example, Katy considered the cycle of her addiction to be a logical consequence of an emotional predicament, with its origins in her troubled relationship with her parents:

> I have always had the blame for everything, always. And of course Dad always told me that her drinking got worse because I was always out. [...] And I don't know, but anyway I had more and more blame, and the more and more blame I had, the more and more guilt I felt, the more I use [...] Vicious circle. (Katy)

Thus, relationship difficulties are understood, by Katy and many other respondents, to provide a rationale that explains, or justifies, future emotional decisions (that is, non-volitional actions). It is worth noting that this is an aspect of the relatedness of our experiences. As we have seen in the introduction to this chapter, 'relatedness' is an important feature of phenomenological psychology. And as is evident here, this is not just important for phenomenologists on purely theoretical grounds; it is because the things that matter to people are features of their relationship to the world, and particularly to other people. In this study, relatedness is especially important in terms of relationship difficulties and the threat or reality of relationships ending. The following excerpt from Paul provides an example of how breakdown in a relationship was experienced as leading to emotional decisions:

> I: *At what point did you start to care then, do you think?*
> R: Ooofff! That's a good one that. About– eight (PAUSE) – about ten weeks ago. My girlfriend left me. I didn't– I just– I couldn't see it coming. [...] I thought things were going smooth and– great. And she left me and I got a phone call saying, 'I ain't coming back until you stop.' And me head was well and truly scattered – really bad. So I started using more – and more – and it just wasn't working [...] Got a bottle of sleeping tablets. Took the lot. Injected a major load of heroin. Collapsed in somebody's house. (Paul)

Here we can see both Paul's abdication of agency ('me head was well and truly scattered' – that is, not a 'rational' decision) and his failed attempt to control or escape the uncomfortable emotions stemming from relationship breakdown ('it just wasn't working'). Although there is an 'I' here, to 'start using more', the agency of that 'I' is effectively disabled (in the last four sentences) by Paul's emotional response to the departure of his girlfriend.

A related strategy, the *pathological decision*, seems to function in a similar manner to the emotional decision. With the pathological decision, however, the dualism is even more overt. Here, agency for the paradoxical action is owned by 'the addict' as an independent entity – a pathological manifestation of the person. For example:

The bulimia never made me feel very good. The bulimia I thought– I remember thinking once, I'll spend the night with my best friend tonight, you know – my bulimia. The only person– it was the only thing I really felt controlled of– in control of. (Jos)

As suggested above, these non-volitional strategies can *both* be connected to dualism (between addict and self, control and self, or emotions and self), but the pathological option is more overtly dualistic.

3. Locked into a cyclical pattern

Collectively, the participants provided an exhaustive catalogue of emotions which they felt to be implicated in their various activities, in the manner described as 'emotional decisions'. In the context of 12-Step, they had come to understand these emotional experiences as the precipitates of their addictions. Most of them were negative, such as guilt, shame, embarrassment, humiliation, disgust, anger. However, the respondents also identified some dangerous positive emotions (which were understood as risky because of their association with complacency), such as success, happiness, completion. For example:

And the great thing about it– or *terrible* thing about it, is that you build your– you build very high, get up very high again, because all your creativity comes back etc. etc. etc. You reach somewhere and then whatever happens, whatever the trigger is, you simply erm go into erm a sort of self-destruct mode – exponential self-destruction. Of– of everything. And then you very quickly – as I say, its exponential – it starts and then all of a sudden you're in warp drive [...] And within two or three weeks you can have blown everything else out of the water – marriages, career, blah blah blah. (George)

For George, success and complacency are key triggers for his out-of-control drinking. However, there are two other emotions in particular – guilt and shame – which were understood to be especially important to the experience of addiction by most of the respondents. This is because guilt and shame are strongly implicated in the non-volitional experience of addiction as a 'cycle of use'. George captures the inevitable, circular progression of this experience as it is typically framed by 12-Step and the respondents:

Eventually it begins to slowly catch up with you, and you– and then you drink more and things begin– and then you begin– *isolation* and you begin to sort– try and sort things out – yourself and in your head – and as you're basically flawed anyway, you're not using family and friends anymore so that your chances of failing [...] get more and more and more, and eventually its just a sort of– like Venn diagrams closing in on each other – *enclosing* – [...] You end up with just yourself [LAUGHS] on a park bench. (George)

There does seem to be a clear connection between George's understanding of his problems and the cyclical understanding of addiction utilized in 12-Step. As we can see above, in the 'cycle', inappropriate actions originate in emotional decisions, and then, because they are paradoxical and are recognized as *inappropriate*, they give rise to strong feelings of guilt, shame, humiliation, disgust, and so on. In order to control or escape these emotions, further engagement in the activity then ensues. Essentially, this account of addiction offers 'addicts' a moral model of their behaviour: if they do not *accept* the moral judgement of their emotionally-inappropriate actions, then their prospects, within the 12-Step framework, are bleak.

In 12-Step, relapse is often described as a 'slippery slope'. Participants in the study frequently stated that any relapse would be worse than the last, as if this were a self-evident truism. There is clearly some danger that the therapeutic ideology may be the source of a self-fulfilling prophecy. Within the recovery centre, the main consequence of this belief in exponentially-severe relapses was seen to be its function as an incentive for *avoiding* relapse. In this context, relapse is to be avoided by adherence to the recovery programme and by close contact with others (and the recovery peer group, in particular). This is fine so far as it goes (or for those to whom it applies positively), but the success of this strategy is not borne out by the participants' accounts, which are littered with relapse stories.

The case of the 'cycle of addiction' demonstrates that the various representations of non-volitional action presented here have to be understood in the context of 12-Step's own framework for making sense of addiction, which must inform the participants' understandings of their experiences to some extent. The centre's own perspective on addiction is very clear: 'All addictions seem to serve the same purpose. This is to anaesthetise our feeling' (from the centre's promotional material). Thus, addiction is understood to be a disease in which emotions are suppressed or evaded – rather than given 'honest' expression – by means of inappropriate engagement in mood-modifying activities. The problem of recovery, in 12-Step terms, is thus how to reclaim and deal with these emotions in more appropriate ways: 'The real difficulty, as with other addictions, is with being able to cope with the feelings that come up once we are "clean"' (from the centre's promotional material).

This understanding of addiction was common in the interviews, but it is obviously difficult to estimate the extent to which it has been 'acquired from' the centre itself. Some participants – Edward, Paul, Frank – *do* offer accounts of their experiences which indicate that emotional suppression and repression *had* been important in the development of their problems, *despite* the fact that they themselves appeared to lack insight into this connection at the time of the interview. This certainly suggests that emotional experiences are important in the transition to problematic use, but there is a problem with this narrow, intra-individual explanation for addiction as an 'emotional disease'. In 12-Step, the symptoms of the disease of 'addiction' are emotional and pathological, so these are the meaningful sources of non-volitional acts – not contextual and relational issues. This may be why Jenny, for example, does not place more emphasis on her childhood abuse as an explanation for her current problems:

> And I was just– I don't think I ever looked anyone in the eye, I was so scared and so depressed. Erm I think it took weeks, I don't know, I was so in denial that when I did my Step One, I did my Step One about four times by the time– because I blamed everybody and blamed everything. (Jenny)

Blaming other people and contexts for one's actions is unacceptable in the 12-Step ideology (Cavanaugh, 1998). There is a tradition of expressing one's feelings about formative events in 12-Step recovery, but this is not to be equated with explanation. In some respects this may be positive, because it helps persons to reclaim responsibility for their lives – but it presumes that such responsibility is within their reach. For example, Paul expects to return from his treatment to a social context in which most of his peers use heroin, and Edward to a job in the alcohol industry. Thus, the individualization and pathologization of addiction can be obstructions to engaging with people who are seeking help. This is because 12-Step does not equip people with a framework for understanding their actions, or re-storying their lives in terms of *context*. Some people may not need this contextual understanding, and that may be one reason why 12-Step's peer-support method works well for some people, but many others drop out quite early in the process.

To summarize, then, I have presented an analysis suggesting that subjective loss of control and paradox are key elements in the experience of addiction. I have suggested that two further understandings of addiction which are prevalent here – the cyclical element of addiction and the inevitability of relapse – must be understood within the local instantiation of 12-Step ideology. I have described two modes for understanding non-volitional action that were utilized by the participants: pathological decisions and emotional decisions. Finally, I have argued that 12-Step's ambivalence about discussions of context here, in accounting for loss of control, represents one limitation of that approach.

Reflection on the example

There are some features of the above account which are worth noticing. The account is not perfect, of course, but I have taken care to include some key features of IPA work. So we have a 'phenomenological core' to the analysis, which is perhaps more descriptive in tone, identifying some key features of the experience of addiction (paradox, loss of control) as they are understood by the participants. Alongside that, we have a more 'interpretative' strand which includes some thoughts about the specific ways in which participants make sense of their experiences ('emotional decisions' and 'pathological decisions' in this case). It is a little compressed here, but I hope that I have made the key points reasonably clearly. There is also some critical leverage (often this would come in the discussion section, but it can be incorporated into an analysis, as it is here), which relates the analysis to a concept or theory in the literature (in this case, the assumption that there is an inevitable, escalating and cyclical quality to relapse and recovery) and offers a fresh perspective on that issue, in the light of the analysis. These are all different levels of analysis in IPA, and while all three do not need to be present in equal measure, it is important that an IPA study moves beyond the 'descriptive' core. It is equally important that this core is established persuasively for the reader; it is difficult to move from personal experience to the wider context if this has not been achieved.

There are also some concrete features of the account that are worth noticing. It is written in the active voice, mostly, and in the first person, where appropriate. That is, there is an authorial presence addressing the reader and it is clearly the author (me, in this case) who is making the claims about the data. There may also be some reflection incorporated in this; for example, recognizing my own discomfort at the participants' dilemmas turned out to be important for me. Coming to understand my discomfort brought *context* into focus. There is also a basic structure – indicated by the theme titles – but there are many links between the themes. The themes capture 'patterns of meaning' in the accounts, not simply 'topics that people talked about'. Substantive verbatim quotes are used to illustrate the points and, on the whole, the intended interpretation of these quotes is made clear either in the introduction to the quote or in the commentary that follows it. There is a direct dialogue with phenomenological concepts (in this case, some brief discussion of relatedness) and there is some degree of idiographic focus (e.g. on George). Often I would incorporate more of the latter by introducing the participants in more detail in the Method section. Sometimes I might take time to discuss a feature of the analysis that is particularly pertinent to understanding one participant's different view of their experiences. Due to constraints of space here, I have relied on the use of some longer quotes and on the consistent use of pseudonyms, in order that the reader can at least accumulate a sense of 'who is who' as the analysis develops.

The reader might like to look at two lists of potential criteria for a 'good' IPA study, one in Larkin and Thompson (2011) and the other, developed as part of a systematic review, by Smith (2011). The two sets of criteria are pitched at different levels, and taken together they do offer a rounded view of what an author – or reader – of IPA work might expect. Neither is simply a checklist intended to provide a formula for a 'good' study, and while it could be difficult to produce a good study without some *consideration* of most of the elements, there will always be innovative and creative exceptions.

Method

There are many published accounts of 'how to do' IPA. In addition to a recent book (Smith et al., 2009), there are many chapters (e.g. Larkin & Thompson,

2011) and papers (e.g. Larkin et al., 2006; Smith, 2007) which give guidance on processes and techniques. IPA is a reasonably flexible approach. The account which follows is not prescriptive, and reading other methods chapters on IPA will provide you with a wider range of strategies which you can use to solve the problems presented by your data. The list itself is adapted from Smith et al. (2009).

1. *Reflection on one's own preconceptions and processes* (e.g. see Smith, 2007). It can be helpful to kick off with the process of analysis by allowing yourself to be wrong. The urge to capture and respond to our intuitions, assumptions, theoretical interests, and personal reactions can be strong. So begin by taking a clean copy of the transcript, reading through it a couple of times, and then writing all over it. *Write whatever you like.* This 'free coding' is partly about getting your initial ideas down, so that you can then proceed with a more systematic and consistent focus (as below). However, it is also partly about identifying and considering the influence of your preconceptions. We cannot bracket these in a genuinely *separate* space, but we can *notice* them and set them deliberately *apart* from our intended focus, so that we are less likely to be directly driven by them. This is an ongoing, reflexive process which runs right through the life of a project, but it begins here.

2. *The close, line-by-line analysis (i.e. coding) of the experiential claims, concerns and stance of each participant* (e.g. see Larkin et al., 2006). This is the most time-consuming part. It is important to put the effort into doing this phenomenologically-focused coding in a detailed, thorough and systematic manner. The rest of the analysis develops from these foundations. Work with a clean copy of the transcript, and take your time. Read the data and make notes on what matters to the participant (*objects of concern*; that is, concepts, ideas and things with significance for the respondent) and what these things mean (*experiential claims*, often accessed through embodied, emotional, evaluative or metaphorical language). This is frequently described as 'line-by-line' coding. Certainly, there will rarely be a line where you cannot say something at this level, and frequently you will be pressed for space to capture all of your thoughts. Often it can be helpful to pull back to a more *global* level of analysis as well, and to characterize the tone or mood of a whole paragraph, page or narrative. At this level, it can be useful to try to characterize the *stance* or '*positionality*' of the participant too.

3. *The identification of the emergent patterns and commonalities (i.e. themes, understandings) within this experiential material, perhaps first for single cases and then subsequently across multiple cases.* Once you have completed the phenomenologically-focused coding for a transcript, it can be a good idea to summarize it. This can involve organizing the work done so far into loose clusters (for example, if 'control' is an object of concern, then put all of the work relevant to the meanings of control in one cluster and ask yourself what it adds up to). Give these clusters rough

working titles (more than one for each cluster, if it helps, which it often does). These are 'emerg*ing* themes' and you will have a lot of them; that is fine at this stage. It is also helpful to review your notes and draw together some reflexive comments at this stage. How would you characterize this participant and their concerns, and how does that resonate with you? For the addictions study, I wrote an idiographic, case-level summary for each participant at this stage. This sort of summarizing can act as a really useful 'staging post' that captures your ideas on each case in order to preserve a 'phenomenological core' to the analysis. You can then move on to work which is either broader, or more interpretative, in focus.

4. *The development of a 'dialogue' between the researchers, their coded data, and their psychological knowledge, about what it might mean for participants to have these concerns, in this context (e.g. see Larkin et al., 2006), leading in turn to the development of a more interpretative account.* This is a reference to the more interpretative stage of coding in IPA. In practice, it often develops in parallel with the more phenomenological forms of coding, but it tends to come to the fore once case-level summaries have been produced. Thus, it is a key stepping stone en route to the pattern-forming and thematizing stages described below. Once you have a summary of each interview or case – something which captures the things that matter for each participant and the meanings that are attached to them – you are then in a position to start developing interpretations across the cases. There are questions you are likely to ask yourself here, such as: 'What does it mean for participants to share these concerns, but not those? What does it mean for them to understand their concerns in this particular way in that context, but in another way when in a different context?' Often this sends you back to the data to do more thinking and coding. This is exactly what happened in the addictions study. Looking across the cases, it was clear that 'loss of control' was important to the participants, but it was also evident that the initial work I had done was not sufficiently focused or consistent to shed light on *how* this was understood. I looked at my case-level notes and they sent me to what I had written about a related issue in another piece of work. Then I went back to the data, and from there the sub-themes about 'emotional decisions' and 'pathological decisions' began to take shape.

5. *The development of a structure (often, but not necessarily, hierarchical) that illustrates the relationships between themes.* Although this part of the process was finalized by the organization of the analytical work in a large spreadsheet table, the early stages were much more low-tech and intuitive. I photocopied all of my notes and coded transcripts, then cut the photocopies up into small segments. I shuffled and sorted these slips of paper into piles, and I used coloured pens, paperclips and sticky notes to record what I was doing. I lost the use of a room for a while, as it was overtaken by this pattern-forming storm of paper. There are computer programs

which can help you to do this, but personally I find that they lack the flex-ibility of 'hands-on' solutions. I also like to be able to stand in the middle of a room and *see* all of this work while it is in progress. It helps me to think about my next move and to shift between the 'whole' analysis and its emerging constituent parts. The analysis should be becoming leaner at this point; the higher-order themes should be subsuming many of the lower-order themes.

6. *The organization of all of this material in a format that allows for coded data to be traced right through the analysis – from initial codes on the transcript, through initial clustering and thematic development, into the final structure of themes.* The thematic structure about which you have been reading (or at least, one part of it) is underpinned by a large cross-referenced spreadsheet that itemizes all of the various levels of themes (superordinate themes, themes, sub-themes and codes). All of the codes (i.e. notes and interpretations) written on the transcripts were trans-posed to this spreadsheet once the patterns within them (i.e. the various levels of themes) had begun to take shape. This organizational process was also part of the *analytic* process. It forced me to examine the extent of the evidence for all of the themes, and also to organize the themes into a structure which had some interpretative logic to it. At this point, the names of the themes can be fine-tuned: Do they capture the *meaning* of the material to which they relate? Would someone understand the basic message of the analysis if they read only the theme titles? Once the *organization* is complete, you should have a structure which can be pre-sented to other people, and about which you can develop narratives and arguments.

7. *The use of supervision, collaboration, audit, or other processes of trian-gulation and credibility-checking to test and develop the coherence and plausibility of the interpretation.* In my case, I did have some triangula-tion with other data to consider. I also had the benefit of feedback from a supervisor (Mark Griffiths), from audiences at conferences where I pre-sented the developing analysis, and from my examiners.

8. *The development of a narrative, evidenced by detailed commentary on data extracts, which takes the reader through this interpretation, usually in a theme-by-theme structure, and often supported by some form of visu-al guide (a simple structure, diagram or table).* All of these features are present in the account of addiction above. What may be less clear is just how important the writing process is – it is not merely 'reporting' on a completed analysis. Instead, it is an integral part of that analytical process. I have pointed out that I have written previously about these data in a thesis (Larkin, 2001), but inevitably, all of the typical processes involved in writing IPA were still present. These include: *selection* (what to include and exclude); *focus and pitch* (e.g. imagining you, the reader of this book, and might what interest you); *re-interpretation and reflection* (the act of writing forces one to make decisions about what to call things

and how to conceptualize them); *argument* (deciding what key points to get across), and *balance* (the phenomenological and the interpretative, but also getting a balance of voices from across the dataset). One good tip is to find a couple of published IPA papers which you like, so that you have a good model of what you are aiming to produce. There are plenty to choose from (Smith's 2011 review shows a year-on-year increase in published IPA papers) and a very wide range of topics are tackled (see Table 10.1 for examples).

Table 10.1   Example papers showing some of the topics approached by IPA researchers in clinical and health psychology

Topic	Example
People's experiences of distress and illness	Rhodes, J. & Smith, J.A. (2010). 'The top of my head came off.' An interpretative phenomenological analysis of the experience of depression. *Counselling Psychology Quarterly*, 23(4), 399–409.
People's experience of interventions and services	Chapman, E., Parameshwar, J., Jenkins, D., Large, S. & Tsui, S. (2007). Psychosocial issues for patients with ventricular assist devices: A qualitative pilot study. *American Journal of Critical Care*, 16, 72–81.
Carers' experiences	Glasscoe, C. & Smith, J.A. (2011). Unravelling complexities involved in parenting a child with cystic fibrosis: An interpretative phenomenological analysis. *Clinical Child Psychology and Psychiatry*, 16(2), 279–298.
Staff experiences	Macran, S., Stiles, W. & Smith, J.A. (1999) How does personal therapy affect therapists' practice? *Journal of Counselling Psychology*, 46, 419–431.
Multiple perspective studies	Rostill, H., Larkin, M., Toms, A. & Churchman, C. (2011). A shared experience of fragmentation: Making sense of foster placement breakdown. *Clinical Child Psychology and Psychiatry*, 16(1),103–127.
Experiences of particular contexts and environments	Larkin, M., Clifton, E. & De Visser, R. (2009). Making sense of 'consent' in a constrained environment. *International Journal of Law and Psychiatry*, 32, 176–183.
Fundamental processes	Meneses, R. & Larkin, M. (in press). The experience of empathy: Intuitive, sympathetic and intellectual aspects of social understanding. *Journal of Humanistic Psychology*.
Contextual processes	Kam, S. & Midgeley, N. (2006). Exploring 'clinical judgement': How do child and adolescent mental health professionals decide whether a young person needs individual psychotherapy? *Clinical Child Psychology and Psychiatry*, 11(1), 27–44.

Concluding thoughts: Why do it?

All qualitative analysis is intensive and conceptually-demanding. It helps to have a topic that you care about, partly to motivate you during the denser periods of work, and partly to give you a position from which to reflect. It also helps to use an approach which fits your *approach* to your research, and which will deliver an answer to your research question. When I work with interpretative phenomenological approaches, I often find that my enthusiasm for research is rejuvenated. Partly, I think that this is about the powerful effect of the particular: these approaches lead you towards a focus on personal accounts, and this is a level of detail that is often missing in psychology. To encounter and work with this is to have one's theoretical imagination and curiosity re-invigorated. And partly, it is due to the opportunities afforded by a thorough analysis of such data: experiential accounts can provide tremendously powerful critical leverage. These are ways of seeing the world differently, of course, but they also offer ways of *showing* that different perspective to others.

Further reading

Finlay, L. (2009). Debating phenomenological research methods. *Phenomenology & Practice, 3*(1), 6–25.
Gallagher, S. & Zahavi, D. (2007). *The Phenomenological Mind: An Introduction to Philosophy of Mind and Cognitive Science.* London: Routledge.
Moran, D. (2000). *Introduction to Phenomenology.* London: Routledge.
Smith, J.A., Flowers, P. & Larkin, M. (2009). *Interpretative Phenomenological Analysis.* London: Sage.

References

Ashworth, P. (2003). An approach to phenomenological psychology: The primacy of the lifeworld. *Journal of Phenomenological Psychology, 34*(2), 145–156.
Boden, Z.V.R. & Eatough, V. (2014). Understanding more fully: A multimodal, hermeneutic-phenomenological approach. *Qualitative Research in Psychology, 11*(2), 160–177.
Cain, C. (1991). Personal stories: Identity acquisition and self-understanding in Alcoholics Anonymous. *Ethos, 19,* 210–253.
Cavanaugh, C. (1998). *AA to Z: Addictionary of the 12-Step Culture.* New York: Doubleday.
Finlay, L. (2009). Debating phenomenological research methods. *Phenomenology & Practice, 3*(1), 6–25.
Giorgi, A. (1995). Phenomenological psychology. In J.A. Smith, R. Harré & L. Van Langenhove (eds), *Rethinking Psychology.* London: Sage.
Harper, D. (2012). Surveying qualitative research teaching on British clinical psychology training programmes 1992–2006: A changing relationship? *Qualitative Research in Psychology, 9*(1), 5–12.

Hefferon, K. & Gil-Rodriguez, E. (2011). Methods: Interpretative phenomenological analysis. *The Psychologist*, 24(10), 756–759.

Kvale, S. & Brinkmann, S. (2008). *InterViews: Learning the Craft of Qualitative Research Interviewing*. London: Sage.

Langdridge, D. (2006). *Phenomenological Psychology: Theory, Research and Method*. Harlow: Pearson.

Larkin, M. (2001). Experiences and understandings: A post-constructionist cultural psychology of addiction and recovery in the 12-Step tradition. PhD thesis. Nottingham: Nottingham Trent University.

Larkin, M. & Griffiths, M.D. (2002). Experiences of addiction and recovery: The case for subjective accounts. *Addiction Research and Theory*, 10, 281–311.

Larkin, M. & Thompson, A. (2011). Interpretative phenomenological analysis. In D. Harper & A. Thompson (eds), *Qualitative Research Methods in Mental Health and Psychotherapy: An Introduction for Students and Practitioners*. Oxford: Wiley-Blackwell.Larkin, M., Eatough, V. & Osborn, M. (2011). Interpretative phenomenological analysis and embodied, active, situated cognition. *Theory and Psychology*, 21(3), 318–337.

Larkin, M., Watts, S. & Clifton, E. (2006). Giving voice and making sense in Interpretative Phenomenological Analysis. *Qualitative Research in Psychology*, 3(2), 102–120.

Orford, J. (2002). *Excessive Appetites: A Psychological View of Addictions* (2nd edn). Chichester: John Wiley & Sons.

Rull, C.P. (2002). The emotional control metaphors. *Journal of English Studies*, 3, 179–192.

Smith, J.A. (2007). Hermeneutics, human sciences and health: Linking theory and practice. *International Journal of Qualitative Studies on Health and Well-being*, 2, 3–11.

Smith, J.A. (2011). Evaluating the contribution of interpretative phenomenological analysis. *Health Psychology Review*, 5(1), 9–27.

Smith, J.A., Flowers, P. & Larkin, M. (2009). *Interpretative Phenomenological Analysis*. London: Sage.

Psychoanalytically Informed Research

Kerry Gibson

11

The work of clinical and health psychologists involves engaging quite specifically with the emotional lives of their clients. In their training they are taught skills that allow them to recognize and monitor their clients' and their own emotions, to deal with emotionally laden subject matter and to help their clients work through difficult emotions. It is ironic, then, that most of the research methods conventionally associated with psychology allow little opportunity to engage with emotion. While the increasing acceptability of qualitative methods in applied psychology has created a valuable space for clinicians to better understand the subjective worlds of research participants (Harper, 2012), emotion has remained largely invisible in this research. As Cromby (2012) notes, the lack of emotion in research writing may be explained by the dominance of linguistic and cognitive models, together with the difficulty of putting emotion into words. What has, however, been called the 'affective turn' in the social sciences (Clough & Halley, 2007) has led to researchers finding innovative ways of trying to capture emotion in their research. Some of the most exciting options for researchers wishing to engage more directly with emotion have come from a psychoanalytically informed approach. This provides an opportunity for researchers to show how emotion permeates people's meaning-making and influences the way in which they experience the world.

There are a number of reasons why a psychoanalytically informed research method might be attractive to health and clinical psychologists. First, its theory and methods emerged out of the consulting room and so are uniquely suited to making sense of the work of therapists and related practitioners. Psychoanalytic theory and practice (usually in the form of psychodynamic psychotherapy) are still commonly taught in many psychology programmes and applied psychologists are likely to have had at least some grounding in the core theoretical concepts associated with this approach. Most significantly for clinical and health psychologists, this unique approach has the potential to bring an emotional 'aliveness' to participants' accounts of their experience that resonates with the focus of our work (Hollway, 2009:2).

In this chapter I describe contemporary researchers' attempts to turn psychoanalysis into a viable research methodology and show how it can be used to explore issues of central concern for clinical and health psychologists. I illustrate this research method with my own research into young clients' accounts of counselling.

Historical background

While psychoanalysis has a long history of research, this has been limited largely to clinical case studies collected during the course of psychoanalytic intervention. As a research methodology, psychoanalysis did not make significant inroads into the mainstream of psychology until the 1990s. This is hardly surprising, since there has been considerable uneasiness in the relationship between psychology and psychoanalysis. On the one hand, those who followed the dominant 'science' paradigm in psychology had been sceptical of the focus of psychoanalysis on subjectivity, meaning and interpretation, seeing it as lacking the objectivity and rigour central to the scientific endeavour (Frosh, 1989). On the other hand, social psychologists had, sometimes with good reason, been cynical about the tendency for psychoanalysis to individualize, pathologize and decontextualize the person (Parker, 2005). Concerns about the 'unscientific' nature of psychoanalysis have largely been answered by the increasing attention paid to rigour in qualitative research more generally (Guba & Lincoln, 1989). The criticisms levelled at psychoanalysis by social psychologists can also be challenged. Many of their claims rest on the historical theory and practice of psychoanalysis and do not recognize the changes in thinking brought about by newer, relational models of psychoanalysis (Rustin, 1991). Rustin also notes that contemporary psychoanalysts have moved away from seeking out causal links that purport to explain pathology to an approach that focuses on the process of meaning-making, consistent with other qualitative methods.

In recent decades psychologists have begun to develop the potential of psychoanalytic ideas to enhance qualitative research. Hollway and Jefferson (2000, 2013) have provided possibly the most coherent account of a research method drawing from psychoanalysis. Although they value, and have indeed been a part of, the social constructionist movement that recognizes the way in which individuals are shaped by their social context (Henriques et al., 1984), they questioned the implicit social determinism in this kind of approach and sought a way of understanding that was able to recognize how people were shaped by psychological as well as social forces. Their psychoanalytic research method grew out of an interest in why people positioned themselves in one culturally available discourse rather than another, and how they imbued these discourses with emotional significance. Drawing from Kleinian psychoanalytic theory, they argued that human beings experience anxiety linked to unpalatable or contradictory experiences. They protect themselves from this anxiety through a variety of psychic defence mechanisms (see Box 11.1). According to

Hollway and Jefferson (2013), it is this psychic motivation that provides the emotional impetus for people to invest in discourse and gives the investment its particular valence and power. They specifically used the word 'investment' to indicate that this was not a conscious choice of one discourse over another, but instead reflected an unconscious selection, the reasons for which were only partially known or not at all known to the person. It is for this reason that they write about a 'defended subject' – one whose own motivations are not always transparent to themselves.

Hollway and Jefferson (2000, 2013) have developed a systematic methodology associated with their conceptual understanding. They use what they call the 'free association narrative interview' (FANI), an open-ended interview that allows participants to follow their own train of thought. This aligns with the psychoanalytic idea that where people are allowed to speak unimpeded, their chain of associations will indirectly reveal ideas that hold unconscious emotional significance. These interviews are then subjected to an analysis that focuses on exploring the research participant's underlying investments by examining unconscious links and contradictions between ideas and the psychic strategies that they use to manage emotional discomfort. These concepts form the core of the approach that I use and they will be discussed in more detail later in the chapter.

Frosh (1999, 2002) has also argued convincingly that in focusing only on words, researchers had neglected the important realm of emotion that gives experiences their texture and valence. His research on how boys talk about issues of importance to them uses psychoanalytic ideas to show how participants manage unconscious emotional conflicts and anxieties through discourses of masculinity (Frosh et al., 2001, 2003). However, in spite of his commitment to the project of developing psychoanalysis as a research method, Frosh points out some important pitfalls in an unthinking application of psychoanalytic ideas to research (Frosh & Baraitser, 2008). Psychoanalysis was developed as a method for exploring possible meanings together with a client in the consulting room. To apply it as a series of technical analytic steps external to this context runs the risk of suggesting that some absolute psychic 'truth' about a person can be discovered outside of the relationship with the client. Frosh and Baraitser argue for the importance of using psychoanalysis in research to open up possible meanings that enrich interpretation, rather than answering a question about the specific 'cause' of any individual's particular psychic investment. Hollway and Jefferson suggest that the term 'psychoanalytically informed' method might be used to avoid implying a direct transfer of psychoanalytic practices to the research context (2013:150).

Social psychologists have been concerned about a psychoanalytically informed research method losing sight of the way in which society shapes individual experience (Wetherell, 2005). While this is an understandable concern for social psychologists, it should also be one for health and clinical psychologists, whose primary models of explanation are often highly individualistic and inadvertently place responsibility on the individual for their own difficulties and the solution of these (Nightingale & Cromby, 2001). Layton (2006, 2008, 2009) has developed an approach to psychoanalytic thinking that seems to avoid this pitfall. She explains how emotional vulnerability does not arise simply from some individual psychic mechanism. Instead, she places the origins of psychic conflict squarely within society itself. Society, through its own discursive and material intolerance for ambiguity, splits up human capacities like masculinity and femininity, autonomy and dependence into one-dimensional categories – some of which are idealized and associated with access to power and others denigrated and linked to positions of relative powerlessness (Layton, 2006). These idealized norms challenge human experience, which is ambiguous and multifaceted. According to Layton, this gives rise to an inevitable sense of 'lack' or inferiority within those who occupy the social world. Thus, women and girls experience themselves as inferior against the normative ideals of masculinity, and men too feel that they lack something when judged against these one-dimensional representations. This helps to create a cycle between individual and society in which people fend off socially unacceptable aspects of their experience to protect themselves against social vulnerability, and their attempts to do this help to maintain and reproduce the very same normative discourses and practices that cause them to feel vulnerable in the first place. The unwanted experiences and their associated feelings, however, remain unconsciously active and liable to return. This creates a need for constant emotional negotiation aimed at managing the anxiety associated with these.

My practical approach to psychoanalytic research methodology draws heavily on the careful and detailed approach advocated by Hollway and Jefferson (2000, 2013). I do, however, shift away from their position in some respects. First, I am mindful of the cautions about the differences between psychoanalysis as therapy and psychoanalysis as research method (Frosh & Baraitser, 2008; Kvale, 2003). For this reason, I try to limit interpretations to the signs of emotion, unconscious conflict and attempts to manage it that are visible in the interview, rather than making claims about characteristic psychic potentials of an individual that apply outside of the research setting. For similar reasons, I do not specifically explore participants' biographical history, a strategy that has been used and recommended by other researchers (Frosh & Saville Young, 2008; Hollway & Jefferson, 2013). This is not to discount the influence of the past, which is one of the strengths of a psychoanalytic approach, but I prefer to work with the idea that elements of the past may be evoked and reconstructed in the present in a way that says as much about current concerns as it does about the actual experiences of the past. This avoids the impression that the historical 'cause' of a participant's emotional investments can be clearly established in the research context. I have also been strongly influenced by Layton (2006, 2008, 2009) in focusing on the social origins of psychic conflict while acknowledging that these are mediated through the personal experiences of the participants.

Theoretical background

Although each of us experiences our life as uniquely personal and private, the context in which we live shapes how we think of ourselves, the sorts of things that are allowed to matter to us and the way that it is acceptable to be, in very powerful if invisible ways. The starting point for a psychoanalytically informed research method is to understand what social and cultural resources people might have available to them at this time and place in history to make sense of their lives. Social constructionists talk about how we are all positioned in discourses that both create opportunities and set limits for how we live and how we understand our lives. These social ideas in which we find and define ourselves (and others define us too) carry strong emotional meaning and significance for the way in which we experience the world and ourselves.

However, from a psychoanalytic perspective our engagement with the social world is recognized also to create powerful emotional responses. As we engage with social discourses that often demand unrealistic standards of normativity from us, we respond with a series of strategies for managing the emotional discomfort that results. It may be that aspects of our experience are so unpalatable to society that we have to disavow them completely. So, for example, the women we interviewed about their experience with HIV/AIDS, in the context of highly stigmatized views of the illness in South Africa at the time, seemed to invest heavily in positive representations of their status and either avoided or minimized any possible negative connotations (Soskolne et al., 2004). In order to protect ourselves from unacceptable aspects of experience, we employ a variety of psychological strategies that have the result of distorting our emotional experience in various ways. Splitting is a commonly used mechanism for fending off emotional threats (see Box 11.1). This reflects an inability to tolerate ambiguity or ambivalence, creating instead one-dimensional representations that define normative identities and behaviour. So, for example, dominant discourses of masculinity might make it difficult to hold both 'strength' and 'weakness' together as aspects of male identity. In this case one pole of the experience is split off from the other, with the outcome of stereotypical, idealized or denigrated representations, saturated with emotional significance (Layton, 2006). When experiences or identities are split in this way, the aspects that are considered most threatening to the self are often attached to another person or group. In psychoanalysis this psychic process is known as projection (see Box 11.1). Projection allows individuals and social groups to attribute threatening aspects of themselves to others. So, for example, men might attribute their own disavowed weakness to women; 'mad people' carry the split-off fears that 'normal people' may have of their own irrationality; and black people help to contain the anxieties that white people have about their privileged place in society. This imaginary way of getting rid of the unwanted aspects of the self or of experience has very real effects on its recipients, who are often treated in ways that reinforce these projections.

BOX 11.1   Key concepts in psychoanalysis

Defences are psychic strategies designed to keep anxiety at bay.

Splitting is a psychic defence that involves dividing split-up experiences so that they appear to be either 'all good' or 'all bad'.

Projection is a psychic defence that involves rejecting unwanted aspects of one's self or experience and attributing these to others.

From a psychoanalytic perspective, one of the curious things about these strategies for managing anxiety is that as much as they are designed to keep threatening experiences and feelings at bay, they seldom achieve this very effectively. First, they tend to be only partly effective, and the underlying concerns against which the person is protecting themselves will often still make themselves known in subtle ways. Secondly, the attempts to avoid unpalatable experiences and their associated feelings reveal as much as they hide. The often quoted phrase 'My lady doth protest too much' is a good example of the way in which an attempt to hide a particular view actually makes it more evident that the person thinks other than what they say. Thirdly, these strategies do not create some kind of end-point resolution. Rather, they are part of a dynamic process in which unacceptable experiences and feelings rise to the surface and the person has then to work to fend off the anxiety associated with this.

Psychoanalysis helps to answer questions about why people might invest in particular kinds of ideas rather than others. They do this not simply because

---

BOX 11.2   Distorting and disavowing experience: An example from society

When it first appeared, HIV/AIDS was thought to be a 'gay disease'. This particular representation solidified into social discourse in spite of much evidence to the contrary and remains one of the most prevalent ideas about the illness. Psychoanalytic ideas help us to understand why people invest in this discourse rather than accepting the evidence that it is, in fact, heterosexual women who are most at risk of contracting HIV. This begins to make sense if we recognize how people who define themselves as heterosexual may be emotionally soothed by the idea that they are less likely to be at risk than gay men. Not only does this allow them to minimize any possible risk to themselves, it also allows them to shed any uncomfortable, negative or contradictory views that they might hold about themselves – and attach these firmly to members of another group (Joffe, 1995). These kinds of strategies have been present throughout history as people disavow unpalatable aspects of themselves or their experiences and attribute these to others in society. Those who occupy less powerful positions, women, black people, minorities and those who identify as gay or lesbian provide excellent receptacles for these unwanted experiences.

these discourses are prevalent, but because they serve an emotional purpose – they help them to manage unacceptable experiences and the uncomfortable emotions associated with these.

Method

Researchers may be put off by psychoanalytically informed research because the ideas seem so complex and often draw on a language that has developed unique meaning in the context of psychoanalysis as a clinical practice. My aim here is to try to pull out some key ideas from psychoanalytic research, with a focus on helping the reader develop a working knowledge of this approach. For this reason, I am setting out the method in a clear, 'step-by-step' fashion. However, as with all qualitative methods, the process is closer to an art than a recipe and must of course be adapted to the particular research situation.

Selecting an appropriate topic

A psychoanalytically informed research method would probably best be used to explore topics that are likely to carry a high degree of emotional significance for participants. This is not an unusual situation in research conducted by clinical and health psychologists, which often deals with issues related to psychological distress, such as becoming ill, experiencing a psychological trauma or challenging life circumstances. Generally, the question asked in this methodology is an open one intended to offer depth to an understanding of how a person experienced some meaningful aspect of their lives. However, while the research question will be broadly about experience, the method leads inevitably towards an exploration of the emotions evoked and the way in which this influences the participants' ability to make meaning of their experience. Psychoanalytic methods have been used to reflect on individuals' accounts of life experience or significant issues, but have also been employed to study organizations and social institutions. Some of this research has provided interesting insights into the functioning of the human services organizations within which psychologists work (Hinshelwood & Skogstad, 2000; Obholzer & Roberts, 1994).

Gathering data

While some researchers employ a multimethod, case-study approach including interviews and observations (Hollway, 2009; Gibson & Swartz, 2001; Gibson, 2003), in this chapter I focus on interviews with individual participants. To obtain data that is sufficiently rich to support an analysis, it is important to work with participants who are relatively verbally fluent and capable of expressing themselves in the language in which the researcher is working. While the interview text can be the focus of a psychoanalytically informed analysis, observations and reflections on the interpersonal context are also considered part of the data in this method.

Conducting the interview

For Hollway and Jefferson (2000, 2013), a highly unstructured interview method is key. Their interviewing method evolved out of their frustration with conventional research interviewing, in which the researchers' agenda and their meanings tend to take priority over those of the participant. To address this potential problem, they propose a narrative-style interview that allows the participant to determine the interpretation of the topic and to steer the direction of the interview. The free association narrative interview (FANI) allows participants to lead the researcher to those ideas in which they have unconsciously invested emotional significance. In contrast to traditional research interviewing, which often assumes that people are experts on their own experience, psychoanalysis works with the idea that people are not fully aware of the emotional significance of aspects of their experience. In this sense, people do not so much 'tell' as 'show' the researcher what is unconsciously significant to them. They reveal this significance through what they say and when and how they say it, as well as what they do not say. In order to capture the more subtle emotional tones of the interview, it is important that the researcher conducts the interviews themselves.

Hollway (2009) provides some specific recommendations for researchers conducting the FANI, including that researchers should use open-ended rather than closed questions. She also suggests that they try to elicit 'stories' rather than abstract commentary, as these detailed personal accounts are more likely to hold and reflect emotional investments. Researchers should furthermore avoid asking 'why' questions, as these often invite attempts to rationalize or justify behaviour and close down the participant's open flow of ideas. Finally, while the interview is clearly a dialogue between two (or more) people, the researcher should try to avoid steering the direction of the conversation. Instead, their follow-up questions should attempt to follow the order and phrasing suggested by the participant. These interviews may be longer than usual qualitative interviews and it may be useful to have more than one interview to develop a deeper understanding of the participant's preoccupations.

Clinical and health psychologists are usually well trained in the art of open-ended interviewing. Kvale (1999, 2003), who has written extensively about the value of using psychoanalytic-style interviews, acknowledges an irony in the fact that therapists do not draw on these strengths in their research, often relying instead on conducting experiments and gathering statistics. My own experience with this style of interviewing, however, suggests some unexpected pitfalls for clinicians. While creating a facilitative environment within which the participant sets the agenda has not been difficult with psychologists trained in non-directive counselling techniques, I have sometimes found myself slipping into a more therapeutic style of interviewing in which empathy is the primary ingredient. While empathy is helpful insofar as it obviously facilitates open communication with a participant, I have found that it can sometimes also forestall a more completely elaborated account elicited by a naïve inquirer stance. There are also some ethical issues associated with adopting a therapeutic interviewing style in the research context, which we will discuss a little later in this chapter (see also Chapter 3).

Conducting the analysis

A psychoanalytically informed analysis begins the way in which most other qualitative methodologies do, with the researcher immersing themselves in the material through reading and re-reading of the transcripts. Hollway (2009), however, talks about the importance of not detaching the transcript from the audio recording, which conveys the emotional meaning more fully through tone, pace and emphasis. I have found it most helpful to read the transcript of interviews while I listen to the original recording. In these early readings it may be useful for the researcher to approach the interview with 'evenly hovering attention' (Freud in Kvale, 2003:27). This idea, which draws from psychoanalytic practice, refers to how the researcher should open their mind to various and new meanings rather than being blinded by their own agenda.

Hollway writes about the value of the researcher's subjectivity as 'an instrument of knowing' (2009:3). The researcher's observations and responses to the participant in the interview and afterwards can be documented in reflexive field notes that include both their and the participants' contributions to the interaction. While Frosh and Baraitser (2008) caution against a direct importation of the psychoanalytic notion of counter-transference, it is helpful for the researcher to be aware not only of the verbal communications that occur between the participant and the researcher, but also the more subtle, non-verbal and emotional communications that provide some insights into the investments of both the researcher and the participant. Given the difficulty of accessing one's own counter-transference reactions, it may be important to involve another researcher in discussion around this who might be able to point out areas of blindness or offer alternative responses.

Hollway and Jefferson (2000, 2013) stress the importance of beginning with the gestalt of the narrative, rather than partitioning it off into words or word clusters, as required in some other methods. Frosh and Saville Young talk about something similar when they recommend finding the 'emotional sense of the story' (2008:114). The premise of the FANI is that emotionally significant issues will unfold through the linkage between ideas as the narrative develops. I have found it helpful to think of these links as forming a kind of 'red thread' – a dominant emotional story that emerges through a narrative. This provides a good starting point for identifying what the participant has 'done' with the topic at hand and how it reveals their underlying preoccupations as well as the social resources they have used to organize these. At this point it is possible to explore actively whether there are any alternative readings, a 'shadow' story, which might suggest aspects of experience that have been disavowed, distorted or minimized in some way. These often only become clear with repeated readings. The contradictions between the dominant and shadow stories may help to illuminate potential areas of unconscious conflict for the participant.

Having developed a sense of the key emotional themes and discourses that make up each narrative, it is then possible to conduct a more detailed microanalysis of the way in which that narrative is structured by the participant's attempts to manage anxiety. At this stage it is helpful to look at how one idea leads to or links emotionally to another; to explore contradictions between ideas; to identify shifts in tone and emphasis, interruptions (like laughter or silence) or overt expressions of emotion; and to hypothesize about possible omissions from the story. All of these phenomena are interpreted through a psychoanalytic lens that identifies the way in which participants might be working unconsciously to protect themselves against anxiety. This not only helps to identify the participants' strategies for managing anxiety, but also illuminates those preoccupations that carry particular emotional significance for them.

Once this groundwork is done, it becomes possible to put together the pieces of the psychoanalytic analysis. This involves hypothesizing about sources of the participants' anxieties and identifying the primary psychological strategies that they use to protect themselves. Finally, these ideas can be considered in the context of the interview, the interview topic and the social and cultural resources available to the participants. This context helps to shed further light on participants' unconscious emotional investments.

A psychoanalytically informed analysis in action: Young clients' emotional investments in counselling

In recent research, we asked young people to tell us about their experience of counselling. We approached the study with an open research question, wanting to find out how our participants made meaning of their experience of counselling and the emotional significance it carried for them.

We were aware that young people could be particularly vulnerable to being disempowered in therapy contexts, which may be dominated by the interests of professionals and other adults (Gibson & Cartwright, 2013). We wondered what kinds of feelings counselling might evoke in young people and how this might affect their engagement in the process. In the example that follows, I show how a psychoanalytic analysis of a narrative interview reveals a young man's conflicted feelings about his emotional vulnerability in counselling.

Joshua was a 16-year-old boy who had used the counselling service at his school intermittently over a period of about three years. He initially represented himself in the interview as a 'tough guy', a swashbuckling anti-hero who might need practical help, but had little need for emotional support. His response to my opening question to tell me about how he had first come to counselling set the scene for this dominant story:

I'd just started at the school. Basically I came in with the attitude that I'm South African and I'm a lot better than everyone. Got me into a few fights and that led me to anger management courses and that led me to counselling. You must have met quite a few South African people and they've all got the same attitude I guess. We think we're better than everyone else. ... I've always been smart and I'd excel at most things. I'm generally sporty as well so I'm quite fit and strong. Anytime somebody would try and beat me at something I'd make sure that they couldn't, whether it's with muscles or with masculinity and all that.

Joshua explained how he had been sent to counselling for 'anger management' after getting into trouble for being 'cocky'. Through this account he conveyed the sense that he was the protagonist, using his superior strength and skill to get himself into trouble and sometimes out of it again. This particular version of his experience used a discourse of 'tough' masculinity similar to those described as defining boys' behaviour in other school contexts (Frosh et al., 2001, 2003; Messerschmidt, 2000).

However, while this was the dominant narrative that ran throughout the interview, it was not the only way in which the events that Joshua described could be read. On listening to his account I imagined an alternative narrative that could be told about a young immigrant boy who came to a new school and was picked on by the other students in his class. Listening to the details of an extract from a little later in the interview, it is possible to visualize Joshua less as a protagonist than as a victim of bullying:

I was in the class with all ... you know the ... the 'wanna be' gangsters. They tried to put me in my place straight away, trying to make out that that group is the best in the school and if you want to be cool you've got to be friends. Then I started to realise that they were bigger arseholes than I was so it got me in trouble with them and then they tried picking on me: the group against me. So I was singled out and then I rebelled and it got me into a fight with one of them, as I remember and I knocked him out clean with one head butt and that got me a name straight away and then the group came back a few weeks later and they tried to get their strongest guy on me and me and him got into a scrap but instead of it just being him, I think three or four of his mates jumped in so I grabbed a weapon and I started swinging away basically and then that got me into anger management.

In the dominant narrative, Joshua presented himself as being on top of the situation that he faced in coming to a new school, both in terms of being able to manage the circumstances and in being 'better than' the other boys. This nevertheless contrasted with this account of his being outnumbered and beaten up by a group of boys. This sense of two contradictory emotional stories within the narrative was echoed in my own responses to Joshua. While I was doing the interview, I was aware of having a mixed counter-transference response to his story. At times I was a little intimidated by Joshua's masculine assertiveness, but as the interview progressed I found myself also resonating increasingly with a sense of his emotional vulnerability. This elicited protective feelings in me, in particular a sense that I should tread gently around him lest I puncture what seemed to be a fairly fragile bubble of grandiosity. I was aware that my own experience as a migrant in a strange country may have heightened my sensitivity to being an outsider, and also that I needed to monitor whether my own experience was helping me understand what Joshua was describing or how I might overinterpret it on the basis of my own experience.

After listening to the recording and carefully reading the transcript several times, the split-off shadow story that alluded to Joshua's vulnerability emerged more clearly. He described how as a young boy he had been shuttled between one parent and another. He missed his mother back in South Africa and felt that he did not live up to his father's expectations that men should be emotionally and physically tough:

> I don't have the most supportive dad and he thinks that men should just plough through this kind of thing and shrug it off. … My brother's the exact clone of him. They've got literally the same job, same interests, rugby and football and all that. They do literally everything together. Me on the other hand, I'm more into art and I'm that kind of guy.

He explained how he felt that he lacked the close relationship he would have liked with his father: 'I guess my dad just never really has been a dad because my family is separated. I've spent time away from my dad.'

When Joshua shifted out of the dominant 'tough guy' narrative, his voice quality also changed from the assertive tone he had adopted earlier, becoming softer and more hesitant. As this occurred, I was touched by an awareness of his vulnerability and responded to him in the interview, saying that this situation must have been hard for him to deal with. My comment seemed, however, to provoke Joshua to swing back into the persona of the 'tough guy' who was invulnerable to emotional pain: 'Yeah, I mean most of it has passed by. When my parents got divorced it was no effect whatsoever. Didn't faze me.'

This alternation between Joshua as a 'tough guy' and Joshua as emotionally vulnerable occurred a number of times through the interview, most particularly when talking about his relationship with his father. The splitting that Joshua used to protect himself was mirrored in my own responses. As I read through the interview transcript, I was able to identify how I vacillated between an acknowledgement of Joshua's vulnerability in phrases like 'that must have been hard for you' and apparent attempts to shore up his 'tough guy' persona by adopting an admiring stance, remarking on how well he had done one thing or another.

At times during the interview I was also struck by Joshua's slightly condescending tone, in talking both about his classmates and about teachers and counsellors he had known in the past. Joshua gave me the impression that he would not suffer fools gladly and I registered some anxiety that I not be judged as one of them. This projection of incapacity onto others also seemed to help Joshua maintain the sense of himself as tough and capable.

While much of Joshua's narrative focused on the experiences that had led him to counselling rather than the experience itself, we might speculate that attending counselling might have posed a significant conflict for him. On the one hand, counselling might offer much-needed support for Joshua's emotional vulnerability, but it could also threaten his investment in being 'tough' like his father and brother. Not surprisingly, Joshua initially seemed to minimize the significance of counselling, describing how he had entered into it with a blasé attitude and few expectations: 'Just the thought here we go again kind of thing.' However, he went on to explain how he had come to value the advice the counsellors offered and their ability to help him out of difficult situations. Nevertheless, even as he explained how they had helped him, he was careful to do this in a way that asserted his control of the counselling situation and minimized his own vulnerability. Rather than talking about the prototype of a supportive relationship with one particular counsellor, Joshua positioned himself as being able to evaluate the various counsellors' strengths and weaknesses and to make choices about who would best meet his particular needs at particular times:

> It depends on the situation you're in I guess. If it's girls ... about girl issues a lot but I've gone to [Counsellor 1] a lot because he knew more. I don't know, he's been through it all. He's older, he's wiser. But say if I was in trouble with guys giving me threats or something like that I know I'd go to [Counsellor 2] because he knows the guys, ... he can give me advice on how to get them to back off. If its family issues, which were happening a lot, I'd go to [Counsellor 3] and would just be able to, she'd give me that retreat away from family.

In this representation Joshua clearly appreciates the support he received from the counsellors, but emphasizes his ability to control when and from whom he receives it. The idea that he is able to choose freely from the array of supports available is also in stark contrast to the lack of support he experiences in his relationship with his father. This reversal of the usual state of affairs in his family may further help Joshua to keep at bay the emotional vulnerabilities that might be evoked by the supportive intimacy of a counselling relationship.

While there are many occasions in the interview when Joshua reveals a degree of vulnerability, towards the end he seems to want to counteract this with a final assertion of his strength and capability:

> I've started to get on top of things. I've got myself a job. I've got myself two jobs. I've got myself three jobs! [I] sorted out relationships with friends and yeah just started to get on top of things. Instead of, I don't

know, I guess when I was younger I wanted all the drama and then when it came to me I'd make a big fuss of it. I've grown past that now.

In this extract Joshua seemed to project his denigrated, vulnerable self back in the past, which protected a current representation of himself as strong and resilient. While it is possible that he really does have 'three jobs', his emphasis here once again seems to assert his superior capability and to hide possible experiences of being vulnerable. Joshua also described how there had been considerable improvement in his relationship with his father:

The thing that changed the most was the relationship towards my dad because instead of still acting like a child, I think that's what got on my dad's nerves the most. I was acting like a kid and I thought I was acting like an adult. I don't know … that's my biggest issue I guess is my dad.

Although this sounded like a promising development, just moments later in the interview he seemed to contradict the idea that his relationship with his father had changed with a poignant admission that his father still did not provide him with the kind of supportive relationship he wished for:

Honestly sometimes it feels like [my father] wants me to fail because he's gone so far out of his way to help my brother. He literally got him a job. He helped him find a truck to start a business, all this stuff. But then the second I turn round and say 'Right. I'm trying to get into university can you give me some advice?', he just went: 'Well I don't believe you can get to university.'

This final insight into Joshua's painful experience of being the less favoured son of his father seems to suggest that his earlier assertion of an improvement in their relationship may involve a degree of disavowal of the reality.

Joshua's account suggests that counselling may involve some challenges, as it forces him to confront the conflict between the toughness required of boys and the emotional vulnerability that he experiences. This conflict is reinforced at the social level by the discourses that define masculinity, but also takes its emotional significance from the way in which these play out in his relationship with his father.

While the participants we interviewed produced narratives that were in some ways unique to each person, many, like Joshua, also showed similar attempts to fend off the anxiety triggered by aspects of the counselling experience. These included the experiences, like Joshua's, that were associated with emotional vulnerability, as well as experiences of dependence or stigmatized abnormality. The young people I spoke with often dealt with the perceived threat of counselling by investing in discourses that allowed them to assert their strength, autonomy or normality, but their interviews also indirectly revealed the disavowed aspects of their experience and the anxieties associated with this. The

---

BOX 11.3   Questions to guide the analysis

Doing the groundwork
- What is the dominant emotional story told in the narrative – the red thread?
- Is it possible to discern a 'shadow' story within the narrative?
- How do you (the researcher) respond emotionally to these different stories?
- How does the interview unfold to reveal the key preoccupations of the participant?
- Are there any experiences that seem to have been omitted or minimized in the participant's dominant story?
- Are there participant-initiated shifts of direction, interruptions, unplanned interactions, hesitations, periods of confusion in the interview?
- Are there contradictions between different parts of the story?
- Are people or events in the story represented in a 'one-dimensional', overly positive or negative way?

Putting the pieces of the puzzle together
- What kinds of experiences do you think the participant is protecting themselves from?
- What strategies do they use to protect themselves against anxiety?
- Are there any clues in the interview as to the participant's motivations for investment in certain discourses rather than others?
- How does the discursive context help to produce the participant's emotional discomfort?
- How is each participant's analysis similar or different? Are there context-specific claims that can be made?
- Are there any general theoretical claims that might be made?

---

analysis provided us with a deeper understanding of the kinds of conflicting emotions that counselling might evoke in young people, and pointed to the importance of counsellors being aware of and working with the ambivalent emotional experiences that may be elicited within a counselling situation.

Issues of quality

Issues around quality in psychoanalytically informed research are similar to those in other qualitative areas of research (see Chapter 5), but there are some particular strengths and challenges in establishing the quality of psychoanalytically informed research. The elaboration of reflexivity beyond theoretical or demographic allegiances to include the subtle emotional investments that researchers may have in their work is a potential benefit for the quality of this approach (Hollway & Jefferson, 2013; Kvale, 2003). Nevertheless, it would be naïve to assume that this kind of self-reflection by researchers would offer direct access to their emotional investments. Like the participant, the researchers' motivations may not be transparent to themselves. To make the most of this potential tool for establishing quality, it is useful for researchers to use supervision or a research team to help them explore and challenge their understanding of their own unconscious investments.

There are also some challenges for quality that centre around the accuracy of psychoanalytic interpretations. As a psychoanalytic approach requires that the researcher 'read behind the text', this has raised a concern about the potential for overinterpretation (Frosh & Baraitser, 2008). Some of the research strategies that have been set up to deal with this situation, such as member checking, may not be entirely appropriate for this method as, by definition, the analysis will depart somewhat from the conscious meanings that the participant may give to their experience. There are two possible ways of trying to address this concern. Kvale (2003) suggests giving the participant an opportunity to 'object' to the interpretations. This may involve a second interview with participants to talk about some of the analytical ideas generated. However, this needs to be done carefully as participants, unlike clients, do not enter into a research process with the aim of developing new self-understanding. It is possible nevertheless to think of ways of generating discussion with participants that would allow for some mutual understanding to develop, provided that the analysis itself was conducted with respect for the participants' perspective. In psychoanalytically informed research that I conducted with people working with high levels of trauma in the human services, I went back to participants and engaged in a valuable discussion with them about the way in which they and the organization protected themselves from the difficulties inherent in their work (Gibson, 2003). This same strategy could also be used with individual participants to help develop a co-constructed understanding of the meaning of their narrative (Hollway & Jefferson, 2013). The second strategy to deal with the potential for overinterpretation is to keep the analysis very close to the data and ensure that it is presented in enough detail to support any claims, or to allow for alternative interpretations. In the end, however, any analysis needs to be recognized as provisional and subject to alternative interpretation. Yet, as Frosh and Saville Young note, there are some readings that are 'better' than others and these can be judged by their 'capacity to communicate experience more richly' (2008:117).

Ethical considerations

Beyond the usual ethics of qualitative research (see Chapter 3) there are some specific concerns that apply when using this method. Given that the method relates directly to a form of intervention, there is the potential for there to be some confusion between a research and a therapy agenda (Kvale, 1999). This is particularly relevant given that the readers of this book are health and clinical psychologists who are likely to use therapy in their everyday practice (Thompson & Russo, 2012). It is important to ensure that both the researcher and the participant are aware of the differences between the two practices and can monitor their responses accordingly.

Hollway and Jefferson (2013) also write about several other specific ethical considerations associated with this method. While informed consent assumes that participants can make a rational decision about the disclosure of information, this method is intended to elicit unconscious material that may go beyond that which the participant believed themselves to be revealing. It may be helpful for researchers to engage in a conversation with their participants about the kind of approach they take in their research, but this openness about the researcher's agenda needs to be weighed against the potential for a participant to become self-conscious in a way that has an impacts on the effectiveness of

---

BOX 11.4   Examples of research using a psychoanalytically informed method

Frosh, S., Phoenix, A. & Pattman, R. (2003). Taking a stand: Using psychoanalysis to explore the positioning of subjects in discourse. *British Journal of Social Psychology*, 42, 39–53.

Gest, Y. (2012). Reflections on resilience: A psycho-social exploration of the life long impact of having been in care during childhood. *Journal of Social Work Practice, Psychotherapeutic Approaches in Health, Welfare and the Community*, 26(1), 109–124.

Gough, B. (2009). A psycho-discursive approach to analysing qualitative interview data, with reference to a father–son relationship. *Qualitative Research*, 9(5), 527–545.

Hollway, W. (2010). Conflict in the transitions to becoming a mother: A psycho-social approach. *Psychoanalysis, Culture & Society*, 15, 136–155.

Hollway, W. & Jefferson, T. (2005). Panic and perjury: A psychosocial exploration of agency. *British Journal of Social Psychology*, 44, 147–163.

Jones, D.W. (2004). Families with serious mental illness: Working with loss and ambivalence. *British Journal of Social Work*, 34, 961–979.

Nicholson, C., Meyer, J., Flatley, M. & Holman, C. (2012). The experience of living at home with frailty in old age: A psychosocial qualitative study. *International Journal of Nursing Studies*, 50(9), 1172–1179.

Nicholson, C., Meyer, J., Flatley, M., Holman, C. & Lowton, K. (2012). Living on the margin: Understanding the experience of living and dying with frailty in old age. *Social Science and Medicine*, 75(8), 1426–1432.

Rohleder, P. (2010). Educators' ambivalence and managing anxiety in providing sex education for people with learning disabilities. *Psychodynamic Practice: Individuals, Groups and Organisations*, 16(2), 165–182.

Rohleder, P. & Gibson, K. (2006). 'We are not fresh': HIV-positive women talk of their experience of living with their 'spoiled identity'. *South African Journal of Psychology*, 36(1), 25–44.

Soskolne, T., Stein, J. & Gibson, K. (2004). Working with ambivalence: Finding a positive identity for HIV/AIDS in South Africa. *International Journal of Critical Psychology*, 10, 123–147.

Van der Walt, H. & Swartz, L.H. (2000). Isabel Menzies Lyth revisited: Institutional defences in public health nursing in South Africa during the 1990s. *Psychodynamic Counselling*, 5(4), 483–495.

the FANI method. While Hollway and Jefferson (2013) acknowledge that in some sense this is an irresolvable situation, they stress the importance of counter-balancing this potential for 'deception' with principles of honesty in their approach to participants and their data and respect, which they define as 'recognition' of the participants' experience. Most importantly, they emphasize the importance of approaching the research with an attitude of 'sympathy' for ordinary human experience.

In any emotionally significant research it is also essential to be mindful of the potential to evoke distress in participants (Thompson & Russo, 2012). Research of this nature requires safeguards for participants, including the opportunity to stop the interview if they feel too distressed or to receive support, from someone other than the researcher, after the interview. However, Thompson and Russo (2012) also point to some of the advantages that professional psychologists may bring in terms of their ability to establish a climate of empathy and understanding within the research, which may make it easier for participants to talk about emotionally significant experiences with some degree of safety.

Further reading

Psychoanalytic concepts

Frosh, S. (2003). *Key Concepts in Psychoanalysis*. New York: New York University Press.

A psychoanalytically informed research method

Frosh, S. & Saville Young, L. (2008). Psychoanalytic approaches to qualitative psychology. In C. Willig & W. Stainton Rogers (eds), *The Sage Handbook of Qualitative Research in Psychology* (pp. 109–126). London: Sage.
Hollway, W. & Jefferson, T. (2013). *Doing Qualitative Research Differently: A Psychosocial Approach*. London: Sage.

References

Clough, P. & Halley, J. (eds). (2007). *The Affective Turn: Theorising the Social*. Durham, NC: Duke University Press.
Cromby, J. (2012). Feeling the way: Qualitative clinical research and the affective turn. *Qualitative Research in Psychology*, 9(1), 88–98.
Frosh, S. (1989). *Psychoanalysis and Psychology: Minding the Gap*. Basingstoke: Macmillan.
Frosh, S. (1999). What is outside discourse? *Psychoanalytic Studies*, 1(4), 381–390.
Frosh, S. (2002). Things that can't be said: Psychoanalysis and the limits of language. In S. Frosh, *After Words: The Personal in Gender, Culture and Psychotherapy* (pp. 134–149). Basingstoke: Palgrave.

Frosh, S. & Baraitser, L. (2008). Psychoanalysis and psychosocial studies. *Psychoanalysis, Culture & Society, 13*, 346–365.

Frosh, S. & Saville Young, L. (2008). Psychoanalytic approaches to qualitative psychology. In C. Willig & W. Stainton Rogers (eds), *The Sage Handbook of Qualitative Research in Psychology* (pp. 109–126). London: Sage.

Frosh, S., Phoenix, A. & Pattman, R. (2001). *Young Masculinities: Understanding Boys in Contemporary Society.* Basingstoke: Palgrave.

Frosh, S., Phoenix, A. & Pattman, R. (2003). Taking a stand: Using psychoanalysis to explore the positioning of subjects in discourse. *British Journal of Social Psychology, 42*, 39–53.

Gibson, K. (2003). Politics and emotion in work with disadvantaged children: Case studies in consultation from a South African clinic. PhD thesis. Cape Town: University of Cape Town.

Gibson, K. & Cartwright, C. (2013). Agency in young clients' narratives of counseling: 'It's whatever you want to make of it'. *Journal of Counseling Psychology, 60*(3), 340–352.

Gibson, K. & Swartz, L. (2001). Psychology, social transition and organizational life in South Africa: 'I can't change the past – but I can try.' *Psychoanalytic Studies, 3*(3/4), 381–392.

Guba, E. & Lincoln Y. (1989). *Fourth Generation Evaluation.* Newbury Park, CA: Sage.

Harper, D. (2012). Surveying qualitative research teaching on British clinical psychology training programmes 1992–2006: A changing relationship? *Qualitative Research in Psychology, 9*(1), 5–12.

Henriques, J., Hollway, W., Urwin, C., Venn, C. & Walkerdine, V. (1984). *Changing the Subject.* London: Methuen.

Hinshelwood, R.D. & Skogstad, W. (eds). (2000). *Observing Organisations: Anxiety, Defence and Culture in Health Care.* London: Routledge.

Hollway, W. (2009). Applying the 'experience-near' principle to research: Psychoanalytically informed methods. *Journal of Social Work Practice, 23*(4), 461–474.

Hollway, W. & Jefferson, T. (2000). *Doing Qualitative Research Differently: Free Association, Narrative and the Interview Method.* London: Sage.

Hollway, W. & Jefferson, T. (2013). *Doing Qualitative Research Differently: A Psychosocial Approach.* London: Sage.

Joffe, H. (1995). Social representations of AIDS: Towards encompassing issues of power. *Papers on Social Representations, 4*(1), 29–40.

Kvale, S. (1999). The psychoanalytic interview as qualitative research. *Qualitative Inquiry, 5*(1), 87–113.

Kvale, S. (2003). The psychoanalytic interview as inspiration for qualitative research. In P. Camic, J. Rhodes & L. Yardley (eds), *Qualitative Research in Psychology: Expanding Perspectives in Methodology and Design.* Washington, DC: American Psychological Association Press.

Layton, L. (2006) Racial identities, racial enactments and normative unconscious processes. *Psychoanalytic Quarterly, 75*(1), 237–269.

Layton, L. (2008). What divides the subject? Psychoanalytic reflections on subjectivity, subjection and resistance. *Subjectivity, 22*, 60–72.

Layton, L. (2009). Who's responsible? Our mutual implication in each other's suffering. *Psychoanalytic Dialogues, 19*(2), 105–120.

Messerschmidt, J.W. (2000). Becoming 'real men': Adolescent masculinity challenges and sexual violence. *Men and Masculinities*, 2(3), 286–307.

Nightingale, D. & Cromby, J. (2001) Critical psychology and the ideology of individualism. *Journal of Critical Psychology, Counselling and Psychotherapy*, 1(2), 117–128.

Obholzer, A. & Roberts, V.Z. (eds). (1994). *The Unconscious at Work: Individual and Organizational Stress in the Human Services*. London: Routledge.

Parker, I. (2005). Lacania discourse analysis in psychology: Seven theoretical elements. *Theory and Psychology*, 15, 163–182.

Rustin, M. (1991). *The Good Society and the Inner World: Psychoanalysis, Politics and Culture*. London: Verso.

Soskolne, T., Stein, J. & Gibson, K. (2004). Working with ambivalence: Finding a positive identity for HIV/AIDS in South Africa. *International Journal of Critical Psychology*, 10, 123–147.

Thompson, A. & Russo, K. (2012). Ethical dilemmas for clinical psychologists in conducting qualitative research. *Qualitative Research in Psychology*, 9(1), 32–46.

Wetherell, M. (2005). Unconscious conflict or everyday accountability? *British Journal of Social Psychology*, 44(2), 169–173.

PART III

Qualitative Methods: Exploring Social Worlds

Conversation Analysis

Chris Walton and W.M.L. Finlay

12

This chapter is an introduction to conversation analysis (CA) as it can be applied to research in health and clinical settings. CA is an analytical method that allows the researcher to study in detail how people talk and interact with each other over a series of conversational turns. It has advantages over other observational methods in that it provides a much richer and more detailed analysis of social behaviour (and social order) than more traditional observational methods.

We start by describing the background of conversation analysis, then move on to describing some CA studies that address clinical issues. A brief description of how an analysis might proceed follows, and we end by providing a short worked example from some of our own research. Readers wishing to pursue this approach are advised to supplement this chapter with the introductory texts and resources listed at the end.

Historical background

No introduction to conversation analysis (CA) would be complete without mention of Harvey Sacks and the key role played by the lectures he gave between 1964 and 1972 at the University of California. Sacks died in a car accident in 1975, but his lectures (edited by Gail Jefferson) were published posthumously (Sacks, 1992) and still form the central text for CA. They lay out what was then a new approach to understanding the coordination of everyday interaction and are a touchstone for those now working within that approach (see Schegloff's introduction to Sacks [1992] for a thorough account).

As a sociologist, the work of Erving Goffman and Harold Garfinkel undoubtedly shaped Sacks's approach. Sacks shared Goffman's concern with everyday social interaction as a site of social order and with the procedures that give it, and the social selves that inhabit it, structure (what Goffman terms the *interaction order*; Goffman, 1983). Goffman was primarily concerned with the *ritual* nature of everyday interaction. What was striking about his ideas at the time was the proposition that this interaction order constituted a viable site for micro-analysis. The influence of Goffman on Sacks is evident in CA's adoption of one modality (speech) as the site for a micro-analysis of social action and the production of social order. Sacks, however, was distinct from Goffman in the systematic manner in which he set about the task of micro-analysis; that is, in the methodology he developed. Whereas Goffman drew on a wide range of sources, Sacks focused on one modality and developed a data-driven approach through his analysis of recordings of naturally occurring *talk-in-interaction* ('the talk produced in everyday situations of human interaction'; Hutchby & Wooffitt, 1998:13). This data-driven approach is still characteristic of CA today. Researchers doing CA remain concerned with the collection and systematic analysis of corpora of naturally occurring talk in everyday and institutional settings.

Sacks also drew from ethnomethodology (Garfinkel, 1967) a concern for the common-sense knowledge on which members of cultures draw in interaction (their 'ethno-methods') and for how people in interaction use those methods to account for their own and others' actions in ways that will make sense to their audience. The problem for Garfinkel was how to make such common-sense knowledge and practices visible so that they could be analysed. He most famously did this through his breaching experiments, in which experimenters were instructed to respond to utterances in ways that undermined normative expectations. For example, in response to an everyday inquiry such as 'How are you?', experimenters would answer with something like 'How am I in regard to what?' (Garfinkel, 1967:44). Such breaches of the common-sense understandings of how such enquiries should be responded to often led to the interaction breaking down, albeit in ways that still somehow accounted for the apparently bizarre behaviour of the experimenter. Garfinkel's breaching experiments were effective in laying bare some of the common-sense knowledge on which everyday actions tacitly rely, but the events themselves were not naturally occurring. In CA, Sacks developed a systematic method for engaging with such common-sense knowledge and practices without the need for breaching; he did this through a focus on the production of naturally occurring, everyday talk-in-interaction. In essence, CA was intended to provide a route to glimpsing the 'machinery' through which everyday talk-in-interaction is produced as orderly, through which social actions can be accomplished (in ways sensible and meaningful to the interactants) and through which speakers can account for their actions and the actions of others. (Readers looking for more detailed accounts of the origins of CA should see Schegloff, 1992 or Hutchby & Wooffitt, 1998.)

Sacks died in 1975, and since then CA has been developed and disseminated by many others, most notably Emanuel Schegloff and Gail Jefferson, co-authors on the 1974 paper 'A simplest systematics for the organization of turn-taking for conversation' (Sacks et al., 1974). That paper is prototypical of the aims and methods of CA. It starts with the seemingly mundane observation that people typically take turns at talking. Through the micro-analysis of naturally occurring talk, it then systematically examines the rules that govern the operation of this fundamental feature of social interaction. The paper exemplifies what we might understand to be *basic*, as opposed to *applied*, CA.

Basic and applied conversation analysis

The distinction between basic and applied CA hinges on both the nature of the data and the aims of the analysis. *Basic* CA is concerned with everyday talk (e.g. telephone and face-to-face conversations between friends or family members, outside of any obvious institutional setting) and has the primary aim of explicating some regular feature of those interactions. Examples of such regular features include the rules organizing turn-taking (Sacks et al., 1974), the occurrence of 'oh' or 'well' in responses to enquiries (Heritage, 1998; Schegloff & Lerner, 2009, respectively) or mechanisms through which 'repairs' (corrections of difficulties in interaction) are made (Schegloff et al., 1977). The aim in these papers is primarily to render that practice visible (that is, the regularities of its location, structure and function within an unfolding interaction) so that it can join the expanding catalogue of interactional practices that conversation analysts have studied.

In contrast, *applied* CA is usually concerned with the analysis of talk in institutional settings, and with how its practices may serve some institutional function, be part of some interactional problem and/or be the object of CA-based intervention. Applied CA is likely to be most relevant to research in health and clinical settings, and it has been used to study many different types of institutional interactions in primary care, social care, psychological therapies, speech therapy and physiotherapy, among others (see Table 12.1 on pg. 202 for examples). Antaki (2011) identified six varieties of applied CA of which two, *institutional* and *interventionist*, are particularly relevant to this volume.

Institutional applied CA tries to understand how the particular tasks and structures of the institution are achieved and maintained through talk-in-interaction. It does not aim primarily to solve any particular problem. It is this problem-solving orientation that characterizes *interventionist* applied CA. Here, CA tries both to understand some interactional problem and to develop a strategy for resolving that problem. Heritage et al. (2007) provides an ideal example of this interventionist applied CA. Addressing the problem of patients who leave GP consultations without having mentioned some of their health concerns, these authors illustrate how CA can identify an intervention to elicit a greater number of patients' concerns within a primary care consultation.

Activities, practices and context

In applied CA there are three key analytical concerns: *activities, practices* and *context*. An *activity* (or *action*) would be a broad type of 'interactional business' such as making an invitation, ending a meeting, offering a formulation or offering a choice. Activities are made up of *practices* (or *conversational devices*), which are smaller units of talk or interactional behaviour such as questions, hesitations, agreements or prompts. For example, the activity of asking a person with aphasia what they want to eat for dinner might be made up of a number of practices such as calling the other person's attention to the choice, asking open questions, suggesting options, rephrasing questions in the event that they have been misunderstood, and offering guesses if the person is unable to articulate their choice clearly. Analysts attempt to identify practices that are reliably found in the performance of a particular activity. For example, Heritage and his colleagues (2007) were interested in how the use of the words 'anything' or 'something' in the question 'Is there anything/something else you want to address in the visit today?' (*practice*) affected the number of unmet concerns reported by patients in a primary care consultation (see later in this chapter for further discussion of this study).

A key feature of the practices identified through CA is that they should be both *context sensitive* and *context free* (Sacks et al., 1974). They should be *context free* insofar as the practices used are not tied to the specific people in a particular situation, but may be used by other actors in more or less similar situations to achieve similar aims. Practices are also *context sensitive* insofar as they are used in a way that is sensitive both to the preceding talk and to the wider situational or institutional context. CA therefore assumes that the practices and actions of the participants demonstrate their concerns with, and understandings of, the immediate interactional and institutional context in which they are situated. The key task of both institutional and interventionist applied CA is to lay bare the practices and the activities of real interactions, and the role they play in creating the institutional context. However, only interventionist applied CA takes the next step to identify how those mechanisms may be changed in order to resolve some previously identified problem.

Uses of conversation analysis in clinical and health settings

Although there are many we could mention, a few examples of CA research in health and clinical settings are summarized in Table 12.1. While certain features of these studies are discussed in greater detail later, it is perhaps worth noting the following features: the diverse clinical and health settings to which CA has been applied; the wide range in sample sizes, some being very large for such a qualitative, micro-analytical approach as CA; and the use of not only audio but video recording of such personal and private interactions as psychiatric or psychotherapeutic consultations in order to capture the full richness of the interactions. All these issues demonstrate the flexibility of applied CA in clinical and health settings in terms of what can be taken as data, how much of it is needed and the topics and phenomena to which it can be applied.

The most common type of applied CA in clinical and health settings is institutional applied CA. Quirk et al. (2012) provide a clear example of such institutional applied CA through their analysis of the activity of shared decision-making (SDM) about changes to anti-psychotic medication in psychiatric consultations. The UK government's National Institute for Health and Clinical Evidence (NICE) states that shared decision-making (SDM) should underlie changes to and the choice of oral anti-psychotic medication (NICE, 2009). Quirk et al. (2012) used CA to study how SDM occurred in practice. Analysis of 92 consultations allowed the identification of three specific forms of SDM, ranging from pressured decisions, characterized by cycles of psychiatrist suggestions and patient resistance with both parties seemingly concerned about potential loss of face, through directed decisions, characterized by the 'diplomacy of the consultant and the absence of resistance by the patient' (2012:105), to open decisions, characterized by a marked lack of psychiatrist pressure, with multiple opportunities to revisit and revise proposed medication changes.

An important area of clinical research in CA is the study of how people with various forms and types of disabilities and/or communication difficulties interact with others, either in their everyday lives or in institutional settings. Although we have only added one of these studies to Table 12.1, others include studies of dementia, dysarthria, deafness, autism, intellectual disabilities and aphasia (for an overview, see Antaki & Wilkinson, 2013).

Research by Antaki and Jahoda (2010), Parry (2005) and Stivers (2002) can also be seen as falling within the category of institutional applied CA, although all are also concerned with the wider implications of the practices and activities identified. For example, Antaki and Jahoda (2010) are concerned with the therapeutic implications of the practices through which therapists treat client contributions as 'off track'. Stivers (2002) is concerned with the implications of parental pressure to prescribe antibiotics in paediatric consultations, and Parry (2005) discusses how the practices that physiotherapists use to correct physical treatment activities might be inconsistent with the UK Chartered Society of Physiotherapy's standards of practice. Parry showed how the subtle practices used by physiotherapists are sophisticated techniques for the maintenance of an effective therapeutic relationship, despite not being 'open, honest, direct and unambiguous' (2005:208). All therefore have important contributions to make to discussions and debates about how applied CA might inform practice. That they did not set out specifically to address these problems and do not advance specific interventions to address them is the reason that they are not categorized here as interventionist applied CA.

In contrast, the study by Heritage et al. (2007) provides a clear example of interventionist CA. It involves the empirical examination of an intervention, derived from CA, designed to elicit greater problem presentation in primary care consultations, thereby allowing more health concerns to be dealt with earlier and more efficiently in a single consultation. The intervention was relatively simple. Physicians would, after seeing four non-intervention patients, ask

Table 12.1 Examples of various types of applied CA research across a range of clinical and health settings

Authors	Setting	Data	Action	Practices	Type of applied CA (based on Antaki, 2011)
Antaki & Jahoda (2010)	Psychotherapy sessions (specifically cognitive behavioural therapy [CBT])	Audio and video recordings of 13 CBT sessions with intellectually impaired (3) and non-impaired clients (10)	Keeping the therapy session 'on track' when client's talk goes 'off track'	Gradient of therapist responses to 'off-track' talk from minimal receipts, through repeats of parts of client's turn, to explicit orientations to need to remain 'on track'	Institutional
Goodwin (1995)	Man with aphasia interacting with his wife and a nurse	Single case study	Co-construction of meaning; word finding	Guess sequences; use of intonation and bodily behaviour	Institutional
Heritage et al. (2007)	Primary care consultations	Audio and video recordings of 224 consultations (plus questionnaire about unmet concerns)	Eliciting patient reports of unmet health concerns	The use of some or any in the question: 'Is there some/anything else you want to address in the visit today?'	Interventionist
Parry (2005)	Physiotherapy sessions	Audio and video recordings of 72 physiotherapy sessions with patients who had suffered strokes	Identifying and correcting errors in the performance of physical treatment activities	Direct indication and correction of problem vs less direct approaches, including the use of 'adjusting' verbal and non-verbal prompts, 'cushioning' and 'perspective display sequences'.	Institutional

Quirk et al. (2012)	Psychiatric outpatient consultations	Audio recordings of 92 consultations	Shared decision-making about changes to anti-psychotic medication	Pressured, directed and open decision-making styles	Institutional
Schwabe et al. (2007)	Neurology consultations about experiences of seizures	Audio and video recordings of 11 consultations	The differential diagnosis of epileptic and non-epileptic seizures	Use of metaphors, patient or consultant initiation of seizures as topic; spontaneous references to attempts at seizure suppression as basis for potential differentiation between epileptic and non-epileptic seizures	Diagnostic
Stivers (2002)	Paediatric consultations	Audio-only (295) or audio and video recordings (66) of 360 acute paediatric consultations	Shared decision-making about the prescription of antibiotics	Direct requests from parents for antibiotics, stated desire for antibiotic treatment, questions about antibiotic treatment and reports of past experiences of antibiotic treatment	Institutional

the next patient one of two randomly assigned questions after the patient had presented their primary health concern. The physician would ask either 'Is there something else you want to address in the visit today?' (SOME condition) or 'Is there anything else you want to address in the visit today?' (ANY condition). Analysis of the consultations allowed identification of the number of extra problems presented. These were also compared with a questionnaire completed by the participants prior to the consultation in which they had listed all 'their "reasons for seeing the doctor today, including the problems and concerns you want to talk about with the doctor"' (Heritage et al., 2007:1430). The researchers found that the SOME condition had the equivalent effect of reducing unmet concerns by 78% relative to the non-intervention condition. In contrast, the ANY condition could not be distinguished, in terms of reducing unmet concerns, from the non-intervention condition. Heritage et al. were therefore able to make clear recommendations as to how physicians should ask this kind of question to make the most effective use of each consultation. It should be noted that the use of CA alongside quantitative measurement and inferential statistical analysis is a controversial feature of applied CA work, but one that is perhaps necessary if it is to be effective in persuading wider audiences of the merits of CA-derived interventions.

Finally, the third and certainly smallest category of applied CA work in clinical and health settings is diagnostic applied CA (from Antaki, 2011), represented in Table 12.1 by the work of Schwabe et al. (2007). These researchers were concerned with using CA-derived findings to differentiate between epileptic and non-epileptic seizures. According to these authors, the task of differentiation can be difficult and time-consuming, taking on average seven years to make an accurate diagnosis and often only achieved through the use of video EEG. This study involved a small sample of 11 patients. A linguist, blind to the patients' diagnosis, was trained to identify the practices hypothesized (from CA work) to be characteristic of descriptions of epileptic and non-epileptic seizures. In all cases, the linguist was able to differentiate reliably between the two types. Such diagnostic use of applied CA is in its early stages, but nonetheless it represents a potentially interesting application of the method and an example of the verification of its reliability through 'blind' techniques.

Doing conversation analysis: The basics

Data collection and ethics

Conversation analysis uses recordings of interactions between people. Since it is concerned with how social life is organized, the best data are recordings of real-life interactions rather than research interviews. While early CA work used audio recordings, video recording is now increasingly employed because it can capture important non-verbal behaviours, which audio cannot. CA does not use traditional observational methods (e.g. on-the-spot coding or note-taking) because the analysis requires a verbatim transcript of the interaction, including such features as intonations, pauses, overlap in turns and so on. An in situ observer is unable to record all of these features. In addition, the analytical process requires repeated examination of interactional sequences, the relevant parts of which might only become apparent later in the analysis. CA also has not traditionally asked people to report what they do in interaction. One reason is that it is impossible to remember accurately all the relevant features of even very short interactions.

A project might involve analysis of publicly available recordings (e.g. televised debates; radio phone-ins) or the researcher might collect their own recordings. If recordings are collected, strict ethical procedures must be followed. Participants might feel uneasy about being recorded, and researchers might find that while some people in a setting are happy to be recorded, others do not wish to participate. This means that the researcher must be able to turn the recording device off when those who have not chosen to participate are present. In addition, participants who do consent must be regularly reminded that they can ask for the recording to be stopped at any time, and can request that their data not be used if they have second thoughts.

Participants need to be informed how the data might be used (e.g. published papers, presentations) and how their identities will be protected. If recordings of extracts are played in presentations, anonymization will involve blurring of faces, removal of identifying names and details and, if necessary, altering the sound of voices and 'beeping out' details. This is particularly important if there is a chance that audience members might be familiar with the institution in which the data was collected. Because video data make people easily identifiable and can be posted on internet video sites, particular care needs to be taken with electronic files involving video or audio recordings. If other computers are used to make presentations or if computers are upgraded, video files need to be deleted in such a way that they cannot be retrieved. See Chapter 3 for further discussion of ethical issues.

Transcription

Depending on the size of the research project, you might either transcribe all the recordings collected, or else select particular types or features of interactions and transcribe only those. A detailed transcription is essential for analysis and includes many features that a standard interview transcript would not (e.g. pauses, overlaps in speech, changes in volume or speed of speech). This can make it difficult to read for those unfamiliar with CA. It is impossible to transcribe every feature of an interaction, so the level of detail you aim for will depend on your approach to analysis. Linguists might use a much more detailed transcript involving, for example, intonation features. Applied CA tends to use the Jeffersonian system (see Box 12.1 for some examples), although analysts tend to adapt this system rather than follow it slavishly. The

---

BOX 12.1 Some features of the Jeffersonian transcription system

(.)	Just noticeable pause
(.3), (2.6)	Examples of timed pauses in seconds
word [word]	
[word]	Speakers' words overlap with another speaker
wor-	Sharp cut-off
wo:::rd	Speaker has stretched the preceding sound
(words)	A guess at what might have been said
( )	Talk too unclear to merit even a guess
word= =word	Words run together
wo̲rd, WORD	Underlined sounds are louder, capitals louder still
°word°	Material between 'degree signs' is quiet
>word word<	Inward arrows show faster speech
wo(h)rd(h)	Shows that the word has 'laughter' bubbling within it
((*smile voice*)	Attempt at representing something hard to write phonetically
→	Analyst's signal of a significant line

Source: ten Have (2007).

---

level of transcription used must be detailed enough for the purposes of the analysis. For example, some analysts might render all words as they sound, while others might adopt conventional spellings unless the speaker clearly diverges from standard pronunciation. In our work with people with limited symbolic communication, we included more detail of the non-verbal features of interaction (e.g. gaze and hand movements) than analysts examining other contexts might do.

An example of a short section of transcribed interaction from one of our studies is provided in Box 12.2. It is crucial for the analysis and the write-up that line numbers are given. You can also see that we have tried to record non-verbal behaviours in italics and round brackets (lines 08 and 10) and have noted with square brackets the many times that overlaps occur (moments when people are speaking over each other or are acting simultaneously). Given the importance attached to the sequential organization of interaction in CA, one of the real challenges of transcription is making clear when one thing occurs relative to another. As you can see, it is not easy to read for the uninitiated.

Analytical approaches

Broadly, there are two approaches to analysis (Hutchby & Wooffitt, 1998). One is to collect a large number of one particular type of phenomenon – this might include a particular type of *practice* (e.g. the use of the phrase 'To be honest'; the use of reported speech) or a particular type of conversational *activity* (e.g. making a complaint; getting caller details during a phone call to

---

BOX 12.2 Example of transcription

```
01  Jill     (off camera) >d'y wanna< another go,
02           (.3)
03  Chris    w'done Jul[ie.
04  Jill               [d'y wan' another go,
05           (.5)
06  (?)      (laughter)) (.3) (              )
07  Jill     c'mon (.3) >sh'we get weighed<
08  Matt     (°nerh°)=      [(Matthew turns away)]
09  Jill     =weighed? (.)  [no (.) we had a clear no: there,
10                          [(Jill drops M's hand, straightens)
11  Chris    Right.
12           (.3)
13  Jill     you don't have to.
```

---

a crisis line). In this case the analyst might have a collection of transcripts involving many different actors, and the goal would be to identify if there were particular patterns to the way such activities were carried out or such practices were used.

The other is more of a case-study approach, where a particular interaction (or a small number of interactions) is examined in depth (e.g. a psychiatrist and patient making a decision about medication). Such analysis is likely to draw on insights from previous CA studies in order to describe how an interaction unfolds over extended sequences. In our work we have found this particularly useful in studying how issues of choice and empowerment might play out in social care services.

In both cases, rather than the analyst knowing or predicting what they will find, the aim is to see what is there, to work up through micro-analysis a description of what actually happens. The aim is to describe patterns in interaction rather than to confirm or disprove theories.

The process of analysis

It is impossible to set out a required set of procedures or steps, as different researchers will take different approaches to their analysis. Rather, conversation analysis requires a certain way of looking at the data. As Hutchby and Wooffitt (1998:94) put it: 'The conversation analytic mentality involves more a cast of mind, or a way of seeing, than a static and prescriptive set of instructions, which analysts brings to bear on the data.' While this might sound rather discouraging to those wishing a quick and clear set of instructions, CA is a skilled activity that requires familiarity with previous research.

Research in this field has been conducted for over 40 years and there is now a sizeable body of literature examining how different activities are performed and how practices occur in different types of activity, as well as a set of terms for different features of conversation. Some of the terms used in CA are also used by other qualitative analysts – for example, three-part list (Jefferson, 1990), extreme case formulation (Pomerantz, 1986), contrast structure (Hutchby, 1992) – while others are not widely known outside the field – for example, adjacency pairs, preference structure, other-initiated repair, turn-constructional unit.

How do you choose which parts of the data to analyse?

In CA, transcripts are not generally analysed in their entirety. There must be an initial process of selection, where a choice is made about which types of activity or practice are to be the focus of the analysis. In some cases, the analyst is clear about what particular feature of interaction they are interested in before the analysis begins. For example, in our work one of our interests was in how choices were offered. This was stated as one of our goals when we applied for our research grant, long before any data were collected. As a result, we began by collecting examples of people offering choices to each other from our videos.

However, in many cases the analyst does not know in advance what they will concentrate on. Most early CA work tended to adopt this approach. It involves examining the transcript and listening to/viewing the recordings without having a clear focus. Often this is done as 'data sessions' with others, where there is a discussion about what is happening in the transcript. It might be that the activity of interest is only identified after a process of examination and discussion.

What does the analysis involve?

Overview

In general, once an activity or practice is decided on, the analyst would analyse a sequence in which it occurs, trying to build up a rich understanding of the turns involved and how the sequence develops. Each turn in the conversation is understood as responding to the previous turn and creating a new context for the next turn. This does not always happen in a clear fashion, however, and the analyst must also see how misunderstandings, counter-normative responses and other conversational 'troubles' form part of the interactional sequence. An important principle in CA is that participants' understandings are visible in the interaction itself. Therefore, you are interested in how participants *treat* each other's turns. For example, Jim asks Julie if she likes the pie he has made. Julie replies, 'Um (1.2) it's ok.' Jim then responds by snatching her plate away and saying, 'Well you don't have to eat it!' We can see how Jim has understood Julie's reply by examining his response to it. We might then go back to examine Julie's turn to understand how its design ('Um (1.2) it's ok') might lead to Jim's angry response. In this case it is important to know that previous CA research has shown that positive evaluations are often given without hesitation and unambiguously (Kitzinger & Frith, 1999). In contrast, a response involving hesitations (Um...), pauses and neutral evaluations (it's ok) may be heard as indicating a negative evaluation.

Having examined one sequence in depth and identified a candidate practice or activity, the researcher would then look for other instances in their recordings and analyse them, examining whether there are general patterns that can be described across the data (that is, whether a particular practice is generally part of a particular kind of activity). Differences should be noted and examined as they provide depth to the analysis: an understanding of how different patterns develop with different actors and across different contexts will lead to a deeper insight into the phenomenon. The temptation to ignore variation should be resisted, as this will oversimplify the relationships between practices and activities.

Breaking the analysis into steps

Drew (2007) provides some suggestions for carrying out CA (see Box 12.3). The starting point here is to *identify the activity* in which the participants are engaged. In applied health or clinical settings, activities might include offering a formulation, gathering background information, carrying out an assessment, explaining a problem, obtaining consent and delivering a complaint, among many other activities. Here it is important to familiarize yourself with the literature, because it may be that we already know something about how these activities are carried out in other contexts.

Drew suggests that the analyst then attempt to see *how the activity is managed* between the participants (that is, which practices the participants use in a turn-by-turn manner). The analyst does this by looking at what happens just before the activities begin (pre-sequences), how the actors propose activities, how they respond to each other and how the interaction unfolds. While examining how the activity is managed, you would pay attention to both the content and the form of what people say, how the actors' understanding of the context and the preceding turn is displayed in their talk, and how turn-taking is managed. (Are there silences? Do people interrupt or talk over each other?)

BOX 12.3 General steps when first looking at a transcript

1. Identify the activity.
2. Is there a sequence leading up to the activity? Does the sequence prepare the way for the activity in any way?
3. Examine how the activity is proposed.
4. Examine how the other person responds.
5. Examine the subsequent turns, paying attention to how each turn responds to the previous turn.

Source: Drew (2007).

If non-verbal behaviour is important, you might also examine how gestures and other bodily movements are used and when they occur relative to the spoken component. The result might be the identification of regular patterns in a certain type of interaction or a rich description of a particular interaction. Often the management of an activity occurs over a number of turns. In cases where a complex decision is made, for example, the activity can occur over several pages of transcript (e.g. Antaki et al., 2006).

A general strategy for exploring the management of activities in an extract is suggested by ten Have (2007). He proposes using a set of four 'organizations' (see Box 12.4) to focus the initial analysis. Although insights can be gained from trying to do this without any prior knowledge of CA, good-quality research will usually require the analyst to have some familiarity with basic CA concepts and research (for introductions see Hutchby & Wooffitt, 1998; ten Have, 2007)

This general strategy allows you to build an understanding of what is happening in the extract through a close inspection of its organizational structure. As you work through the extract, you would note the practices relevant to this organizational work (e.g. how turns are handed over; how overlaps are resolved; how topics are initiated and closed down). Write notes as you notice things. Finally, try to come up with some general descriptions that summarize your observations. Remember, the aim is to develop an in-depth understanding of what actually happens in practice when people interact in particular settings, and to identify the patterns to these activities. In applied

---

BOX 12.4 Looking in more detail at the turns in the interaction

1. *Turn-taking organization.* The set of practices by which speakers manage turns in conversation. The analyst would look at such features as pauses, overlaps and how changes from speaker to speaker are coordinated.

2. *Sequence organization.* Utterances are usually designed for particular 'slots' in conversation. For example, some utterances invite particular kinds of responses (e.g. question–answer). When the response is not normative, this might be marked in the interaction in various ways and lead to further turns.

3. *Repair organization.* Repairs are ways of dealing with 'trouble' (e.g. misunderstandings, relevance problems, lack of clarity). There are a range of ways of signalling trouble as well as initiating repair in which either party in a conversation might engage.

4. *Organization of turn design.* This is a further set of general concepts that help us understand turns in conversation: ten Have includes ideas such as 'recipient design' and 'preference structure'. For example, recipient design concerns how one actor might design their utterance to take into account who the other person is (for example, using simplified vocabulary to a young child).

Source: ten Have (2007).

work, this can help us see where problems arise and how people attempt to solve them, how people position each other (e.g. as more or less competent), how things 'work' and how what happens might or might not conform to broader institutional goals.

In applied CA research, it is also important to note the wider *social context* of the activities. For example, a doctor might be recommending a particular treatment to a particular patient, and the management of this activity is the focus of the analysis. However, there may be an institutional focus on 'patient-centred care' or 'shared decision-making' (SDM) that is relevant to such interactions. Conversation analysts might disagree about the extent to which bringing in the wider institutional or ideological context is acceptable, but research aimed at practitioners would need to understand how the management of such interactions is relevant to the normative models of doctor–patient interaction found in professional and institutional discourse (Peräkylä & Vehviläinen, 2003). For example, an analysis might look at how particular types of turns seem to be in line with the principles of SDM, while others might appear to go against such principles (see Quirk et al., 2012).

Worked example

This example is from a project we carried out that might be described as institutional or interventionist applied CA (Antaki et al., 2008; Finlay et al., 2011). This recording was made in a staffed social care home for adults with intellectual disabilities during a meeting to plan meals for the week (for a full analysis, see Antaki & Finlay, 2012). Two staff members and five residents are sitting around a table, on which are various food packets and photos of food. Tim and Kath (staff members) are asking resident Alec what he would like for dessert.

EXTRACT 12.1   CHW Peaches

```
1 Tim:    Alec (.5) what d' you want for pudding look there's (.3)[prunes,
2 Tim:                                                             [((touches prunes tin))
3 Tim:    [peaches, (.8)
4 Tim:    [((points at peaches tin)) ((to Kath, aside)) we haven't got Angel Delight
5 Alec:       [peaches
6             [((taps peaches tin))
7 Kath:   Angel Delight we haven't got, no.
8 Alec:   [Tim, this one
9         [((picks up & holds peaches tin, shakes it))
```

We start by identifying the activity: Tim is asking Alec to decide which pudding he would like for the meal. This can be understood in terms of the wider institutional goal of promoting self-determination among residents by eliciting their preferences in everyday areas of their lives. This relates to the government policy of promoting 'choice and control' in social care services. What we are examining, then, is how policy gets translated into practice.

Tim begins this activity by naming Alec. This is understandable in the context – there are several other residents at the table and the discussion immediately before this extract involved a different resident. Use of Alec's name nominates him as the next speaker. This might seem trivial, but later in the extract we will see names being used for other purposes.

The next thing we notice is how the question is posed: 'what d' you want for pudding'. This open question seems to be clear and not to require any further elaboration. In CA terms it is a *turn constructional unit* (an utterance that could be a complete unit and would allow the next speaker to begin). Alec could therefore answer after the word 'pudding' (a place where a speaker changes is called a *transition relevance place*). However, Tim does not allow a space for Alec to reply (for example, by leaving a pause) and Alec does not jump in with an answer at this point. Rather, Tim continues to speak. He points out two options (prunes and peaches) and he offers these two options both verbally and by tapping the relevant tins. Here we see an instance of *recipient design* – Tim is designing his utterance for Alec and is orienting to potential difficulties in comprehension by using both verbal language and physical prompts.

At this point (line 4), Tim's attention is turned to the other staff member, Kath, and he asks her a question. Alec then responds 'peaches' and combines the word with a physical prompt (he taps the tin of peaches – lines 5 and 6). In line 7 Kath replies to Tim's question about Angel Delight. Alec then says 'Tim this one' and uses a more emphatic physical prompt – he picks up the tin and shakes it.

We would look at this and note that Alec has repeated his choice of peaches. Repeating what you have said is one way of addressing 'trouble' in a conversation – in this case Alec is treating Tim as either not having heard or not having attended to his earlier utterance. Repeating what you have already said is a form of 'repair' (an attempt to fix the trouble).

Seeing where in the sequence Alec does this also gives us a clue as to what is happening – it is reasonable to suppose that Tim's attention might be elsewhere, since Alec's first attempt to give his choice (lines 5 and 6) occurs between Tim asking Kath a question (line 4) and Kath answering it (line 7). That Alec is engaged in a form of repair is also seen in the way he expresses his choice this second time – he begins his turn in line 8 by using Tim's name ('Tim this one'). While we saw in line 1 that Tim used Alec's name to nominate him as the next speaker, here Tim's name is used to call him to attention after he has been distracted by Kath. Secondly, Alec then picks up and shakes the tin, which is a more emphatic way of indicating his choice than simply tapping it. When we look at such fine-tuned aspects of social behaviour in a setting like this, we often note the sophisticated social understandings demonstrated by people labelled as having 'intellectual disabilities' (for a discussion of this issue, see Rapley, 2004). This type of practical and flexible social skill is often neglected in more formal clinical assessments of expressive communication.

So far, we have seen how Tim offers a choice, how Alec offers an initial reply and then how Alec reformats his reply in a more emphatic way. His choice seems clear – he has named it, pointed to it, called Tim's attention to it, picked up the tin and shaken it. We might expect the sequence to end there – Tim would notice and accept Alec's choice and the discussion would move on to something else. However, this is not what happens.

EXTRACT 12.2   CHW Peaches (cont.)

10	Kath:	There's [semolina as well
11	Kath:	[(*points across table with pen*)
12	Tim :	You want (.) there's [Angel Delight
13	Tim:	[(*picks up Angel Delight packet and drops on table*)
14	Alec:	[(*puts down tin of peaches, picks up a pile of dessert*
15		*packets*)
16	Tim:	or there's [Semolina (.) or you can
17	Tim:	[(*picks up and puts down Semolina packet on table*)
18	Tim:	have [prunes (.)
19	Tim:	[(*touches prunes tin*)
20	Alec:	[(*puts a pile of dessert packets on table*)
21	Kath:	Which one do you want Alec
22	Alec:	(*picks up packet of Angel Delight, holds it toward Kath*) that one

---

Instead of accepting Alec's choice of peaches, Kath and Tim offer further options: semolina, Angel Delight and prunes (lines 10, 12, 16, 18). Normally when offers are made, or questions are asked, an answer is expected. This is the principle of *adjacency pairs* – that conversation often involves regular structures whereby the first part of a pair (e.g. a question, an offer) is followed by a particular type of response (e.g. an answer, an acceptance or a refusal). However, this process does not work so clearly here. Alec offers a response of peaches, but this is ignored. Kath and Alec then offer further options, but Alec seems to offer no response. We might suppose that having failed in his attempt to provide an answer earlier, he has for the moment given up. However, the form of these offers is ambiguous – Kath and Tim are not using questions in their standard forms, but rather are pointing out options. They are telling him 'there's semolina' or 'you can have prunes'. These options, then, are not phrased as questions.

Given both what has gone before (his choice was ignored) and the verbal format of these offers, it is not clear whether Alec is expected to provide a response at this point, and we can see that indeed he does not respond. However, he does do something non-verbally – he drops the tin of peaches (line 14) and picks up a pile of packets of dried dessert, which he then puts back on the table in line 20. It is only when Kath returns to an open question, 'which one do you want Alec' in line 21, that Alec again attempts a response. Before we look at this, we should just note in passing that Kath has used Alec's name in a similar way to line 1 – she is nominating him as the next speaker and therefore indicating to him that now he is expected to respond.

His response is to pick up a packet of Angel Delight and say 'that one'. Alec seems to have changed his mind. The dilemma for staff is to decide which is his real choice – is it peaches or is it Angel Delight? CA can help us understand what has happened here by looking at what happens turn by turn in the sequence. Alec has been asked to make a choice. He makes a clear choice of peaches, but his choice is not recognized. Instead, further options are offered (to which he does not respond). Finally, he is asked more directly to make a choice and he chooses something different to his initial choice. It seems plausible to suggest that the change in his choice from peaches to Angel Delight follows from the fact that his initial choice is ignored. In ordinary conversation, when a person offers a clear opinion or preference twice and their interlocutor ignores it and offers alternative suggestions, this can be seen as an indication that the initial opinion is faulty in some way. This seems to be what happens here – Alec treats the lack of even a minimal acknowledgement of his first choice (which he has repeated emphatically) as an indication that he must try again.

We have examined the sequence in terms of its activities (offering and making choices), the practices involved (e.g. open questions, nominations, use of gestures, offering a range of options) and its sequential progress. Because this is applied CA, we would then want to try to make sense of it in its institutional context, and here we bring in details from our knowledge of the local setting. One of the goals of the residential unit is to promote residents' choice in aspects of their lives, and this is a clear example of staff trying to achieve this. Choosing meals in a formal meeting also provides written evidence for inspectors that the residents do have choice in the food they eat. Conversations with staff also revealed that they shared a level of uncertainty when communicating with Alec – they worried that sometimes he merely repeated back to them things they had said without making a 'real choice'. We can also bring in our observations from other interactions we recorded – and this phenomenon of offering multiple choices, and of residents changing their choices, happened in a number of situations.

At this point, we could go a step further and make an observation that we think might improve practice in this social care setting. In their efforts to offer Alec a full range of options so that he can make an informed choice, members of staff often make the expression of choice more difficult for Alec, particularly when he responds before they have offered the full range of options. In effect, by ignoring his early choices, they treat them as faulty, leading him to change them. An interaction designed to empower Alec seems to disempower him. When we played extracts like this to the staff group in a workshop, they were able to see these problems straightaway. They decided to try to reduce their use of verbal multiple-option formats, to pay more attention to initial indications of choice from service users and to make more use of non-verbal methods of offering choices (e.g. providing objects from which to select).

This example demonstrates how a close inspection of the details of interactional practice in a health/clinical setting can help us understand some of the difficulties of translating policy into practice, and at the same time lead to direct advice as to how practice might be improved.

Concluding comments

CA is a powerful tool for understanding practice in real-life clinical settings. It allows the examination of how institutional policies or professional goals are translated into everyday practice. Applied CA can provide the basis for interventions to improve practice and better meet those policies and goals. CA is a method that depends on experience and familiarity with the literature and the terminology used to describe already identified practices and activities. Although it may seem daunting at first, what CA requires most of all is a willingness to engage with the mechanics of everyday interaction.

Note

The data in the worked example were collected with Charles Antaki as part of a project funded by ESRC grant Res-148-25-0002. We remain grateful to the NHS Trust in which the research took place and the staff and residents involved.

Further reading

Charles Antaki has created a useful online tutorial: http://homepages.lboro.ac.uk/~sscal/sitemenu.htm

Paul ten Have has a useful set of links and resources: http://www.paultenhave.nl/resource.htm

Forrester, M. (2002) *How to Do Conversation Analysis: A Brief Guide*.
A good introduction to doing CA that can be downloaded from the resources section of the HE Academy website: http://www.heacademy.ac.uk

References

Antaki, C. (2011). *Applied Conversation Analysis*. Basingstoke: Palgrave Macmillan.

Antaki, C. & Finlay, W.M.L. (2012). Trust in what others mean: Breakdowns in interaction between adults with intellectual disabilities and support staff. In C.N. Candlin & J. Crichton (eds), *Discourses of Trust*. Basingstoke: Palgrave Macmillan.

Antaki, C. & Wilkinson R. (2013). Conversation analysis and the study of atypical populations. In T. Stivers & J. Sidnell (eds), *Handbook of Conversation Analysis* (pp. 533°550). Oxford: Wiley-Blackwell.

Antaki, C. & Jahoda, A. (2010). Psychotherapists' practices in keeping a session 'on-track' in the face of clients 'off-track' talk. *Communication & Medicine*, 7(1), 11–21.

Antaki, C., Finlay, W., Walton, C. & Pate, L. (2008). Offering choices to people with intellectual disabilities: An interactional study. *Journal of Intellectual Disability Research*, 52(12), 1165–1175.

Antaki, C, Finlay, W.M.L., Sheridan, E., Jingree, T. & Walton, C. (2006). Producing decisions in service-user groups for people with an intellectual disability: Two contrasting facilitator styles. *Mental Retardation*, 44(5), 322–343.

Drew, P. (2007). Conversation analysis. In J.A. Smith (ed.), *Qualitative Psychology: A Practical Guide to Research Methods* (pp. 133–159). London: Sage.

Finlay, W.M.L., Walton, C. & Antaki, C. (2011). Giving feedback to staff about offering choices to people with intellectual disabilities. In C. Antaki (ed.), *Applied Conversation Analysis*. Basingstoke: Palgrave Macmillan.

Garfinkel, H. (1967). *Studies in Ethnomethodology*. Englewood Cliffs, NJ: Prentice Hall.

Goffman, E. (1983). The interaction order: American Sociological Association, 1982 presidential address. *American Sociological Review*, 48, 1–17.

Goodwin, C. (1995). Co-constructing meaning in conversations with an aphasic man. *Research on Language and Social Interaction*, 28(3), 233–260.

Heritage, J. (1998). Oh-prefaced responses to inquiry. *Language in Society*, 27(3), 291–334.

Heritage, J., Robinson, J.D., Elliott, M.N., Beckett, M. & Wilkes, M. (2007). Reducing patients' unmet concerns in primary care: The difference one word can make. *Journal of General Internal Medicine*, 22(10), 1429–1433.

Hutchby, I. (1992). The pursuit of controversy: Routine skepticism in talk on 'talk radio'. *Sociology*, 26(4), 673–694.

Hutchby, I. & Woofitt, R. (1998). *Conversation Analysis*. Cambridge: Polity Press.

Jefferson, G. (1990). List-construction as a task and a resource. In G. Psathas (ed.), *Interaction Competence* (pp. 63–92). Washington, DC: University Press of America.

Kitzinger, C. & Frith, H. (1999). Just say no? The use of conversation analysis in developing a feminist perspective on sexual refusal. *Discourse & Society*, 10(3), 293–316.

National Institute for Health and Clinical Excellence (NICE). (2009). *Schizophrenia: Core Interventions in the Treatment and Management of Schizophrenia in Primary and Secondary Care*. Guideline 82. London: NICE.

Parry, R. (2005). A video analysis of how physiotherapists communicate with patients about errors of performance: Insights for practice and policy. *Physiotherapy*, 91(4), 204–214.

Peräkylä, A. & Vehviläinen, S. (2003). Conversation analysis and the professional stocksof interactional knowledge. *Discourse & Society*, 14(6), 727–750.

Pomerantz, A.M. (1986). Extreme case formulations: A way of legitimizing claims. *Human Studies*, 9, 219–230.

Quirk, A., Chaplin, R., Lelliott, P. & Seale, C. (2012). How pressure is applied in shared decisions about antipsychotic medication: A conversation analytic study of psychiatric outpatient consultations. *Sociology of Health & Illness*, 34(1), 95–113.

Rapley, M. (2004). *The Social Construction of Intellectual Disability*. Cambridge: Cambridge University Press.

Sacks, H. (1992). *Lectures in Conversation*. Oxford: Blackwell.

Sacks, H., Schegloff, E.A. & Jefferson, G. (1974). A simplest systematics for the organization of turn-taking for conversation. *Language*, *50*(4), 696–735.

Schegloff, E.A. (1992). Introduction. In H. Sacks, *Lectures in Conversation*, ed. G. Jefferson. Oxford: Blackwell.

Schegloff, E., & Lerner, G. (2009). Beginning to respond: Well-prefaced responses to Wh- questions. *Research on Language and Social Interaction*, *42*(2), 91–115.

Schegloff, E.A., Jefferson, G. & Sacks, H. (1977). The preference for self-correction in the organization of repair in conversation. *Language*, *53*(2), 361–382.

Schwabe, M., Howell, S.J. & Reuber, M. (2007). Differential diagnosis of seizure disorders: A conversation analytic approach. *Social Science & Medicine*, *65*(4), 712–724.

Stivers, T. (2002). Participating in decisions about treatment: Overt parent pressure for antibiotic medication in pediatric encounters. *Social Science & Medicine*, *54*(7), 1111–1130.

ten Have, P. (2007). *Doing Conversation Analysis: A Practical Guide*. London: Sage.

Discourse Analysis

Jane M. Ussher and Janette Perz

13

Historical background

Providing an exact definition of discourse analysis is a matter fraught with difficulty, as there are a number of competing schools of thought, as well as ongoing debates and developments in both theory and practice. Discourse analysis (DA) evolved within a range of diverse disciplinary contexts, including literary criticism, linguistics, cognitive psychology, philosophy and sociology. The influence of these disciplines shapes the various strands of discourse analysis practised in psychology today. For example, within linguistic psychology, the focus is on fine-grained sentence structure and utterances; within cognitive psychology, attention is paid to the role of mental schemas and scripts in the comprehension of language (see Potter, 2004). However, the two strands of DA that originated within literary theory, sociology and philosophy have had the greatest influence on the discipline and are the most widely used methods of DA in health and clinical psychology. They will thus form the focus of this chapter.

The 'turn to language' that introduced discourse analysis to psychology in the 1980s was well underway in sociology, philosophy and communications in the 1950s and 1960s. This 'turn' marked a shift from the conceptualization of language as a reflection of thought or experience to seeing language as both performative and productive, central to the construction of social reality and subjectivity. Two seminal publications introduced this body of work to psychology: *Discourse and Social Psychology: Beyond Attitudes and Behaviour* (Potter & Wetherell, 1987) and *Changing the Subject: Psychology, Social Regulation and Subjectivity* (Henriques et al., 1984). It is not an understatement to say that these texts spearheaded a revolution within social and feminist psychology, challenging cognitivism and realism, and placing the focus of research on the role of language in the constitution of the social realm, rather than on the internal cognitions or behaviour of the individual psychological subject. Discourse analysis has therefore always been more than a method – it stands as a critique of mainstream psychology (see Potter, 2012).

The decades that followed have been marked by rich and vigorous debate about the nature and function of discourse analysis, leading to a range of interpretations and developments of this early work (Billig, 2012; Edwards & Potter, 1992; Hollway, 1989; Parker, 1992; Parker, 2012; Wetherell, 1998). This has crystallized into two identifiable, but overlapping, schools of thought, described as discursive psychology (DP) and Foucauldian discourse analysis (FDA). In this chapter, I will examine the theoretical and conceptual framework of both approaches, their commonalities and differences, and their applicability for clinical and health psychology.

Discursive psychology

The strand of discourse analysis now referred to as 'discursive psychology' (Edwards & Potter, 1992) was first introduced to psychology through the publication of *Discourse and Social Psychology* (Potter & Wetherell, 1987). Influenced by poststructuralist literary theory, as well as the sociology of scientific knowledge (Potter, 2012), DP focuses on the analysis of 'interpretive repertoires' or 'discourses': sets of statements that reflect shared patterns of meaning. DP draws on the practices of ethnomethodology and conversation analysis, and focuses on the *action orientation* of talk and text in social practice: what is the text *doing*, rather than what does the text mean or 'what is the text saying?' (Willig, 2008:98). Topics recognized in mainstream psychology, such as 'memory', 'causal attribution', 'script' and knowledge, are reframed as 'discourse practices' (Edwards & Potter, 2005:241). Thus, for example, the study of attitudes is replaced by analysis of argumentative practices in discourse (Potter & Wetherell, 1987).

Discursive psychologists are concerned with the management of issues of 'stake or interest' within talk (Potter, 2004). For example, an individual may say 'I've got nothing against gay people, but I don't agree with gay marriage' as a way of disclaiming a homophobic identity, then legitimate their position by appealing to a higher authority: 'scientific research makes it clear that children need to be brought up by a man and a woman'. Within DP, attention is also paid to the *negotiation* of meaning within language, and to the interaction between speakers in everyday situations. The *form* of language is also of interest, in order to examine 'what people do' with language (Potter, 2004:203) and how they manage social interactions. Emphasis is thus placed on the rhetorical or argumentative nature of talk and texts (Billig, 1991), metaphors and analogies, extreme case examples, graphic descriptions and consensus formulations (see Edwards & Potter, 1992). The association of gay marriage with bestiality and polygamy within political and media debate in both the United Kingdom and Australia would provide ideal fodder for discursive analysis of extreme cases. Analysis is frequently focused on the often contradictory interpretative repertoires on which individuals draw in their accounts (Wetherell, 1998) and the rhetorical context within which such repertoires are deployed.

While many discursive psychologists conduct interviews as a means of analysing discourse, naturally occurring talk is often the focus of analysis, as research questions centre on how people account for themselves and interact in everyday life, with the intention of achieving personal objectives (Willig, 2008). For example, Curl and Drew (2008) examined language use in phone calls to emergency services; Rowe and colleagues (2003) investigated representations of 'depression' in the print media in Australia; and Brown (1999) conducted a critical analysis of self-help literature. In a health or clinical context, interactions between patients and health professionals, therapists and clients, or lay people discussing health issues on the radio or television also provide appropriate material for investigation. For example, Mark Rapley examined the social construction of intellectual disability, identifying the ways in which talk and text actively constitute the truths about being 'mental' as well as 'disabled' (2004:10) through the analysis of 'official' texts and the interactions of health professionals with people described as intellectually disabled. In a further study, McHoul and Rapley (2005) examined the transcript of a diagnostic session involving a young boy, his parents and a paediatrician, to contest the diagnosis of attention deficit disorder (ADHD). In Extract 13.1, the mother's account of how she came to bring her son to see the paediatrician is analysed.

EXTRACT 13.1

Mo: >I j's think< (I was) just picking up
     (.) things along the way
Dr: Mm hm
Mo: We (.) just basic'ly decided to eliminate
Dr: Mm hm
     Mo: the possibility
Dr: Mm hm
     (0.7)
Dr: So you really hadn't got– had great problems
     until he'd got to schoo:l (mm) °is'at right°

The interaction within this account is interpreted as representing the mother adopting a scientific process of deduction through collecting data and evidence, 'just picking things up along the way', in order to refute the conjecture that she was overly concerned. 'Problems' are identified and tied to school, but not, as yet, identified as ADHD. In combination with analysis of the remainder of the interview, this local instance of talk-in-interaction is used to examine how routine and mundane it is for children to be positively diagnosed and medicated merely on presentation with the possibility of ADHD, even when parents are manifestly sceptical about the diagnosis (McHoul & Rapley, 2005:419).

Foucauldian discourse analysis

Foucauldian discourse analysis (FDA) originates within poststructuralist theory, influenced by the philosophical work of Michel Foucault (1972, 1984). Within FDA, discourses are described as 'sets of statements that constitute objects and an array of subject positions' (Parker, 1994:245) that are 'a product of social factors, of powers and processes, rather than an individual's set of ideas' (Hollway, 1983:231). Language is deemed to be constitutive of social life, making available certain subject positions that influence and regulate subjectivity and experience – the way we think or feel, our sense of self and the practices in which we engage (Gavey, 1989). FDA is thus concerned with identifying discourses, the subject positions they open up (or disallow) and the implications of such positioning for subjectivity and social practice, rather than the form or structure of interaction within talk or text. This includes analysis of expert discourse and institutional practice, talk generated through interviews, diaries or group discussions, and broader cultural representations.

In contrast to the focus of DP on interpersonal communication, FDA centres on the examination of the relationship *between* discourse, subjectivity, practice and the material conditions within which experience takes place (Willig, 2008). This leads to attention being paid to wider social processes and power, and how social order and the political realm are produced and reproduced through discourse (Burman & Parker, 1993). For example, the biomedical discourse, which positions health professionals (in particular doctors) as all-knowing and powerful and health problems as pathologies to be eradicated through expert intervention, has been identified as one of the most powerful discourses in the field of health and illness (Foucault, 1987). Legitimating the subject positions 'expert' and 'patient', it leads to a focus on somatic or psychological 'symptoms', which are deemed to be located within the individual and conceptualized in a realist manner as existing outside of language or cultural interpretation (Fee, 2000). Thus, individuals who experience changes in mood, sleep patterns or energy, and who report such changes to a medical practitioner, are positioned as 'depressive' and their future experiences interpreted through a medical lens, when they may have previously normalized or accepted such changes (LaFrance, 2007). This positioning of emotional and behavioural changes as psychiatric illness, or madness, can be identified as serving to maintain the boundaries of normality, leading to self-policing on the part of the individual, in order to avoid diagnosis (Ussher, 2011) or return to 'normality' after diagnosis is given (LaFrance, 2009).

In this vein, FDA has been used to examine expert accounts of diagnosis or treatment (Johnstone, 1999; Larsson et al., 2012; Malson, 1998), broader cultural representations (Bilić & Georgaca, 2007) and lay experiences of psychological distress or diagnosis (Guise et al., 2010; LaFrance, 2007), identifying the multiple and sometimes contradictory subject positions adopted, the implications of these subject positions for subjectivity and their association with broader social discourse. Physical health and health behaviour have also been subjected to FDA, including a deconstruction of the meaning of being an un/healthy fat woman (Tischner & Malson, 2012), young women's negotiation of smoking (Gilbert, 2008), internet discussions of mothers' choices regarding infant feeding practices (Callaghan & Lazard, 2012), sexual behaviour (Hollway, 1989; Mooney-Somers & Ussher, 2010), negotiating sexual changes after cancer (Ussher et al., 2013a) and cultural representations of menopause (Hvas & Gannik, 2008).

As part of an FDA analysis, attention is often paid to the relationship between discourse and institutions, or institutional practice, described as 'ways of organising, regulating and administering social life' (Willig, 2008:113). For example, the proliferation of psychiatric diagnosis through the Diagnostic and Statistical Manual of the American Psychiatric Association (DSM) serves to maintain the authority of the 'psy-professions' – psychiatry and psychology – the experts who are legally empowered to execute psychiatric judgement and administer 'treatment' (Rose, 1996). The development of new diagnostic categories in every edition of the DSM also serves to shore up the power and profits of BigPharma, the drug companies that sponsor the experts, who create the diagnostic categories, which new drugs are then developed to treat (Cosgrove & Wheeler, 2013).

Within FDA, attention is also paid to the ways in which discourses change over time, the *genealogy* of discourse and discursive practice (Arribas-Ayllon & Walkerdine, 2008). For example, the development of the modern clinical diagnosis 'anorexia nervosa' can be traced to historical accounts of 'fasting girls' (Malson, 1998) and the diagnostic category premenstrual dysphoric disorder (PMDD) traced to diagnoses of hysteria and neurasthenia, as well as to nineteenth-century pronouncements on the vagaries of menstruation (Ussher, 2006). This genealogical analysis identifies continuities in both discourse and discursive practice – in both of the examples cited above, these practices centre on the pathologization and regulation of the female body, and the maintenance of the boundaries of acceptable femininity. FDA has been influential in feminist psychological research (Gavey, 1989; Hollway, 1989) because of its ability to be used in the analysis of the gendered construction of subjectivity, power relations and social practice. However, feminist psychologists have also adopted DP in analysing expert and lay accounts (Sheriff & Weatherall, 2009; Weatherall & Priestley, 2001), as discursive practice is also often gendered, and thus research arising from both DP and FDA traditions is described as 'feminist discourse analysis'.

Synthesis or divergence: Debates about variations in discourse analysis

While many reviewers and discourse analysts distinguish between discursive psychology and FDA (for example, Burr, 2003; Potter, 2004; Willig, 2008), it has also been argued that the two strands should not be differentiated so

Table 13.1 Uses of discourse analysis in clinical and health psychology

Focus of analysis	Examples
Expert discourses and institutional practices Representations of health and illness, or of expert intervention, in: • medical or psychological texts • health campaigns • self-help guides • health promotion • sex education • treatment management guidelines • media representations • drug company advertising • self-help guides • interviews with health professionals	**FDA** • Exploration of representations of infant feeding and infant feeding choices in UK public debates, through analysis of two threads chosen from the debating board of an online parenting community (105 and 99 individual posts, respectively; Callaghan & Lazard, 2012). • Analysis of the ways in which patients are constructed within an influential published paper on the experience of electroconvulsive therapy (ECT; Johnstone, 1999). • Examination of Australian anti-smoking campaigns to investigate how medical knowledge, imagery and language legitimate and confirm the 'expert' status of medicine in regard to smoking conduct (Gilbert, 2008). **DP** • Investigation of representations of 'depression' in the print media in Australia during 2000 that produce unhappiness as individualized pathology in need of management (Rowe et al., 2003). • Analysis of the texts of 10 interviews with care staff, to explore the discourses used in constructing the aggressive challenging behaviours of men and women with learning disabilities (Wilcox et al., 2006). **Combination of FDA and DP** • Critical feminist discourse analysis of constructions of gender and relationships in two 'Men are from Mars, Women are from Venus' relationship self-help texts (Crawford, 2004). • Exploration of how counselling psychologists working with schizophrenia experience the work and construct the diagnosis, based on eight interviews with psychologists (Larsson et al., 2012).
Lay accounts – everyday talk • The extent to which expert discourses are reflected in lay people's accounts • Constructions of health and illness in lay accounts • Constructions of clinical interventions or health information in lay people's accounts	**FDA** • Analysis of ME/CFS (chronic fatigue syndrome) sufferers' descriptions of interactions with medical professionals taken from an asynchronous, online sufferers' support group (Guise et al., 2010). • Analysis of discursive constructions of the dying body in relation to anorexia nervosa, in interviews with 23 women diagnosed with the disorder (Malson & Ussher, 1997). **DP** • Case study to examine critically the health benefits of talking or writing about emotional experiences, to assess the emotional disclosure paradigm (EDP; Ellis & Cromby, 2012).

Continued overleaf

Table 13.1 *Continued*

Focus of analysis	*Examples*
Lay accounts – everyday talk • Negotiation and resistance of subject positions associated with health and illness	**FDA** • Analysis of construction of sex work through interviews with 19 people working in the industry (Weatherall & Priestley, 2001). **Combination of FDA and DP** • Exploration of psychological repercussions of living with Type 1 diabetes, through interviews with four individuals, analysed case by case (Watts et al., 2009). • Analysis of how young men used their talk to make sense of their own masculinity in the context of their health-care visits, through interviews with seven men (Jeffries & Grogan, 2012).
Interactions between experts and lay people • Interactions in health settings • Evaluation of process or efficacy in therapy	**FDA** • Exploration of power dynamics in therapy through analysis of interviews with eight therapists (Guilfoyle, 2002). • Health professional (HP) constructions of sex, and of discussion of sex with cancer patients and their partners, analysed through interviews with 38 HPs (Ussher et al., 2013). **DP** • Investigation of how change is constructed or 'performed' in therapeutic interactions, through analysis of family therapy interaction between an adolescent, his parents and the therapist (Couture & Strong, 2004). • Critique of diagnosis of attention-deficit/hyperactivity disorder (ADHD), through analysis of a transcript of a diagnostic session involving a young boy, his parents and a paediatrician (McHoul & Rapley, 2005). **Combination of FDA and DP** • Examination of three cross-cultural family therapy sessions in order to consider what constitutes culturally sensitive practice (Pakes & Roy-Chowdhury, 2007).

sharply, and that the analysis of discursive practices and resources should be combined (Rapley, 2004; Sims-Schouten et al., 2007). For example, Wetherell has argued for a synthesis of the two approaches, 'which reads one in terms of the other' (1998:388). Sims-Schouten and colleagues (2007) have combined discursive psychology and FDA in their description of a critical realist discourse analysis; and Rapley (2004) used a combination of discursive psychology and Foucauldian theory in analysing constructions of disability. These approaches examine both discursive practices, the performative qualities of discourse and the role of discourse in the constitution of subjectivity, selfhood and power relations (Willig, 2000).

At the same time, across both DP and FDA, differences can be identified between those who conduct fine-grained analysis of selected sections of talk or text, using either DP or FDA (for example, Guise et al., 2010; McHoul & Rapley, 2005; Potter, 2004), and those who combine elements of thematic analysis (see Chapter 7) with discourse analysis. The latter focuses on identifying discursive themes across accounts (see Gurevich et al., 2004; Ussher & Perz, 2008), through thematic decomposition (Stenner, 1993) or within individual cases, described as thematic composition (Watts et al., 2009).

Table 13.1 summarizes the uses of discourse analysis in clinical and health psychology, with examples of research examining expert discourses and institutional practices, lay accounts of health and illness, and interactions between experts and lay people.

Defining discourse analytical methods

This leads to the question: How do you do discourse analysis and how does it differ across the different strands? There is no simple recipe, which can make discourse analysis seem daunting to the novice researcher. Parker (1992) provides a detailed, twenty-step guide for conducting FDA, which Willig (2008) has simplified into a six-stage guide, as well as providing three steps for DP analysis. Potter and Wetherell (1987) provide details of ten stages of discourse analysis, which later came to be known as DP, but also argue that it is reliant on 'intuition', craft skills and tacit knowledge, and that there is 'no analytic method' (1987:169). Similarly, Hollway (1989) emphasizes her own intuitive feelings about the identification of discourse; and Billig (1997) argues that discourse analysis cannot be simply learned as a procedure, separate from its wider theoretical critique of psychology, and that methodological guidelines should not be followed too rigidly. It has also been argued that the processes of analysis and writing are not separate, as analysis will be refined and clarified throughout the writing process (Potter & Wetherell, 1987).

With these caveats in mind, Table 13.2 offers a general summary of steps in the process of conducting discourse analysis, drawing on the guidelines provided by Willig (2008) and Potter and Wetherell (1987), with distinctions between DP and FDA indicated in the analysis section. I then provide a description of a

Table 13.2   Components of discourse analysis

Reading

Read through transcripts, and listen to interview recordings, to gain an overview of the data and what the text is doing. For textual analysis, read through texts or representations.

Coding

Select the material for analysis, using the research questions as the basis for selection. Develop a coding frame, based on reading and re-reading of the data. Highlight and select relevant text and file it under the coding frame. Computer software, such as NVivo, can be used to manage the organization of coded data.

Analysis

Read through the coded data, paying attention to the functional aspects of discourse: How does the text construct subjects and objects? What is the discursive context within which the account is produced? Are there contradictions or variability in the accounts? Can particular discursive themes, or interpretative repertoires, be identified?

Discursive psychology

Focus of analysis: How are particular versions of reality manufactured, negotiated and deployed in conversation?

Steps: What terminology is used; what are the stylistic and grammatical features, the preferred metaphors and figures of speech? What is the action orientation of the account – what people do with language? How is meaning negotiated in local interaction?

Foucauldian discourse analysis

Focus of analysis: Examine the social, psychological and physical effects of discourse, the availability of discourses within a culture and the implications for those within.

Steps: Discourse and discursive constructions: Locate the various discursive constructions of the object and identify their association with wider cultural discourses. If conducting a genealogy, examine the historical development of such discourses and discursive practices. *Function*: What is the function of such constructions? What is gained by constructing the object in this way?

Positioning: What subject positions are offered by the text?

Practice: How does discourse open up or close down opportunities for action? What are the implications in terms of power relations?

Subjectivity: What are the consequences of taking up, or resisting, the subject positions made available? What can be thought, felt or experienced from within various discourses?

Writing

Contextualize your research in the context of other DA studies using a similar method. Provide details of the theory and method adopted: how you did the analysis. Depending on the research question, focus the analysis on the identification of discourses (or interpretative repertoires) in talk or representation; on the discursive construction of objects (such as menopause) and/or subject positions (such as 'ageing woman'); or on discursive strategies and their consequences. Illustrate each with examples from the data. Analysis and discussion sections are often combined, with a separate, shorter conclusion section drawing out the wider theoretical implications and suggestions for future research.

discourse analysis of women's negotiation of negative pre-menstrual change, as an illustration of how this analysis can function in practice.

The construction and negotiation of premenstrual change: A feminist Foucauldian discourse analysis

Study aim and method

The aim of this study was to examine women's construction and negotiation of negative pre-menstrual change. The research involved 60 heterosexual and lesbian women who were taking part in a mixed-methods study examining the construction and experience of pre-menstrual change in self-diagnosed PMS sufferers (Ussher & Perz, 2008, 2010, 2013a, b). We conducted one-to-one semi-structured interviews, which lasted between 45 and 90 minutes. We kept the interview questions open and general to avoid being leading, and conducted the interview as a discussion between interviewer and participant. The interviewer began by asking women to describe a typical experience of PMS and how this varied across relational contexts, and then explored strategies of coping. In the analysis, we adopted a feminist FDA approach, which examines the role of discourse in the constitution of subjectivity and social practice, while also acknowledging the material conditions that influence such experiences and the role of discourse in wider social processes of legitimation and power (Gavey, 1989, 2011).

Reading and coding
All of the interviews were transcribed verbatim. A sub-set of the interviews was then read and re-read by both authors and a research assistant to identify first-order codes, such as 'embodied changes', 'emotional distress', 'relational issues', 'PMS at work', 'coping' and 'triggers for pre-menstrual distress'. The entire dataset was then coded using NVivo, a computer package that facilitates the organization of coded qualitative data.

Analysis
All of the coded data were then read through independently by both authors, who made detailed notes of patterns, commonalities, variability across the data and uniqueness within cases. This was a reflexive process that allowed us to interpret participant accounts from our different perspectives: as a woman who experienced pre-menstrual change (Ussher) and one who did not (Perz). Through a process of discussion we then identified the discursive constructions of PMS and pre-menstrual change in the context of broader cultural discourse. These constructions included PMS as an illness, as a sign of weakness, as natural and as a relational experience. The function that these discourses served for women and for their partners was identified and attention paid to the subject positions made available through various discursive

constructions of pre-menstrual change. The implications of discursive constructions for practice, in particular for styles of coping and power relations in
both a relational and a broader social context, were also examined. Finally, the
consequences of taking up or resisting subject positions, in terms of women's
subjectivity, were attended to: women's accounts of thoughts or feelings, and
of selfhood, from various discursive positions. The genealogy of discursive
constructions of PMS is examined elsewhere (Ussher, 2006).

Women's descriptions of pre-menstrual change

All of the women interviewed described pre-menstrual change as 'PMS', characterized by heightened pre-menstrual irritability, intolerance of others and
oversensitivity, using terms such as 'irritable', 'cranky', 'short-tempered', 'snap-
py', 'confrontational', having a 'short fuse', 'bitey', 'impatient', 'grumpy',
'stroppy', 'frustrated', 'stressed', 'annoyed' or 'teary' (Ussher & Perz, 2013a).
However, how women discursively positioned these changes, and the implications for subjectivity, self-positioning and practice, varied. Two discursive constructions of PMS identified in women's accounts are summarized in Table 13.3:
PMS as pathology, drawing on biomedical discourse, and leading to a victim or
monster subject position; and PMS as an understandable reaction, drawing on
a feminist life-stress discourse, which facilitated tolerance and self-care.

Table 13.3   A feminist Foucauldian discourse analysis of PMS

Discursive construction	PMS as pathology	PMS as an understandable reaction
Discourses	Biomedical	Feminist psycho-social
Function	PMS as a thing that causes distress Locates PMS within the body Exonerates women from unacceptable anger	Locates PMS within relationships or life stress Legitimates expression of pre-menstrual needs and emotions Tolerance and normalization of pre-menstrual change
Positioning	Woman as out of control Victim of hormonal imbalances Woman as monster; abject	Woman as agentic and rebellious Woman as sensitive or vulnerable pre-menstrually
Practice	Pharmaceutical interventions Avoidance to protect others Pre-menstrual self-control and self-silencing	Legitimating time-out and avoidance for self-care Attention to situational issues associated with distress Rejection of acquiescent femininity
Subjectivity	Self-blame and guilt Shame	Acceptance of pre-menstrual emotions Catharsis

Pre-menstrual change as pathology: Woman as victim or monster

> When you're being taxed physically by the PMS, because it does some-
> thing, I don't know what it does, whether it ... I know it depletes certain
> vitamins and you've got low magnesium and this and this and this and
> that, and your hormones can be off, and not where they should be. And
> I think just that being taxed with those things helps you, or makes you
> not be able to handle other things, where if you're not taxed with all that,
> you can handle other difficulties that you'd normally be able to handle.

Discourse and discursive constructions
The construction of pre-menstrual change as pathology, drawing on a biomedical discourse, is illustrated in the account just quoted. PMS is described as a
thing ('the PMS') that results in the woman's inability to handle daily stresses
with which she is 'taxed', and which she would 'normally' be able to handle.
PMS is blamed for depleting 'certain vitamins' and for causing hormones to be
'off'. This 'thingifying' of PMS has been previously identified in published
expert accounts (Ussher, 2003), demonstrating that women are drawing on
wider cultural discourses in adopting this construction of pre-menstrual
change. This serves to position PMS as the *cause* of women's pre-menstrual
distress, rather than a label that is given to an array of pre-menstrual changes
that women may report.

Function and positioning
We asked what the function is of such constructions and what is gained, or
lost, by constructing pre-menstrual change in such a manner. One of the implications of the adoption of a biomedical discourse is the self-positioning of the
pre-menstrual woman as 'out of control' and a victim of her hormonal 'imbalances', as is evident in this account:

> the imbalances were happening in the body and all that sort of stuff that
> I had absolutely no control over. I mean, sure, I had other issues I had to
> contend with, but I was dealing with that so, to me, this was something
> that was so out of my control that I felt like I was being blamed for actu-
> ally knowing how to deal with it, and it's like, 'Well, I don't.'

Through reading the coded data, we identified a process of splitting, wherein
women discursively separate their normal sane selves from the abhorrent
nature of pre-menstrual emotion, thus exonerating themselves from what they
construe to be mad or bad behaviour. Extreme descriptions of the pre-menstrual self were used to illustrate the dramatic nature of this change, including
'crazy', 'mad', a 'nut case', 'absolute psycho', 'Schizo', 'out of my mind' or 'a
complete loony'. Positioning the pre-menstrual self as mad serves to reinforce
the notion of pre-menstrual changes as outside of the woman's agency, and of
the sufferer as someone whose behaviour is a sign of pathology:

you're like a person that's probably, you know a crazy drunk that's had a lot of alcohol or on pot, really high on drugs and they just snap and you can't control their anger. I would um react like that, without having had anything.

However, the expression of pre-menstrual irritation or anger was invariably followed by reports of guilt and self-criticism, suggesting that self-positioning as afflicted by hormones pre-menstrually is not effectively serving to exonerate women from 'bad' behaviour, as previously suggested (Elson, 2002). Thus, one woman told us, '(Y)ou feel horrible about it the next week ... it makes you feel sick' and another said that she feels 'really upset' and 'angry' with herself. This is associated with shame and with a sense of the need to apologize, which involves the woman taking up a position of abjection:

There's fair bit of violence coming through in all of this isn't there. Throwing things, um, venting a frustration and trying to learn to control these things so that people don't look at you funny and you don't make a fool of yourself which you later regret. When you come back to normality, you think, um, I've got to go around and apologise to all these people I've just bitten their heads off over absolutely nothing. No, it's, in the back of your head you know what's normal.

Practice
We asked what the implications are of this positioning in terms of women's coping strategies in the face of negative pre-menstrual change. What opportunities for action are made available by the subject positions that women adopt?

Biomedical constructions of PMS leave women with one obvious opportunity for action: pharmaceutical interventions. In this vein, we identified that women who adopted a biomedical discourse talked of taking self-prescribed herbs (such as St John's wort, Vitex or evening primrose oil), and vitamins or minerals (in particular B complex and magnesium), as part of their pre-menstrual self-care. A small minority of women had also been prescribed the contraceptive pill, with one participant prescribed antidepressants, to reduce pre-menstrual distress. The majority reported satisfaction with such remedies, reinforcing the positioning of PMS as a biomedical phenomenon that can be treated: 'I know that I wouldn't cope too well if I wasn't on St Johns Wort which has helped me 100%'; 'I think if I remember to take them, like, as I should, I mostly get away without almost without any symptoms'.

Implications for power relations
These strategies served to position women as dependent on medical advice and intervention; as 'patients' whose bodies are the focus of intervention. However, all of these dietary supplement or pharmaceutical coping strategies were also accompanied by psychological or behavioural strategies, demonstrating that

the adoption of a biomedical discourse does not inevitably preclude women's agency. This is analogous to the 'tight-rope talk' identified by McKenzie-Mohr and LaFrance, wherein women construct themselves as both 'agents and patients: both active and acted upon' (2011:64), enabling credit for agency in coping and deflection of blame for 'having' PMS.

The coping strategy most commonly reported by participants was avoidance of people or situations that had the potential to provoke anger and irritation. For example, one woman told us, 'the kids ... I try not to get into conflict, into confrontation with them'. Anticipation or avoidance of stressful situations is not always possible, however, and many participants gave accounts of experiencing unexpected situations that elicited pre-menstrual anger or irritation. As a result, they described coping with occurrences of negative premenstrual emotion through the exertion of self-control, leaving a situation in which they had become angry in order to avoid the escalation of conflict.

> I usually feel stressed in the lead up. If it gets to the point where I actually need to say that, I know the pressure cooker, little thing on the top bouncing up and down, you know, um at that point and it's almost like a last resort for me. If I know I'm going to explode, I try to train myself to step back and chill.

In some accounts, self-control was described as necessary for the protection of others, reinforcing the positioning of the woman as monstrous and out of control. For example, one woman described 'hibernating' because of a fear of not being able to 'rein yourself in' and wanting to avoid 'hurting people with words' because 'it's not their fault'.

Subjectivity
The consequence of constructing pre-menstrual change as pathology, and adopting a biomedical discourse, was that women reported shame and dislike of the self during the pre-menstrual phase of the cycle. The body was a focus of negative emotion, being blamed for women's distress and disconnected from the self: 'I feel quite odd and almost out of body'; 'you feel like you're a blimp um even though you feel ugly and this is this is all PMS'.

PMS as an understandable reaction: Facilitating agency and self-care

> P. I get very snappy and short with people I know ... you know ... um ... yeah, things that normally don't bother me, bother me. It tends to be about housework, and my role as a woman, and why do I have to do all of this and ... yeah. Things that I kind of repress ... come out to the surface.
> I. Okay.
> P. That's what I've found.

I. Okay. So they're not things that aren't there the rest of the time and suddenly they appear, they're things that you think are ...?
P. They're underlying. They're underlying issues and I just kind of tick along nicely and think, 'Well, you know, it's okay, I can deal with it,' and then, PMS comes and I can't deal with it. Yeah.

Discourse and discursive constructions
In contrast, in the account above, pre-menstrual emotion is described as a reflection of a woman's anger or frustration with the 'underlying issues' associated with domestic concerns and her 'role as a woman'. This reflects the adoption of a feminist psycho-social discourse, wherein gendered inequalities and over-responsibility are positioned as causes of women's distress, and anger or frustration is deemed to be a legitimate reaction. A similar construction of PMS was adopted in accounts of intolerance or anger towards male partners pre-menstrually. For example, one woman described her husband as 'a bit of a hoarder and a collector, and 3 weeks of the month that does not bother me'. However, when pre-menstrual, she said, 'it bothers me a lot and I want to throw everything out, to put everything into plastic bags and dump it on his desk [laughs]'.

Function
One of the primary functions of the adoption of a feminist psycho-social discourse was to position pre-menstrual emotions as understandable and reasonable, resisting the discursive positioning of the pre-menstrual woman as mad, bad or dangerous (Chrisler & Caplan, 2002). Thus, one woman described the awareness of pre-menstrual sensitivity as 'a weight off my mind. 'Cause at first I used to think I was going a little crazy ... it's helped me deal with, "those are PMS feelings".' Similarly, another woman told herself, 'Oh, OK, I know now, you're not actually the wicked witch.' This construction of PMS was also associated with tolerance of negative pre-menstrual change, which could then be normalized or embraced as an 'opportunity' to 'be emotional':

> I think I embrace it as an opportunity to, um, just rest and, um, be more in tune with myself, and be emotional. I think I was probably fighting being emotional in the past, and that's what caused so much discomfort and stress.

Recognition and acceptance of negative pre-menstrual change can also function to give women permission to engage in coping strategies to avoid or reduce pre-menstrual distress without a sense of guilt. Thus, one woman told us: 'I'll actually give myself permission to actually go and lie down for half an hour. Even half an hour will make substantial amount of difference.'

Positioning and subjectivity
In these accounts, women not only avoid taking up a subject position of victim or patient, wherein their bodies (or minds) warrant medical treatment;

they also subvert the self-surveillance that they adopt for the remainder of the month (see Ussher & Perz, 2010). Implicit in these accounts is the transgression of self-silencing, which is broken when PMS 'comes along'.

Implications for power relations

Pre-menstrual emotional expression is associated with a sense of catharsis. In this way, 'PMS' signifies rebellion and resistance, rather than weakness and pathology, and breaks in self-silencing are a sign of women's agency.

This case example illustrates the ways in which discourse analysis can be used to understand the construction and experience of a specific health issue, as well as the role of language in the course of distress and in facilitating coping.

Concluding comments

Discourse analysis has a relatively short history in psychology, but has had a significant impact on the conceptualization of the psychological subject and on the conduct of qualitative research. While its impact is most notable in social, critical and feminist psychology, its utility in clinical and health psychology has also been widely demonstrated. Discourse analysis offers the opportunity to explore the construction of health and illness within a range of cultural representations and expert accounts, the meaning and experience of health and illness for lay people, and the implications of discursive constructions of health and illness for subjectivity. There is no one correct method of discourse analysis, as multiple methods have been identified (Wetherell, 2001) and practitioners interpret and present analyses in a range of different ways. This flexibility is its strength in clinical and health psychology, given the uniqueness of health problems. This chapter has summarized two identifiable strands of DA, discursive psychology and Foucauldian discourse analysis, and presented one interpretation of feminist FDA as an example. However, the specific form of DA adopted will always be determined by the research questions that drive a project, with the mode of analysis and presentation influenced by the theoretical orientation, skills and creativity of the researcher.

Further reading

Potter, J. & Wetherell, M. (1987). *Discourse and Social Psychology: Beyond Attitudes and Behaviour*. London: Sage.

Wetherell, M. (2001). Debates in discourse research. In M. Wetherell, S. Taylor & S.J. Yates (eds), *Discourse Theory and Practice: A Reader*. London: Sage.

Willig, C. (2008). *Introducing Qualitative Methods in Psychology: Adventures in Theory and Method*. Maidenhead: McGraw-Hill, Chapters 6 and 7.

References

Arribas-Ayllon, M. & Walkerdine, V. (2008). Foucauldian discourse analysis. In C. Willig & W. Stainton Rogers (eds), *The Sage Handbook of Qualitative Research in Psychology* (pp. 91–109). London: Sage.

Bilić, B. & Georgaca, E. (2007). Representations of 'mental illness' in Serbian newspapers: A critical discourse analysis. *Qualitative Research in Psychology*, 4(1–2), 167–186.

Billig, M. (1991). *Ideologies and Beliefs*. London: Sage.

Billig, M. (1997). Rhetorical and discursive analysis: How families talk about the royal family. In N. Hayes (ed.), *Doing Qualitative Analysis in Psychology*. Hove: Psychology Press.

Billig, M. (2012). Undisciplined beginnings, academic success, and discursive psychology. *British Journal of Social Psychology*, 51(3), 413–424.

Brown, S. (1999). Stress as regimen: Critical readings of self-help literature. In C. Willig (ed.), *Applied Discourse Analysis: Social and Psychological Interventions* (pp. 22–43). Buckingham: Open University Press.

Burman, E. & Parker, I. (1993). *Discourse Analytic Research*. London: Routledge.

Burr, V. (2003). *Social Constructionism* (2nd edn). London: Routledge.

Callaghan, J.E.M. & Lazard, L. (2012). 'Please don't put the whole dang thing out there!' A discursive analysis of internet discussions around infant feeding. *Psychology & Health*, 27(8), 938–955.

Chrisler, J.C. & Caplan, P. (2002). The strange case of Dr. Jekyll and Ms. Hyde: How PMS became a cultural phenomenon and a psychiatric disorder. *Annual Review of Sex Research*, 13, 274–306.

Cosgrove, L. & Wheeler, E.E. (2013). Industry's colonization of psychiatry: Ethical and practical implications of financial conflicts of interest in the DSM-5. *Feminism & Psychology*, 23(1), 93–106.

Couture, S.J. & Strong, T. (2004). Turning differences into possibilities: Using discourse analysis to investigate change in therapy with adolescents and their families. *Counselling and Psychotherapy Research*, 4(1), 90–101.

Crawford, M. (2004). Mars and Venus collide: A discursive analysis of marital self-help psychology. *Feminism & Psychology*, 14(1), 63–79.

Curl, T.S. & Drew, P. (2008). Contingency and action: A comparison of two forms of requesting. *Research on Language and Social Interaction*, 41(2), 129–153.

Edwards, D. & Potter, J. (1992). *Discursive Psychology*. London: Sage.

Edwards, D. & Potter, J. (2005). Discursive psychology, mental states and descriptions. In H. Molder & J. Potter (eds), *Conversation and Cognition* (pp. 241–259). Cambridge: Cambridge University Press.

Ellis, D. & Cromby, J. (2012). Emotional inhibition: A discourse analysis of disclosure. *Psychology & Health*, 27(5), 515–532.

Elson, J. (2002). Menarche, menstruation, and gender identity: Retrospective accounts from women who have undergone premenopausal hysterectomy. *Sex Roles*, 46, 37–48.

Fee, D. (2000). *Pathology and the Postmodern: Mental Illness as Discourse and Experience*. London: Sage.

Foucault, M. (1972). *The Archeology of Knowledge and the Discourse on Language*. New York: Pantheon Books.

Foucault, M. (1984). The order of discourse. In M.J. Shapiro (ed.), *Language and Politics* (pp. 108–138). Oxford: Blackwell.

Foucault, M. (1987). *Mental Illness and Psychology*. Berkley: University of California Press.

Gavey, N. (1989). Feminist poststructuralism and discourse analysis: Contributions to feminist psychology. *Psychology of Women Quarterly*, 13(1), 459–475.

Gavey, N. (2011). Feminist poststructuralism and discourse analysis revisited. *Psychology of Women Quarterly*, 35(1), 183–188.

Gilbert, E. (2008). The art of governing smoking: Discourse analysis of Australian anti-smoking campaigns. *Social Theory & Health*, 6(2), 97–116.

Guilfoyle, M. (2002). Power, knowledge and resistance in therapy: Exploring links between discourse and materiality. *International Journal of Psychotherapy*, 7(1), 83–97.

Guise, J., McVittie, C. & McKinlay, A. (2010). A discourse analytic study of ME/CFS (Chronic Fatigue Syndrome) sufferers' experiences of interactions with doctors. *Journal of Health Psychology*, 15(3), 426–435.

Gurevich, M., Bishop, S., Bower, J., Malka, M. & Nyhof-Young, J. (2004). (Dis)embodying gender and sexuality in testicular cancer. *Social Science and Medicine*, 58(9), 1597–1607.

Henriques, J., Hollway, W., Urwin, C., Venn, C. & Walkerdine, V. (1984). *Changing the Subject: Psychology, Social Regulation and Subjectivity*. London: Methuen.

Hollway, W. (1983). Heterosexual sex: Power and desire for the other. In S. Cartledge & J. Ryan (eds), *Sex and Love: New Thoughts on Old Contradictions* (pp. 124–140). London: Women's Press.

Hollway, W. (1989). *Subjectivity and Method in Psychology: Gender, Meaning and Science*. London: Sage.

Hvas, L. & Gannik, D.E. (2008). Discourses on menopause – Part I: Menopause described in texts addressed to Danish women 1996–2004. *Health*, 12(2), 157–175.

Jeffries, M. & Grogan, S. (2012). 'Oh, I'm just, you know, a little bit weak because I'm going to the doctor's': Young men's talk of self-referral to primary healthcare services. *Psychology & Health*, 27(8), 898–915.

Johnstone, L. (1999). Adverse psychological effects of ECT. *Journal of Mental Health*, 8(1), 69–85.

LaFrance, M.N. (2007). A bitter pill: A discursive analysis of women's medicalized accounts of depression. *Journal of Health Psychology*, 12(1), 127–140.

LaFrance, M.N. (2009). *Women and Depression: Recovery and Resistance*. London: Routledge.

Larsson, P., Loewenthal, D. & Brooks, O. (2012). Counselling psychology and schizophrenia: A critical discursive account. *Counselling Psychology Quarterly*, 25(1), 31–47.

Malson, H. (1998). *The Thin Woman: Feminism, Post-structuralism and the Social Psychology of Anorexia Nervosa*. London: Routledge.

Malson, H.M. & Ussher, J.M. (1997). Beyond this mortal coil: Femininity, death and discursive constructions of the anorexic body. *Mortality*, 2(1), 43–61.

McHoul, A. & Rapley, M. (2005). A case of attention-deficit/hyperactivity disorder diagnosis: Sir Karl and Francis B. slug it out on the consulting room floor. *Discourse & Society*, 16(3), 419–449.

McKenzie-Mohr, S. & LaFrance, M. (2011). Telling stories without the words: 'Tightrope talk' in women's accounts of coming to live well after rape or depression. *Feminism and Psychology*, 21(1), 49–73.

Mooney-Somers, J. & Ussher, J.M. (2010). Sex as commodity: Single and partnered men's subjectification as heterosexual men. *Men and Masculinities*, 12(3), 353–373.

Pakes, K. & Roy-Chowdhury, S. (2007). Culturally sensitive therapy? Examining the practice of cross-cultural family therapy. *Journal of Family Therapy*, 29(3), 267–283.

Parker, I. (1992). *Discourse Dynamics: Critical Analysis for Social and Individual Psychology*. London: Sage.

Parker, I. (1994). Reflexive research and the grounding of analysis: Social psychology and the psy-complex. *Journal of Community and Applied Social Psychology*, 4(4), 239–252.

Parker, I. (2012). Discursive social psychology now. *British Journal of Social Psychology*, 51(3), 471–477.

Potter, J. (2004). Discourse analysis as a way of analysing naturally occuring talk. In D. Silverman (ed.), *Qualitative Research: Theory, Method, Practice* (pp. 200–221). London: Sage.

Potter, J. (2012). Re-reading discourse and social psychology: Transforming social psychology. *British Journal of Social Psychology*, 51(3), 436–455.

Potter, J. & Wetherell, M. (1987). *Discourse and Social Psychology: Beyond Attitudes and Behaviour*. London: Sage.

Rapley, M. (2004). *The Social Construction of Intellectual Disability*. Cambridge: Cambridge University Press.

Rose, N.S. (1996). *Inventing Our Selves: Psychology, Power, and Personhood*. New York: Cambridge University Press.

Rowe, R., Tilbury, F., Rapley, M. & O'Ferrall, I. (2003). 'About a year before the breakdown I was having symptoms': Sadness, pathology and the Australian newspaper media. *Sociology of Health & Illness*, 25(6), 680–696.

Sheriff, M. & Weatherall, A. (2009). A feminist discourse analysis of popular-press accounts of postmaternity. *Feminism & Psychology*, 19(1), 89–108.

Sims-Schouten, W., Riley, S.C.E. & Willig, C. (2007). Critical realism in discourse analysis: A presentation of a systematic method of analysis using women's talk of motherhood, childcare and female employment as an example. *Theory & Psychology*, 17(1), 101–124.

Stenner, P. (1993). Discoursing jealousy. In E. Burman & Parker, I. (eds), *Discourse Analytic Research* (pp. 114–134). London: Routledge.

Tischner, I. & Malson, H. (2012). Deconstructing health and the un/healthy fat woman. *Journal of Community and Applied Social Psychology*, 22(1), 50–62.

Ussher, J.M. (2003). The role of premenstrual dysphoric disorder in the subjectification of women. *Journal of Medical Humanities*, 24(1/2), 131–146.

Ussher, J.M. (2006). *Managing the Monstrous Feminine: Regulating the Reproductive Body*. London: Routledge.

Ussher, J.M. (2011). *The Madness of Women: Myth and Experience*. London: Routledge.

Ussher, J.M. & Perz, J. (2008). Empathy, egalitarianism and emotion work in the relational negotiation of PMS: The experience of lesbian couples. *Feminism and Psychology*, 18(1), 87–111.

Ussher, J.M. & Perz, J. (2010). Disruption of the silenced-self: The case of pre-menstrual syndrome. In D.C. Jack & A. Ali (eds), *The Depression Epidemic: International Perspectives on Women's Self-silencing and Psychological Distress* (pp. 435–458). Oxford: Oxford University Press.

Ussher, J.M. & Perz, J. (2013a). PMS as a gendered illness linked to the construction and relational experience of hetero-femininity. *Sex Roles*, 68(1–2), 132–150.

Ussher, J.M. & Perz, J. (2013b). PMS as a process of negotiation: Women's experience and management of premenstrual distress. *Psychology & Health*, 28(8), 909–927.

Ussher, J.M., Perz, J., Gilbert, E., Wong, W.K.T. & Hobbs, K. (2013). Renegotiating sex after cancer: Resisting the coital imperative. *Cancer Nursing*, 36(6), 454–462.

Ussher, J.M., Perz, J., Gilbert, E. et al. (2013). Talking about sex after cancer: A discourse analytic study of health care professional accounts of sexual communication with patients. *Psychology & Health*, 28(12), 1370–1390.

Watts, S., O'Hara, L. & Trigg, R. (2009). Living with Type 1 diabetes: A by-person qualitative exploration. *Psychology & Health*, 25(4), 491–506.

Weatherall, A. & Priestley, A. (2001). A feminist discourse analysis of sex 'work'. *Feminism & Psychology*, 11(3), 323–340.

Wetherell, M. (1998). Positioning and interpretative repertoires: Conversation analysis and post-structuralism in dialogue. *Discourse & Society*, 9(3), 387–412.

Wetherell, M. (2001). Debates in discourse research. In M. Wetherell, S. Taylor & S.J. Yates (eds), *Discourse Theory and Practice: A Reader*. London: Sage.

Wilcox, E., Finlay, W.M. & Edmonds, J. (2006). 'His brain is totally different': An analysis of care-staff explanations of aggressive challenging behaviour and the impact of gendered discourses. *British Journal of Social Psychology*, 45(1), 197–216.

Willig, C. (2000). A discourse-dynamic approach to the study of subjectivity in health psychology. *Theory and Psychology*, 10(4), 547–570.

Willig, C. (2008). *Introducing Qualitative Methods in Psychology: Adventures in Theory and Method*. Maidenhead: McGraw-Hill.

Ethnography

Juliet Foster

14

Ethnography involves observation, which may entail differing levels of participation, and usually also includes other methods such as interviews and documentary analysis. As Duveen and Lloyd say, 'The ethnography is aiming ... to describe the collective life of a society – to articulate, among other things, the beliefs which are shared by the members of this culture' (1993:97). Its purpose, then, is to try to gain a deeper understanding of a group, a community or a situation. The researcher usually aims for a thick description that details many aspects of this, including the practices, rituals and organization of behaviour, as well as the interpretations of those involved. That allows the researcher the possibility of developing their ideas about what might be going on, and why, and then reflecting on these with the participants. Common roles that might be associated with that of the ethnographic researcher include the learner (Agar, 1980) and the novice (Hammersley & Atkinson, 2007): these roles both imply inexperience and the need to familiarize oneself as a researcher with something that is more familiar to existing participants.

Ethnography is often used in combination with other qualitative and quantitative methods (Agar, 1980; Savage, 2000): for example, a researcher might additionally undertake more formal interviews in order to check details learned from the ethnographic work, or to ask about information that is harder to glean from observation. Pope and Mays (2000) point out that observation has always played a vital role in the practice of medicine; as such, the principles of ethnography should not be unfamiliar to medical professionals, although its practice might be.

History

Ethnography is a method more associated with anthropology than with psychology, and it is certainly here that its roots lie. Before the First World War, anthropologists generally did not engage directly in their own ethnographic fieldwork, but remained 'armchair anthropologists', often using missionaries to do the practical side of their work (Pratt, 1986). This had some advantages: missionaries often spent long periods in the field and were fluent in relevant languages. However, the issue that still dogs much ethnography – that of the role of the ethnographer and their own ideas in the perception and interpretation of other situations – was already relevant (Clifford, 1986): missionaries often approached local beliefs as matters of heathen superstition rather than as belief systems to be understood in their own context. Additionally, at this time it was more common for ethnographic work to be used to test and support existing theory rather than to generate it. Anthropologists at home would devise questionnaires to send out to the field to be completed. In many ways this was symptomatic of the commitment to structuralism that was common at this time in anthropology; as such, there was often an assumption that there was an underlying (universal and cognitive) social structure that generates observable social phenomena (Hammersley & Atkinson, 2007).

A change began to come about when professional anthropologists started to do their own fieldwork, but this was a gradual process. The Torres Strait expedition in 1898 is often cited as a key turning point in the history of ethnography (and indeed in the social sciences in general): those involved came from many disciplines and brought something of an interdisciplinary approach to their work. Alfred Haddon combined anthropology with a career as a naturalist; W.H.R. Rivers, C.S. Myers, C.G. Seligman and William McDougall were all also experimental psychologists. While in many ways continuing to display a commitment to the notion that theory leads to ethnography, which is used to confirm and strengthen the theory, Rivers also contributed to a significant methodological clarification of the ethnographic method. In his detailed work on kinship, he maintained a fairly positivist approach towards ethnography, seeing it as an objective scientific study of reality, but at the same time he advocated a long-term and intensive study of the societies concerned, and a more empathetic and extensive questioning of and interaction with his subjects.

In Rivers's (1912) *Notes and Queries on Anthropology*, 'A general account of method', he highlights several important points, including:

- The importance of learning the local language.
- The problems of translation that mean that direct questions are not always sufficient.
- The need to pay attention to volunteered information.
- The need to get corroboration from others.
- The need for the ethnographer to corroborate their own witnessing of ceremonies with verbal accounts.
- The need for sympathy and tact.

As Stocking (1983) points out, this had a huge influence on Malinowski, who is usually credited with being the author of the revolution in ethnography and indeed in anthropology more generally, and the principles set out by Rivers still hold true today. However, it is also interesting to note that Rivers, who remains a celebrated figure in anthropology, is better known as a psychologist, and indeed psychiatrist; the links of ethnography to health and clinical psychology are therefore not necessarily tenuous from the outset.

Sociology was probably the next discipline to engage seriously with ethnography, and it was here that researchers began to engage in research not only in cultures other than their own, but also in those that were closer to home. The Chicago School is often credited with playing a major role in this, exemplified in Whyte-Foote's (1943) classic study of an Italian working-class community in Boston, in which he lived for four years during the process of his research.

However, it was some time before psychology really engaged with ethnography. There have, of course, been some notable exceptions, such as Festinger et al.'s (1956) study of a doomsday cult; health and clinical psychology (and nursing studies) have also engaged with it on occasions. Mental health has received particular attention, including high-profile ethnographic studies such as Rosenhan's (1973) infamous 'On being sane in insane places'. Some of these examples will be discussed in more depth later in this chapter. Nevertheless, it is probably true that ethnography struggles a little to be seen as a valid method in health and clinical psychology, partly due to concerns over the effects (and interpretations) of the researcher, and partly due to other issues, such as ethical concerns. Although interest in research using qualitative methods, including ethnography, in health-care settings has steadily increased (Pope & Mays, 2000), some uncertainty remains regarding the practicalities and implications of using such methods. Jones (1995) points out the problems inherent in attempting to integrate qualitative research into the format of conventional scientific journals. Although some headway has been made over the past 20 years, there is still more to be done and questions relating to ethical issues remain outstanding (Quirk & Lelliott, 2002). Qualitative methods – arguably, ethnography especially – do not necessarily fit into established medical research procedures or the guidelines for the ethical conduct of conventional research in health-care settings, and, as such, can be misunderstood or rejected. I shall return to some of these issues later in the chapter.

Theoretical and conceptual background

Ethnography can be undertaken from a variety of different philosophical perspectives; indeed, in its history it has been associated with a number of positions, including positivism, naturalism, structuralism, functionalism and constructionism (for more discussion of this point, see Hammersley & Atkinson, 2007). However, despite their very significant differences, ethnographies that draw on all these theoretical backgrounds have one thing in common: they are based on the conviction that observing what goes on in a group within society (and participating in it to various differing extents; see the discussion later in this chapter) leads to valuable information about that particular group and to a greater understanding of their way of life.

The use of ethnography in health psychology and clinical psychology

As already mentioned, and indeed as Griffin and Bengry-Howell (2007) point out, ethnography has been used much more frequently in sociology and in other social sciences than in psychology; indeed, in health-care settings in general it has also been underused (Savage, 2000). Still, we should not underestimate its influence here; any search engine will reveal that a large amount of ethnographic work is undertaken in nursing research, for example, and Robinson (2013) has recently made a concerted argument for its relevance in this area in particular. Ethnography is gaining in popularity in health research, as testified to by a variety of studies (see, for example, Smith et al., 2003; The et al., 2002).

Additionally, as already mentioned, dating back to the 1950s we also see a strong tradition of ethnographic research in mental health settings. Much of this is associated (not always correctly) with the anti-psychiatry movement that sought to challenge the way in which 'madness' was conceptualized and treated within society. Goffman's (1961) work on asylums and the 'moral career of the mental patient' involved a year's worth of ethnographic observation in St Elizabeth's Hospital in Washington, DC. Another classic study that used ethnography was Rosenhan's (1973) study in psychiatric hospitals (see Box 14.1).

Even before this in the 1950s, a number of social scientists were also conducting what might be seen as ethnographic studies in psychiatric facilities, including Stanton and Schwarz (1954) and Caudill (Caudill et al., 1952; Caudill, 1958). Particularly interesting is Caudill, who studied all aspects of hospital life covertly, exaggerating existing mental health problems in order to

---

BOX 14.1   On being sane in insane places

Rosenhan's (1973) study of psychiatric diagnosis has rightly become a classic, praised and criticized in equal measure for its methodological approach. Rosenhan sent a number of research confederates posing as potential patients to a number of psychiatric hospitals. These 'pseudo-patients' claimed to be hearing voices saying things like 'hollow'. All were admitted to hospital, and all but one was given a diagnosis of schizophrenia. After their admission, the pseudo-patients stated that they could no longer hear the voices and answered all the other questions truthfully. Rosenhan's conclusions centred on the fact that the pseudo-patients' 'normal' life histories and behaviours were seen as being further symptomatic of their diagnosis. Ethnography formed a significant part of the methods used in this study, as the pseudo-patients kept careful notes of their experiences while in hospital. It is interesting that this was also seen as a possible symptom of schizophrenia, as it was noted on one occasion that the 'patient exhibits writing behaviour'.

gain admission. Many of these studies do raise important ethical questions, which will be returned to later in this chapter. One of the classic studies that initiated the process of grounded theory (see Chapter 8) also involved ethnographic work in a health-care setting: Glaser and Strauss (1965) observed practices surrounding death and dying in hospitals in order to gain a better understanding of what was not only a sensitive but also a much under-researched topic.

The utility of ethnography in health and clinical psychology, however, is not in question, especially in situations where the issue being researched plays an important role in the everyday lives of those being observed (Duveen & Lloyd, 1993), which is clearly often the case within these fields. We are often interested in patients' and service users' day-to-day lives, in how they approach issues related to their health and treatment, and these issues are consequently likely to be highly salient to those participants. Ethnography allows access to the ordinary activities and discourses in the everyday lives of participants that are 'shot through' with their health-related ideas and beliefs. It also provides an opportunity to examine the non-verbal expression of representations and ideas (Becker & Geer, 1957), something that may be important in some health-care settings. Although this may not be relevant in every instance, participants might not always be able to express themselves fully verbally, due to medication or other factors associated with their experiences, illnesses or disabilities.

It has also been claimed that participant observation is especially appropriate in situations where less is known about an area, where it is somehow obscured from public scrutiny and where there are significant differences between insiders and outsiders (Jorgensen, 1989). This may well be relevant in many health-care settings and regarding the different people who operate within them.

BOX 14.2   Researching the unsaid

Jodelet (1991) studied a community in central France in which patients from a psychiatric hospital lodged in the homes of villagers, who were referred to as 'foster families'. Her project involved extended ethnography and comprised observations, interviews with foster families and mental health professionals, and extensive documentary analysis of material relating to the history and organization of the 'colony', as it was called. She found that although the foster families explicitly denied the possibility that mental health problems were contagious, they organized their daily routines within their homes around rituals of separation, especially of bodily fluids. For example, they kept separate sets of crockery for the patients, which they would not wash in the same water as the crockery that they themselves used. Similarly, laundry was always washed separately. Jodelet traced this back to ancient beliefs regarding contagion through the humours. Such crucial issues might not have been uncovered without the direct observation of everyday life that ethnography involves.

Overall, then, ethnography can allow the researcher access to issues that might otherwise be hard to research. It enables access to the everyday meaning of health and illness to participants, and to their lived experiences of it; it is particularly suited to examining patient perspectives (Buston et al., 1998; Charmaz & Olsen, 1997). Health beliefs and representations are not merely held in the abstract but influence action and interaction (Leventhal et al., 1997) and are enshrined in habits and practices (Gervais & Jovchelovitch, 1998). Often, such beliefs might even be taken for granted and not consciously expressed by a participant, as in Box 14.2. Ethnography may help to access what would otherwise be missed using other methods.

Outline of the method

As already mentioned, ethnography can be used in a variety of different ways. This section will first consider issues of access and the role of the researcher, before focusing on the collection of data and then moving on to consider the interpretation and analysis of that data. Particular attention will be paid to the ethical issues that ethnography raises.

Access

Assuming that a research question has been defined, and that ethnography seems to be an appropriate method for addressing that question, the first issue any researcher will face is finding a suitable location for that research. Of course, if the research question is specific (for example, how do patients experience waiting times at a particular hospital clinic?), then this location may be obvious; if the question is more general (for example, how do users of mental health services understand mental health and illness?) then this might not be so immediately obvious. Much of the discussion regarding ethnography centres on negotiating access with 'gate-keepers' (Hammersley & Atkinson, 2007); that is, individuals responsible for the management and organization of a location. Within a health-care setting, this is likely, at least in the first instance, to involve management, senior clinicians, staff and ethics committees. Discussions with ethics committees can take some time; indeed, the processes within such committees have themselves recently been the subject of ethnographic research (de Jong et al., 2012). In most cases it is likely that consent will need to be obtained from all of these different levels before any potential participants can be directly considered; consent within ethnographic work is indeed complex (Savage, 2000). However, negotiating consent with individuals within the setting is an extremely important subsequent stage of negotiating access, and it is crucial that potential research participants are given as much information as possible regarding a research project, enabling them to make an informed decision about whether to take part or not. This can be done in a number of ways. In more permanent locations, for example day centres or regular groups, meetings can be arranged to present the project to all individuals concerned, distribute information sheets and answer questions. In locations that also cater for more transient populations, such as wards or surgeries, posters and information sheets can be displayed detailing the project. If such meetings and information meet with the favour of the potential participants, researchers should make an effort to introduce themselves to individuals on a one-to-one basis, allowing prospective participants to ask questions before seeking individual consent. Obtaining written informed consent from each participant should be regarded as paramount. However, the way in which this is done should reflect the non-threatening and non-invasive character of the method itself. Care should be taken to ensure that signing the consent form does not become an issue of more concern to participants than participation in the study itself. Given the ongoing nature of ethnographic work, the researcher must also recognize that the participant's consent is not automatically a blanket assent to participate throughout the research (see Chapter 3 for further discussions about ethics).

Bengry-Howell and Griffin (2011) have given recent careful consideration to many of these difficult questions. It can be complicated to obtain written informed consent from all potential participants in an ethnographic situation. Take the example of a hospital ward: should the researcher gain written consent from all individuals on the ward, staff, patients, visitors, passers-by and so on, before beginning the ethnography? How should the researcher deal with new patients, emergency admissions, temporary staff, people making deliveries? Is it feasible to expect written consent from every individual who comes onto the ward and, if this is not possible, have the crucial principles of informed consent been violated? Similarly problematic is the issue of non-consent: all individuals on the ward have the right to decline to participate in the research, but if one individual exercises this right, must the entire research project be abandoned? Does the presence of the researcher on the ward violate that individual's rights? These are complicated questions, but I would argue that there are ways of addressing these, and even that ethnographic research can allow a more ethical relationship to develop between researcher and participant, as long as particular care is taken. In such health-care settings, a more ongoing approach to consent is necessary, and it is also possible for the researcher to find an appropriate way of dealing with non-participants. Ethnographers often take a passive role, especially at the outset of a project, waiting for individuals to approach them; should an individual not wish to participate, it would therefore be possible for the ethnographer not to approach that individual, nor any groups of which that individual is a part. The ethnographer should not include any reference to such an individual in their notes or subsequent discussions of the data. Researchers should, however, behave in a friendly manner to such individuals, so as not to make them feel that their participation is required or engender any undue stress. However, the answer to these questions is likely to be dependent on the situation, and different approaches and solutions might be needed in different situations.

Relationships between researcher and participants

Ethnography involves sustained interaction between researcher and participant; as such, both parties have the opportunity to become more acquainted with one another over several weeks, months or even years. For instance, Estroff (1981) spent two years engaged in ethnographic research in a community care programme in the United States. This chance to establish a longer research relationship, in turn, has numerous ethical advantages.

First, it gives the researcher the time to explain the purpose and practice of the research, and it gives the participant the opportunity to ask questions informally. Any subsequent questions about the research can be addressed in depth during later interaction. This may give the participant the opportunity for greater reflection and consideration of the research project, something that might be important if participants are ill, taking medication or vulnerable. There is also the potential for continued reassurance should the participant have any concerns regarding the project. There is perhaps a fine line here between the benefits for the researcher in gaining access to data and the participants' rights; Bengry-Howell and Griffin (2011) make reference to such an ambiguity in referring to this process as a kind of 'methodological grooming'.

Additionally, much of the success of an ethnographic study rests on the quality of the relationship between researcher and participants (Jorgensen, 1989). As Pope and Mays (2000) comment, the researcher is very much a research tool in ethnographic work and attempts to build trusting research relationships with participants. Such relationships have a twofold function. First, they can make the research situation less stressful and potentially more enjoyable for the participant. Second, they can establish a reciprocity between researcher and participant that leads to a greater depth of data, which arguably allows for the potential for greater collaborative effort: participants are able to tell the researcher what they feel is the most relevant issue, rather than the researcher assuming what this will be. This means that participants may feel a greater sense of long-term commitment to the research, wanting to express their points of view on issues. In my own experience of conducting ethnographic research into the ideas that clients of the mental health services have of mental health and illness (Foster, 2007), clients would regularly refuse to be interviewed by medical students who came to the ward as part of their training, but were enthusiastic about discussing similar issues with me, on the basis that they understood my research project and purpose and, indeed, wanted their views to be heard. Ethnographic work, then, can allow the researcher to engage with participants in a reciprocal and fruitful way. However, the way in which the relationship develops between researcher and participant can be emotionally very difficult in some circumstances. Gross (2012) discusses her complex experiences in an ethnographic study of a brain oncology unit, especially in relation to one patient with whom she became friends; there is extreme tension between her role as researcher and as friend, and the way in which this affected her interaction and approach to the information she received in clinical meetings and so on.

It is also the case that any researcher engaging in ethnography should expect to be viewed with suspicion by many participants, especially if the location is one that might be more usually hidden from view or the topic is a sensitive one. Accusations of being a spy are common (Lee, 1995) and researchers need to take special care if they intend to involve participants from different groups in the ethnography in situations where there is a clear hierarchy, as is often the case in the health services. Having said this, it is also often the case that key informants will strike up particularly important relationships with the researcher, such as Doc in Whyte-Foote's (1937) study: key informants are often participants who show early interest in a project and can act as intermediaries, introducing the researcher to other participants and so on. Care should, of course, be taken to ensure that the researcher is able to gain more than merely that one perspective, however; this will be discussed in more detail later in this chapter.

One final point that merits consideration here is also whether the researcher should be an 'insider' or 'outsider' to the situation that they are researching. Traditionally, as noted above, ethnographies were carried out in situations far from the researcher's own culture and experience. Even as ethnography 'came home' and researchers began to work in their own countries, it was still more usual to research populations to which one was an outsider. Some theorists, however, have argued that research should be much more wholly participatory (e.g. Dockery, 2000; Tones & Tilford, 1994), which raises some important questions for ethnography. While it may be more unusual to advocate that researchers should *only* engage in ethnographic research in their own cultures/groups, and indeed problematic given that this might well mean that the taken-for-granted assumptions of a group may not be fully visible to the researcher, there is a long tradition of autobiographically related ethnography (for a review of this and also a consideration of analytical autoethnography, see Anderson, 2006). Whether one agrees with this position or not, it is certainly the case that researchers should carefully consider the research questions that participants in any given situation believe to be important. Indeed, returning to the point made at the start of this section, this opportunity is, in many ways, built into the ethnographic process.

The role of the researcher

Another important question is the role that the researcher should take in the process of ethnography. In a rather dated, but still important paper, Gold (1958) describes four possibilities: complete participant, participant as observer, observer as participant and complete observer.

Although covert research has been practised in mental health services in particular in the past (Caudill et al., 1952; Rosenhan, 1973), and in a few cases a little more recently (Parr, 1998 on depression self-help groups) with researchers faking or exaggerating mental health problems in order to be admitted to mental institutions, this is now generally regarded as unacceptable (British Sociological Association, 1992; Francis, 1999): it makes informed consent an impossibility, thereby violating honesty and openness, crucial parts of the relationship between the researcher and the researched. Covert research also removes any possibility for questioning research participants, either informally or in a more structured way, meaning that researchers only have access to their own perspective on the situation and are unable to attempt to uncover others. Caudill et al. (1952) and Redlich (1973) also point out that covert research risks interfering with the therapeutic process of treatment for real patients and places a significant strain on the researcher. It is clearly not a viable option for ethnographic research in health and clinical psychology nowadays.

The role of complete observer can also be problematic: it implies that the researcher is in some kind of objective, neutral and omniscient position, which is hard to sustain from a constructionist perspective; although if a different conceptual approach is taken, then it may be feasible. However, it also has problems from an ethical point of view, especially in any study where there is already a significant imbalance of power between clients and others. Much research within health or clinical psychology deals with participants in difficult and distressing circumstances, and it is crucial that research with any already disempowered groups does not add further to their disempowerment through its methods (Duckett et al., 2000). It can also be argued that it is impossible to act as a complete observer in the sense that the researcher's presence inevitably affects any situation, and this influence is impossible to remove (Hammersley & Atkinson, 2007). One particular advantage of the ethnographic method is its position with regard to the relationship between researcher and researched discussed earlier: it acknowledges the reflexivity of the research process and calls for the researcher to take their own feelings and biases into account. Ways of doing this will be discussed later in this chapter.

However, it is at this point that I take issue with Gold's (1958) roles, and would concur with Jorgensen (1989) that the distinction between participant and observer is overexaggerated. We take a number of different roles in interaction, some more participatory and some more observing, and it is artificial to try to separate them. In most studies, the researcher is likely to act as both participant and observer in any study, at once acknowledging the differences between researcher and researched, while also attempting to gain access to routines and understanding. It may even be the case that researchers move from a more passive role to a more participatory one, as they gain more familiarity with the situation and are accepted more within it.

Doing ethnography

Once access has been granted to a field situation and consent has been gained, the researcher will then spend some time gaining participants' trust. Taking note of the surroundings, and the way in which they are used, is also crucial, and this is important in the process of familiarization too. The researcher can then add to these observations with more interactions with participants and with a developing appreciation of rituals, practices and routines. Ethnography, as the study of people and social situations in their natural context, is undertaken for the purpose of gaining a deeper understanding of the phenomena at work that shape those situations. It may involve multiple forms of data collection, including interviews, informal discussions, consideration of relevant documents and other artefacts and so on (Hammersley & Atkinson, 2007).

Keeping a comprehensive selection of notes, or a 'field diary', is essential and this will later form the basis of the analysis. This document needs to be as accurate as possible; indeed, one of the criticisms of ethnography is often that it relies too much on the recollections of ethnographers, and therefore may be flawed. Writing up notes during interaction is usually off-putting for participants and can also mean that the ethnographer misses out on other details. However, notes should certainly be written up as soon as possible and the researcher should expect this process to take a considerable amount of time. Some ethnography is more focused and therefore looks only at specific issues within any situation, whereas other studies might be more general; at the early stages the researcher may not know what will or will not be relevant at any later stage. Many ethnographic researchers resort to carrying a piece of paper and a pencil in their back pocket to jot down brief notes to aid their memory until the notes can be written up comprehensively; more recently, in some situations, some researchers have found that making a quick note on a mobile phone is easier and can be done during some interactions quite naturally (Morton, 2012). Video or audio recording may be possible in some situations, but this raises its own ethical questions and may be considered too intrusive in many sensitive situations.

However, the researcher will not only be relying on observations of what is said and done in each situation. Careful notes can be made of the way in which space is used by different groups, of any documents that may be displayed and of any other artefacts. As these observations and conversations build, the researcher is likely to develop ideas and theories about why certain practices may occur, or to have questions about the different processes that take place. It is here that conversations with multiple participants play a particularly important role: they allow the researcher the opportunity to check their own interpretation, to gain more information and so on. In many ways, the triangulation that Flick (2007) and others see as being so important to qualitative analysis is inbuilt into ethnography in this way; multiple perspectives are always under consideration.

Ethnographers may also combine their observation and participation in daily routines with interviews of various kinds with participants, which can be useful to check details and to gain more information on issues that might be harder for an outsider to understand without more direct questioning. These may be unstructured, semi-structured or narrative interviews, or focus group interviews might even be suitable (see Flick, 2009 for more discussion of all of these interviews; see also Chapter 6). Again, this will depend very much on the individual situation and on the research questions. Documents might also be available that could be analysed: these may be formal policy documents, histories of the location, diaries kept by participants and so on. In some studies, photographs have either been taken by participants or brought along for discussion so as to add to an understanding of their daily lives (Gillespie, 2006). Surveys and questionnaires can also be devised to gain more information. Again, the suitability of these methods will very much depend on the location and topic under consideration.

Analysis

The overall aim of analysis of ethnographic data is a greater understanding of the themes and patterns in situations, actions and interactions, and the meanings behind these. Careful analysis of the corpus of data that is collected is essential. There are numerous ways of approaching this issue and it is not necessarily the case that all of these will be qualitative: it is perfectly possible to approach the analysis of many of the sources of data that might emerge from an ethnographic project with a more quantitative analysis (for example, comparing the frequency of events). As discussed earlier in this chapter, much of the historical approach to ethnography was indeed much more positivist and quantitative.

However, the ethnographic method is usually more associated with qualitative analysis. In many ways, the various documents that are likely to emerge from an ethnographic project can be analysed in a similar way to any other textual data: field notes, interviews, documents and so on can be coded thematically (Attride-Stirling, 2001) or taking a grounded theory approach (Braun & Clarke, 2006). Flick (2009) discusses moving from an open to a selective coding approach, which allows the researcher the opportunity to gain an overall understanding of the data before moving in to focus on aspects that are of particular interest. It is often the case that the researcher will have particular research questions in mind at the outset, so a coding frame can be established that rests partially on several inductive codes, but is also open to novel and new ideas, and therefore allows deductive codes to emerge. The process of data analysis in this kind of work is always both cyclical and iterative (Bauer, 2000). Different kinds of data may need different kinds of analysis or coding, but it is important to be able to compare and contrast both within and across data sources, while also looking for wider patterns and examining unexpected or unusual instances that do not fit in with these overall themes. It is important not to see the coding frame as an end in itself and to be able to employ one's 'sociological imagination' to suggest interpretations and possibilities (Provencher, 2011). This calls not only for describing the data, but also for developing broader suggestions and claims about what is going on, linking data from one study to existing theory and empirical work.

Assessing the quality of ethnographic research

There has been much discussion of ways of assessing qualitative analysis in health-related areas (e.g. Pope & Mays, 2000; Savage, 2000) and ethnographic work does not present a particularly different case. It is, of course, still possible formally to calculate inter-rater reliability for coding frames or to engage in a data audit (Flick, 2009) as an alternative. Coherence and consistency must drive the analysis at all stages (Duveen & Lloyd, 1993) and transparency of decision-making in all phases of the research is particularly appropriate. It may also be possible to employ communicative validation in many cases of ethnographic work in health and clinical psychology (Gaskell & Bauer, 2000), with the researchers either returning to the location to discuss findings and interpretations with participants, or sending summaries to interested participants for their comments if populations are more transient.

There is an important question that must be raised as to how well received ethnographic work is likely to be in some health-care settings. Most ethnographers would agree that the research that comes from this method is particularly dependent on the combination of time, place and participants; as such, questions of reliability, validity and generalizability are not easily answered. Some researchers argue that these traditional measures should be mapped directly onto qualitative work (e.g. Krippendorff, 1980 on content analysis) and concern themselves with methods for doing this. However, such a process is often viewed as practically and philosophically problematic. More often than not, in practice such traditional quality indicators are used to cast qualitative work as inadequate, sub-standard or deficient in comparison with more obviously 'testable' quantitative work (Clarke, 1992), and attempting to deal in concepts of validity and reliability in qualitative work that stems from a constructionist perspective has been seen as a mistake (Murray & Chamberlain, 1999). In fact, Jorgensen (1989) has claimed that ethnography is very high in validity: few assumptions are made at the outset; nothing is being tested as such; and ethnographers make attempts to learn and use the vocabulary of the participants, asking for clarification as they progress. However, questions of reliability and generalizability cannot be so easily answered, and this is why so many theorists, including Flick (2009) and Gaskell and Bauer (2000), have suggested that new ways of assessing qualitative analysis are required. It is important to note that even though results from one ethnographic study may not be generalizable to another, they can still be relevant to others (Geertz, 2000), as can theoretical or conceptual insights. We may not be dealing with absolute rules, but there is a great deal to be said both for understanding the detail of one situation and location, and being able to consider how far some of these details may be relevant and useful in considering other similar situations. Meta-ethnographic approaches can be used here, which aim to combine and compare results across a number of studies to look for overall themes. Clark et al. (2012) employ such an approach when looking at factors that influence attendance at rehabilitation programmes for

---

BOX 14.3   Summary: Ethnographic research

- Ethnography involves observation and participation in a particular setting, and may also involve other methods such as interviews and documentary analysis.
- Ethnography aims to access the rituals, practices, representations and ideas that guide daily life, and may be particularly appropriate in situations that are not well researched.
- Access and consent are particularly complicated issues within ethnography and must be carefully negotiated.
- The relationship between researcher and participants can be a particularly fruitful tool.
- Notes of all kinds must be very carefully recorded for later analysis.
- Similar principles apply to the analysis of data that emerges from ethnographic research and evaluation of findings, as with other kinds of qualitative analysis.

---

patients with heart disease; Heinze and Nolan (2012) do likewise on parental decision-making in end-stage childhood cancer.

Users' understanding of mental health problems

In the late 1990s there was a considerable gap in the literature on understandings of mental health problems and their implications. Work using a variety of methodological approaches had considered the understandings held by the general public and by professionals, and there was a substantial amount of work (much of it undertaken outside academia within the mental health service user movement) that examined the views of people who use mental health services on those services (see, for example, the discussion of user-focused monitoring in Rose, 2001). My own study (Foster, 2003, 2007) aimed to examine the understandings and experiences of people who use mental health services about mental health and illness, and to consider the implications of these understandings. Drawing on the social constructionist perspective of social representations theory (Moscovici, 2000), a qualitative mixed-methods approach that allowed access to the meaning of mental health problems in the context of the mental health services seemed particularly appropriate.

I therefore made contact, initially through an interested psychiatrist, with four different mental health services (two day centres and two hospital wards) to discuss the possibility of engaging in ethnographic research for around eight weeks in each location. Access had to be negotiated on several levels, first with the consultant psychiatrists, then with ward managers and then with the rest of the staff. At this stage, one ward decided not to participate, leaving two day centres and one acute ward involved in the project. In tandem, the project was also submitted to the local National Health Service ethics committee (now the National Research Ethics Service); explaining ethnographic work, and its purpose and analysis, to this committee took some time. Once ethical approval had been granted and all staff had agreed to the project, I was then able to meet the service users themselves and explain my project. This was done at group meetings and also through a series of posters. The ethics committee had insisted on written consent from each participant, so information sheets were prepared and discussed with service users and written consent was sought. However, as discussed earlier, consent was an ongoing process in this project.

At each location I spent the first few days taking something of a back seat, observing the layout of the space and how it was used, and getting used to the routines. At this stage, many service users began to approach me to find out more about who I was and what I was doing. In many cases, services were used to having student nurses or other trainees doing placements, and many service users saw my role as akin to these: I was there to learn about what life was like from their perspective. This also meant that many participants were keen to explain other aspects of the mental health services and how a service fitted in to the wider area, which was particularly useful. I tried to match the routines of the service users themselves: this meant arriving roughly when they did in the morning and leaving when they did, although the ward required more flexibility, including some work in the evenings and at weekends to gain a full perspective. Immediately after leaving the services each day, I would write up comprehensive notes on a secure computer, including information on the events of the day, conversations in which I had participated, my own thoughts and feelings, and the questions that I was starting to develop about each location. Many of the conversations I had did not directly involve discussion of mental health: sometimes these were a part of rapport-building, but at other times they yielded other interesting data. Towards the end of the eight-week period in each service, I approached service users to see if they would be interested in speaking to me on a one-to-one basis in an interview, which began by asking each participant how they came to be using that particular service, and then followed this up as appropriate.

All data was thematically analysed, a process that is discussed in detail elsewhere (Foster, 2007). What was particularly interesting was how the ethnographic work allowed me to build up relationships with participants and to gain an insight into their lives and service use. It also allowed me to compare across the three services: this was ultimately one of my main conclusions, as although all the participants in my study were engaged in a 'project' of getting through mental health problems, this was conceptualized and operationalized in different ways in the three services. Indeed, this involved different aspects of understandings of mental health problems, such as how important medication might be, the differing values of talking treatments, ideas regarding longevity and so on. The notion of self-defined recovery was essential in all services, and relations with professionals could therefore be complex. It was through ethnography that the subtle differences between the projects in which service users were engaged became evident: both explicitly and implicitly, the service users in the different locations conveyed slightly different ideas of mental ill-health and demonstrated their shared understandings of how to approach these problems. In one of the day centres, which catered largely for people who had been using mental health services for some time and who were considered by professionals to have long-term chronic mental health problems, research participants talked about 'coming round' from mental health problems. This had parallels with coming round from unconsciousness, but it would be wrong to see this as a passive process, since participants did see a role for themselves in this, albeit one that was shared with roles played by professionals, medication and so on. At the acute ward, in contrast, participants discussed the need to 'get it together' and then 'keep it together'. This was a much more active project and participants felt that medication and service use might only provide a temporary solution, or in some cases mask the real problems that they needed to work through themselves. An ethnographic approach allowed me to understand how these ideas and understandings were developed and maintained in interaction, informal conversations, practices within the services and so on. It also allowed me to consider whether these ideas were, in practice, supported or thwarted by staff.

Concluding comments

Ethnography has a rich history not only within anthropology but also within a range of other disciplines, and has continuing relevance in considering questions related to clinical and health psychology. It is certainly not without practical and ethical challenges, and is a time-consuming process. However, the detail and richness that can be accessed through using ethnography is significant, and has real potential to help psychologists understand important aspects such as the day-to-day lived experience of health, illness and service use.

Further reading

Flick, U. (2009). *An Introduction to Qualitative Research*. London: Sage.
Glaser, B.G. & Strauss, A.L. (1965). *Awareness of Dying*. Chicago, IL: Aldine.
    A seminal work using ethnography.
Hammersley, M. & Atkinson, P. (2007). *Ethnography: Principles and Practice*. London: Routledge.
Jodelet, D. (1991). *Madness and Social Representations* (trans. T. Pownall). Hemel Hempstead: Harvester Wheatsheaf.
    An excellent example of a comprehensive ethnography.
Jorgensen, D.L. (1989). *Participant Observation: A Methodology for Human Studies*. Newbury Park, CA: Sage.

References

Agar, M.H. (1980). *The Professional Stranger: An Informal Introduction to Ethnography*. New York: Academic Press.

Anderson, L. (2006). Analytic autoethnography. *Journal of Contemporary Ethnography*, 35(4), 373–395.

Attride-Stirling, J. (2001). Thematic networks: An analytic tool for qualitative research. *Qualitative Research*, 1(3), 385–405.

Bauer, M.W. (2000). Classical content analysis: A review. In M.W. Bauer & G. Gaskell (eds), *Qualitative Researching with Text, Image and Sound* (pp. 131–151). London: Sage.

Becker, H.S. & Geer, B. (1957). Participant observation and interviewing: A comparison. *Human Organisation*, 16(3), 28–32.

Bengry-Howell, A. & Griffin, C. (2011). Negotiating access in ethnographic research with 'hard to reach' young people: Establishing common ground or a process of methodological grooming? *International Journal of Social Research Methodology*, 15(5), 403–416.

Braun, V. & Clarke, V. (2006). Using thematic analysis in psychology. *Qualitative Research in Psychology*, 3(2), pp. 77–101.

British Sociological Association. (1992). *Statement on Ethical Practice*. London: British Sociological Association.

Buston, K., Parry-Jones, W., Livingston, M., Bogan, A. & Ward, S. (1998). Qualitative research. *British Journal of Psychiatry*, 172, 197–199.

Caudill, W. (1958). *The Psychiatric Hospital as a Small Society*. Cambridge, MA: Harvard University Press.

Caudill, W., Redlich, F., Gilmore, H. & Brody, E. (1952). Social structure and interaction processes on a psychiatric ward. *American Journal of Orthopsychiatry*, 22, 314–334.

Charmaz, K. & Olsen, V. (1997). Ethnographic research in medical sociology. *Sociological Methods and Research*, 25(4), 452–494.

Clark, A., King-Shier, K., Thompson, D., Spaling, M., Duncan, A., Stone, J., Jaglal, S. & Angus, J. (2012). A qualitative systematic review of influences on attendance at cardiac rehabilitation programs after referral. *American Heart Journal*, 164(6), 835–845.

Clarke, L. (1992). Qualitative research: Meaning and language. *Journal of Advanced Nursing*, 17, 243–252.

Clifford, J. (1986). Introduction: Partial truths. In J. Clifford & G.E. Marcus (eds), *Writing Culture: The Poetics and Politics of Ethnography* (pp. 1–26). Berkeley: University of California Press.

de Jong, J.P., van Zwieten, M.C.B. & Willems, D.L. (2012). Ethical review from the inside: Repertoires of evaluation in Research Ethics Committee meetings. *Sociology of Health and Illness*, 34(7), 1039–1052.

Dockery, G. (2000). Participatory research: Whose roles? Whose responsibilities? In C. Truman, D.M. Mertens & B. Humphries (eds), *Research and Inequality* (pp. 95–110). London: UCL Press.

Duckett, P., McCall, F. & Fryer, D. (2000). Interactional asymmetry in research interviews: Some attempts to reduce the imbalance of power between interviewers and interviewees. Paper presented at the *Fifth International Conference on Logic and Methodology*, Cologne, 3–6 October.

Duveen, G.M. & Lloyd, B. (1993). An ethnographic approach to social representations. In G. Breakwell & D. Canter (eds), *Empirical Approaches to Social Representations* (pp. 90–109). Oxford: Oxford University Press.

Estroff, S.E. (1981). *Making It Crazy: An Ethnography of Psychiatric Clients in an American Community*. Berkeley: University of California Press.

Festinger, L., Riecken, H.W. & Schachter, S. (1956) *When Prophesy Fails*. Minneapolis: University of Minnesota Press.

Flick, U. (2007). *Managing Quality in Qualitative Research*. London: Sage.

Flick, U. (2009). *An Introduction to Qualitative Research*. London: Sage.

Foster, J.L.H. (2003). Beyond otherness: Controllability and location in mental health service clients' representations of mental health problems. *Journal of Health Psychology, 8*(5), 632–644.

Foster, J.L.H. (2007). *Journeys through Mental Illness: Clients' Experiences and Understandings of Mental Distress*. Basingstoke: Palgrave Macmillan.

Francis, R.D. (1999). *Ethics for Psychologists: A Handbook*. Leicester: BPS Books.

Gaskell, G. & Bauer, M.W. (2000). Towards public accountability: Beyond sampling, reliability and validity. In M.W. Bauer & G. Gaskell (eds), *Qualitative Researching with Text, Images and Sound* (pp. 336–350). London: Sage.

Geertz, C. (2000). Anti anti-realism. In C. Geertz (ed.), *Available Light: Anthropological Reflections on Philosophical Topics* (pp. 42–67). Princeton, NJ: Princeton University Press.

Gervais, M.-C. & Jovchelovitch, S. (1998). *The Health Beliefs of the Chinese Community in England*. London: Health Education Authority.

Gillespie, A. (2006). *Becoming other: From social interaction to self-reflection*. Charlotte, NC: Information Age Publishing.

Glaser, B.G. & Strauss, A.L. (1965). *Awareness of Dying*. Chicago, IL: Aldine.

Goffman, E. (1961). *Asylums: Essays on the Social Situation of Mental Patients and Other Inmates*. London: Penguin.

Gold, R.L. (1958). Roles in sociological field observations. *Social Forces, 36*, 217–223.

Griffin, C. & Bengry-Howell, A. (2007). Ethnography. In C. Willig & W. Stainton Rogers (eds), *Sage Handbook of Qualitative Methods in Psychology* (pp. 15–31). London: Sage.

Gross, S. (2012). Biomedicine inside out: An ethnography of brain surgery. *Sociology of Health and Illness, 34*(8), 1170–1183.

Hammersley, M. & Atkinson, P. (2007). *Ethnography: Principles and Practice*. London: Routledge.

Heinze, K. & Nolan, M. (2012). Parental decision making for children with cancer at the end of life: A meta-ethnography. *Journal of Pediatric Oncology Nursing, 29*(6), 337–345.

Jodelet, D. (1991). *Madness and Social Representations* (trans. T. Pownall). Hemel Hempstead: Harvester Wheatsheaf.

Jones, R. (1995). Why do qualitative research? *British Medical Journal, 311*, 2.

Jorgensen, D.L. (1989). *Participant Observation: A Methodology for Human Studies*. Newbury Park, CA: Sage.

Krippendorff, K. (1980). *Content Analysis: An Introduction to Its Methodology*. London: Sage.

Lee, R.M. (1995). *Dangerous Fieldwork*. Newbury Park, CA: Sage.

Leventhal, H., Benyamini, Y., Brownlee, S. et al. (1997). Illness representations: Theoretical foundations. In K.J. Petrie & J.A. Weinman (eds), *Perceptions of Health and Illness: Current Research Applications*. Amsterdam: Harwood Academic.

Morton, C. (2012). Understandings and experiences of living with an acquired brain injury (ABI): An ethnographic and interpretative phenomenological analysis. Dissertation. Cambridge: University of Cambridge.

Moscovici, S. (2000). The phenomenon of social representations. In S. Moscovici, *Social Representations: Explorations in Social Psychology* (pp. 18–77). Cambridge: Polity Press.

Murray, M. & Chamberlain, K. (1999). Health psychology and qualitative research. In M. Murray & K. Chamberlain (eds), *Qualitative Health Psychology: Theories and Methods* (pp. 3–15). London: Sage.

Parr, H. (1998). Mental health, ethnography and the body. *Area, 30*(1), 28–37.

Pope, C. & Mays, N. (2000). *Qualitative Research in Health Care Settings*. London: BMJ Books.

Pratt, M.L. (1986). Fieldwork in common places. In J. Clifford & G.E. Marcus (eds), *Writing Culture: The Poetics and Politics of Ethnography* (pp. 27–50). Berkeley: University of California Press.

Provencher, C. (2011). Lauri on organ donation or how to teach the theory of social representations using a quality empirical study. *Papers on Social Representations, 20*(2). http://www.psych.lse.ac.uk/psr/PSR2011/PSR2011_Issue_2.htm, accessed 2 May 2014.

Quirk, A. & Lelliott, P. (2002). Acute wards: Problems and solutions: A participant observation study of life on an acute psychiatric ward. *Psychiatric Bulletin, 26,* 344–345.

Redlich, F. (1973). The anthropologist as observer: Ethical aspects of clinical observations of behaviour. *Journal of Nervous and Mental Disease, 157*(5), 313–320.

Rivers, W.H.R. (1912). A general account of method. In W.H.R. Rivers, *Notes and Queries on Anthropology* (ed. British Association for the Advancement of Science, 4th edn, pp. 108–127). London: RAI.

Robinson, S.G. (2013). The relevancy of ethnography to nursing research. *Nursing Science Quarterly, 26*(1), 14–19.

Rose, D. (2001). *Users' Voices: The Perspectives of Mental Health Service Users on Community and Hospital Care*. London: Sainsbury Centre for Mental Health.

Rosenhan, D.L. (1973). On being sane in insane places. *Science, 179,* 250–258.

Savage, J. (2000). Ethnography and health care. *British Medical Journal, 321,* 1400–1402.

Smith, A., Goodwin, D., Mort, M. & Pope, C. (2003). Expertise in practice: An ethnographic study exploring the acquisition and use of knowledge in anaesthesia. *British Journal of Anaesthesia, 91*(3), 319–328.

Stanton, A.H. & Schwarz, M.S. (1954). *The Mental Hospital: A Study of Institutional Participation in Psychiatric Illness*. London: Tavistock.

Stocking, G.W. (1983). The ethnographer's magic: Fieldwork in British anthropology from Tylor to Malinowski. In G. Stocking (ed.), *Observers Observed: Essays on Ethnographic Fieldwork* (pp. 70–120). Madison: University of Wisconsin Press.

The, A.-M., Pasman, R., Onwuteaka-Philipsen, B., Ribbe, M. & van der Wal, G. (2002). Withholding the artificial administration of fluids and food from elderly patients: Ethnographic study. *British Medical Journal, 325,* 1326–1330.

Tones, K. & Tilford, S. (1994). *Health Education: Effectiveness, Efficiency and Equity*. London: Chapman and Hall.

Whyte-Foote, W. (1943). *Street Corner Society*. Chicago, IL: University of Chicago Press.

Participatory Research

15

Cathy Vaughan

Most health research requires the 'participation', in some way, of research participants (who participate in interviews, undertake clinical experiments, complete surveys and allow themselves to be observed) and of researchers (who conduct these interviews, experiments and observations). However, there is increasing recognition that when the involvement of research participants is limited to that of being a 'subject' in health research, the knowledge thus generated about health is also limited. Therefore, many health researchers are looking towards participatory approaches to the production of knowledge.

Participatory research can be broadly defined as 'systematic inquiry, with the collaboration of those affected by the issue being studied, for purposes of education and taking action or effecting change' (Green et al., 1995). Participatory research is primarily differentiated from conventional research in the alignment of power within the research process, with differences between participatory and conventional approaches being made evident in 'who defines research problems and who generates, analyses, represents, owns and acts on the information which is sought' (Cornwall & Jewkes, 1995:1668). As Cornwall and Jewkes (1995) highlight, however, there is considerable fluctuation between the ideal type of a participatory and conventional approach, with differences often being more of degree than of kind. Most research endeavours will involve varying degrees of participation by different actors at different stages of the research process.

Traditionally, researchers make decisions about research processes, such as what questions to ask, how to ask them, what methods to use and what the data generated mean, without the input of research participants or subjects. The objectivity and expertise of researchers are emphasized. All research aims to produce new knowledge about a particular issue; however, with this conventional approach, the knowledge that is produced will be shaped and limited by what the researcher already knows. Research questions, for example, will be grounded in the 'literature', seeking to extend the current state of evidence about what is known about the health issue under study. Questions will seek to generate knowledge about what the researcher knows to be gaps in the literature, or the 'known unknowns', to borrow from Donald Rumsfeld. What is missed with a conventional approach to research are the 'unknown unknowns', those factors that are beyond the current state of evidence and for which the researcher is unaware that they should even be looking. Researchers can begin to learn more about some of these factors by working collaboratively with research participants, drawing on their different knowledge systems, perspectives, experiences and priorities. Extending the horizons of the knowledge that can be generated through research is one important rationale for a participatory approach.

Participatory approaches to research are oriented towards action. When research participants are not involved in the design of the research process, there is a risk that findings may be theoretically interesting (answering the abstract questions identified by the researcher from gaps in the literature), but unusable for taking action or making change in the 'real world' of participants. Research findings that are disconnected from the practical concerns of participants (and policy-makers and practitioners) have too often been dismissed as irrelevant, inappropriate and impractical. Ensuring that research activities are grounded in the priorities and day-to-day challenges of those best placed to use the knowledge generated is another key reason for using a participatory approach.

Participatory research approaches also explicitly aim to build the skills and confidence of participants through the process. Participatory researchers value different ways of knowing. This valuing of participant knowledge and perspective can contribute to participants themselves recognizing the worth of what they have to say, and that they are indeed the experts in their own lives. This can build participant confidence in sharing this expertise in a range of forums and in taking action to make changes to address their priorities and concerns. Sometimes participatory researchers will also work with participants to identify what specific skills the members of the research team (academics, practitioners and participant researchers) require to take effective action for change, and work collaboratively with participants to develop these skills.

Origins of participatory research approaches

Participatory research methodologies are not new. Since the early 1970s, participatory approaches to research have been increasingly used in a wide range of settings. Kurt Lewin's action research experiments in the 1940s, and the work of the Tavistock Institute from the same period, are often highlighted as underpinning the development of participatory approaches to research. However, participatory research has broad origins.

The 1950s through to the 1970s saw collectives of people pursuing their rights in movements as diverse as the independence movements in the colonized 'third world', the civil rights movement in the United States and 'second-wave' feminism. In this climate, Marx's 1845 observation that the point is not merely to interpret the world but to change it informed the work of a range of researcher-practitioners. Researchers were developing new ways of engaging in action-oriented research processes in various settings, but particularly in contexts of poverty, inequality and exclusion. Throughout this period there was a growth in the number of researcher-practitioners seeking to work with communities in more equal and inclusive ways to achieve progressive social change collaboratively. This includes researcher-activists in developing countries, such as Paulo Freire (in Brazil and elsewhere) and Orlando Fals Borda (in Columbia), and also those working in richer if unequal countries, such as Myles Horton and others at the Highlander Center in Tennessee and a number of early feminist researchers. Key historical and theoretical influences on approaches to participatory research are outlined in the next section.

Kurt Lewin and action research

Action research is generally described as having its origins in the work of social and experimental psychologist Kurt Lewin in the 1940s. Lewin's background as a Jewish scholar who had fled Nazi Germany heavily informed his commitment to understanding group behaviour, and to supporting cultural and organizational change. Lewin was deeply committed to the resolution of social conflicts and the position of minorities or disadvantaged groups. This ethos, and his position that 'one cannot understand an organization without trying to change it' (Schein, 1996:64), continue to inform participatory research practitioners.

Lewin described his action-oriented approach to research as being based on 'a spiral of steps, each of which is composed of a circle of planning, action, and fact-finding about the result of the action' (Lewin, 1946/1948:206). While Lewin has been criticized for neglecting complexity and the non-linear nature of social change (Burnes, 2004), the notion of a spiral of reflection, action and reflection about the outcomes of the action has been a central pillar of participatory research endeavours in health for more than 50 years.

Lewin's description of an 'action research spiral' is both an asset and a source of considerable difficulty for action researchers. The metaphor of the spiral is one that is straightforward to explain and as a heuristic device is intuitive. However, it has also been misused to reduce action research to simply a *procedure* involving a cycle of reflection, planning for action, action and then going back to reflecting on the impact of that action. Action researchers argue that this misinterprets Lewin's intent to highlight the dynamic nature of action research and its relationship with practice (McTaggart, 1996). McTaggart emphasizes that 'it is a mistake to think that slavishly following the "action research spiral" constitutes "doing action research"', highlighting the more fundamental feature of 'collective reflection by participants on systematic objectifications and disciplined subjectifications of their efforts to change the way they work (constituted by discourse, organization and power relations, and practice)' (McTaggart, 1996:207). Others have emphasized that the procedure of the action research cycle is less important than the principle of working with, rather than on or for, people in efforts to transform complex situations (Chevalier & Buckles, 2013).

Feminist theories

Feminist theories emphasize that historically, health research practices have been based on the research questions, health experiences and bodies of men (Bird & Rieker, 2008), with feminist authors demonstrating ways in which 'traditional' approaches to research obscure and silence women's experiences (Maguire, 1996). While public health researchers and psychologists have long acknowledged the impact of inequality on health, feminist theorists have drawn attention to the impact of gender inequality and the intersections of oppressions and inequalities based on gender, class, sexuality, race and postcolonialism (Crenshaw, 1991). Feminist theories illuminate the way in which these intersecting inequalities have been overlooked or misunderstood by researchers using traditional research approaches. In intentionally countering dominant theories about human experiences and strategies for change, feminist theories have highlighted the way in which researchers need to 'unlearn' their privileges, to enable them to listen to and gain knowledge from the diverse experiences of those who are less privileged (Frisby et al., 2009).

Feminist theories share an emphasis on achieving social change through a focus on power and how this manifests in gender inequalities. These social change goals resonate with the 'action' orientation of participatory research. Participatory research draws on feminist theories in attempting to unsettle the 'taken for granted' (Frisby et al., 2009). By supporting research participants to question why things are as they are in their communities, participatory research builds on the feminist notion that participation in knowledge-making has the potential to empower actions that seek to change the status quo.

Feminist authors recognize that research participants should be viewed as actors in the world rather than objects of study (Letherby, 2003). However, feminist theorists also remind us that the world in which research participants act is inherently unequal and unfair. The act of participating in a research project can potentially build participants' critical thinking, confidence and skills, contributing to their capacity to take meaningful action in the world. However, Fraser reminds researchers to recognize, and work to address, the limitations to genuine participation in the public sphere, given that communities' 'discursive arenas are situated in a larger societal context that is pervaded by structural relations of dominance and subordination' (1990:65). The experience of feminist theorists such as Fraser grounds the sometimes lofty rhetoric associated with participatory research, forcing attention back to the difficult and entrenched inequalities that shape and bound many research participants' lives.

Paulo Freire and critical pedagogy

Participatory research, in various forms, had been going on for some time in both the majority world (Fals Borda, 2006) and parts of the United States (Gaventa & Horton, 1981) by the time Paulo Freire's *Pedagogy of the Oppressed* was published in English in 1970. However, it was Freire's view of research as a form of social (collective) action that increased attention towards the emancipatory potential of an approach to research that incorporated a broader societal analysis (Herr & Anderson, 2005).

Paulo Freire's theory of how marginalized communities can act collectively to produce social change, detailed in *Pedagogy of the Oppressed*, is based on the notion of *conscientização* (Freire, 1970). *Conscientização*, most often translated as 'conscientization' or the development of critical consciousness, is a process that emerges in dialogical relations. Conscientization is fostered through dialogue about the contexts in which people live, where interlocutors co-construct a reflective and critical understanding of the broad range of (social, economic, cultural, psychological) factors shaping local circumstances.

Freire's pedagogy utilizes a problem-posing approach to stimulate the dialogue fundamental to conscientization, encouraging reflection on, and the critique of, the inherent relationship between the construction of knowledge and power (Freire, 2005[1974]). This is in stark contrast to the problem-solving techniques often 'taught' to community members in traditional health interventions. Problem-posing instead has the potential to interrupt assumptions (of both health workers and community members) and re-define the nature of 'problems'. Participatory researchers using a problem-posing approach encourage formally trained researchers and community member participants to bring their different knowledge systems and perspectives together to reflect on why situations in the community are as they are, in order to co-construct new knowledge for action.

Freire's pedagogy, based on bringing the knowledge of different actors into dialogue, confirms that knowledge is an expression of historically, socially and psychologically situated lived experience. When one actor's knowledge is brought into dialogue with that of another, the process illuminates the 'diversity, expressiveness and limitations' inherent in all knowledge (Jovchelovitch, 2007). When actors recognize the partial nature of knowledge, the social order can be seen as arbitrary and possible alternatives can emerge. As such, 'the world becomes one which is open to change' (Cornish, 2004). Recognition of the contextual nature of knowledge enables interlocutors to critically reflect on their lived experience – how and why each of them knows what they know – and to co-construct a new understanding of the world from which to act on this context: 'Integration results from the capacity to adapt oneself to reality *plus* the critical capacity to make choices and to transform that reality' (Freire, 2005[1974]:4). For Freire, the development of critical consciousness through reflection is inextricably linked with critical action. This action–reflection dynamic, which both emerges from and gives support to conscientization,

Freire calls *praxis*. This clearly resonates with an action research approach based on planning, action and reflection.

Participatory rural appraisal

A range of practitioners working in international development were heavily influenced by Freire's approach to working with disempowered communities, and began to develop participatory approaches to generating knowledge based on their development practice. Chief among these was Robert Chambers, widely acknowledged as a leading proponent of participatory development practice and the architect of an approach to knowledge production known as participatory rural appraisal (PRA).

In the late 1970s and early 1980s, an approach to generating knowledge for community development initiatives was developed known as RRA (rapid rural appraisal). This was developed in response to the costs and biases associated with using traditional research methods to evaluate or design projects in developing countries. RRA was based primarily on qualitative tools such as key informant interviews, focus group discussions, structured observations and informal surveys. It was intended to be a quick process to generate sufficiently accurate information to inform programmes.

While RRA was focused on outsiders' information needs, in the late 1980s the process of PRA emerged and focused on building local people's knowledge and skills to change their own situation, and gave recognition to local people's analytical capacities. The methods used in PRA are many and varied (for examples, see Pretty et al., 1995), but are characterized by visual tools and techniques for mapping, ranking and prioritizing that are often done in small groups and are not dependent on literacy. While often initiated and/or facilitated by outside development practitioners, PRA can enable local people to design, collect, analyse and act on data that they have generated (Chambers & Guijt, 2011). Despite criticisms, based on some researchers' excessive focus on the tools themselves (rather than the process) or sloppy practice, the approach continues to be widely used in international development practice and research.

Key principles of participatory research

The diverse threads of inquiry and theory that have historically informed the development of participatory research mean that rather than 'a method', it should be seen as a group of approaches that share an orientation towards inquiry (Bradbury & Reason, 2003). 'Participatory research' is an umbrella term inclusive of a broad range of tools, methods and processes – including community-based participatory research, participatory learning and action, appreciative inquiry, empowerment evaluation and many others – that share some key principles. These have been outlined by a diverse range of authors

---

BOX 15.1   Features of participatory research

- Knowledge generated is oriented towards action.
- Research questions are based on participant priorities and practical concerns.
- Collaborative partnerships are formed between formally trained researchers and participants who may not have had research training.
- Participants are involved in deciding the most appropriate questions and methods for answering these questions.
- Methods are chosen not only to answer research questions, but to enable local learning and build participants' confidence and skills.
- Participants are involved in analysis and interpretation of the data generated.
- Participants and researchers jointly 'own', use and disseminate the findings.
- Process is prioritized, not just outcomes.
- Process builds on existing community strengths and resources.

(for example, Green et al., 1995; Israel et al., 1998; Fetterman & Wandersman, 2005; Cargo & Mercer, 2008), but across the various guidelines and overviews a number of consistent elements can be identified (see Box 15.1).

How has participatory research been used in clinical and health psychology?

While sometimes seen as the 'domain' of social or community psychologists, participatory approaches to research are well established in health research more broadly, and have been used to examine a range of health issues relevant to psychologists from a range of sub-disciplines. These include anxiety and depression, acquired brain injury, community mental health practice, disaster recovery, housing and health, psychiatric disabilities, schizophrenia, school health, substance abuse and suicide prevention, as outlined in Table 15.1.

Psychologists have used a participatory research approach to engage with service users, carers and community members to generate knowledge collaboratively about patient experience and local mental health priorities. Psychologists have also used participatory research approaches to engage with service providers from a range of disciplines, as well as health services management, to improve the structure and function of clinical and community services.

A wide range of approaches to participatory research have been used in the health sector. These include appreciative inquiry, citizen monitoring, community arts initiatives and participatory video, among others. An example of a tool or approach to participatory research that is increasingly used by health and clinical psychologists is Photovoice. This method will be discussed as a case study to examine some of the processes, strengths and limitations associated with participatory research.

Table 15.1 Participatory research in clinical and health psychology

Health issue	Example	Key outcomes
Acquired brain injury	Gauld, Smith & Kendall (2011)	Development of locally appropriate resources for prevention and care in relation to ABI Community representation in policy-making forums Increased support for culturally appropriate services in remote indigenous communities
Anxiety and depression	Doornbos, Zandee, DeGroot et al. (2013)	Identification of resources to support communities with high levels of depression Identification of most appropriate leadership and providers for mental health responses in different communities
Community mental health practice	Fieldhouse (2012)	Identification of common ground between mental health service users and service providers and managers Changed skills and attitudes of practitioners Increased access to community mental health services
Disaster recovery	Springgate, Wennerstrom, Meyers et al. (2011)	Tailored training for mental health service providers Adaptation of training and resources to meet evolving community needs Increased access to, and utilization of, clinical services for mental health
Housing and health	Grieb, Joseph, Pridget et al. (2013)	Community exhibitions and development of a website exhibiting community members' photographs, engaging policy-makers and service providers Development of an intervention responding to family instability Engagement of local political actors in addressing impacts of incarceration on communities
Mental health promotion	Kermode, Devine, Chandra et al. (2008)	Improvement in participants' quality of life, mental health and experience of somatic symptoms Greater economic participation, and reduced social exclusion, of participants
Psychiatric disabilities	Delman (2012)	Change to policies and practices affecting transition-age youth with psychiatric disabilities Vocational support for young people with psychiatric disabilities
Schizophrenia	Davidson, Stayner, Lambert et al. (1997)	Identification of alternative approaches for addressing inpatient recidivism in serious mental illness Reduction in recurrent admissions after patient participation in design of new intervention
School health	Potvin, Cargo, McComber et al. (2003)	Collaborative development of a code of research ethics Capacity building of community members, such that individuals were appointed to national Aboriginal leadership positions Sustained school health promotion/diabetes prevention programme
Suicide prevention	Mohatt, Singer, Evans et al. (2013)	Participatory public art (large public mural, storytelling and art workshops, storytelling website) as a basis for engaging diverse groups in a suicide-prevention initiative Increased social connectedness and reduced stigma among participants

Photovoice

Photography has long been used to document and draw attention to social issues. Traditionally, however, images are taken by professionals (such as photographers, documentalists and journalists) from their point of view, rather than from the perspective of insiders. In contrast, in recent years a range of techniques have been developed by qualitative researchers to enable community members to tell their own stories through audio-visual media (Harrison, 2002; Ramella & Olmos, 2005). One such tool, Photovoice, has been used in a range of settings to enable participants to represent their everyday realities through photographs. It is a technique that does not require complex recording or editing equipment and, as such, is particularly appropriate for use in communities with minimal access to audio-visual technology or expertise.

As developed by Wang and Burris (1997), Photovoice draws on Freire's approach to education for critical consciousness and is a 'method by which people can identify, represent, and enhance their community' (Wang & Burris, 1997:369). From its early development, Photovoice has been described as having three goals:

■ To enable people to record and reflect their community's strengths and concerns.
■ To promote critical dialogue and knowledge about important issues through large and small group discussion of photographs.
■ To reach policy-makers. (Wang & Burris, 1997:369)

These goals, clearly aligned with the principles of participatory research methods, are based on three theoretical traditions: Freire's pedagogy of critical consciousness, feminist theory and documentary photography (Wang & Burris, 1997).

While the method has been modified to be appropriate in different settings (for example, see Castleden et al., 2008) and adapted to explore health issues with particular population groups (for example, Jurkowski & Paul-Ward, 2007), key elements of the method remain relatively consistent across projects. These key elements include the training of participants as co-researchers and photographers; the taking of photographs; the selection of illustrative images; and the drafting of textual captions or explanations by the participants; group discussion of themes then emerges from the images and preparation of public exhibitions of images aimed at community leaders and decision-makers.

Key steps in a Photovoice process

Building relationships
As with any participatory approach to research, a Photovoice process is grounded in the relationships that are built between researchers and participants. Efforts to engage with the community or group involved in the study,

prior to moving to the photography-based aspects of a Photovoice project, can enable researchers and participants to begin to make transparent the different types and amounts of power held by the diverse partners involved in the project.

Identification of the research question

In some Photovoice projects the research question, or area of focus, is decided by the researchers prior to engagement with the community (for example, when a research team receives funding to examine a particular health issue in a particular location). In others, the area of research focus is jointly decided through a process of negotiation at the time of initial community engagement. More rarely, the area of focus is determined by the participants or the community, who then lead the conceptualization and development of the project.

Training of participants

Consistent with Wang and colleagues' approach, most Photovoice projects involve some training of participants in basic photography skills and in the many ethical (and safety) issues that may be associated with photography in local communities. This may include building participant skills to ask for permission to take photographs, to explain the project to others and to consider issues associated with the representation of people and places. Some Photovoice projects have also provided broader training for participants over time, building skills in qualitative data analysis, report writing and public speaking.

Documentation

All Photovoice projects involve participants producing photographs to illustrate their perspectives on a particular issue. In some projects, participants also produce written material to accompany their photographs, which can range from a caption for the photograph to a textual explanation or story that may be several paragraphs long. When participants are not able to write, these explanations have been dictated to others or recorded by the researcher.

Discussion

For Photovoice projects committed to high levels of participation by participants, and often drawing on Wang and colleagues' original approach, small- and large-group discussion of the participant photographs is an important element in the process. These discussions seek to illuminate why participants took a particular image and selected it for discussion, often generating debate and questioning among participants as to the shared relevance of the image. Discussions may be recorded for later analysis and can occur in a cycle of photography and discussion over several months. Some researchers using Photovoice do not facilitate group discussion of photographs, but rather interview participants individually about the images that they have produced.

SHOWeD

Wang (1999) suggests that the discussion of participant photographs be framed around specific questions such as: What do you See here? What is really Happening here? How does this relate to Our lives? Why does this situation, concern or strength exist? What can we Do about it? Other authors have adapted these questions as appropriate to the context in which they were working, noting that set questions may constrain discussion. The intent of the SHOWeD questions is to encourage participants and researchers to take a critical stance on the material presented and to try to identify factors underlying the situations depicted. The questions also orientate participants and researchers towards possible actions (to change situations depicted) that may arise from the project.

Analysis

Data available for analysis include photographs and any accompanying text, transcripts of discussions and interviews, and notes from any researcher and/or participant field observations. Many researchers using Photovoice engage in participatory analysis of the data produced through the project with participants. Researchers may use PLA tools to support this participatory analysis process (thereby producing more data for later analysis). In most instances, researchers do not undertake an in-depth analysis of the entire corpus of photographs themselves (using, for example, approaches drawn from visual anthropology). The usual rationale for this decision is that researchers choose not to privilege their interpretation of the photographs produced over the interpretations and selection process of participants.

Exhibition of images aimed at decision-makers

In the majority of Photovoice projects, researchers and participants organize advocacy-oriented exhibitions of photographs (and accompanying text or captions) in their local communities. Guests invited to the exhibitions include policy-makers and community leaders, with the explicit aim of the participants' images influencing decision-making about the issues raised in the photographs. The exhibitions also provide what may be a rare opportunity for participants and leaders to engage directly in conversation about the participants' priorities (for example, see Vaughan, 2010).

Community action

In a smaller proportion of Photovoice projects, participants may initiate and/or lead local initiatives in response to issues raised in the project. These may include awareness-raising campaigns, protests, local 'clean-up' events and applications for funding to address specific issues.

Consistent with the participatory ethos and theoretical underpinnings of Photovoice, participation of local community members is prioritized throughout the various stages of a Photovoice project. However, there is considerable variation in the degree to which this is achieved. For further discussion of the extent and limitations to 'participation' in the various elements of a Photovoice process, see Catalani and Minkler's (2010) comprehensive review of Photovoice projects described in the health and public health literature.

Photovoice in practice: The Tok Piksa project in Papua New Guinea

I recently facilitated a Photovoice project working with young people in Papua New Guinea (PNG), one of the largest Pacific countries. PNG is facing a range of development challenges and rapid social change. This case study highlights some of the strengths, as well as limitations, of a participatory approach to research.

Young people living in PNG are often 'targeted' by HIV-prevention programmes claiming, to varying degrees, a participatory approach. Programmes describe activities to increase youth participation with a focus on peer-to-peer dissemination of information, awareness raising, referral of young people to health services, and youth leadership. However, it is often unclear what is meant by 'participation' in the varied contexts in which these programmes operate, and the processes by which this participation is achieved are assumed rather than made explicit.

After a number of years working as a youth health adviser on development projects in PNG, I became concerned that the projects in which I was involved to improve young people's health and wellbeing might not be addressing the needs and priorities of the very young people who they were supposedly 'targeting'. These projects, funded through international development assistance, were primarily focused on the prevention of HIV, and yet little work had been done with young people to identify how they thought about HIV and health more broadly. What did young Papua New Guineans think were the most important influences on their health? What did they think needed to change to enable them to live healthy lives generally, and to reduce their vulnerability to HIV specifically? In order to answer these questions I began working with three youth groups in the Highlands of PNG to explore young people's priorities in relation to health through Photovoice.

The Tok Piksa ('Photovoice' in Tok Pisin, one of PNG's national languages) project grew from a process of discussion and negotiation with groups of young volunteers involved in HIV-prevention activities in three different Highlands communities. In total, 38 young people participated in one week of training on basic photography, and in a context of high levels of crime and violence, on safety, ethics and power associated with photography in communities. The participants then took photographs in and around their communities to illustrate what they thought were the most important positive and negative influences on their health and wellbeing. After a period of several weeks, we ran a two- to three-day workshop at which the young people selected the images that they wanted to discuss, wrote short pieces of text to accompany their images (resulting in photo-stories, a combination of words and image) and discussed these in small and later large groups.

Figure 15.1 Godfrey Mal taking photographs in his local community near Banz, in the Western Highlands Province of PNG

This cycle of taking photographs, discussion of images and production of photo-stories was repeated over a period of five months. Over this time, participants and I collectively analysed themes that we identified in the body of photo-stories. PLA tools, such as problem trees, ranking tools and causal diagrams, were used to facilitate this participatory analysis process. The participants then identified key decision-makers and leaders in their communities, who were invited to an exhibition of their work. Participants prepared speeches and drama performances about the health issues that they had identified as priorities to perform at the exhibition launch.

Each of the youth groups identified specific actions that they could feasibly undertake to address some of the health issues that they identified in their photo-stories, and were provided with some small seed funding to facilitate this over the next four months. Some of these planned actions came to fruition (such as community clean-up days, International Women's Day advocacy activities, awareness raising in schools), but others did not.

There is often an implicit assumption in the participatory research literature that participation and the development of critical thinking will inevitably lead to critical action on health. However, findings from the Tok Piksa project demonstrate that participation is necessary but not sufficient for achieving health-related change in settings of decision-makers' disinterest (Vaughan, 2011). Whether the young people were able to 'get to action' seemed to depend less on the participatory Photovoice process in which the young people had been involved, and more on characteristics of the community and environment in which they were working. Collective action was strongly influenced by the pre-existing symbolic, material and relational contexts of each of

Figure 15.2 Young women in Goroka developing a causal diagram to analyse the factors underlying youth substance abuse, an issue identified as a priority in their photo-stories

Figure 15.3 Mike Ano presenting his photo-stories to community leaders invited to a local exhibition of participants' work

the communities (Campbell et al., 2005). Key factors undermining young people's collective action included the poor reputation and stigmatizing representations associated with particular communities, a lack of community cohesion, unstable and contested local leadership, and a pre-existing model of 'participation' that was not based on self-organization, but rather on the patronage of an international NGO.

While the relationship between a Photovoice process and collective action was contextually dependent, the impact of the process on individual participants was more consistent. In personal narratives written during the project and interviews conducted afterwards, the majority of participants reported the development of psycho-social resources (such as self-confidence, respect and a positive view of the future), new knowledge and skills (including photography skills, communication skills and a new understanding of their community) and changes in their relationships (expanded social networks). These changes suggest that a participatory research process such as Photovoice could be viewed as an intervention to improve health and wellbeing in and of itself.

Strengths and limitations of a participatory approach to research

Strengths of participatory research

Often researchers using traditional methods spend considerable time and energy after a research project trying to ensure the 'translation' of the knowledge that they have produced into a form useful for government, communities and other stakeholders. However, in a participatory research process, the knowledge that is generated is valued by, and useful to, those who will need to use it to change a given situation – it is more clearly and immediately 'translateable' to policy and practice.

Another strength of a participatory research process is that it can support the formation of 'subaltern counterpublics' (Fraser, 1990) in which marginalized groups can work together, and with researchers, to negotiate priorities and identify concrete actions that they can take to make change. Often groups that are marginalized in our communities have had few opportunities to work together to clarify and articulate their perspectives on how to address the health problems that are then 'targeted' by government, service providers and researchers. By using a participatory approach, researchers have the opportunity to create a space in which community groups can work together to discuss priorities, and in so doing can draw on the knowledge and expertise of community members. The positive impact that this recognition has on participants' psycho-social resources and wellbeing means that research can be seen as a health intervention in and of itself, and can potentially support communities' self-determination.

By bringing diverse knowledge systems into dialogue, participatory research has the potential to stimulate innovation and elicit more creative responses to health problems. This is particularly valuable for research on health problems that are seen as 'intractable' or where traditional approaches have proved ineffective.

Limitations and challenges

While there are substantial benefits linked with participatory research, there are also considerable costs associated with the approach. One of participatory research's strengths is recognition of local expertise, but it can be difficult, particularly at the beginning, for researchers to strike a balance between recognizing and respecting local knowledge, and recognizing and respecting their own knowledge and skills as researchers. There is a risk that local knowledge will be reified and professional skills dismissed – a throwing of the highly trained baby out with the bathwater. Dialogical research requires that *both* community members and researchers bring their perspectives to the project.

The time that is required to foster genuine participation is another obvious challenge associated with a participatory approach. It is difficult to develop genuine partnerships, based on trust and respect, in environments of exclusion and where interactions between researchers and others have historically been based on exploitation, extractive research approaches or oppression and racism. It also takes considerable time to build consensus between different actors as to the research purpose and to build the capacity of all for meaningful participation – this may mean training community members in basic research methods and training researchers in culturally appropriate ways to engage with communities. Without taking the time that is required to build an understanding of community groups, researchers may inadvertently reinforce pre-existing power imbalances and inequalities that are present in communities. However, researchers are often under time pressure because of tight timelines from funding bodies, and may also have inadequate resources to sustain community engagement throughout a participatory action research project.

It can be difficult for researchers working in (often) conservative academic settings, as their organizations may not provide the necessary institutional understanding and support for participatory endeavours. Universities may deem participatory research to be insufficiently 'publishable', though review of the reference list for this chapter confirms that this is an inaccurate assessment.

Ethical challenges for the 'outside' researcher have been extensively described (for example, see Minkler, 2004). There can in particular be challenges in obtaining timely clearance from ethics boards when adopting the iterative approach that is called for in participatory action research. This is particularly the case when there are tensions between what a community and its advocates may consider to be 'ethical practice' and the requirements of university-based ethics committees. The time taken to negotiate 'ethics' should not be underestimated.

Concluding comments

Participatory research offers clinical and health psychologists the opportunity to work with research participants to generate a different kind of knowledge than that produced by traditional approaches to research. Knowledge derived through a participatory approach is oriented towards contributing to social change, and can enable researchers the opportunity to draw on different knowledge systems and life experiences to co-construct a new understanding of health. This is particularly valuable for researchers seeking innovative approaches to addressing the thorny health problems associated with marginalization.

Participatory research approaches also offer psychologists the opportunity to challenge themselves, to question their own assumptions, and to learn from perspectives far more diverse than those normally encountered in organizations providing health services or leading health research. Changing the relations between researchers and participants contributes to shifts in power, to growth of mutual respect and to personal transformation for both parties. Such transformation is inevitably associated with challenges, but represents a particularly rewarding way of contributing to health knowledge and improved health outcomes in our communities.

Further reading

Participatory research

Chevalier, J. & Buckles, D. (2013). *Participatory Action Research: Theory and Methods for Engaged Inquiry.* London: Routledge.

Cornwall, A. (ed.). (2011). *The Participation Reader.* London: Zed Books.

Herr, K. & Anderson, G. (eds). (2005). *The Action Research Dissertation: A guide for Students and Faculty.* Thousand Oaks, CA: Sage.

Israel, B., Eng, E., Schulz, A. & Parker, E. (eds). (2005). *Methods in Community-Based Participatory Research for Health.* San Francisco, CA: Jossey-Bass.

Reason, P. & Bradbury, H. (eds). (2008). *Handbook of Action Research: Participative Inquiry and Practice* (2nd edn). Thousand Oaks, CA: Sage.

Photovoice

Catalani, C. & Minkler, M. (2010). Photovoice: A review of the literature in health and public health. *Health Education & Behavior*, 37(3), 424–451.

Lal, S., Jarus, T. & Suto, M. (2012). A scoping review of the Photovoice method: Implications for occupational therapy research. *Canadian Journal of Occupational Therapy*, 79(3), 181–190.

Wang, C. (1999). Photovoice: A participatory action research strategy applied to women's health. *Journal of Women's Health*, 8(2), 185–192.

www.PhotoVoice.org: website of a UK not-for-profit organization that specializes in photography-based community projects.

References

Bird, C.E. & Rieker, P.P. (2008). Gender differences in health: Are they biological, social or both? In C.E. Bird & P.P. Rieker (eds), *Gender and Health: The Effects of Constrained Choices and Social Policies* (pp. 16–53). New York: Cambridge University Press.

Bradbury, H. & Reason, P. (2003). Action research: An opportunity for revitalising research purpose and practices. *Qualitative Social Work*, 2(2), 155–175.

Burnes, B. (2004). Kurt Lewin and complexity theories: Back to the future? *Journal of Change Management*, 4(4), 309–325.

Campbell, C., Foulis, C.A., Maimane, S. & Sibiya, Z. (2005). The impact of social environments on the effectiveness of youth HIV prevention: A South African case study. *AIDS Care*, 17(4), 471–478.

Cargo, M. & Mercer, S. (2008). The value and challenges of participatory research: Strengthening its practice. *Annual Review of Public Health*, 29, 325–350.

Castleden, H., Garvin, T. & First Nation, H. (2008). Modifying Photovoice for community-based participatory Indigenous research. *Social Science & Medicine*, 66, 1393–1405.

Catalani, C. & Minkler, M. (2010). Photovoice: A review of the literature in health and public health. *Health Education & Behavior*, 37(3), 424–451.

Chambers, R. & Guijt, I. (2011). PRA five years later. In A. Cornwall (ed.), *The Participation Reader*. London: Zed Books.

Chevalier, J. & Buckles, D. (2013). *Participatory Action Research: Theory and Methods for Engaged Inquiry*. London: Routledge.

Cornish, F. (2004). Making 'context' concrete: A dialogical approach to the society-health relation. *Journal of Health Psychology*, 9(2), 281–294.

Cornwall, A. & Jewkes, R. (1995). What is participatory research? *Social Science & Medicine*, 41(12), 1667–1676.

Crenshaw, K. (1991). Mapping the margins: Intersectionality, identity politics, and violence against women of color, *Stanford Law Review*, 43(6): 1241–1299.

Davidson, L., Stayner, D., Lambert, S. et al. (1997). Phenomenological and participatory research on schizophrenia: Recovering the person in theory and practice. *Journal of Social Issues*, 53(4), 767–784.

Delman, J. (2012). Participatory action research and young adults with psychiatric disabilities. *Psychiatric Rehabilitation Journal*, 35(3), 231–234.

Doornbos, M., Zandee, G., DeGroot, J. et al. (2013). Desired mental health resources for urban, ethnically diverse, impoverished women struggling with anxiety and depression. *Qualitative Health Research*, 23(1), 78–92.

Fals Borda, O. (2006). Participatory (action) research in social theory: Origins and challenges. In P. Reason & H. Bradbury (eds), *Handbook of Action Research* (pp. 27–37). London: Sage.

Fetterman, D. & Wandersman, A. (2005). *Empowerment Evaluation Principles in Practice*. New York: Guilford.

Fieldhouse, J. (2012). Mental health, social inclusion, and community development: Lessons from Bristol. *Community Development Journal*, 47(4), 571–587.

Fraser, N. (1990). Rethinking the public sphere: A contribution to the critique of actually existing democracy. *Social Text*, 25/26, 56–80.

Freire, P. (1970). *Pedagogy of the Oppressed*. Harmondsworth: Penguin Education.

Freire, P. (2005[1974]). *Education for Critical Consciousness*. London: Continuum.

Frisby, W., Maguire, P. & Reid, C. (2009). The 'f' word has everything to do with it: How feminist theories inform action research. *Action Research*, 7(1): 13–29.

Gauld, S., Smith, S. & Kendall, M. (2011). Using participatory action research in community-based rehabilitation for people with acquired brain injury: From service provision to partnership. *Disability and Rehabilitation*, 33(19–20), 1901–1911.

Gaventa, J. & Horton, B. (1981). A citizen's research project in Appalachia, USA. *Convergence*, 14(3), 30–42.

Green, L.W., George, A., Daniel, M. et al. (1995). *Study of Participatory Research in Health Promotion: Review and Recommendations for the Development of Participatory Research in Canada*. Ottawa: Royal Society of Canada.

Grieb, S., Joseph, R., Pridget, A. et al. (2013). Understanding housing and health through the lens of transitional housing members in a high-incarceration Baltimore City neighbourhood: The GROUP Ministries Photovoice Project to promote community redevelopment. *Health and Place*, 21, 20–28.

Harrison, B. (2002). Seeing health and illness worlds – using visual methodologies in a sociology of health and illness: A methodological review. *Sociology of Health and Illness*, 24(6), 856–872.

Herr, K. & Anderson, G. (2005). *The Action Research Dissertation: A Guide for Students and Faculty*. London: Sage.

Israel, B., Schulz, A., Parker, E. & Becker, A. (1998). Review of community-based research: Assessing partnership approaches to improve public health. *Annual Review of Public Health*, 19, 173–202.

Jovchelovitch, S. (2007). *Knowledge in Context: Representations, Community and Culture*. London: Routledge.

Jurkowski, J. & Paul-Ward, A. (2007). Photovoice among vulnerable populations: Addressing disparities in health promotion among people with intellectual disabilities. *Health Promotion Practice*, 8(4), 358–365.

Kermode, M., Devine, A., Chandra, P. et al. (2008). Some peace of mind: Assessing a pilot intervention to promote mental health among widows of injecting drug users in north-east India. *BMC Public Health*, 8, 294.

Letherby, G. (2003). *Feminist Research in Theory and Practice*. Buckingham: Open University Press.

Lewin, K. (1946/1948). Action research and minority problems. In G.W. Lewin (ed.), *Resolving Social Conflicts* (pp. 201–216). New York: Harper & Row.

Maguire, P. (1996). Proposing a more feminist participatory research: Knowing and being embraced openly. In K. De Koning & M. Martin (eds), *Participatory Research in Health: Issues and Experiences*. London: Zed Books.

McTaggart, R. (1996). Issues for participatory action researchers. In O. Zuber-Skerritt (ed.), *New Directions in Action Research* (pp. 203–213). London: Falmer Press.

Minkler, M. (2004). Ethical challenges for the 'outside' research in community-based participatory research. *Health Education & Behavior*, 31(6): 684–697.

Mohatt, N., Singer, J., Evans, A. et al. (2013). A community's response to suicide through public art: Stakeholder perspectives from the Finding the Light Within project. *American Journal of Community Psychology*, 52(1–2), 197–209.

Potvin, L., Cargo, M., McComber, A. et al. (2003). Implementing participatory intervention and research in communities: Lessons from the Kahnawake Schools Diabetes Prevention Project in Canada. *Social Science & Medicine*, 56(6), 1295–1305.

Pretty, J., Guijt, I., Thompson, J. & Scoones, I. (1995). *Participatory Learning and Action: A Trainer's Guide*. London: IIED.

Ramella, M. & Olmos, G. (2005). Participant authored audiovisual stories (PAAS): Giving the camera away or giving the camera a way? LSE Papers in Social Research Methods, Qualitative series no. 10. Methodology Institute. http://www2.lse.ac.uk/methodology/pdf/qualpapers/ramella_and_olmos.pdf, accessed 2 May 2014.

Schein, E.H. (1996). Kurt Lewin's change theory in the field and in the classroom: Notes towards a model of management learning. *Systems Practice*, 9(1), 27–47.

Springgate, B., Wennerstrom, A., Meyers, D. et al. (2011). Building community resilience through mental health infrastructure and training in post-Katrina New Orleans. *Ethnicity and Disease*, 21(3 Suppl 1), S120–S129.

Vaughan, C. (2010). 'When the road is full of potholes, I wonder why they are bringing condoms?' Social spaces for understanding young Papua New Guineans' health-related knowledge and health-promoting action. *AIDS Care*, 22(Suppl. 2), 1644–1651.

Vaughan, C. (2011). A picture of health: Participation, Photovoice and preventing HIV with Papua New Guinean youth. PhD thesis. London: London School of Economics and Political Science.

Wang, C. (1999). Photovoice: A participatory action research strategy applied to women's health. *Journal of Women's Health*, 8(2), 185–192.

Wang, C. & Burris, M. (1997). Photovoice: Concept, methodology, and use for participatory needs assessment. *Health Education & Behavior*, 24, 369–387.

PART IV

Combining Qualitative and Quantitative Data

Q Methodological Research

16

Wendy Stainton Rogers

Q methodological research is very different from mainstream psychological research – when you start out you are never quite sure where you will end up! There is no initial plan to test a pre-determined hypothesis. Rather, you start with minimalist research questions (like 'What is going on here?'), an open mind and a sense of discovery. You do not want to test anything, but rather to gain real insight and understanding. You 'boldly go' about your research with a sense of adventure, to discover 'new worlds' of meaning and meaning-making. Q methodological research is abductive (as opposed to inductive or deductive). The crucial difference is that it is hypothesis *generating* rather than testing. Instead of looking for systematic patterns of results (in order to establish 'laws of human nature'), abduction focuses instead on things that are puzzling or surprising and 'need explanation'. By seeking to explain, the researcher generates a hypothesis ('a best initial guess') that provides insight into what may be going on.

A good illustration of this adventurous, abductive nature of Q research is a study conducted by Baker (2006) into the alternative strategies that are available to people with Type 2 diabetes for how to manage their condition. Baker's Q study is outlined in detail in Box 16.1 and I will be using it throughout the chapter to illustrate what Q methodology can do, how to do a Q study properly, how to judge a 'good' Q study, the basic features of the statistical techniques involved, and practical information to help you get started on a study of your own. As you will see, Q methodology involves a great deal of specialist terminology. Box 16.2 offers you a translation of some of the terms in the text, to help make the approach clearer.

Historical background

Q methodology was devised in the 1930s by William Stephenson. Ahead of his time, he wanted to concentrate on what makes people different from each other rather than what they have in common. But first, a quick diversion to the question everybody asks: Why did he give his methodology such a meaningless label

---

BOX 16.1 Economic rationality and health and lifestyle choices for people with diabetes

A health economist, Baker wanted to challenge the assumption of the *rational* model of behaviour employed by traditional economists that people simply act 'rationally'. There is evidence enough that people's behaviour in relation to their health is often not at all 'rational' but involves taking risks. What she wanted to do was to discover some of the *alternative* strategies that diabetes patients adopt and, specifically, to gain insight into why they do so.

Using Q methodology allowed Baker to identify three distinct strategies for managing diabetes and describe each of them in detail; crucially, Q enabled her to gain insight into the different values, priorities and concerns on which each strategy is based. Baker's 'lifestyle strategies' study identified three alternative ways of dealing with Type 2 diabetes, which were:

Baker's label for the strategy	The focus of the strategy
Taking responsibility for future health	Preventing problems in the future, by restricting your diet and complying with a regime of 'being careful'
A holistic view of health and lifestyle	Getting a workable balance between 'being good' and 'living a normal life'
Being a good patient	Following 'doctor's orders' diligently, to demonstrate you are a 'good patient'

Baker's research highlighted that although people's choices regarding managing diabetes might be irrational within a narrow biomedical view, they 'can be understood in terms of a coherent rationale, grounded in the accounts of respondents' (2006:2341). This has implications for diabetes management.

Source: Baker (2006).

– 'Q'? The answer is horribly obscure and reflects a time when a great deal was going on in the development of statistical techniques. These all needed labels and so were given definitive letters. Examples include Fisher's z-scores and Student's t-test. Stephenson chose a q for his methodology and we are stuck with it – though it has led to inventive punning among the Q community, as in 'Q tips' (helpful handouts), 'tea and Q' (informal get-togethers of the UK Q community) and 'joining the Q' (workshops on how to do Q research). Will Stephenson gained two PhDs, his first in Physics (at a time when Newtonian ideas were being challenged by ideas about relativity) and his second in Psychology. This latter was supervised (in part) by Charles Spearman, world famous as the inventor of standard factor analysis, and its use to explore questions about human intelligence alongside figures like Cyril Burt.

Stephenson's inventiveness was in adapting factor analysis (more on this later in this chapter) for entirely novel goals. In a paper published in *Nature* in 1935, Stephenson speculated that, if applied in an 'inverted' manner, factor

---

BOX 16.2   Q methodology terminology

Abduction	An alternative logic of inquiry to induction and deduction. The crucial difference is that it is hypothesis *generating* rather than testing. Instead of looking for systematic patterns of results, abduction focuses on things that are puzzling or surprising and 'need explanation'.
Concourse	All the things that can be said and thought about the topic in question among the population that the study is about.
Conditions of instruction	Where participants adopt different positions from which to sort – such as 'as I saw things as a teenager', 'how my therapist would see it', 'as I see it when I am happy'.
Exemplificatory Q sort	Those Q sorts that only correlate significantly with just one factor, used (generally with others) as the basis for constructing a 'best estimate' of the sorting pattern for that factor.
Factor account	A short summary outlining the key elements that distinguish the viewpoint or discourse being expressed by the factor.
Q factor analysis	The form of regular factor analysis devised by William Stephenson, where whole patterns of Q sorting are correlated with each other.
Q grid	See Figure 16.2.
Q items	Usually statements, selected as a sample of the concourse for the study. These are what are sorted.
Q set	The set of Q items that will be presented to participants.
Q sort	The pattern produced when the completed set of items are placed onto the Q grid and recorded.
Q sorting	The process of placing the items of the Q set into the positions on the Q grid.
Variance	A statistical term indicating how much of the variability in the whole dataset can be 'explained' by the factor.

---

analysis can be used as what we would now call a 'pattern analytic'. This, he argued, can apply when considering subjective judgements (such as opinions, explanations and representations of what things are), which cannot be measured. It makes no sense to ask whether a diabetes management strategy of 'preventing future health problems' is 'better' than one stressing life-quality aspects like 'family life' and 'enjoying your lifestyle'. What *can* be claimed, of course, is that these two are *qualitatively* different from each other.

Stephenson was not the first to try this sort of inversion of factor analysis, but he was the first to recognize its real potential. Laurence Kohlberg (Stephenson's student and then research assistant when he worked at the University of Chicago) describes how

> many of us got the sense of a general logic of discovery, hypothesis formation and classification that needed exploration ... a basic set of problems that Q technique opened up involved the logic of the humanities, the logic of interpretation of art and literature. (Kohlberg, 1972:xiii)

Stephenson's problem pretty well throughout his life was that he was 'before his time' in championing qualitative research to gain insight, as opposed to hypothesis testing. Both theoretically and methodologically, his were not popular positions to adopt in an academic establishment dominated by hypothetico-deductive logic and quantitative methods. In 1936 he was appointed to the post of assistant director of the Oxford Institute of Experimental Psychology, where he became a key player in the establishment of psychology as a discipline at the University of Oxford in the 1930s and 1940s. It is hardly surprising that in his lifetime Stephenson's influence gradually faded. His career ended in the 1980s, having spent his last years as a lowly (but much loved and admired) professor of journalism at Missouri, a relatively obscure university in the United States. He died in 1989.

Stephenson's influence endures, especially through the work of his many clever and articulate graduate students. Through them Q research is flourishing, albeit still very much 'on the fringe' in the United States where the stranglehold of quantitative approaches persists. Most important of these scholars has undoubtedly been Steven R. Brown, whose text *Political Subjectivity* (1980) became and remains the standard text for anyone wanting to understand the technical detail involved in Q factor analysis. Brown currently maintains and sustains the Q-METHOD discussion list (Q-METHOD@LISTSERV.KENT.EDU), continually updates the Q research bibliography and has taken Q around the world, with groups of Q methodologists highly active in Norway, South America and South Korea, to name but some. He instigated the ISSSS (the International Society for the Scientific Study of Subjectivity), which has an annual conference and a journal, *Operant Subjectivity*.

A number of psychologists in the United Kingdom (of which I am one) have, since the 1980s, developed Q methodology rather differently, as a 'discursive, constructivist, and hence as an essentially qualitative method' (Stenner et al., 2009). Q, in this context, has become a form of discourse analysis (Curt, 1994:128; Stainton Rogers, 1991, 1998). Our sphere of influence has been more European, especially in the United Kingdom but also including Cataluña, the Netherlands, Slovakia and Sweden.

There are certainly differences between the two approaches and our readings of what Q methodology 'is' and 'is for' (see, for example, Stainton Rogers & Stainton Rogers, 1990). However, we have a common purpose, which is to conduct and promote Q methodology as a potent and unique way of carrying out qualitative research, with real potential to have an impact on theory, policy and practice as well as making substantial contributions to our knowledge and understanding.

As we end this brief historical review, it is important to note that, early in its history, Q methodology was appropriated by those who sought to 'improve' it by making it 'properly quantitative' and hence to *measure* such things as the impact of therapy and to 'assess personality'. James Block, probably the best-known proponent of (mis)using Q in this way, began by devising a standardized Q set (the 'California Q-set'; Block, 1961, 2008) to depict what constitutes a 'mentally healthy' person (as defined by 'experts in the field'). He then got people to complete a Q sort to describe their own mental state, and compared this sort to the idealized 'mentally healthy' Q sort pattern. In this way he assessed their state of mental health by how close their sort was to the 'mentally healthy' template. Indeed, among the psychotherapy research community it is generally Block's version that is popularly known and used. Whatever the merits (or not) of using Q sorting in this way, we should recognize that such a use of Q is based on epistemological and ontological assumptions that are entirely contrary to what Stephenson intended. The Block approach is particularly refuted by those who adopt a social constructionist approach to Q. This is because among social constructionists, knowledge is not seen as in any way absolute, but multiple, contingent on time and place and purpose. What is more, it is socially situated, changing according to context and circumstance.

What is distinctive about Q methodology?

There are two distinctive elements in a Q study that make it different from other qualitative approaches: Q sorting as a means of data collection; and Q factor analysis as an initial stage in interpreting the data.

Q sorting

Q sorting involves participants ranking items along a dimension such as 'most agree' to 'most disagree', just like the way judges rank contestants – winner, runner-up and so on. In this way people express their opinion (or whatever is being studied) on a particular topic, question or representation by sorting a set of items in a particular way. Examples of the sorts of items used by Baker in her study of strategies for managing Type 2 diabetes are:

---

4   Following a 'diabetic lifestyle' (diet, exercise etc.) would spoil my pleasure in life.
5   I think it is important to follow medical advice.
24 I live for today, I don't think that much about my health in years to come.
42 I do want to do the healthy thing for my diabetes, but I don't always do it.

You can get an even better idea by looking at the complete list of 46 items that she used in her study by referring to her paper (Baker, 2006), where they are given in full. These items were derived from a range of sources, including interviews with people with Type 2 diabetes, patient resources, medical textbooks and journal articles.

You can see what Q sorting entails in Figure 16.1 (though often now it is carried out via computer). The participant is placing the items from 'most agree' on the right to 'most disagree' on the left.

Figure 16.1   Q sorting

Mostly strongly agree   Most strongly disagree

−6	−5	−4	−3	−2	−1	0	+1	+2	+3	+4	+5	+6

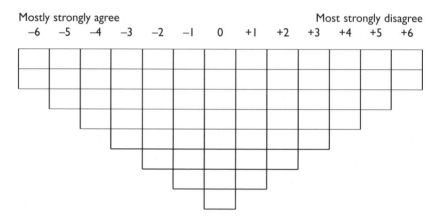

Figure 16.2   The Q response grid

Mostly strongly agree   Most strongly disagree

−6	−5	−4	−3	−2	−1	0	+1	+2	+3	+4	+5	+6
1	6	26	30	5	2	18	3	19	23	16	4	12
32	7	31	38	8	10	22	20	46	36	24	13	52
	9	37	44	15	11	28	25	48	39	27	47	
		51	45	41	14	34	29	50	42	33		
		55	49	17	35	43	56	53				
			58	21	40	60	59					
				62	54	61						
					57							

Figure 16.3   A Q grid completed

To guide their sorting, participants follow a grid, as shown in Figure 16.2. When completed, the item numbers are recorded in the spaces on the grid, as shown in Figure 16.3.

Factor analysis as used in Q methodology

Q factor analysis is a variant on standard factor analysis but, in the Q version, the sorting patterns of each participant's sort are compared with the sorting patterns of all the other participants. This more gestalt approach makes it possible to identify and describe the different viewpoints, beliefs, understandings and worldviews being expressed by the pattern as sorted.

Traditional factor analysis

To explain what is so different about Q, we need to start with traditional factor analysis. This was developed for studies investigating 'traits', such as whether intelligence is a single capacity of 'cleverness' or is made up of separate traits like 'cleverness with words' and 'mathematical ability', each independent of the other. If just one factor is identified, this indicates that intelligence is a single capacity. However, if several different factors are found, this indicates that, say, verbal intelligence and mathematical intelligence are two, separate capabilities. In this traditional approach, large numbers of people are given tests to do, each designed to tap a different kind of ability. The data, when entered into the factor analysis programme, would look like Table 16.1, although in real life there would be an awful lot more of it.

Factor analysis here begins with correlating the scores on the different tests and looking for clusters of tests that are highly correlated. Working systematically to parcel up the inter-correlating tests into clusters, factor analysis first identifies and extracts from the calculation the cluster that explains most of the variance in the dataset – Factor 1. The analysis then moves on to account for the variance that is left, again seeking the cluster of inter-correlation that explains the most variance within this depleted set – Factor 2. Although this process continues until all the variance is accounted for, researchers usually stop looking for factors once they no longer provide useful information to answer the research question(s) or develop insight into the topic.

Table 16.1 Hypothetical data for an R methodological design

People	Test scores			
	Verbal test 1	Verbal test 2	Maths test 1	Maths test 2
Jane	15	19	8	11
Maya	3	8	9	5
Olu	20	19	10	18

Table 16.2   Hypothetical data for a Q methodological design

	Q sort placement of item		
	Alvi's Q sort	Dan's Q sort	Celia's Q sort
Q sort items			
1. When I make choices about my diabetes and health behaviour, I think through all the consequences of my actions.	+1	−4	−1
2. I would rather leave the decisions to the experts and follow the advice they give.	+4	−3	0
3. I am especially worried about having injections.	−2	0	−5
4. Following a 'diabetic lifestyle' (diet, exercise etc.) would spoil my pleasure in life.	0	+2	−2

Q factor analysis

Q factor analysis works in the same sort of way, but there is a crucial difference. The numbers indicating the placement of items in the Q sort are not keyed in as though they are the results of 'tests'. Instead the placement is reversed, as shown in Table 16.2, though again, there would be much more data. Thus, Q factor analysis is not 'by person' but rather 'by sorting pattern'.

Theoretical and conceptual framework

Heath psychology is primarily the study of people's behaviour in relation to their health, and the thinking that underpins this behaviour. Health psychologists are particularly concerned with practical outcomes: informing public policy and professional practice in promoting wellbeing, preventing ill-health, treating illness and improving quality of life for those suffering from chronic conditions. Much the same aims apply to clinical psychology, but with a specific focus on mental health and ill-health. Some examples of Q methodology research in clinical psychology are provided in Box 16.3 later in this chapter.

A major concern in this field is with an apparent paradox: given that, by and large, people know what is healthy and what is not, why do they take risks with their health? Why do they overeat when they know that this leads to obesity, or smoke when they know how dangerous it is to their health? In the following sections I draw on health psychology examples to illustrate the value of a Q methodological approach to research in this field.

Traditional approaches: Social cognition

Historically, health psychologists have turned to social cognition models for explanations, such as models of 'reasoned action', 'planned behaviour' and 'stages of change' (Prochaska & DiClemente, 1983). Quantitative research is used, generally based on questionnaires in which variables (such as 'attitudes', 'normative beliefs' and 'social norms') are manipulated to test the model in question. The problem is that these studies frequently fail to predict behaviour and fail to impress. As I commented some time ago:

> It is hardly surprising that you can predict fairly accurately what somebody will do if you ask them just before they do it whether they think doing it is a good idea, if they think other people will approve, and whether they care what other people think. ... But getting consistent answers does not mean that you understand very much about their thinking except at a very trivial level, and then only under highly constrained circumstances. (Stainton Rogers, 1991:53)

More recently, Mielewczyk and Willig (2007) have criticized the whole social cognition approach more fundamentally, noting that most studies employ only one theoretical framework and thus one methodological approach. Consequently, they argue that this research

> is dominated by applications of models in which social cognitions such as attitudes and control beliefs are combined and assessed according to specific algorithms aimed at maximizing the proportions of variance explainable (by means of multiple regression analyses) in the performance of target health behaviours. (2007:812)

Alternative approaches: 'Health behaviour' as situated social practices

Mielewczyk and Willig (2007) argue persuasively that the reason these models have such trouble predicting 'health behaviour' is because 'health behaviour' is a made-up phenomenon. In conventional health psychology, 'health behaviours' are theorized and written about as if they are 'easily identifiable, unitary entities whose meaning does not change across the diverse contexts and settings within which they may be carried out' (Mielewczyk & Willig, 2007:824). But they are not.

To illustrate the point being made here, consider one specific example of 'health behaviour': condom use. Social cognition theorists study this 'behaviour' completely out of context (see, for example, Hertzog, 2005; Sutton, 2005), as a kind of 'cognitive algebra' that is decoupled from time and place, salience and meaning. The studies imply that condom use is a single kind of action with a single kind of cause; that whenever and wherever it occurs, the same set of influences are in play, and involve an individual weighing up specific costs and benefits in their decisions to use a condom. Consider, by contrast, the way in which qualitative research studies in this field have come up with a whole host of reasons for *not* using condoms in a variety of different socio-cultural settings. For instance, using a condom can be 'a moment killer' (Williamson et al., 2009):

> And then all the magazines that tell you they can become a fun part of foreplay. Lies! Lies! They're the worst things. I've been having sex since I was 14 years old and I still can't put one on somebody properly. ('Kathy', quoted in Williamson et al., 2009:564)

Yet in another situation – in a committed relationship, for instance – insisting on using a condom can scream 'I don't trust you':

> Because it's a very tricky thing, there's pride and there's suspicion and there's jealousy and there's all these terrible things, all mixed up together, and these are the things that kill a marriage, and therefore it's very delicate ground that you are treading on. (cited in Willig, 1995:81)

Just these two examples make a powerful case: that deciding whether or not to use a condom when having sex is not a matter of cognitive algebra calculations, but is profoundly about what using a condom 'means' in the circumstances. Add to this that, for many people, there are moral and/or religious rules to be followed. Mielewczyk and Willig therefore argue that rather than trying to predict de-contextualized actions and behaviours related to health, it might be better – and more meaningful – 'to focus on the wider social practices of which such actions form a part' (2007:829). This approach recognizes that

> health-related behaviours acquire their meaning and significance on the basis of their relationship to the particular social practice of which they form a part and that, therefore, what appears to be the 'same' behaviour can take on radically different meanings within different contexts. (2007:829)

Q methodology to investigate situated social practices

Qualitative researchers in health and clinical psychology investigate 'health behaviour' as a complex of socially situated actions. Their work entails some form of analysis of what people think and say: texts of various kinds, including transcripts from interviews and focus groups, role plays, conversation and narrative analyses. The aim is to gain insight into 'what is going on' in these situated social praxes: what matters, what is valued, what identities are being played out, how power is being deployed and so on. This is precisely what Q methodology was devised to do, and does so well.

Q is often mistaken for a quantitative method, mostly because it uses numbers and analyses them statistically. However, the numbers are not used to *measure* anything. They are ordinal, arising from judgements about the relative value of items. So, even though Stenner and Stainton Rogers (2004) offered the compromise term of *qualiquantological*, I prefer to stick with the standard terminology and place Q method firmly within the range of qualitative methods. Q shares a common purpose with more easily recognizable qualitative approaches similar to those taken by narrative, discourse analytical and phenomenological research. Like them, its goals and underpinning ontological and epistemological assumptions are qualitative in nature.

Subjectivity and intersubjectivity

One of the disputes among the scholars who use Q methodology is about *what* is being studied. To simplify a contrary and complex situation, this is usually a matter of whether Q methodology enables us to explore subjectivity or intersubjectivity.

Q to study subjectivity

Within the Q community (mainly in the United States), Q methodology is often referred to as a way of studying *subjectivity*; that is, the subjective thinking and experience of individuals. This standpoint is reflected in the title of the Q community's main membership organization, the International Society for the Scientific Study of Subjectivity (ISSS). Certainly, Q enables people to express their own point of view about a whole range of topics related to personal subjectivity, such as what it feels like to experience depression. Q allows such subjective aspects to be mapped out in fine detail, providing researchers with a novel and powerful tool for interrogating subjective experience.

Q is often used like this by clinical psychologists and psychotherapists to conduct fine-grained, case-study investigations of an individual's subjective experiences, self-perceptions, aspirations and the like, mapping out their client's subjectivity over time and across various aspects of their emotional and cognitive mental life. Here, the Q set is drawn from statements made by the client in question in therapy sessions. Goldstein and Goldstein (2005) did so to investigate the subjective self-esteem of a client whom they call L. They constructed a Q set on self-esteem based on L's own conversations in therapy sessions and her writings. Then they had her carry out 12 separate Q sorts, each under a different condition of instruction, including 'the way I am as a parent', 'when I am riding a bike', 'how I am in my dreams' and 'when I was divorced'. Goldstein and Goldstein identified four different self-esteem perceptions experienced by L and used these in subsequent therapy sessions with L, enabling her to become more self-aware and, hence, more able to resolve some of the issues for which she had sought therapy.

Q sorting makes people think carefully about and reflect on their own thoughts. It, almost literally, puts their thinking 'on the line', where sorting entails resolving a whole range of differing (sometimes conflicting) ideas, emotions and concerns. In so doing, the person becomes much more self-aware. A number of researchers have capitalized on this aspect of Q sorting as an aid to reflexive practice, a way for people to gain personal insight into their own values, beliefs and emotional investments. This insight can then be used as a means to becoming a more reflexive practitioner, thus improving their professional competence.

McKeown et al. (1999) used just such an approach to investigate the alternative ways in which mental health professionals thought risk should be managed in the delivery and management of mental health services. As well as being a Q study in itself, the impact of doing the Q sort was also used as part of a training programme for managers working in the service. Doing the Q sort allowed these managers to grapple with the contradictions and ambiguities they faced when considering how the service should be run. Importantly, it also helped them to gain real insight into, and greater empathy with, alternative opinions and strategies. This further improved the overall competence of delivery systems, since practitioners became more willing to make compromises.

Q to study intersubjectivity

Among researchers adopting a social constructionist stance, Q studies are primarily used to find out about 'what is going on' in the conversations and other forms of social interplay operating *between* people – including communicative processes like education, journalism, advertising, entertainment and, these days, increasingly through people's interactions on the web and in the virtual worlds made possible by it. For us (and I place myself very much in this camp) Q research provides a powerful technique for studying *intersubjectivity*: how argument and truth claims are deployed within and between the competing positions taken by groups with different stakes to claim, statuses to defend, values to endorse and realities to construct. This approach is consistent with the 'situated social practice' standpoint taken by Mielewczyk and Willig in their 2007 paper.

Q is a very effective way to explore the dynamics operating in human meaning-making, in a whole range of contexts. It can enable researchers to survey and scrutinize how power is being exercised: for example, within the broad 'marketplace' of alternative standpoints and positions that are taken on a particular topic (such as mental health) and within a designated population, whether focused (such as between the different professions working in mental health for a particular local authority) or more broadly based (such as across the UK population as a whole). In this approach, Q methodology is being used less as a means to interrogate individual subjectivities and more as a taxonomic tool. This approach is rather like the field trip a biologist might take, venturing into unknown territory to identify and describe the various plants and animals that occupy it (hence the analogy I used at the beginning of the chapter in which I described Q methodological research as an *adventure*). Nevertheless, there is more to it than simple taxonomy. More ecologically, Q methodology offers a means to explore the complex inter-plays among and between the 'species' (that is, opinions, viewpoints or what-ever) occupying the various 'habitats' within an eco-system. It thus provides a means to discover how the actions of each one determine the ecological niches that are available for the others to occupy. Or, taking a geological analogy, alternative discourses can be seen to operate like tectonic plates, in constant flux, moulding and shaping one another. All these metaphors reflect a different aspect of what Q can enable us to do; that is, name and depict the textuality of the discourses in play and, through further interpretation, map out their tectonics (see Curt, 1994 for a more detailed exposition of the tex-tuality and tectonics of discourses).

Watts and Stenner (2005) liken Q to some features of narrative analysis, in that its analytical approach treats data in a gestalt manner rather than frag-menting it thematically (as does, say, much interpretative phenomenological analysis). Like narrative analysis, the interpretation of Q data allows us to observe how themes that are common across alternatives can be articulated in quite different ways. Unlike narrative analysis, however, Q method produces data that offer a 'snapshot' view of what is going on (as opposed to a life his-tory or account where timescale is an important analytical frame).

Operant subjectivity

What is often not understood among those conducting Q methodological research is that the opinions expressed in the form of a Q sort are *not* seen as synonymous with the person doing the sorting. Q methodology is not done as a means to classify people (as a personality test would do). Rather, it is con-ducted to identify alternative ways of 'seeing the world' or, in some circles, as a form of discourse analysis. The participants in a Q study are simply vehicles for the expression of one or more discursive position(s). Q factor analysis is *not* 'by person' but rather 'by sorting pattern'. People are not the 'exemplars', but their Q sorts are.

Just now I am doing some participant/observer research of my own. Unlike Baker's participants, I do not have Type 2 diabetes, but I do have (temporarily, I hope) 'short bowel syndrome' and I face similar dilemmas about living with a stoma bag, a very restricted diet and a 500 ml per day curb on how much fluid I can drink other than rehydration fluids (which taste totally foul).

I am very much aware of veering between all three of the strategies Baker identified, especially between being prudently determined to conform to all the restrictions imposed on me in order to prevent damage to my kidneys, and not allowing my condition to dominate my life. On most days, I am unable (or more precisely, unwilling) to give up my morning cup of coffee because it will increase the output from my stoma, though I do indulge in only a very small cup. Q methodology acknowledges that it is a familiar thing to be 'in two minds' about what action to take, in ways that social cognitive modelling is not.

Research questions, within such an epistemology, are necessarily minimalist. They cannot take the form of a hypothesis to be tested. Rather, they are open-ended. What is going on here? What different versions of reality are in play? By whom and for what purpose? Which ones are dominant and which ones hidden? How is power being exercised? As such, these questions are abductive: they create opportunities to generate plausible hypotheses and hunches that will offer useful insights – for instance, in how to improve therapeutic interventions.

Using Q methodology for research in clinical and health psychology

By now you should have realized that there are some things that Q research cannot do, including testing hypotheses of any kind. It has to be used in research with an abductive 'logic of inquiry', which is exploratory and about gaining insight. Within this broad approach it can be employed for a number of different purposes, the main ones being gaining insight into:

- An individual's subjective experience and thinking.
- Alternative ways in which people *represent* a particular phenomenon.
- Alternative ways in which people *understand and/or explain* a particular topic or phenomenon.
- Alternative views about what should be done about a particular issue or problem.

Box 16.3 outlines illustrative studies for each of these purposes and sources for more information about each one. If you are planning to conduct a Q study of your own, a great way to start would be to chase up the papers for all of these studies and read them carefully. A 'good enough' start would be simply to look at the paper on the study in Box 16.3 that is most like the one you would like to do. It is worth noting that many of these studies have mistakes and misunderstandings in them. The next section provides a general overview about the practicalities of doing a study.

How to do a Q methodological study

Q methodology is relatively easy to do once you get the hang of it, but it does, at times, involve doing things that 'break the rules' for a quantitative study. In this chapter I have only limited space, so this section offers a bare outline. For more detail, the chapter by Stenner et al. (2009) offers an excellent 'how to do

BOX 16.3 Example studies illustrating different uses for Q methodological research

Purpose – to gain insight into	Examples	Exploration of	Aspirations to
an individual's subjective experience and thinking	Goldstein & Goldstein (2005)	a particular patient's (L) subjectivity around her self-esteem in different social settings, contexts and relationships	fine-tune therapy for L and thus to improve her mental health
alternative ways in which people *represent* a particular phenomenon	Gleeson (1991)	what constitutes 'madness' – alternative images of what constitutes 'a mad person'	challenge preconceptions about 'madness' for polemical reasons and also inform professional practice and social policy in services provided for mental health
alternative ways in which people *understand and/or explain* a particular topic or phenomenon	Baker (2006)	strategies to manage Type 2 diabetes, specifically as understood by patients with this condition	inform patients about alternative ways of managing their condition; inform policy and practice in services provided for patients with Type 2 diabetes
	Jones et al. (2003)	different explanations of why people 'hear voices'	enable practitioners working in the field to widen their understanding of this phenomenon and recognise socio-cultural influences
	McKeown et al. (1999)	alternative strategies for managing the provision of mental health services	act as an opportunity for participants who did the Q-sort to gain insight into each other's viewpoints in ways that improve teamwork in managing these services, in addition to informing professional practice and policy-making
alternative views about what should be done about a particular issue or problem	Eccleston et al. (1997)	alternative explanations of chronic pain, as understood by sufferers, their carers and the professionals who work with them, and the strategies that need to be adopted to cure or ameliorate the condition	offer insight into the way pain specialist doctors see chronic pain as due to a failure to manage what has become a 'lifestyle' and see a solution in patients' behavioural change. Patients themselves see a solution in doctors acknowledging that chronic pain is a physical condition, then finding better ways to diagnose and treat it by medical means. Insight can be gained by medical staff, their patients and their carers

it' guide, a flow-chart map of the process and a clear example to illustrate the stages and steps.

Q methodology is done in discrete stages. These are:

1. Preparation of materials.
2. Collecting the data.
3. Statistical analysis and identification of factors.
4. Factor interpretation.
5. In-depth analysis of the textuality and tectonics of the discourses involved.

Preparation of the materials

These comprise the Q set, the Q response grid and other means to gather information about participants. The Q set is the set of (usually) statements that are to be sorted. The Q response grid is the actual or virtual pattern of responses specified by the researcher, so that all participants in a study sort to a common pattern. With computer-delivered Q sorting (see later in this chapter), these materials are provided in a form for the researcher to customize. In order to manage issues of confidentiality and practicality, a more general participant questionnaire also needs to be constructed.

Designing the Q set

This is a surprisingly demanding and time-consuming task. It is well worth taking the trouble to do this properly and get a balanced and wide-ranging set of items, since its quality is a major determinant of the quality of the data obtained. A surprising number of Q studies yield a single factor, because the researcher has failed to take steps to enable a real diversity of opinion to be expressed. The aim is to 'sample the concourse', that being all the things that can be expressed about the topic in question among the population the study is about. Ways of doing this include wide-ranging reading (magazines and novels as well as academic journals) and scrutiny of what people say and write on the internet, Twitter and the like; keeping a research notebook and recording conversations and especially arguments and debates; conducting interviews and/or focus groups. A good strategy is to ask participants to put you in contact with somebody with very different views from their own. It is quite usual to gather several hundred statements in estimating the scope of the concourse. Then standard techniques can be used to reduce the number of items to a manageable number (somewhere around 40–50 is about right) and to avoid duplication and spot gaps.

Selecting the right language for the statements also needs to be done carefully and systematically, again following the principles of good questionnaire design. For example, each statement should express a single idea, negatives must be avoided (as statements pose problems if sorted in negative categories) and the language must be accessible and appropriate for the participants. With suitably simple language and relatively low numbers of statements, Q studies have been carried out that include as participants quite young children and people with a learning disability (McKenzie, 2009).

It is usual to obtain feedback on an initial sample of items, usually two or three times as many as needed for the Q set. Information is sought on whether there is a numerical balance between statements likely to be agreed or disagreed with, whether they are easy to understand and whether any items are duplicated or omitted. This feedback helps to refine the items, reduce them and work towards a rough balance of positive and negative statements. It is good practice, where possible, to pilot test the Q set, running a full analysis to identify items that are good and poor discriminators. This allows for a final fine-tuning of the Q set.

Designing the Q response grid

Using a response grid standardizes responses, making the analysis more straightforward. But, most importantly, it makes the task of ranking large numbers of items manageable. It is relatively easy simply to rank order up to about 20 statements in a long line; more than that and the process becomes more difficult. Using a grid as shown in Figure 16.2 makes the task relatively easy to do. The grid design is dependent on the number of items in the Q sort and the degree of differentiation required, although researchers seldom use more than 13 categories (–6 to +6).

Designing the participant questionnaire

Many Q researchers seek additional information from participants to help in factor interpretation. It is usual (but not essential) to gather demographic information (gender, age etc.), although other information may be more relevant (such as membership of a church or use of mental health services) and should be gathered. Some researchers observe participants sorting and interview them afterwards. Others gather written comments on reasons for item placement, interpretation and so on. One approach that works well is to ask participants directly what they think has influenced their views. You will also need to include a consent form, no different from those used in other studies.

Collecting the data

This stage entails two main tasks:

- Strategically selecting and recruiting participants.
- Participants completing the Q sort.

Selecting and recruiting participants

It is here where many 'newbie' Q studies go wrong, since novices have had hammered into them the importance of getting a *representative* sample of participants (in terms of demographics like age and gender). In Q such representativeness is not necessary for the Q set. For selecting participants the strategy needs to be *strategic*; that is, deliberately seeking out people who have as diverse a set of opinions or understandings as possible. The criteria depend on the research question. In my own study (Stainton Rogers, 1991) into alternative explanations for health and illness, I recruited a range of medical professionals (including alternative practitioners of various kinds), people who were suffering from a range of health problems and conditions, people of different religious faiths and different political and ideological persuasions. All of these, I believed, were characteristics likely to influence the views that people hold on what causes ill-health, good health and recovery from illness. In some Q studies (such as that of Baker, 2006) the population is restricted, in order to focus specifically on a particular group; in others (such as that of Eccleson et al., 1997) some groups (chronic pain sufferers and the professionals who treat them) are deliberately selected in order to see what kind of difference this distinction may make. Given the growing interest in participatory research (see Chapter 15), Q has a real advantage, as it specifically seeks participation of health-care service users at every stage: in the design of the Q set; selection of participants as participants in the study itself; and, crucially, in interpreting the factors.

Q sorting

Historically, sorters were provided with a pack in which each item is printed on a small card or slip of paper of a manageable size (see Figure 16.1). Many Q researchers continue to use this technique. It has the advantage of being low key and low tech, making it accessible to people who are unwilling or unable to respond to a computer-generated task. However, there is now a choice of software (see the next section) that delivers the sorting task online, usually as a series of binary choices. The result is the same: a numerical record of the items that have been placed in a pre-specified grid pattern, as shown in Figure 16.3. Each statement is given a number and it is this number that is entered into the grid.

There are no set rules about how to deliver and receive back Q sorts (personally, by post, online etc.). Participants can sort on their own or as a group and with or without the researcher present. Each method has advantages and disadvantages. Response rates differ in similar ways to standard questionnaire research, often with lower returns, as Q sorting is demanding and time-consuming. Usually a few sorts are returned incorrectly coded or with data missing. These are normally excluded from the data analysis.

Statistical analysis

Data from the completed grids is entered into appropriate software for analysis. This can be done using a package like SPSS for the factor analysis with some additional calculation (see Brown, 1980 for details). Q researchers these days mostly use dedicated software programs such as *PQmethod* (http://www.lrz.de/~schmolck/qmethod/index.htm) and *PCQ for Windows* (http://www.pcqsoft.

com/). These offer a range of choices about the ways in which the data can be manipulated and described. Other software delivers Q sorts online and then performs the analysis.

All three strategies yield the same basic output: a number of factors are identified, together with a 'best estimate' of the Q sort associated with that factor. Each depicts a holistic pattern of response, from which the particular viewpoint or discourse can be interpreted.

These are arrived at in three stages:

■ First, the *factors are established* through a sequence of calculations involving correlation and data rotation. Different statistical procedures are possible, each with their own advocates in the Q community. Many Q researchers simply use the software following a standardized procedure that makes all the choices for them. Others prefer to 'play around' with the data in different ways in order to consider alternative interpretations.

■ Next, *exemplificatory Q sorts are selected* for each of the factors – these are the ones that correlate significantly with just *this* factor. Here, 'significance level' is selected much as in more familiar tests of statistical significance.

■ Finally, a weighting procedure is used to *generate a 'best estimate' Q sort* for that factor. It is usual at this stage to do some preparatory interpretation, to identify the factors to be interpreted.

Brown (1980) and Watts and Stenner (2005) are both good places to start in understanding the technicalities of all this statistical analysis. However, if statistics are not your forte, do not worry. The software packages will do these stages for you, offering you more or less choice about what strategies to use. There is also plenty of advice and help available via the Q-METHOD list, and a growing number of offline and online tutorials and workshops.

Interpreting the factors

In Q, factor interpretation is similar to the way in which researchers 'immerse themselves' in the data in other thematic, discourse or narrative analytical methods' interpretations. The Q sort pattern for each factor is the starting point for the next stage, producing a factor account (sometimes called explication or exegesis), one for each of the factors chosen for further interpretation. Not all factors need to be interpreted (though there are disputes among Q researchers about when to stop). When writing for a doctorate or publication in which space is at a premium, it is good to be selective and to aim to tell a good story around only some factors, preferably those most relevant to the research question. Each factor account summarizes the key elements of the viewpoint expressed.

Next comes an exploration of the significance of the viewpoint, its origins and the influences that have shaped it, as well as its implications and/or applications. Interpretation involves drawing on a whole range of information: common characteristics among the people whose Q sorts were exemplificatory; expla-nations for why certain items are placed in one column rather than another; accounts from the literature expressing the same argument. Shank (1998) identifies this as researchers making use of the sense-making skills that all of us develop through our life experiences, and use every day to navigate through and manage our relationships and our lives.

In Q research it is usual to give each factor a label; these can be re-ordered if this makes for a more coherent account. This is possible because the order of the factors can be arbitrary. The amount of variance explained may well be as much of a reflection of the participants selected as the relative popularity or importance of the viewpoint expressed. For instance, in my own study of explanations for health and illness (Stainton Rogers, 1991), Factor 1 was all about the role of 'willpower' – spiritual strength to maintain health and fend off disease, a relatively rare understanding. Its ranking was an artefact, arising from the disproportionate number of 'alternative' practitioners among the participants in the study.

Principles of a good Q study

Good Q studies identify a number of clearly alternative viewpoints (or what-ever) on the matter in question. The Q set is well designed: comprehensive of 'what is said and thought', each item expressing a single opinion or depiction, in language accessible to and appropriate for the diversity of participants included. To ensure this quality, preparation is thorough and thoughtful. Interpretation is equally insightful and done with a determination to recognize and solve the riddles presented by hard-to-interpret factors. Often the best studies are done collectively, with a diversity of experience and expertise, espe-cially to the tasks of designing the Q set and interpreting the factors.

Technically speaking, there is a fair amount of (sometimes very heated) debate between Q researchers about the 'best' way to undertake this method. Possibly what matters more is to give a clear account of what you have done and the choices you have made, and to back these up with an informed justi-fication of 'doing it your way'. It is important to follow appropriate research principles such as those used in questionnaire design and thematic analysis. What every Q researcher agrees you *cannot* do is to make claims that are unjustified by the method (such as its being able to tap into every alternative viewpoint) or the analysis (claiming that you can say anything about what proportion of the population hold particular views).

I began by selling Q methodology hard – with words like 'adventure', 'dis-covery' and 'boldly going'. I will end by reminding you that what is best about Q is that, if it is done well, you will genuinely find out things that you did not know before, and that is great fun (not a word commonly used about research), especially if you carry out a study with others. I hope that this chapter has inspired you to try.

Further reading

Brown, S. (1980). *Political Subjectivity: Applications of Q Methodology in Political Science*. New Haven, CT: Yale University Press.
This is Q methodology's 'classic' text. It can be hard going at times, but it is meticulously good at the technical stuff.

Stainton Rogers, W. (1991). *Explaining Health and Illness: An Exploration of Diversity*. Hemel Hempstead: Harvester Wheatsheaf.
Chapter 6 of this text gives an account of the study that I did for my own PhD. It contains much detailed information of a kind not available elsewhere.

Stenner, P., Watts, S. & Worrell, M. (2009) Q methodology. In C. Willig & W. Stainton Rogers (eds), *The Sage Handbook of Qualitative Methods in Psychology*. London: Sage.
This contains a great illustrative study, carried out specifically for the chapter, about viewpoints on qualitative methods. It offers real insight into what Q can do and also has much more technical detail than is in the current chapter.

Watts, S. & Stenner, P. (2005). Doing Q methodology: Theory, method and interpretation. *Qualitative Research in Psychology*, 2, 67–91.
This short paper is a great resource for getting started on your own study.

References

Baker, M.R. (2006). Economic rationality and health and lifestyle choices for people with diabetes. *Social Science & Medicine*, 63, 2341–2353.

Block, J. (1961). *The Q-Sort Method in Personality Assessment and Psychiatric Research*. Springfield, IL: Charles Thomas.

Block, J. (2008). *The Q-Sort in Character Appraisal: Encoding Subjective Impressions of Persons Quantitatively*. Washington, DC: APA Books.

Brown, S. (1980). *Political Subjectivity: Applications of Q Methodology in Political Science*. New Haven, CT: Yale University Press.

Curt, B. (1994). *Textuality and Tectonics: Troubling Social and Psychological Research*. Buckingham: Open University Press.

Eccleston, C., De Williams, A. & Stainton Rogers, W. (1997). 'Patients' and professionals' understandings of the causes of chronic pain: Blame, responsibility and identity protection. *Social Science & Medicine*, 45(5), 699–709.

Gleeson, K. (1991). 'Out of our minds': The deconstruction and reconstruction of madness. PhD thesis. Reading: University of Reading.

Goldstein, D.M. & Goldstein, S.E. (2005). Q methodology study of a person in individual therapy. *Clinical Case Studies*, 4(1), 40–56.

Herzog, T.A. (2005). When popularity outstrips the evidence: Comment on West. *Addiction*, 100(8), 1040–1041.

Jones, S., Guy, A. & Omrod, J.A. (2003). A Q-methodological study of hearing voices: A preliminary exploration of voice hearers' understanding of their experiences. *Psychology and Psychotherapy: Theory, Research and Practice*, 76, 189–209.

Kohlberg, L. (1972) Introduction. In S.R. Brown & D.J. Brenner (eds), *Science, Psychology and Communication: Essays Honouring William Stephenson*. New York: Teachers College Press.

McKenzie, J.A. (2009). Constructing the intellectually disabled person as a subject of education: A discourse analysis using Q methodology. PhD thesis. Grahamstown: University of Grahamstown.

McKeown, M., Hinks, M., Stowell-Smith, M., Mercer, D. & Forster, J. (1999). Q methodology, risk training and quality management. *International Journal of Health Care Quality Assurance*, 6(12), 254–266.

Mielewczyk, M. & Willig, C. (2007). Old clothes and an older look: The case for a radical makeover in health. *Theory and Psychology*, 17, 811–837.

Prochaska, J.O. & DiClemente, C.C. (1983). Stages and processes of self-change in smoking: Toward an integrative model of change. *Journal of Consulting and Clinical Psychology*, 51, 390–395.

Shank, G. (1998). The extraordinary powers of abductive reasoning. *Theory and Psychology*, 8(6), 841–860.

Stainton Rogers, R. & Stainton Rogers, W. (1990). What the Brits got out of the Q and why their way may not line up with the American way of getting into it! *Electronic Journal of Communication/Revue Electronic de Communication*, 1(1). http://www.cios.org/EJCPUBLIC/001/1/00113.html, accessed 2 May 2014.

Stainton Rogers, W. (1991) *Explaining Health and Illness: An Exploration of Diversity*. Hemel Hempstead: Harvester Wheatsheaf.

Stainton Rogers, W. (1998). Using Q as a form of discourse analysis. *Operant Subjectivity*, 21(1/2), special edn.

Stenner, P. & Stainton Rogers, R. (2004). Q methodology and qualiquantology: The example of discriminating between emotions. In Z. Todd, B. Nerlich, S. McKeown & D. Clarke (eds), *Mixing Methods in Psychology: The Integration of Qualitative and Quantitative Methods in Theory and Practice* (pp. 101–120). New York: Psychology Press.

Stenner, P., Watts, S. & Worrell, M. (2009). Q methodology. In C. Willig & W. Stainton Rogers (eds), *The Sage Handbook of Qualitative Methods in Psychology*. London: Sage.

Stephenson, W. (1935). Technique of factor analysis. *Nature*, 136, 279.

Sutton, S.R. (2005). Another nail in the coffin of the transtheoretical model? A comment on West. *Addiction*, 100, 1043–1045.

Watts, S. & Stenner, P. (2005). Doing Q methodology: Theory, method and interpretation. *Qualitative Research in Psychology*, 2, 67–91.

Williamson, L.M., Buston, K. & Sweeting, H. (2009). Young women and limits to the normalisation of condom use: A qualitative study. *AIDS Care*, 21(5), 561–566.

Willig, C. (1995). 'I wouldn't have married the guy if I'd have to do that': Heterosexual adults' constructions of condom use and their implications for sexual practice. *Journal of Community and Applied Social Psychology*, 5, 75–87.

Mixed-Methods Research and Personal Projects Analysis

17

Kerryellen Griffith Vroman

Underpinning mixed-methods research methodology is the premise that there are many ways to explore, examine and make sense of the social world (Johnson et al., 2007; Greene, 2008). By occupying the middle ground between qualitative and quantitative research paradigms, this methodology offers researchers multiple perspectives on what is important, relevant and of value when examining a phenomenon and/or seeking answers to health-related questions (Dures et al., 2013). Yardley and Bishop (2008) capture the essence and scope of the appeal of mixed methods for psychologists and cite Maxcy to argue that as a pragmatic approach, mixed methods embraces the assumption that

> *all* human inquiry involves imagination and interpretation, intentions and values but must also necessarily be grounded in empirical, embodied experience ... [Hence] the aim of inquiry is not to seek a truth that is independent from human experience, but to achieve a better, richer experience – whether through scientific analysis, artistic exploration, social negotiation, or any productive combination of these different approaches. (Maxcy, 2003:359)

In this chapter, mixed-methods research is defined and salient methodological issues are examined. To illustrate the approach, *personal projects analysis* research is presented as an example and the tenets of such analysis are discussed. The processes involved in selecting and implementing this methodology are provided, using examples from the author's and other researchers' work.

Clarification of terminology: Mixed-methods research

Mixed-methods research or the mixed-methods approach describes study designs that employ quantitative and qualitative methods in one or more phases of research that investigates the same underlying phenomenon (Hesser-Biber, 2010; Johnson & Onwuegbuzie, 2004; Tashakkori & Creswell, 2007;

Tashakkori & Teddlie, 2010). Johnson et al. offer the following inclusive definition after surveying leading mixed-methods researchers:

> [Mixed methods is] the type of research in which a researcher or team of researchers combines elements of qualitative and quantitative research approaches (e.g., use of qualitative and quantitative viewpoints, data collection, analysis, and inference techniques) for the broad purposes of breadth and depth of understanding and corroboration. (2007:123)

They make a further distinction between a mixed-methods study, which is the use of qualitative and quantitative methods within a single study, and a mixed-methods programme of research, which involves methods from both paradigms that are used across a 'closely related set of studies' (Johnson et al., 2007:123). Other terms used to refer to mixed-methods research include triangulation and complementary or embedded design (Flick, 1992, 2002).

The terms mixed methods should not be confused with multimethods; these terms are *not* synonymous. A *multimethods* study design uses a variety of either qualitative or quantitative techniques or procedures from a single research paradigm (Hesse-Biber, 2010; Morse, 2003). An example of multimethods design is the use of in-depth interviews, participant journals and participant observations in a qualitative design study. Alternatively, when the design paradigm is quantitative, surveys and quasi-experimental procedures may be used (Hesser-Biber, 2010; Flick, 2002). *Mixed-methods design*s, as defined above, use both qualitative and quantitative research methods and strategies *within* or *across* the phases of the research process, either sequentially or concurrently.

In health and clinical psychology, the use of mixed-methods research designs yields conceptually informative and clinically relevant research data (Dures et al., 2013). As a methodological approach, it addresses a common conundrum in health and clinical psychology research, namely how to deal with the tension between the authentic representation of individuals and their contextualized experiences, while also being responsive to pressure from the health-care environment, stakeholders and/or funding sources for quantifiable objective generalizable data, typically yielded by positivistic quantitative methodologies. One of the primary advantages of mixed-methods research is thus that psychology researchers are not constrained conceptually or methodologically by a single paradigm in the quest to understand humans and their behaviours.

Historical background

The current conceptualization of mixed-methods research in psychology as well as the other sciences emerged in the 1980s (Plano Clark, 2010). Since the mid-1990s, the combining and synthesis of qualitative and quantitative theoretical perspectives and methodological strategies to investigate complex social and health-related issues have been accepted as a legitimate and, at times, innovative approach (Denzin, 2010; Small, 2011). The growth of mixed-methods research has been supported by publications dedicated to this field, such as the *Journal of Mixed Methods Research*, and by the development of qualitative data analysis software programs that also have the capacity to analyse quantitative data (Annechino et al., 2010). A further example of the universal acceptance of mixed-methods research occurred in 2010, when in response to the interest and expansion in mixed-methods research the National Institutes of Health (NIH) Office of Behavioural and Social Sciences Research in the United States commissioned a report to guide NIH investigators to 'rigorously develop and evaluate mixed methods research' (Creswell et al., 2010:1; Plano Clark, 2010). This initiative acknowledged a place for mixed-methods designs within federally funded health-related research in the United States.

In psychology, the emergence and recognition of mixed-methods research as a definable intellectual movement, and the use of mixed methodologies, might be viewed as an inevitable response to the polarization that occurred among and within qualitative and quantitative researchers (Denzin, 2010; Guba, 1990; Howe, 1988). While the acceptance of mixed methods is not without debate, the community of researchers in health and clinical psychology and other scientists who embrace the blending of qualitative and quantitative design and methodologies continues to grow (Tashakkori & Creswell, 2007; Dures et al., 2013; Johnson et al., 2007; Mertens & Hesse-Biber, 2013; Sale et al., 2002). Even Guba and Lincoln (2005), ardent qualitative proponents of a purist approach, concur that there is a place for pluralism in research that is achieved by thoughtful blending of the elements of the qualitative research paradigm with those from the quantitative research paradigm in order to engage in research that represents the best of both worldviews.

Conceptual framework: The third research paradigm

Mixed-methods research is more than the combination of qualitative and quantitative research methods. It is positioned as a research paradigm or as the 'third methodological movement' (Guba, 1990; Hesse-Biber, 2010; Johnson & Onwuegbuzie, 2004; Johnson et al., 2007; Tashakkori & Teddlie, 2003:ix). As a research methodology, it encompasses philosophical assumptions (that is, beliefs, values), specific designs and methods regarding the nature of and way to conduct research (Creswell & Plano Clark, 2011). Therefore, in addition to being well versed in the assumptions, aims and methods of qualitative and quantitative research paradigms, a researcher must be cognizant of the particular epistemologies and theoretical assumptions of mixed-methods research (Mertens & Hesse Biber, 2013; Greene, 2007). Maxwell and Loomis (2003) specifically caution researchers not to view mixed-methods research as merely borrowing the procedures and techniques from the quantitative and qualitative paradigms. The process must extend to the language, the framing of the study and/or adopting a perspective for the interpretation of findings from the respective paradigms. Consequently, mixed-methods researchers mindfully situate their research within a framework of knowledge and follow its presumptions, its theoretical scope and its validity to shape the nature of questions and their interpretation of the data (Dures et al., 2013; Mertens & Hesse-Biber, 2013). The parameters of the mixed-methods paradigm assume that the research design will be informed by theoretical tenets and include methods of *both* qualitative and quantitative research when selecting methods, strategies, techniques or procedures (Creswell et al., 2003; Dures et al., 2013). Authentic use of a mixed-methods paradigm is methodological decision-making that is *always* underscored by a sound rationale for employing mixed methods.

In a mixed-methods study, design elements of qualitative and quantitative paradigms may be given equal status or one paradigm may have dominant status. Equally important to the emphasis of a research paradigm is the timing or staging of qualitative and quantitative dimensions in the research design. The methods may be sequential; that is, using qualitative methods to explore and clarify or refine the research question followed by quantitative data collection. In the analysis phase of the study, qualitative data strategies may be quantified for statistical analysis procedures, a process that some qualitative software will perform. Alternatively, qualitative and quantitative methods may be used concurrently. For example, data is collected using methods that are either fully or partially integrated. The emphasis of the qualitative or quantitative paradigm and staging of the methods is represented in the typologies in Figure 17.1.

Typologies of mixed-methods designs

Mixed-methods typologies assist us to understand, evaluate and design mixed-methods research because the potential variations of designs challenge both a novice researcher and researchers new to mixed methods (Leech & Onweuegbuzie, 2009). In response to potential mixed-methods designs and the need for guidance in designing studies, numerous typologies are offered (Creswell & Plano Clark, 2011; Johnson & Onwuegbuzie, 2004; Maxwell & Loomis, 2003; Tashakorri & Teddlie, 2003). Leech and Onwuegbuzie (2009) sought to meet the need for an integrated typology of mixed-methods research design with a three-dimensional typology. They differentiate between partial and fully integrated mixed-methods designs and propose that a comprehensive 'fully' mixed-methods design, regardless of whether the methods used are sequential or concurrent, is one that encompasses characteristics of both qualitative and quantitative methods research

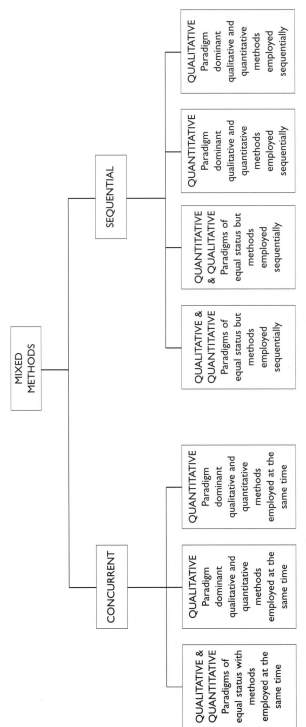

Figure 17.1 Typologies of mixed methods by paradigm dominance and order of methods

within one or more components of a single study. This delineation of a fully mixed-methods design provides us with the following useful checklist of questions that researchers can ask themselves:

☑ Do the objectives represent qualitative and quantitative research such that they are both exploratory and predictive?

☑ Are the types of data and operations used from both paradigms or are the strategies and procedures of one paradigm more dominant?

☑ Are the analysis procedures integrated or are they drawn from each paradigm to triangulate as complementary data?

☑ Are the types of inferences and/or interpretations informed by both paradigms?

In a fully integrated mixed-methods design, a researcher will in one or more phases of the study use qualitative *and* quantitative techniques and methods together; whereas in a partial mixed-methods study design the expectation is that a qualitative and quantitative method is used in the research process prior to the interpretation of all the data. Both partial and fully mixed-methods designs can be either sequential or concurrent. In summary, there are three critical dimensions to consider when planning a mixed-methods study:

■ The emphasis that will be given to the qualitative and quantitative paradigms (i.e. are they equally weighted or is one paradigm dominant?).

■ The extent to which the qualitative and quantitative methods will be integrated (i.e. full vs. partial).

■ The timing of the qualitative and quantitative methods (i.e. concurrent or sequential).

Figure 17.1 was developed from similar figures and matrices produced by Johnson and Onwuegbuzie (2004), Leech and Onweuegbuzie (2009) and Tashakorri and Teddlie (1998). More complex models are available.

Guide to designing a mixed-methods study

In designing a mixed-methods study, a researcher takes into consideration a number of aspects, starting with the phenomenon being studied and the nature of the study question(s). These will both determine if the study design will be mixed methods and if it will be a full or partial design (see Table 17.1 for guidelines on choosing and designing a mixed-methods study). Research standards for rigour, credibility and validity dictate adherence to principles associated with, but not exclusive to, mixed-methods research. Harper (2008) also states that psychologists employing mixed methods should ensure that the methods that are selected share epistemological assumptions.

Table 17.1   Guidelines for choosing and designing a mixed-methods study

Consider the benefits and advantages of mixed methods relative to other approaches
- Is the nature of the problem or question not able adequately to be understood, developed or investigated using solely a qualitative or quantitative perspective? For example, qualitative methods elicit idiographic data as a precursor to developing quantitative measurement strategies (Creswell et al., 2010).
- Is there added value in the triangulation or cross-validation of data? For example, will combining two or more sources of data or using one or more theories yield a more comprehensive understanding of a phenomenon than would be gained using a solely qualitative or qualitative study design (Sale et al., 2002)?
- Are there advantages in using one method to augment another method? For example, will a breadth of perspective be achieved because a phenomenon is viewed from corresponding, yet different, paradigmatic assumptions?

Uses and advantages of mixed-methods research in clinical and health psychology

In 1996, Spicer and Chamberlain called for health psychologists to use integrative strategies in their research. Today, we frequently see clinical, counselling and health psychology studies in which researchers employ integrative strategies in mixed-methods research designs. Similarly, numerous articles, chapters and books outline the utilization of mixed methods as a legitimate, useful methodological and conceptual approach (e.g. Dures et al., 2013; Hanson et al., 2005; Yardley & Bishop, 2008).

The appeal of mixed methods largely lies in its pragmatism, and in the flexibility and breadth of methods that a clinical or health psychology researcher can access, in order to understand the complex dimensions of socially constructed realities drawing from both qualitative and quantitative research. Complex and multifaceted issues and lines of inquiry pursued by health and clinical psychology researchers are suited to research from a mixed-methods paradigm. Positivistic/postpositivistic research affords strong internal validity through the use of reliable measures and experimental designs. The results permit us to draw causal inferences (Yardley & Bishop, 2008). However, the strength of quantitative (deductive) research for testing theory-based hypotheses comes at the cost of ecological validity, the application to and relevance of the results to the 'messy' nature of everyday life. Qualitative (inductive) research gives psychologists the contextual nature of a phenomenon. Situated and interpreted within everyday life, it captures the nuances of context, meanings and relationships. For example, quantitative methods in randomized clinical trials determine the efficacy of therapeutic interventions and afford the capacity to predict patient outcomes. This level of internal validity is essential for policy development and decision-making with regard to resource planning and measuring the cost effectiveness of health-promotion and illness-prevention

Table 17.2 Examples of health and clinical psychology mixed-methods design studies

Authors	Objectives	Design and methods	Key findings
Single studies			
Yardley et al. (2010)	To develop and evaluate a web-based behavioural intervention to reduce the risk of transmission of colds and flu.	Sequential study: i) qualitative studies (pen and paper and interview) to examine website users' (n=28) responses to materials; ii) survey (n=129) to assess assumptions about hand washing.	Hygiene behaviours are influenced by 'socio-cultural customs and social approval'. Hand washing viewed as most feasible preventative strategy and beliefs about hand washing confirmed; strong correlation identified between intentions and current behaviours.
Park et al. (2011)	To examine dietary beliefs, preferences and practices among Hispanic women.	Sequential study: i) semi-structured interviews (n=28); ii) Interview data used to formulate hypotheses for the development of a Food Frequency Questionnaire (FFQ) (n=345).	Minimal discussion of nutritional content of healthy food, which was defined in interviews by freshness, source, purity and naturalness. Availability of fresh local produce/meat may influence Hispanic urban women's healthy diet.
De Visser & McDonnell (2013)	To examine how 'masculine capital' is accrued via traditionally masculine behaviours and used to permit non-masculine behaviour among university students.	Sequential study: i) online survey assessing personal importance of gender identity, gender role stereotypes and beliefs about the gender of various health behaviours (n=731); ii) semi-structured interviews (n=16 heterosexual students) using a stratified 2×2 design.	Positive relationship between perceived masculinity and engagement in traditionally masculine health behaviours. Patterns clearest among students who endorsed gender role stereotypes and gave greater importance to their own gender identity.

Programme of studies			
Peterson et al. (2013)	To assess a positive affect and self-affirmation (PA/SA) intervention to increase physical activity and to improve medication adherence among African Americans with hypertension and adults with coronary artery disease or asthma.	Sequential programme: i) a qualitative phase explored participant values and beliefs; ii) a pilot study of the PA/SA intervention; iii) three randomized controlled trials with a parallel study design (combined PA/SA versus informational control) (n =1056).	45.1% of PA/SA participants versus 33.6% of informational control participants achieved successful behaviour change. PA/SA intervention a significant predictor of achieving behaviour change after controlling for other variables, e.g. co-morbidity.
Dures et al. (2010, 2011)	To examine the impact of working with individuals with epidermolysis bullosa (EB), to explore the psychosocial impact of EB on affected adults and to identify support needs.	Two-part qualitatively driven integrated sequential design: i) semi-structured interviews with healthcare professionals (n=7); ii) online survey based on the themes generated in part one to triangulate the findings (n=26); iii) semi-structured interviews to gain access to participants' (people with EB) experiences, feelings and social worlds.	Working with people with EB affects wellbeing. Team member support, supervision and the rewards of working with people with EB made work worthwhile. Disabling affect, understanding and beliefs about the effect of EB describe the personal, inter-personal and socio-cultural ways in which EB influences daily lives and support needs. EB differentiated from other skin disorders.

programmes. When we draw on mixed methods we are provided with conceptual depth and methodological breadth to investigate complex phenomena. This is particularly beneficial when beginning a novel line of inquiry or programme of research or when we are engaging in theory and/or measurement development. Frequently, qualitative methods are used in the initial exploratory phase of a study in which the quantitative paradigm is dominant. For example, Dibb and Yardley (2006) employed a sequential mixed-methods approach to expand the understanding of social comparison and to validate the identification–contrast model in relation to people with a chronic illness. Exploratory qualitative findings informed the development of the Social Comparison in Illness Scale, which was employed in conjunction with the Identification–Contrast Social Comparison scale and SF 36 Health Status Questionnaire in a subsequent quantitative component of the study. There are also specific epistemological and methodological mixed-methods approaches being developed, such as personal project analysis (PPA).

Results from clinical and health psychology mixed-methods design studies are reported in the literature in two main ways. The first is as one comprehensive report that describes the findings obtained through integrated qualitative and quantitative methods (see Table 17.2 for a range of research examples). The second is when the qualitative findings are reported in publications that are predisposed towards this research paradigm and quantitative results are reported in a second article in a more quantitative venue (see Tables 17.2 and 17.3). For example, Dures's doctoral research employed a mixed-methods design to study epidermolysis bullosa and was published in two separate publications, one reporting the mixed-methods data, analyses and findings, and the other the qualitative findings only (Dures et al., 2010, 2011).

Example of a mixed-methods research approach: Personal projects analysis

Personal projects analysis (PPA) is an integrated sequential mixed-methods design. It is viewed as an ecological approach; namely, personal projects are person-in-context units of analysis. They are modular, flexible and contextually embedded in the reality of a person's performance and reveal people's pattern of interaction with their environment (Cantor & Zirkel, 1990; Little, 1999; Vroman et al., 2009a). In these sets of personally relevant actions, researchers can explore multiple factors related to wellbeing and a person's process of adaptation or maladaptation to life events such as changes in health status.

The premise that underscores PPA is that people consciously engage in information processing and purposive acts and that the meaning and purpose of one's life are unfolding phenomena. Epistemologically qualitative, the constructivist perspective of PPA places the individual central in the research process as a collaborator, rather than an 'object' of study. People's lives are presumed to be ongoing stories structured by setting, striving and pursuing goal-directed activities that are meaningfully embedded in the subjective reality of day-to-day lives (Little, 2000; Ryan et al., 1996). The self is distributed within these deliberate purposive acts. It is a product that is actively constructed and negotiated through the conative processes of choosing, planning, implementing and revising personally meaningful projects. In these volitional and motivational processes to exert control over a person's self and environment, a constructivist view of self-agency is articulated (Little, 1993, 2000).

As visible representations of the intention to engage in self-directed actions, or of that engagement, personal projects reflect cognitive, affective and behavioural aspects of human conduct and people's beliefs, concerns, aspirations and identities (Little, 1989). In their purposive actions, people actively construct their perceptions of self and their place in the world; projects are an expression of their present and imagined future selves (Little, 1993; Sheldon & Elliot, 1999). Therefore, personal projects as units of 'measurement' represent the dynamic, adaptive processes of day-to-day changes, striving and struggles of self-appraisal. As such, they can be used in clinical and health psychology to explore and investigate the complex ways in which people experience, adapt and navigate health, illness, trauma and/or disability. For example, PPA research has explored the effect of health on the personal goals and psychological wellbeing of young adults with cystic fibrosis and those who are cancer survivors, as well as the relations of goals to the psychological wellbeing and diabetes health of adolescents with Type 1 diabetes. Table 17.3 provides more examples of mixed-methods research in clinical and health psychology.

In summary, personal projects analysis is a way to obtain a recounting of the active self. Personal projects represent people's adaptive processes of negotiating their evolving and stable internal and external dimensions of self over time and situations. Furthermore, they are cognitive representations of motives, self-regulation and agency processes that are initiated and coordinated in volitional acts (Austin & Vancouver, 1996; Cantor & Zirkel, 1990; McAdams, 1996). They can reflect short-term changes as well as enduring patterns of behaviour and goals that develop, are achieved or abandoned over time. Personal projects as the intent to and the engagement in goal-directed actions have a versatility that can represent a person's adaptation to health problems and/or wellbeing and the disruption of poor health. Researchers gather rich material as they explore the content (nature of projects identified), structure (how projects are cognitively construed and described), context and intentions of people's actions. In people's appraisal of projects, the internal states that arouse and direct their actions and their appraisals of their actions can be understood. When all this information is viewed in relation to health behaviours or psychopathology, people's behaviour that contributes to their health, and their responses and projects related to health-related issues (that is, adjustment or adaptive/maladaptive behaviours) in context, is revealed (Little, 1989; Vroman et al., 2009a).

Table 17.3 Examples of health and clinical psychology studies of personal projects analysis using mixed-methods designs

Authors	Objectives	Design and methods	Key findings
Schwartz & Drotar (2009)	To examine content of personal goals, health-related hindrance (HRH) and relations of HRH to health status and wellbeing among young adults with cystic fibrosis (n=48), cancer survivors (n=57) and healthy peers (n=105).	PPA and measures of life events, quality of life and health and psychological wellbeing.	HRH was significantly related to subjective wellbeing and distress after controlling for other variables. Cancer survivors without cancer late effects had significantly less HRH than the other groups. Health status may affect pursuit of personal goals and relate to wellbeing of young adults.
Helgeson & Takeda (2009)	To examine the relationships between adolescents with (n=110) and without (n=117) Type 1 diabetes with goals of psychological wellbeing and diabetes health.	PPA (dimensions: progress, stress, typicality, happiness, extent desired by others) and measures of psychological wellbeing (e.g. Children's Depression Inventory) and diabetes health (e.g. Multidimensional Diabetes Questionnaire, the Self-Care Inventory and lab measures of metabolic control).	Adolescents with diabetes more likely to identify appearance projects. Healthy adolescents more likely to identify self-improvement projects. Project progress associated with better psychological and diabetes health; project stress associated with poor psychological and diabetes health. Goals adolescents' set may have implications for their psychological wellbeing and self-care of diabetes.
Vroman et al. (2009a, b)	To investigate adaptation to low back pain (LBP) in relation to project participation and dispositions, perceptions of pain and their functioning and wellbeing (n=143).	PPA (dimensions: integrity, personal agency, social visibility, stressfulness and pain salience), functioning, health and wellbeing, pain-perception measures and open-ended question (LBP experience).	All five dimensions predicted function, disruption of roles and wellbeing. Pain salience strongest predictor of function and stressfulness best predictor of wellbeing. Narrative themes: challenges to the authenticity of LBP; disruption of life due to physical limitations; and emotional distress incurred. LBP narratives told as chaos narratives.

Application of personal projects analysis methodology

As described above, in eliciting idiographic data about individuals' personal projects, where projects are done and with whom, the multidimensionality of people's everyday lives is captured (Mason, 2006; Little, 1989; Presseau et al., 2008; Vroman et al., 2009a). This inclusion of physical, social and cultural contextual information about people's personal projects provides an ecologically representative perspective.

In PPA, the research process begins with qualitative methods of gathering participant information. This includes generating idiographic items (personal projects) to which nomothetic methods are subsequently applied. Statistical procedures are performed to measure the strength of evolving malleable characteristics (that is, dispositional attributes) of the person in relation to their projects or characteristics of those projects. The data generated by quantitative procedures are collapsed across participants to yield data that can be statistically analysed to examine the strength of the relationships among the variables of interest and to make predictions. The findings of a study can thereby be generalized to populations or clinical settings. The procedural steps for implementing a personal projects analysis study are outlined in Figure 17.2.

Step 1
The first phase involves eliciting an individual's personal projects. Personal projects are defined for study participants as 'activities, tasks and goals' and it is explained that 'everyone has a number of projects at any one time that they are thinking about, planning and doing'. Participants are given examples to highlight the diverse nature of personal projects and are then asked to spend 15 minutes generating a written list of their own personal projects. These projects can range from the mundane (e.g. *walk the dog* or *do the laundry*) to the more serious (e.g. *be a good parent* or *come to terms with my father's death*). In contrast to selecting projects from a pre-determined inventory, the project-elicitation process has participants describe their personal projects in their own idiosyncratic language. This process yields rich, personally informative material, which ranges along different dimensions and may be present or future oriented, abstract or concrete, and superordinate or subordinate in nature.

The second phase of Step 1 involves the identification and selection of five to seven projects from the elicited pool. The selection is based on criteria determined by the nature of the research question(s). For example, participants might be asked to select their most important health projects, those projects they perceive to be most affected by symptoms, social projects that are most associated with their sense of wellbeing, most significant social projects, preferred leisure projects or most stressful projects. Studies often ask participants to choose their most important projects, assuming that people's personally salient projects are particularly representative.

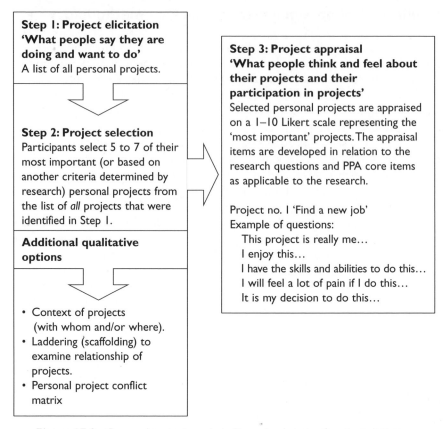

Step 1: Project elicitation
'What people say they are doing and want to do'
A list of all personal projects.

Step 2: Project selection
Participants select 5 to 7 of their most important (or based on another criteria determined by research) personal projects from the list of *all* projects that were identified in Step 1.

Additional qualitative options

- Context of projects (with whom and/or where).
- Laddering (scaffolding) to examine relationship of projects.
- Personal project conflict matrix

Step 3: Project appraisal
'What people think and feel about their projects and their participation in projects'
Selected personal projects are appraised on a 1–10 Likert scale representing the 'most important' projects. The appraisal items are developed in relation to the research questions and PPA core items as applicable to the research.

Project no. 1 'Find a new job'
Example of questions:
This project is really me...
I enjoy this...
I have the skills and abilities to do this...
I will feel a lot of pain if I do this...
It is my decision to do this...

Figure 17.2 Personal projects analysis: Procedural steps of project elicitation and appraisal

Step 2

In this step, quantitative methods are employed, which involve the appraisal of participants' selected personal projects on a set of items (dimensions) chosen for theoretical reasons and/or applied utility. A set of core dimensions is frequently used in PPA research (McGregor & Little, 1998) and these measure the characteristics and dispositional attributes of individuals towards their projects, such as perceived stress, autonomy, difficulty of project, perceived social support, self-efficacy, competence and/or congruence with self-identity. Ad hoc items are added to measure dimensions that are specific to the research questions, such as the perceived influence of health status or symptoms.

Participants rate each of their selected 'important' personal projects on the same set of dimensions using a Likert scale (0, 'strongly disagree', to 10, 'strongly agree'). A matrix (usually one page of 15–25 dimensions) is completed for each project. Table 17.4 provides a sample of dimensions used in the Vroman et al. (2009) study, which investigated the trajectory of low back pain. The dimensions included self-efficacy, autonomy and the stress that people experienced in relation to engaging in their personal projects, their perception of the role of their pain in relation to their projects, concordance between self and personal projects, and the social connectedness, visibility and involvement of other people. In this study dimensions were presented as first-person statements, although other researchers have sought to carry out dimension appraisal using a question format (e.g. 'How difficult do you find it to carry out this project?'). The individual's dimensions are averaged across projects and aggregated across participants. Factor analysis is then performed to determine theoretically relevant factors (domains) for subsequent analysis. In PPA research the domains are often used as predictor variables with health and wellbeing measures. For the most part, people's actual personal projects are dynamic. However, evidence suggests that the dimensions can demonstrate stability (Salmela-Aro & Nurmi, 1997). When project dimension ratings are aggregated and entered into factor analysis, the interpretation of factor loadings as disposition characteristics is found to demonstrate a relatively high level of stability over time (Little, 2000; see also Little & Gee, 2007 for further discussion of the psychometric properties of PPA).

Additional procedures for data collection in PPA may include inter-project conflict, which assesses the negotiation of the competing demands of one's

Table 17.4 Sample of personal project dimensions

Dimensions	Dimension items
1. Self-identity	This is 'really me'.
2. Future self	Doing this helps me become the person I want to be.
3. Enjoyment	I enjoy doing this.
4. Value congruency	This fits in with the values and/or beliefs that guide my life.
5. Self-worth	This makes me feel good about myself.
6. Control	I feel in control of this…
7. Commitment	I am committed to this
8. Decision self-initiated	It is my decision to do this.
9. Time adequacy	I have enough time to work on this.
10. Stress	I find this is stressful.
11. Difficulty	I find this difficult.
12. Progress	To date, I have been successful with this.
13. Competence	I have the abilities and skills to finish this.
14. Involvement of others	I choose to do this with other people
15. Social support	Other people are helpful with this.
16. Hindrance of others	Other people make it difficult to do this.

Example of ad hoc dimensions

1. Pain avoidance	I avoid doing this because it would cause back pain.
2. Pain intensity	I feel a *lot* of back pain if I do this.
3. Pain disruption	My back pain will prevent me from achieving this.

Source: Vroman et al. (2009a).

How do projects conflict with each other?
This chart is to examine how doing each of your projects conflicts with another.
For example, project A may highly conflict with project B but the reverse may not be true.

Rating Scale   0 = Does not conflict at all
                  10 = Conflicts extremely

To what extent does doing these projects ⟶ *conflict with actively doing these projects* ↓	*Gaining a promotion at work*	*Exercising regularly*	*Completing my graduate studies*	*Being a good parent*
Getting a promotion at work		5	3	6
Exercising regularly	6			4
Completing my graduate studies	5	7		8
Being a good parent	7	3	5	

Figure 17.3   Example of a personal projects analysis conflict matrix

personal projects. Participants evaluate the extent to which they consider that engaging in one project conflicts with or supports one another using a matrix (Figure 17.3). For example, *getting promoted at work* may conflict with the project *being a good parent to my children*.

Example of a health psychology study using a personal projects analysis approach

Low back pain is a complex disorder characterized by the loss of ability to carry out everyday tasks, the disruption of life plans, psychological distress, persistent pain and for some people long-term disability. We undertook a comprehensive study to understand further the trajectory of acute low back pain (LBP) by using personal projects analysis, an integrated mixed-methods design with sequential and concurrent qualitative and quantitative elements. The objective was to examine the relations of individuals' dispositional attributes towards projects and their functional adaptation to LBP in the context of their day-to-day goal-directed activities. Additional measures of health, emotional and cognitive wellbeing and pain avoidance were included, as well as an open-ended question to elicit low back pain narratives.

It was proposed that a functional personal project model in which individuals whose project dispositions were highly concordant with sense of self, perceived competence and social orientation would exhibit better function and health and report navigating the experience of low back pain with less disruption to activities and psychological and social sequelae. Thus, we expected that these dispositional attributes would enhance adaptation. Conversely, poor adaptive abilities, such as difficulties with physical function and self-reported poor health, would be predicted by project dispositions such as condition-specific perceptions of pain and negative appraisals of project stress, low social connection and visibility of projects. The open-ended question was intended to provide data to triangulate (see Chapter 5) and validate the findings of the PPA data. Content analysis of these data yielded rich descriptive material about people's emotional distress and the disruption of life due to LBP, and narrative analysis revealed that the dominant narrative was a chaos narrative.

A functional project system was not found to have adaptive benefits; instead, the results further supported functional self-efficacy and pain-related fear models of LBP and disability trajectory. Viewing one's pain as salient to the progress and success of personal projects and perceiving one's projects as stressful were predictive of having limited social and physical functioning in activities and overall poor health, even when traditional predictors of LBP disability, pain severity or pain-related fear were controlled for. The perceived salience of pain and stressfulness of projects outweighed any advantages of other dispositional attributes of participants towards their projects in their everyday lives.

Concluding comments

In summary, mixed methodology potentially leads to a richer and more complete understanding of a phenomenon than does a single approach (Yardley & Bishop, 2008; Johnson et al., 2007). Selecting a mixed-methods study design is a choice that provides 'the most informative, complete, balanced and useful research results' (Burke et al., 2007:129). Recognizing the potential that the breadth of mixed-methods approaches offers for accessing the different layers and dimensions of complex and constructed social realities also brings questions regarding ontology, epistemological tenets, theoretical frameworks and practical applications. Even though this chapter embraces mixed-methods design, its endorsement comes with a cautionary note that the theoretical or methodological application of mixed-methods research to a question or line of inquiry is undertaken intentionally because it optimally meets the objectives of the study (Sale et al., 2002). The choices of methods in a mixed-methods design are predicated on a fundamental understanding of the two traditional research paradigms. Furthermore, regardless of the structure of the design (that is, sequential or concurrent, triangulation or complementary), the study should be anchored within a theoretical paradigm (Denzin, 2010).

Further reading

Mixed methods research

Creswell, J.W. & Plano Clark, V.L. (2011). *Designing and Conducting Mixed Methods Research*. Thousand Oaks, CA: Sage.

Creswell, J.W., Klassen, A.C., Plano Clark, V.L., Clegg Smith, K. (2010) *Best Practices for Mixed Methods Research in the Health Sciences*. Bethesda, MD: Office of Behavioral and Social Sciences Research. http://obssr.od.nih.gov/mixed_methods_research/, accessed 3 May 2014.

Hesse-Biber, S.N. (2010). *Mixed Methods Research: Merging Theory with Practice*. New York: Guilford Press.

Tashakkori, A. & Teddlie, C. (eds). (2010). *Handbook of Mixed Methods Research* (2nd edn). Thousand Oaks, CA: Sage.

Yardley, L. & Bishop, F. (2008). Mixing qualitative and quantitative methods: A pragmatic approach. In C. Willig & W. Stainton Rogers (eds), *The SAGE Handbook of Qualitative Research in Psychology* (pp. 352–372). Thousand Oaks, CA: Sage.

Special journal issues on mixed-methods research
Research Schools, 2006, *13*(1).
International Journal of Multiple Research Approaches, 2010, *4*.
Qualitative Inquiry, 2010, *16*(6).

Personal projects analysis methodology

Little, B.R. (2011). Personal projects and motivational counselling: The quality of lives reconsidered. In W.M. Cox & E. Klinger (eds), *Handbook of Motivational Counselling: A Goal-Based Approach to Assessment and Interventions with Addition and Other Problems* (2nd edn; pp. 73–86). Chichester: John Wiley & Sons.

http://www.brianrlittle.com provides articles, PPA workbooks and other resources.

References

Annechino, R., Antin, M.J. & Lee, J.P. (2010). Bridging the qualitative/quantitative software divide. *Field Methods*, *22*(115–124). doi: 10.1177/1525822X09360760.

Austin, J.T. & Vancouver, J.B. (1996). Goal constructs in psychology: Structure, process, and content. *Psychological Bulletin*, *120*, 338–375.

Burke, J.R., Onwuegbuzie, A.J. & Turner, L.A. (2007). Toward a definition of mixed methods research. *Journal of Mixed Methods Research*, *1*, 112–133.

Cantor, N. & Zirkel, S. (1990). Personality, cognition, and purposive behavior. In L.A. Pervin (ed.), *Handbook of Personality, Theory, and Research* (pp. 135–164). New York: Guilford Press.

Creswell, J.W. & Plano Clark, V.L. (2011). *Designing and Conducting Mixed Methods Research*. Thousand Oaks, CA: Sage.

Creswell, J.W., Clark, V.L.P., Gutmann, M.L. & Hanson, W.E. (2003). Advanced mixed methods research designs. In A. Tashakkori & C. Teddlie (eds), *Handbook of Mixed Methods Research in Social and Behavioural Research* (pp. 209–240). London: Sage.

Creswell, J.W., Klassen, A.C., Plano Clark, V.L. & Clegg Smith, K. (2010). *Best Practices for Mixed Methods Research in the Health Sciences*. Bethesda, MD: Office of Behavioral and Social Sciences Research.

Denzin, N.K. (2010). Moments, mixed methods, and paradigm dialogs. *Qualitative Inquiry*, *16*, 419–427.

De Visser, R.O. & McDonnell E.J. (2013). 'Man points': Masculine capital and young health. *Health Psychology*, *32*, 5–14.

Dibb, B. & Yardley, L. (2006). How does social comparison within a self-help group influence adjustment to chronic illness? A longitudinal study. *Social Science & Medicine*, *63*, 1602–1613.

Dures, E., Morris, M., Gleeson, K. & Rumsey, N. (2010). 'You're whatever the patient needs at the time': The impact on health and social care professionals of supporting people with epidermolysis bullosa (EB). *Chronic Illness*, *6*, 215–227.

Dures, E., Morris, M., Gleeson, K. & Rumsey, N. (2011). The psychosocial impact of epidermolysis bullosa. *Qualitative Health Research*, *21*, 771–782.

Dures, E., Rumsey. N., Morris, M. & Gleeson, K. (2013). Mixed methods in health psychology. *Journal of Health Psychology*, *16*, 332–341.

Flick, U. (1992). Triangulation revisited: Strategy of or alternative to validation of qualitative data. *Journal for the Theory of Social Behavior*, *22*, 175–197.

Flick, U. (2002). *An Introduction to Qualitative Research*. London: Sage.

Greene, J. (2007). *Mixed Methods in Social Inquiry*. San Francisco, CA: John Wiley & Sons.

Greene, J. (2008). Is mixed methods social inquiry a distinctive methodology? *Journal of Mixed Methods*, *2*, 7–22.

Guba, E.G. (1990). The alternative paradigm dialog. In E.G. Guba (eds), *The Paradigm Dialog* (pp. 17–27). Newbury Park, CA: Sage.

Guba, E.G. & Lincoln, Y.S. (2005). Paradigmatic controversies, contradictions and emerging confluences. In N.K. Denzin & Y.S. Lincoln (eds), *The Sage Handbook of Qualitative Research* (3rd edn; pp. 191–215). Thousand Oaks, CA: Sage.

Hanson, W.E., Creswell, J.W., Plano Clark, V.L., Petska, K.S. & Creswell, J.D. (2005). Mixed methods research designs in counseling psychology. *Journal of Counseling Psychology*, *52*, 224–235.

Harper, D. (2008). Clinical psychology. In C. Willig & W. Stainton Rogers (eds), *The SAGE Handbook of Qualitative Research in Psychology* (pp. 352–372). Thousand Oaks, CA: Sage.

Helgeson, V.S. & Takeda, A. (2009). Brief report: Nature and implications of personal projects among adolescents with and without diabetes. *Journal of Pediatric Psychology*, *34*, 1019–1024.

Hesse-Biber, S.N. (2010). *Mixed Methods Research: Merging Theory with Practice*. New York: Guilford Press.

Howe, K.R. (1988). Against the quantitative–qualitative incompatibility thesis or dogmas die hard. *Educational Researcher*, *17*, 10–16.

Ivankova, N.V., Creswell, J.W. & Stick, S. (2006). Using mixed methods sequential explanatory designs: From theory to practice. *Field Methods*, *18*, 3–20.

Johnson, R. & Onwuegbuzie, A. (2004). Mixed methods research: A research paradigm whose time has come. *Educational Researcher*, *33*, 14–26.

Johnson, R., Onwuegbuzie, A. & Turner, L. (2007). Towards a definition of mixed methods research. *Journal of Mixed Methods Research*, *1*, 112–133.

Leech, N.L. & Onwuegbuzie, A.J. (2009). A typology of mixed methods research designs. *Quality & Quantity*, *43*, 265–275.

Little, B.R. (1989). Personal projects analysis: Trivial pursuits, magnificent obsessions, and the search for coherence. In D.M. Buss & N. Cantor (eds), *Personality Psychology* (pp. 15–31). New York: Springer-Verlag.

Little, B.R. (1993). Personal projects and the distributed self: Aspects of a conative psychology. In J. Suls (ed.), *Psychology Perspectives on the Self* (Vol. IV, pp. 157–185). Hillsdale: Lawrence Erlbaum.

Little, B.R. (1999). Personality and motivation: Personal action and the conative evolution. In L.A. Pervin & O.P. John (eds), *Handbook of Personality, Theory and Research* (2nd edn; pp. 501–524). New York: Guilford Press.

Little, B.R. (2000). Free traits and personal contexts: Expanding a social ecological model of well-being. In W.B. Walsh, K.H. Clark & R.H. Price (eds), *Person-Environment Psychology: New Directions and Perspectives* (2nd edn; pp. 87–116). Mahwah, NJ: Lawrence Erlbaum.

Little, B.R. & Gee, T.L. (2007). The methodology of personal projects analysis: Four modules and a funnel. In B.R. Little, K. Salmela-Aro & S.D. Phillips (eds), Personal Projects Pursuits: Goals, Actions and Human Flourishing (pp. 51–93). Mahwah, NJ: Lawrence Erlbaum.

Mason, J. (2006). Mixing methods in a qualitatively driven way. *Qualitative Research*, *6*, 9–25.

Maxcy, S.J. (2003). Pragmatic threads in mixed methods research in the social sciences: The search for multiple modes of inquiry and the end of the philosophy of formalism. In A. Tashakkori & C. Teddlie (eds), *Handbook of Mixed Methods in Social and Behavioral Research* (pp. 51–89). Thousand Oaks, CA: Sage.

Maxwell, J.A. & Loomis, D.M. (2003). Mixed methods design: An alternative approach. In A. Tashakkori & C. Teddlie (eds), *Handbook of Mixed Methods in Social and Behavioral Research* (pp. 241–271). Thousand Oaks, CA: Sage.

McAdams, D.P. (1996). Personality, modernity and the storied self: A contemporary framework for studying persons. *Psychological Inquiry*, *7*, 295–321.

McGregor, I. & Little, B.R. (1998). Personal projects, happiness and meaning: On doing well and being yourself. *Journal of Personality and Social Psychology*, *74*, 494–512.

Mertens, D. & Hesse Biber, S. (2013). Mixed methods and credibility of evidence in evaluation. In D.M. Mertens & S. Hesse Biber (eds), Special issue: Mixed methods and credibility of evidence in evaluation. *New Directions for Evaluation*, *138*, 5–13.

Morse, J.M. (2003). Principles of mixed methods and multimethod research designs. In A. Tashakkori & C. Teddlie (eds), *Handbook of Mixed Methods in Social and Behavioral Research* (pp. 189–208). Thousand Oaks, CA: Sage.

Park, Y., Quinn, J., Florez, K., Jacobson, J., Neckerman, K. & Rundle, A. (2011). Hispanic immigrant women's perspective on healthy foods and the New York City retail food environment: A mixed-method study. *Social Science & Medicine*, *73*, 13–21.

Peterson, J.C., Czajkowski, S., Charlson, M.E., Link, A.R., Wells, M.T. & Jobe, J.B. (2013). Translating basic behavioral and social science research to clinical application: The EVOLVE mixed methods approach. *Journal of Consulting and Clinical Psychology*, *81*, 217–230.

Plano Clark, V.L. (2010). The adoption and practice of mixed methods: U.S. trends in federally funded health-related research. *Qualitative Inquiry*, *16*, 428–440.

Plano Clark, V.L. & Creswell, J.W. (2008). *The Mixed Methods Reader*. Thousand Oaks, CA: Sage.

Presseau, J., Sniehotta, F.F., Francis, J.J. & Little, B.R. (2008). Personal projects analysis: Opportunities and implications for multiple goal assessment, theoretical integration and behaviour change. *European Health Psychologist*, *10*, 32–36.

Ryan, R.M., Sheldon, K.M., Kasser, T. & Deci, E.L. (1996). All goals are not created equal: An organismic perspective on the nature of goals and their regulation. In P.M. Gollwitzer & J.A. Bargh (eds), *The Psychology of Action: Linking Cognition and Motivation to Behavior* (pp. 1–26). New York: Guilford Press.

Sale, J.E.M., Lohfeld, L.H. & Brazil, K. (2002). Revisiting the quantitative–qualitative debate: Implications for mixed methods research. *Quality & Quantity*, *36*, 43–53.

Salmela-Aro, K. & Nurmi, J.E. (1997). Goal content, well-being and life context during transition to university: A longitudinal study. *International Journal of Behavioural Development*, *20*, 471–491.

Schwartz, L.A. & Drotar, D. (2009). Health-related hindrance of personal goal pursuit and well-being of young adults with cystic fibrosis, pediatric cancer survivors, and peers without a history of chronic illness. *Journal of Pediatric Psychology*, *34*, 954–965. doi: 10.1093/jpepsy/jsn144.

Sheldon, K.M. & Elliot, A.J. (1999). Goal striving, need satisfaction, and longitudinal well-being: The self-concordance model. *Journal of Personality and Social Psychology*, *76*, 482–497.

Silverman, D. (2005). *Doing Qualitative Research* (2nd edn). London: Sage.

Small, M.L. (2011). How to conduct a mixed methods study: Recent trends in a rapidly growing literature. *Annual Review of Sociology*, *37*, 57–86.

Spicer, J. & Chamberlain, K. (1996). Developing psychosocial theory in health psychology: Problems and prospects. *Journal of Health Psychology*, *1*, 161–171.

Tashakkori, A. & Creswell, J.W. (2007). The new era of mixed methods research. *Journal of Mixed Methods Research*, *1*, 3–7.

Tashakkori, A. & Teddlie, C. (1998). Mixed Methodology: Combining Qualitative and Quantitative Approaches. Applied Social Research Methods Series, 46. Thousand Oaks, CA: Sage.

Tashakkori, A. & Teddlie, C. (2003). *Handbook of Mixed Methods in Social and Behavioral Research*. Thousand Oaks, CA: Sage.

Tashakkori, A. & Teddlie, C. (eds). (2010). *Handbook of Mixed Methods Research* (2nd edn). Thousand Oaks, CA: Sage.

Vroman, K., Chamberlain, K. & Warner, R. (2009a). A personal projects analysis: Examining adaptation to low back pain. *Journal of Health Psychology*, *14*, 696–706. doi: 10.1177/1359105309104916.

Vroman, K., Warner, R. & Chamberlain, K. (2009b). Now let me tell you in my own words: Narratives of acute and chronic low back pain. *Disability & Rehabilitation*, *31*, 976–987.

Yardley, L. & Bishop, F. (2008). Mixing qualitative and quantitative methods: A pragmatic approach. In C. Willig & W. Stainton Rogers (eds), *The SAGE Handbook of Qualitative Research in Psychology* (pp. 352–372). Thousand Oaks, CA: Sage.

Yardley, L., Miller, S., Teasdale, E. & Little, P. (2010). Using mixed methods to design a web-based behavioural intervention to reduce transmission of colds and flu. *Journal of Health Psychology*, *16*, 353–364.

Index